Decision Theory and the Legal Process

Decision Theory and the Legal Process

Stuart S. Nagel
Marian G. Neef
University of Illinois

Lexington Books
D.C. Heath and Company
Lexington, Massachusetts
Toronto

Library of Congress Cataloging in Publication Data

Nagel, Stuart S   1934-
   Decision theory and the legal process.

   Bibliography: p.
   Includes indexes.
   1, Justice, Administration of—United States—Decision making.
2. Bail—United States. 3. Plea bargaining—United States. 4. Jury—United States.
   I. Neef, Marian, joint author. II. Title.
KF9223.N34   345'.73'05   78-20348
ISBN 0-669-02742-1

Copyright © 1979 by D.C. Heath and Company.

All rights reserved. No part of this publication may be reproduced or transmitted in any form or by any means, electronic or mechanical, including photocopy, recording, or any information storage or retrieval system, without permission in writing from the publisher.

Published simultaneously in Canada.

Printed in the United States of America.

International Standard Book Number: 0-669-02742-1

Library of Congress Catalog Card Number: 78-20348

This book is dedicated to improving the
effectiveness, objectivity, and understanding
of the legal process.

Contents

	Introduction	xv
Part I	*The One-Person Decision Situation: Bond Setting*	1
Chapter 1	**The Bond-Setting Decision in Individual Cases**	7
	I. The Release or Hold Decision	7
	A. Nonmonetary Values	7
	B. Applications and Variations	10
	C. Monetary Values	15
	II. The Bond-Setting Decision	21
	III. Increasing the Expected Value of Releasing in Individual Cases	24
	A. The General Perspective	24
	B. Raise and Clarify the Probability of Appearance	26
	C. Make More Visible the Errors and Costs of Holding Defendants Who Would Appear	27
	D. Decrease the Costs of Releasing Defendants Who Fail to Appear	30
Chapter 2	**The Bond-Setting Decision Across Cases**	45
	I. Nondiscretionary Bond Schedules	45
	A. The Problem	45
	B. The Goal and a Solution	46
	C. Variations on the Solution	48
	II. The Optimum Percentage to Release	50
	III. Some Tentative Conclusions	50
	Appendix 2A. Glossary of Symbols	59
	Appendix 2B. Basic Formulas Used	61
Part II	*The Two-Person Bargaining Situation: Plea Bargaining*	63
Chapter 3	**Decision Theory Applied to the Defendant and the Prosecutor**	71

	I. The Payoff Matrices as Perceived by the Bargainers	71
	A. Interpreting the Matrices	71
	B. Deriving the Matrices	73
	C. Translating the Matrices into Satisfaction Units	74
	II. The Bargaining Limits of the Bargainers	76
	A. Determining the Likely Sentences at Varying Conviction Probabilities	76
	B. Determining the Bargaining Limits from the Likely Sentences	78
	C. Determining the Conviction Probabilities	82
	D. Determining the Bargaining Limits where Nonsentence Goals Are Involved	88
Chapter 4	**Equilibrium Models Applied to the Defendant and the Prosecutor**	111
	I. Results of Clashes between Different Bargainers	111
	A. General Equilibrium	111
	B. Equilibrium under Special Conditions	115
	II. The Dynamics of Converging toward Equilibrium	120
	A. The Time Path Graph	120
	B. Initial Offers and Bluffing	122
	C. Calculating Counteroffers	127
	D. Convergence: Its Occurrence, Meaning, and Likelihood	130
Chapter 5	**Civil Analogies and Implications for Policy and Research**	141
	I. Out-of-Court Civil Settlements	141
	A. From the Payoff Matrices to the Dynamic Equilibrium	141
	B. Time Discounting	143
	C. The Decision to Sue and Other Analogies	144
	II. Practitioner and Policy Implications	146
	A. Scholars, Lawyers, and Society	146
	B. The Role of Discovery, Defense, Bail, and Delay	147
	C. Changes in Conviction Probabilities and Sentencing Payoffs	149

Contents ix

	III.	Future Research	153
		A. Plea Bargaining Research	153
		B. Other Decision and Game Theory Applications	155
		C. Other Equilibrium Modeling Applications	157
		Appendix 5A. Glossary of Symbols	175
		Appendix 5B. Basic Formulas Used	179

Part III   *Other Applications of Decision Theory to the Legal Process*   181

Chapter 6   **Decision Theory and Juror Decision Making**   187

    I. The Basic Decision Theory Model   187
    II. Measuring the Variables   191
    III. Characteristics of the Jurors and Cases that Influence the Model Inputs and Outputs   196
    IV. Judicial Instructions to Increase Objectivity, Conformity with the Law, and Accurate Decision Making   200
    Appendix 6A. Glossary of Symbols and Terms   213
    Appendix 6B. Basic Formulas Used   215

Chapter 7   **Allocating Resources among Court Cases by Legal Counsel**   217

    I. A Basic Example   217
        A. Defective Strategies   217
        B. Equalizing Marginal Rates of Return   219
    II. Simplifying and Varying the Basic Model   221
        A. Constant, Linear, and Nonlinear Relations   221
        B. Other Ways of Conceiving the Basic Equations   223
    III. More Cases and More Types of Law Practice   226
        A. From a Personal Injury Plaintiff's Perspective   226
        B. From Other Law Practice Perspectives   229
    IV. Related Problems   232
        A. The Decisions to Accept a Client and to Go to Trial   232
        B. Implementing the Model   235

	C. Other Applications of Portfolio Analysis to the Legal Process	239
	V. Some Conclusions	241
	Appendix 7A. Glossary of Symbols	249
	Appendix 7B. Basic Formulas Used	251
Chapter 8	**Using Decision Deterrence Theory to Encourage Socially Desired Behavior**	255
	I. Criminal Law Applications	255
	A. Clarifying the Payoff Matrix	257
	B. Determining the Threshold Values	258
	C. Increasing Compliance	259
	II. Business Regulation Applications	262
	III. Applications to Noncomplying Public Officials	265
	IV. Some Conclusions	269
	Bibliography	275
	Index of Names	283
	Index of Subjects	289
	About the Authors	5

List of Figures

1-1	Decision Theory Payoff Matrices as Perceived by Two Arraignment Judges Deciding Whether to Release a Defendant	8
1-2	Some Questions for Obtaining a Judge's Values regarding Pretrial Release Decisions	11
1-3	Decision Theory Payoff Matrices Involving Two Contingent Events and Monetary Values	16
1-4	Determining the Maximum and Minimum Probability for Each Contingent Possibility with Two Contingent Events	17
1-5	Decision Tree Involving Two Contingent Events and Monetary Values	20
1-6	Some Questions for Obtaining a Judge's Propensities regarding Bond-Setting Decisions	23
1-7	Increasing the Percentages of Defendants Released in the Pretrial Release Decision	25
2-1	The Relation between Level of Bond and Both the Probability of Appearing in Court and the Probability of Being Held in Jail	47
3-1	The Likely Sentences which Correspond to Various Conviction Probabilities (Strategies Graph)	77
4-1	Dynamic Plea Bargaining from Initial Offers to Counteroffers to Equilibrium (Time Path Graph)	121
5-1	The Impact of Judicial Process Changes on Plea Bargaining Settlements	152
6-1	The Basic Decision Theory Model of Juror Decision Making	188
6-2	Some Questions for Obtaining a Person's Values regarding a Conviction-Acquittal Decision	192
8-1	Increasing Compliance in the Criminal Law Context	256
8-2	Increasing the Likelihood that Prosecutors Will Reach Time-saving Decisions	267

List of Tables

3-1	The Payoff Matrices as Perceived by a Defendant and a Prosecutor	72
4-1	The Bargaining Limits of Certain Types of Defendants and Prosecutors (The Limits Matrix)	116
4-2	Results of Clashes between Certain Types of Defendants and Prosecutors (The Results Matrix)	199

Introduction

In recent years, a great deal of substantive concern has been shown by scholars, students, people in government, reformers, lawyers, and others for improving and understanding the legal process. Also there has been considerable methodological concern for trying to determine the effects of legal policy changes before the policies are adopted and for arriving at a set of policies to maximize given legal process goals under varying conditions. This book combines those two concerns for the substance of the legal process and the methods of decision-making analysis. As such, the book is designed to appeal to a variety of audiences, including the people mentioned above who are interested in improving and understanding the legal process. The book is also intended to be used in classrooms of undergraduate and graduate students in political science, sociology, psychology, economics, and law. The book is further intended for use by researchers, practitioners, and others oriented toward the substance, the methods, or both.

The specific purpose of this book is to analyze decision making by judges, defense attorneys, prosecutors, jurors, would-be law violators, and others involved in the procedures whereby legal rules are applied to specific cases. The analysis emphasizes a decision theory perspective. That perspective assumes that individuals seek to maximize their perceived benefits minus costs, where both the benefits and the costs are discounted by the probability of their occurrences. That assumption or perspective enables one to deduce how the decisions of individuals would change as a result of system changes that affect their perceived benefits minus costs. That assumption also enables one to deduce what decisions ought to be reached in light of what the individuals consider to be benefits and costs. Decision theory is a form of axiomatic modeling or deducing from basic axioms or assumptions. The above-mentioned uses of decision theory (1) describe or predict current or future empirical behavior and (2) prescribe or optimize normative behavior that ought to be.

The idea of decisions being affected by the probability that uncertain events will occur is particularly applicable to the legal process since it involves many such decisions. Examples emphasized in this book include (1) a judge trying to decide whether to hold or release a defendant prior to trial, contingent on the probability that the defendant will appear in court without committing a crime while released; (2) defense attorneys and prosecutors trying to decide whether to accept a compromise out-of-court settlement or to go to trial, partly contingent on the probability that the defendant will be convicted if the case does go to trial; (3) jurors trying to decide whether to convict or acquit, contingent on the probability that the defendant is actually guilty; (4) a would-be law violator trying to decide whether to engage in wrongdoing, contingent on the probability that he or she will be caught, convicted, and penalized; and (5) lawyers deciding how to allocate their scarce time among a number of cases where each case has a separate probability of victory. The first three examples involve decision making in the adjudicative stages of the legal process, where the emphasis is on the due process problem of separating the guilty from the innocent. The last two examples relate to the preadjudication stages of the legal process, where the emphasis is both on preventing wrongdoing or other events that might lead to litigation and on the allocation of scarce resources to more effectively deal with the wrongdoing or litigation that does occur. Other important examples in the legal procsess could include (1) the decision of a police officer to make an arrest, contingent on the probability of approval from superior officers, peers, and the states' attorney; (2) the decision of a judge to grant a jail sentence or probation to a convicted defendant, contingent on the defendant's recommitting a crime while on probation or shortly afterward; and (3) the similar decision of a parole board in which granting parole is analogous to a judge's granting probation.

Instead of talking in terms of the specific subject matter of the decisions being reached, such as pretrial release, plea bargaining, and convicting, one could speak in terms of a broader typology of decision making. Such a typology might emphasize whether the decision making primarily involves a single decision maker, a pair of interacting decision makers, or group decision making. In that context, the pretrial release decision can be thought of as illustrating the one-person decision situation; the plea bargaining decision, as illustrating the two-person bargaining situation; and the jury voting, as illustrating group decision making. Thus, one can extrapolate by analogy from these specific topics to other examples of those decision-making situations or types. Another general classification asks whether the decision-making problem involves discrete alternatives, as in an either-or dichotomy, or a continuum of alternatives, such that it is meaningful to talk in terms of an optimum policy level or an optimum mix across policies. Discrete decision making is involved in trying to decide whether to release or hold a defendant, settle out of court or go to trial, and convict or acquit. Continuum decision making is involved in trying to allocate a lawyer's time among a set of court cases. That situation involves a continuum of possibilities regarding the optimum level of time to allocate to a given case or the optimum mix of time to allocate to a set of cases, with each case having a separate probability of victory.

This book is the companion volume to the Nagel and Neef *Legal Policy Analysis: Finding an Optimum Level or Mix* (D.C. Heath, Lexington Books, 1977). That book dealt with legal policy problems more at the level of the legislature, chief executive, other lawmakers, or the total judicial system, rather than problems emphasizing individual grass roots decision making in the legal and judicial process. Specific contrasting examples include (1) finding the optimum percentage of defendants to release prior to trial, rather than the decision of whether to release a specific defendant; (2) determining the optimum jury size and fraction required to convict, rather than the decision of a given juror to convict or acquit; (3) optimally allocating resources for civil rights activities without contingent probabilities, rather than alloting time in individual cases each of which has its own probability of victory; (4) optimally allocating anticrime dollars among aggregate places and activities, rather than concentrating on the decision making of the individual would-be law violator; and (5) optimally balancing conflicting legal values such as free press versus fair trial, rather than balancing conflicting decision makers such as defense attorneys and prosecutors in the plea bargaining situation. Given its orientation, that earlier book emphasized continuum policies for which it is meaningful to find an optimum level or mix, rather than discrete decisions for which it is more meaningful to find an optimum choice. Both that earlier book and this one analyze in detail the problems with which they deal rather than the more abbreviated summary material which is included in Nagel and Neef, *The Legal Process: Modeling the System* (Sage, 1977).

This book presupposes no mathematical knowledge beyond high school algebra. One nice thing about decision theory (as contrasted with optimal level and mix analysis) is that it involves finite mathematics, rather than the calculus-related methods associated with optimization. Finite mathematics often is closely associated with logic and thus appeals to lawyers, nonquantitative social scientists, and others who like puzzles and parlor recreations that are simultaneously fun, challenging, and socially useful. Also decision theory can often be applied to obtain insights into important kinds of decision making (including one's own decisions) without requiring data that may be difficult to obtain and process with sophisticated statistical methods. Many of the chapters of this book are data-based or are designed to lead to future data-based applications in a book being developed by the authors entitled *Testing Models of the Legal Process*. Nevertheless, the usefulness of most of what is presented depends not on the illustrative data, but rather more on the logic of the analysis, the nonobviousness of the conclusions, and the importance of the subject matter.

We are indebted to many people and organizations for their help in making this book possible, in addition to those cited in the footnotes. Funds to conduct the research were provided by the Ford Foundation Public Policy Committee, the LEAA National Institute of Law Enforcement and Criminal Justice, the Illinois Law Enforcement Commission, the University of Illinois Law and Society Program, and the University of Illinois Research Board. None of those organizations, however, is responsible for the ideas advocated here. Chapters 1 and 2 were coauthored with Sarah Slavin

Schramm of the George Washington University Political Science Department. Chapter 6 was coauthored with David Lamm of the Georgetown University Law School, and chapter 7 was coauthored with James Stengel of the Stanford University Law School. Joyce Nagel helped assemble and process materials for all the chapters for which we are grateful. Thanks are also owed to the *University of Miami Law Review,* the *Indiana Law Journal,* and Bruce Sales (ed.), *The Jury, Judicial, and Trial Processes* (Plenum, 1978), for allowing us to use ideas from previous versions of our work. Thanks are especially owed to numerous teachers, students, researchers, judges, lawyers, and others who over the years have raised questions and suggested answers to the coauthors with regard to the logic of decision making in the legal process.

Part I
The One-Person Decision Situation: Bond Setting

Introduction to Part I

In recent years, much concern has been expressed about the lack of uniformity and effectiveness of sentencing in criminal cases. As both a cause and a result of that concern, the number of studies of the sentencing decision has increased, especially studies seeking to describe, explain, and decrease the nonuniformity and studies seeking to determine the effects of diverse sentences, including benefit-cost analyses of would-be criminal behavior in light of the deterrent effect of possible conviction and sentencing.[1] The sentencing stage of the criminal justice process, however, may be a marvel of uniformity and effectiveness in comparison to the pretrial release stage. In spite of that fact, there has been little analysis of the great diversity from judge to judge with regard to pretrial release. Likewise, there has been little analysis of the effects of bond setting on the probability of a defendant appearing in court. For awhile, though, a flurry of studies did deal with release on recognizance and preventive detention.[2] A major purpose of the following chapters is to analyze the pretrial release decision from a decision theory perspective which emphasizes the possible benefits and costs to arraignment judges and to society under various circumstances.

More specifically, decision theory can be defined as the study of which of various available decisions should or will be reached in order to maximize benefits minus costs in light of the probable occurrence of uncertain events.[3] In the context of pretrial release, the available decisions are basically to release on a low bond or on the defendant's own recognizance, or to hold on a high bond or on a nonbondable charge. The key probabilistic events are whether the defendant will appear in court and whether the defendant will commit a crime while released. Although these chapters are concerned primarily with the pretrial release decision, much of the analysis can be applied by analogy to other stages in the criminal justice process which also involve probabilistic decisions. Those stages include a police officer's decision to make an arrest contingent on the approval of superior officers, a prosecutor's decision to plea-bargain contingent on the probability of obtaining a conviction, a juror's decision to convict contingent on the probability that the defendant is guilty, and a parole board's decision to release contingent on the inmate's likelihood of repeating the crime, especially while on parole.

In addition to providing a better understanding of decision theory and the pretrial release decision, the analysis presented in these chapters serves a number of functions relevant to improving the pretrial release process. In using decision theory as the basis for gathering data from arraignment judges, a researcher can indicate to the judges various types of biases they might have in their pretrial release decisions but not be clearly aware of, especially with regard to their relative concern to avoid holding someone who would appear rather than release someone who would have failed to appear. The decision theory perspective also provides a means for determining the implicit threshold probabilities which various judges have in making pretrial release decisions. Revealing those probabilities to a set of judges on the same court may help to bring the more deviant judges closer to the average. Knowing these probabilities may also be a step to explaining the causes of the variation among judges, cases, and places. That kind of causal analysis can aid in determining the effects on decisions of changes in benefits, costs, or probabilities, or of changes in their visibility. The benefit-cost aspects may also clarify the need for more pretrial release of marginal defendants. The complete analysis may be especially useful in developing objective bond schedules or charts analogous to the objective decision-making charts used in workmen's compensation cases and increasingly being proposed for flat sentencing in criminal cases. Such bond schedules could conceivably make more specific the bonds that should be set for various crimes in order to maximize the benefits of defendants appearing in court minus the costs of having to hold defendants in jail.

Notes

1. On disuniformity in sentencing, see M. Frankel, *Criminal Sentences: Law without Order* (1973). On the lack of effectiveness of sentences designed to rehabilitate, see Martinson, "What Works? Questions and Answers about Prison Reform," 35 *The Public Interest* 22 (1974). On the possible effectiveness of sentences designed to deter, see F. Zimring and G. Hawkins, *Deterrence* (1973).

2. Ares, Rankin, and Sturz, "The Manhattan Bail Project: An Interim Report on the Use of Pre-Trial Parole," 38 *N.Y.U.L. Rev.* 67 (1963); "Preventive Detention: An Empirical Analysis," 6 *Harv. Civil Rights, Civil Lib. L. Rev.* 289 (1971); and Wald, "The Right to Bail Revisited: A Decade of Promise without Fullfillment," in *The Rights of the Accused: In Law and Action* ed. Nagel (1972), pp. 177-205.

3. For general discussions of one-person decision theory, see S. Richmond, *Operations Research for Management Decisions* 527-560 (1968); W. Baumol, *Economic Theory and Operations Research* 550-568 (1965); H. Raiffa, *Decision Analysis: Introductory Lectures on Choice under Uncertainty* (1968); R. Mack, *Planning on Uncertainty: Decision Making in Business and Government Administration* (1971); R. Behn and J. Vaupel, *Analytical Thinking for Busy Decision Makers* (1978); and W. Lee, *Decision Theory and Human Behavior*.

For discussions of decision theory applied to pretrial release and other criminal justice matters, see Landes, "The Bail System: An Economic Approach," 2 *Journal of Legal Studies* 79 (1973); G. Tullock, *The Logic of the Law* (9171); J. Locke et al., *Compilation and Use of Criminal Court Data in Relation to Pre-Trial Release of Defendants: Pilot Study* 112-115 (1970); G. Monkman, *Readings in Correctional Economics* (1973); Fried et al., "Jury Selection: An Analysis of Voir Dire," in *The Jury System: A Critical Analysis,* ed. Simon (1975); and Stover and Brown, "Reducing Rule Violations by Police, Judges, and Corrective Officials," in *Criminal Justice Modeling,* ed. Nagel (1977).

1 The Bond-Setting Decision in Individual Cases

The bond-setting decision is an especially good decision situation to illustrate various aspects of decision theory because it involves many contingent events, many alternative decisions rather than a simple dichotomy, both monetary and nonmonetary values, both individualized cases and different case types, and both descriptive and optimizing elements.[1] These features of the bond-setting decision will be defined and clarified in chapter 2. We begin with the individual case where judicial discretion is important; later we deal with nondiscretionary bond schedules where legislatures or state supreme courts specify fixed bonds for various case types. Within the individual case, first we treat the release versus hold decision from both a nonmonetary and a monetary perspective, and then we deal with the bond-setting decision which is more complicated than the simple dichotomy of releasing or holding.

I. The Release or Hold Decision

A. *Nonmonetary Values*

The decision to release a defendant can take the form of releasing the defendant on his own recognizance (ROR) without any bond or setting a bond low relative to the defendant's ability to pay. The decision to hold can take the form of labeling the case a "no bond allowed" case or setting a bond high relative to the defendant's ability to pay. Figure 1-1 gives the payoff matrices for two hypothetical judges in the same case. A payoff matrix shows the satisfaction or dissatisfaction received or perceived by a decision maker or a collectivity from each available decision and each possible occurrence of some uncertain event. A payoff matrix is a useful way of analyzing decisions, not necessarily a way of explicitly making them. In the pretrial release context, two alternative decisions are available, namely release or hold. Likewise, there are two alternative categories on the contingent event, namely the defendant would appear or fail to appear if released. The cells indicate the relative satisfaction or dissatisfaction received by each judge if he releases the defendant who then fails to appear (cell *a*), if he releases the defendant who does appear (cell *b*), if he holds the defendant who would have failed to appear if released (cell *c*), and if he holds the

8   Decision Theory and the Legal Process

a. A Judge Who Is More Worried about Holding a Good-Risk Defendant than Releasing a Bad-Risk Defendant (oriented toward avoiding type 1 errors)

	Probability of Appearance (PA)		Expected Value if PA = .6
Alternative Decisions Available	Would Fail to Appear	Would Appear	
Release via ROR or Low Bond	a −50	b +100	$(.4)(-50) + (.6)(+100) = +40$
Hold via No or High Bond	c +75	d −100	$(.4)(+75) + (.6)(-100) = -30$

b. A Judge Who Is More Worried About Releasing a Bad-Risk Defendant than Holding a Good-Risk Defendant (oriented toward avoiding type 2 errors)

	Probability of Appearance (PA)		Expected Value if PA = .6
Alternative Decisions Available	Would Fail to Appear	Would Appear	
Release via ROR or Low Bond	a −100	b +25	$(.4)(-100) + (.6)(+25) = -25$
Hold via No or High Bond	c +100	d −10	$(.4)(+100) + (.6)(-10) = +34$

Cells indicate relative satisfaction of each occurrence with the most satisfying anchored at +100 and the most dissatisfying anchored at −100.

Figure 1-1. Decision Theory Payoff Matrices as Perceived by Two Arraignment Judges Deciding Whether to Release a Defendant.

defendant who would have appeared if released (cell *d*). The most satisfying occurrence is anchored at + 100, and the most dissatisfying is anchored at − 100. The cell entries shown in figure 1-1 are hypothetical, but figure 1-2, discussed later, deals with how such values may be empirically derived.

The judge in figure 1-1*a* is more worried about holding a good-risk defendant than releasing a bad-risk defendant, as indicated by the fact that he gets the most dissatisfaction from cell *d*. On the other hand, the judge in figure 1-1*b* is more worried about releasing a bad-risk defendant than about holding a good-risk defendant,[2] as indicated by the fact that he gets the most dissatisfaction from cell *a*. We assume that both judges are hearing the same case in the same city, so that the differences in their perceived payoff values reflect their attitudinal differences. Otherwise, the differences might reflect the severity of the defendant's criminal behavior since the same judge could have a payoff matrix like figure 1-1*b* for a homicidal maniac but a payoff matrix like figure 1-1*a* for a jaywalker. Likewise, a judge in a city that has high holding costs relative to releasing costs might have a payoff matrix like that in figure 1-1*a*, but judge in a city that has high releasing costs relative to holding costs might have a payoff matrix like figure 1-1*b*. In this context holding costs might refer to jail upkeep, lost earnings, and bitterness due to misarrests, whereas releasing costs refer to the costs of rearresting no-shows and the monetary and psychological costs of crime committed by released defendants.

Suppose both judges perceive the defendant as having a probability of appearing (or *PA*) of about .60. If either judge were to be confronted with ten such defendants, this means about six would appear for their trial date and four would fail to appear. If the same defendant were to be given ten opportunities, this means that about six times he would appear and four times he would not. Thus, the expected values for the judge in figure 1-1*a* of releasing ten such defendants would be as follows: four times he would suffer a − 50 dissatisfaction; six times he would receive a + 100 satisfaction; and thus we would average a + 40 expected value from releasing the hypothetical defendant. Likewise, the expected values for the judge in figure 1-1*a* of holding ten such defendants would be these: four times he would receive a + 75 satisfaction; six times he would suffer a − 100 dissatisfaction; and thus he would average a − 30 expected value from holding the hypothetical defendant, assuming in both the releasing and the holding situation that he could be made aware of the consequences of his actions. The same kind of expected-value calculations could be done with the judge in figure 1-1*b*. In general, an *expected value* is the benefits or costs associated with an action or decision discounted by or multiplied by the probability that the benefits or costs will occur.

Given the logical assumption that any judge or any person will prefer to choose the action that yields the highest expected value, the judge in figure 1-1*a* will prefer to release the hypothetical defendant with a probability of appearing of .60, and the judge in figure 1-1*b* will prefer to hold such a hypothetical defendant. Rather than ask whether a given judge will release or hold a particular defendant, the more interesting question is, What is the threshold proability of appearance (or PA^*) that has to be met before the judge in figure 1-1a or 1-1b will release a defendant? To calculate PA^* for either judge, all we have to do is solve for PA in

$$(1 - PA)(a) + (PA)(b) = (1 - PA)(c) + (PA)(d)$$

since at that PA level the expected value of releasing exactly equals the expected value of holding.[3] Thus, for the judge in figure 1-1a, his PA^*, or threshold probability of appearance, equals .385, whereas for the judge in figure 1-1b PA^* equals .851. This means the judge in figure 1-1a will release (or should release if he wants to maximize the expected values) any defendant who has a .39 or higher chance of appearing and will hold any defendant who has a .38 or lower chance of appearing. On the other hand, the judge in figure 1-1b will release (or should release if he wants to maximize his expected values) any defendant who has a .86 or higher chance of appearing and will hold any defendant who has a .85 or lower chance of appearing. The judge in figure 1-1a probably releases a substantially higher percentage of the defendants than the judge in figure 1-1b if their judicial behavior reflects their differential values and they face roughly the same defendants.

B. Applications and Variations

Actual judges could be positioned with regard to their orientation toward avoiding type 1 errors versus avoiding type 2 errors by calculating for each judge his threshold or equilibrium PA^*. The higher his PA^* is, the more he is oriented toward holding defendants. To obtain the values of judges for insertion into matrices such as those shown in figure 1-1 would involve asking them questions like those shown in figure 1-2. The questions are in a form that facilitates pencil-paper mailed responses, although they could be administered in person also. Asking judges directly what probability of appearance they require in order to release a defendant is likely to yield less valid responses than this more indirect approach, although both approaches can be used.[4] The questionnaire also can contain other questions relating to the bond-setting process including hypothetical bond-setting situations as described in section II.

Instead of having both an upper anchor at +100 and a lower anchor at −100, one might use just an upper anchor at +100 or just a lower anchor at −100. Doing so allows more freedom at the other end of the scale rather than sometimes artificially saying that the worst payoff has the same value as the best payoff but is opposite in sign. The worst payoff, however, is the

The Bond-Setting Decision/Individual Cases

General Statement: There are two things that could happen if you *release* someone. One is that he will appear in court when he is supposed to (possibility *a*); the other is that he will fail to appear in court when he is supposed to (possibility *b*). There are, likewise, two things that could have happened when you *hold* someone in jail. One is that he would have appeared in court if he had been released (possibility *c*); the other is that he would have failed to appear if he had been released (possibility *d*).

1. Which of these four possibilities would give you the most satisfaction? Let's score this one +100 to have an upper anchor point.
   _____ (*a, b, c,* or *d*)

2. Which of these four possibilities would give you the most *dis*satisfaction? Let's score this one −100 to have a lower anchor point.
   _____ (*a, b, c,* or *d*)

3. Which of these four possibilities would give you the next to the most satisfaction?
   _____ (*a, b, c,* or *d*)

4. In view of the satisfaction you receive from the most satisfying occurrence, how would you rate this next most satisfying occurrence on a scale from 0 to +100, where 0 means neutral, and +100 means most satisfying?
   _____ (a number from 0 to +100)

5. Which of these four possibilities would give you the next to the most satisfaction?
   _____ (*a, b, c,* or *d*)

6. In view of the dissatisfaction you receive from the most dissatisfying occurrence, how would you rate this next most dissatisfying occurrence on a scale from 0 to −100, where 0 means neutral and −100 means most dissatisfying?
   _____ (a number from 0 to −100)

7. Are you sure you want your next to the best choice to be that close or that far away from the best choice, and that close or that far away from the neutral position? If not, please revise your answer accordingly.
   _____ (possible revised number for question 4)

8. Are you also sure you want your next to the worst choice to be as close or as far away from your worst choice as you initially put it? If not, please revise that evaluation accordingly.
   _____ (possible revised number for question 6)

Figure 1-2. Some Questions for Obtaining a Judge's Values Regarding Pretrial Release Decisions.

same as the best payoff but opposite in sign if a judge says that the cost of a type 1 error (of holding a defendant who would show up) is the holding costs incurred minus the releasing costs saved, and that the cost of a type 2 error (of releasing a defendant who fails to show) is the releasing costs incurred minus the holding costs saved. Generally it would not be meaningful to assign the worst payoff a value of zero because doing so might result in the next to the worst payoff having a positive value even though it is an undesirable payoff in an absolute as well as a relative sense.[5]

As an alternative to the set of questions shown in figure 1-2, which some respondents may find difficult to handle because of the abstract nature of the numbers and the sometimes undesirable tendency to make the worst payoff the same as the best payoff but opposite in sign, one can talk in terms of dollars willing to be paid for each result. Thus, each judge would be asked, How much money would you be willing to pay out of your own pocket in order to avoid whatever hurt you might feel if a defendant you release fails to appear in court (possibility *a*)? Likewise, how much would you be willing to pay in order to ensure that a defendant you release will appear in court (possibility *b*)? How much would you pay to ensure that the defendant you hold would have failed to appear in court (possibility *c*)? Finally, how much would you pay to avoid the hurt of knowing that the defendant you hold would have appeared in court if he had been released (possibility *d*)?[6] The positive and negative signs would be the same as in figure 1-1*a* and 1-1*b*, but subjective monetary amounts would appear in the cells. This method may be alright for determining the relative distances between each payoff for a given judge. But it is not meaningful for making comparisons across judges because the amount of money a judge will pay to avoid a dissatisfying alternative or to receive a satisfying one is partly dependent on how much a dollar is worth to him as well as how much dissatisfaction or satisfaction he feels from various outcomes. The idea of personally paying something, no matter how small, to avoid dissatisfaction or receive satisfaction also may seem too unrealistic for a judge to think about, although the approach may be made more manageable if the most satisfying alternative is automatically valued at $10 in order to provide a base line.

Another alternative to the type of questions posed in figure 1-2 is simply to ask two questions instead of eight in order to arrive at a judge's threshold probability for cases in general or for a specific type of hypothetical case. The two questions would be as follows:

> 1. If you set a bond that *releases* a defendant prior to trial, he might subsequently fail to appear in court. This is undesirable result *B*. If you set a bond that *holds* a defendant prior to trial, he might have appeared in court if he had been released. This is undesirable result *A*. Which of those two undesirable results would you consider more undesirable in the average case, *A* or *B*?
>
> *Answer:* _____
> (*A* or *B*)

The Bond-Setting Decision/Individual Cases 13

2. If we anchor the more undesirable of those two results at -100 on a scale that goes from -100 to 0, then approximately where would you position the result that is not the more undesirable? In other words, what relative number from -100 to 0 would you assign to B if you thought A were more undesirable, or to A if you thought B were more undesirable?

Answer: _____
(0 to -100)

With those two items of information, we can now determine the judge's threshold probability. Suppose, for example, the judge were William Blackstone who said that it is ten times as bad to convict an innocent person (a type A undesirable result) as it is to acquit a guilty person (a type B undesirable result.)[7] Suppose, further, that Blackstone applied the same rule to holding and releasing in pretrial release decisions. In effect, then, he would be saying that a type A result is worth 100 points on an undesirability scale and a type B result is worth 10 points on the same undesirability scale.[8] Thus Blackstone would have a threshold probability of $10/(100 + 10)$, or .09, meaning that he would release any defendant who had an appearance probability better than .09 and hold any defendant with a probability less than .09. That .09 decision rule would, in effect, enable Blackstone to maximize his net satisfaction or expected values in his pretrial release decision making.[9] The advantage of this alternative is that it is simpler. Its disadvantage is that the respondent can thereby more easily see what he thinks are the legally right answers and thus give those answers rather than his true attitudes.

One purpose for obtaining data like those asked for in figure 1-2 would be to determine what kinds of background or attitudinal characteristics correlate with being a holding- or a releasing-oriented judge. That kind of information could be helpful in enabling persons involved in the judicial selection process to choose judges whom they consider as having a more appropriate or balanced orientation. Another purpose might be to provide the judges from a given court system with an analysis of how they stand on this pretrial release dimension relative to their fellow judges. Then they could decrease their releasing or holding orientation in order to come closer to the average judge in their system or to come closer to a threshold of .50 or whatever other threshold that might be considered desirable. Such a use would be analogous to informing the judges in a given court system how they compare in sentencing with the average judge in their system, as is sometimes done among judges in order to produce more uniformity in their sentencing practices.

This uniformity-producing use of data from payoff matrices logically raises the question as to the desirability of seeking uniformity among judges with regard to any PA^* level or threshold probability of appearance other than .50. One might argue that if a defendant has a better than a .50 chance of appearing in court, then he should always be released; and if he has less than a .50 chance of appearing in court, then he should be held in jail pending a speedy trial. As previously implied, however, that reasoning may ignore the severity of the defendant's behavior and his likelihood of recommitting his crime before he is tried and sentenced, with the homocidal maniac and the jaywalker used as extreme examples. More important, that reasoning may ignore the relation within the court system between the cost of holding an average defendant in jail and the cost of rearresting a released defendant. If the holding cost is substantially greater than the rearrest cost, then the system should be willing to release an average defendant even if his probability of appearing is substantially less than .50. Likewise, if the releasing cost is substantially greater than the average holding cost, then the system should be willing to hold an average defendant even if his probability of appearing might be greater than .50. State statutes specifying prerelease procedures normally allow discretion to deviate from a .50 figure, especially in view of the difficulty of determining what figure a judge is operating under.[10]

There is no way of determining the PA^* threshold that a judge is using simply by observing his behavior. For example, if a judge releases 50 percent of two defendants, that judge may be operating at a .75 threshold level since he may have perceived one of the defendants as being above the .75 level and one as being below. On the other hand, that judge may be operating at a .25 level since he may have perceived one of the defendants as being above the .25 level and one as being below. In other words, by observing the percentage of defendants a judge releases, we cannot predict his threshold probability-of-appearing criterion unless we know what he perceived as the probability-of-appearance figure for each of those defendants. If we had that information, we could observe above what PA figure he begins to release and below what figure (that is, the same figure unless there is a gray area) he begins to hold. With that information, we could assign each judge a behavioral PA^* figure rather than just an attitudinal PA^* figure which the questionnaire in figure 1-2 generates, although one's behavior generally follows one's attitudes.[11]

If we knew a given judge's perceived probability-of-appearance figure for each defendant, then we might find that above a certain PA figure he releases most, but not all, defendants and below that figure he holds most, but not all, defendants even though that figure involves the fewest inconsistencies. Those inconsistencies, however, may simply reflect the fact that the judge is not considering just one contingent event in making the release or hold decision. A second contingent event that he might be considering is the probability that the defendant may commit a crime while released—although under most statutes the probability of appearing in court is supposed to be the main or even exclusive criterion for releasing or holding defendants prior to trial. We could prepare a payoff matrix like those shown in figure 1-1 in order to indicate how a given judge or type of judge

The Bond-Setting Decision/Individual Cases

feels in a given case or type of case about releasing or holding a defendant in light of the probability that he might commit a certain type of crime while released. From that four-celled matrix we could obtain for the judge a threshold PN^*, where PN stands for the probability of not committing a serious crime. For a defendant to be released under this multiple-contingency perspective, he would have to have a probability of appearing greater than PA^* and a probability of not committing a crime greater than PN^*. If the defendant flunks either test, he does not get released.

C. Monetary Values

One might ask how the multiple-contingency approach can take into consideration that more weight is supposed to be given to the probability of appearing in court than to the probability of committing a crime. This is difficult to do under the nonmonetary approach, partly because a -100 in the crime-committing payoff matrix is treated as being as undesirable as a -100 in the court-appearing matrix. Likewise, the nonmonetary approach would treat a -100 in a payoff matrix dealing with committing murder as being as undesirable as a -100 in a payoff matrix dealing with a substantially lesser crime. What we need is a common measurement unit for showing values across payoff matrices regardless of the contingent event with which we are dealing. Ideally, such a unit measures psychological utility, but that kind of unit is too difficult to express. As a substitute, at least we can tentatively try working with dollars.

Figure 1-3 shows a decision theory payoff matrix involving two contingent events and monetary values. The two contingent events are appearing or failing to appear in court and committing or not committing a crime while released. The monetary values include two releasing costs and three holding costs. The *releasing costs* are the cost of rearresting an average defendant, estimated at $200, and the cost of a crime committed by an average defendant while released, estimated at $1,000. The *holding cost* consists of (1) the maintenance cost for keeping an average defendant in jail for an average pretrial period, figured at $4.43 per day for 2.28 months, (2) the lost gross national product for an average defendant, figured at $360 per month for 2.28 months, and (3) the bitterness cost that society might be willing to pay to avoid having a defendant sit in jail prior to trial for an average 2.28 months and then be found not guilty, estimated at $300 per month given that 12 percent of the defendants held in jail prior to trial are found not guilty.[12] Those figures come from a survey of police chiefs, prosecutors, defense attorneys, and bail administration officials in a sample of twenty-three cities, analyzed in more detail in another study.[13] The two releasing cost are symbolized RC_1 and RC_2, respectively, in figure 1-3*a*, and

16   Decision Theory and the Legal Process

a. Releasing and Holding Costs

Alternative Possibilities with Point Probabilities

	(D) Would Fail to Appear and Commit Crime	(C) Would Appear and Commit Crime	(B) Would Fail to Appear and No Crime	(A) Would Appear and No Crime
	.08(.15) = .01	.92(.15) = .14	.08(.85) = .07	.92(.85) = .78
Release	RB = +1,206 RC_1 = −200 RC_2 = −1,000 ——— $6	RB = +1,206 RC_2 = −1,000 ——— $206	RB = +1,206 RC_1 = −200 ——— $1,006	RB = +1,206 ——— $1,206
Hold	HC = −1,206 HB_1 = +200 HB_2 = +1,000 ——— −$6	HC = −1,206 HB_2 = +1,000 ——— −$206	HC = −1,206 HB_1 = +200 ——— −$1,006	HC = −1,206 ——— −$1,206

b. Expected Values

Alternative Possibilities with Range Probabilities

	Would Fail to Appear and Commit Crime	Would Appear and Commit Crime	Would Fail to Appear and No Crime	Would Appear and No Crime	Total Expected Value
	.00 to .08	.07 to .15	.00 to .08	.77 to .85	
Release	$.06 0 to .48	$29 14 to 31	$70 0 to 80	$941 (or $1,206 × .78) 929 to 1025 (or, $1,206 × .77)	$1,040 943 to 1,136
Hold	−$.06 0 to −.48	−$29 −14 to −31	−$70 0 to −80	−$941 −929 to −1,025	−$1,040 −943 to −1,136

Figure 1-3. Decision Theory Payoff Matrices Involving Two Contingent Events and Monetary Values.

the three holding costs are collectively symbolized *HC*. Costs are shown as negative amounts, and benefits are shown as positive amounts. Releasing benefits (*RB*) are holding costs saved, and holding benefits (HB_1 or HB_2) are releasing costs saved.

The same questionnaire data from which most of the cost figures were obtained also indicated that 92 percent of the released defendants appeared in court, and 85 percent of the released defendants were not known to have committed a crime while released.[14] Given that there are two contingent events, there are four possible occurrences which are labeled *A, B, C,* and *D* in figure 1-3*a*. To determine the probability that a released defendant

The Bond-Setting Decision/Individual Cases 17

would both appear in court and not commit a crime, we could simply multiply .92 by .85 if we are willing to assume that those two subpossibilities are independent of each other. We know, however, that they are not likely to be completely independent because defendants with certain characteristics are likely to both appear and not commit crimes, whereas defendants with opposite characteristics are more likely both to fail to appear and to commit crimes. Even though we do not know how close related our two contingent events are, from the data we have we can determine a maximum and a minimum probability somewhere between .00 and 1.00 for the A, B, C, and D possibilities. This is done in figure 1-4. For example, if possibilities A and C must constitute 92 percent of our released defendants (since those two possibilities constitute all the defendants who appear and only the defendants who appear), then that equality alone indicates that either possibility A or possibility C (but not both) can have a maximum probability of .92. The second equality tells us, however, that possibility A can be no higher than .85 and not .92. Applying that same reasoning to A, B, C, and D in figure 1-4a, we can take those four maximum probabilities and the four equalities

a. Determining the Maximum Probability for Each Possibility

Given This Equality	Then max D is	Then max C is	Then max B is	Then max A is
$A + C = .92$	X	.92	X	.92
$A + B = .85$	X	X	.85	<u>.85</u>
$C + D = .15$	.15	<u>.15</u>	X	X
$B + D = .08$	<u>.08</u>	X	<u>.08</u>	X

(The lowest maximum for each possibility is underlined.)

b. Determining the Minimum Probability for Each Possibility

Given This Equality and the Above Maximums	Then min D is	Then min C is	Then min B is	Then min A is
$A + C = .92$	X	.07 (or, .92 − .85)	X	.77 (or, .92 − .15)
$A + B = .85$	X	X	.00 (or, .85 − .85)	.77 (or, .85 − .08)
$C + D = .15$	.00 (or, .15 − .15)	.07 (or, .15 − .08)	X	X
$B + D = .08$	.00 (or, .08 − .08)	X	.00 (or, .08 − .08)	X

(An X means the equality does not apply.)

Figure 1-4. Determining the Maximum and Minimum Probability for Each Contingent Possibility with Two Contingent Events.

to figure 1-4*b* to determine the minimum probabilities. Thus, *A* could not be lower than .77. Otherwise, *A* + *C* could not add up to .92, since .15 is as high as *C* can be.[15]

Now that we have that cost and probability data, what do we do with them? That is where figure 1-3*b* comes in. The logical thing to do is to determine for each of the four alternative possibilities the expected values for releasing or holding this hypothetical average defendant. The *expected value* for any one of the eight cells in the payoff matrix is the total value or cost of that cell times the probability that the combination of contingent events will occur which that cell represents. Thus, the expected value for releasing an average defendant who would fail to appear and not commit a crime (possibility *B*) is $70. That figure represents $RB + RC_1$ sum (or $1,006) multiplied by the .07 probability. If one rejects the independent-probability approach for handling two contingent events, one can say the expected value is from $0 to $80. That range represents the $RB + RC_1$ sum multiplied by the .00 minimum probability, and the $RB + RC_1$ sum multiplied by the .08 maximum probability for alternative possibility *B*.[16]

After we have obtained expected values for each payoff cell, the next logical thing is to sum the expected values across each row to obtain the total expected value for releasing the average defendant; then that value can be compared with the total expected value for holding the average defendant. Doing so with the data given shows that our judicial system would maximize its benefit-cost picture by releasing the average defendant. This is what our judicial system does do, at least as indicated by the same questionnaire data from which the costs and probabilties were taken. Those data show the average defendant has a .73 chance of being released since the average city in the sample reported a 73 percent release rate. Many defendants, however, are not average, which possibly explains why 27 percent of the defendants are held in jail pending trial. Perhaps the judges in those specific cases implicitly perceive the probability of appearing, the probability of crime committing, the releasing costs, and the holding costs to be such that the expected value of holding those defendants is greater than the expected value of releasing them, rather than the more common reverse order.[17] Perhaps some of those cases also involve other contingent events (such as the probability that a defendant, although "guilty," will be acquitted) or other costs (such as the opportunity cost of not taking advantage of the opportunity of holding a defendant in order to teach him and others a lesson—not to get arrested).

The decision rule generated by an analysis of figure 1-3 is this: Release a defendant when the expected value of releasing him, given his specific probabilities and costs, is greater than the expected value of holding him. An alternative way of conceptualizing the release-hold decision would be to say this: Release the defendant if the expected holding costs are greater than the expected releasing costs. The expected holding costs for our hypothetical average defendant are $1,206, or *HC*, assuming he is held. The expected releasing costs are $(PF)(RC_1) + (PC)(RC_2)$, where *PF* is the probability of failing to appear (that is, 1.00 − *PA*) and *PC* is the probability of committing a crime while released (that is, 1.00 − *PN*). The expected releasing costs are thus (.08)($200) + (.15)($1,000), or $166. That alternative conceptualizing could also be stated thus: Release the defendant if the expected releasing benefits are greater than the expected holding benefits. Given the data, the expected releasing benefits for the average defendant would be $1,206 saved, and the expected holding benefits would be $166 saved.[18] We also can combine those two concepts by saying that the defendant should be released if releasing benefits minus releasing costs (that is, $1,206 − $166) is greater than holding benefits minus holding costs (that is, $166 − $1,206). In other words, the $1,040 expected value of releasing the average defendant is greater than the −$1,040 expected value of holding.[19] Either the expected-value approach via the payoff matrix or the expected-net-benefit approach (that is, expected benefits minus expected costs) should yield the same result, which in this case is a decision in favor of releasing the average defendant prior to trial.[20]

Another insight-generating way of analyzing the data in figure 1-3 is to use a decision tree perspective like that shown in figure 1-5. The left trunk end of the decision tree shows that we are trying to determine the value of a decision to release versus a decision to hold. Releasing can result in appearance or nonappearance and in no crime or a crime. Likewise, the held defendant could have resulted in appearance or nonappearance and in no crime or a crime if he had been released. At the right end of each branch are given the *A, B, C,* and *D* possibilities listed in figure 1-3, along with the benefits minus costs from figure 1-3. A prime sign is used to distinguish those possibilities for held defendants versus released defendants. The expected value of any branch that is not an end branch is equal to the sum of the values of the subsequent branches discounted or multiplied by the probability of their occurring, as indicated by the equations given at the bottom of the figure. Those calculations are referred to as "folding back" because they involve working backward from the values on the horizontal end branches and the probabilities on the diagonal branches to the expected values in the previous circles.

The decision tree shows that the expected value of releasing an average defendant is substantially greater than the expected value of holding one, as was previously indicated. That result is not affected by whether the decision tree branches first on appearance and then on crime committing, or first on crime committing and then on appearance. That result, however, assumes that the probabilities of appearing and crime committing are not affected by whether we release or hold someone. In other words, if an average defen-

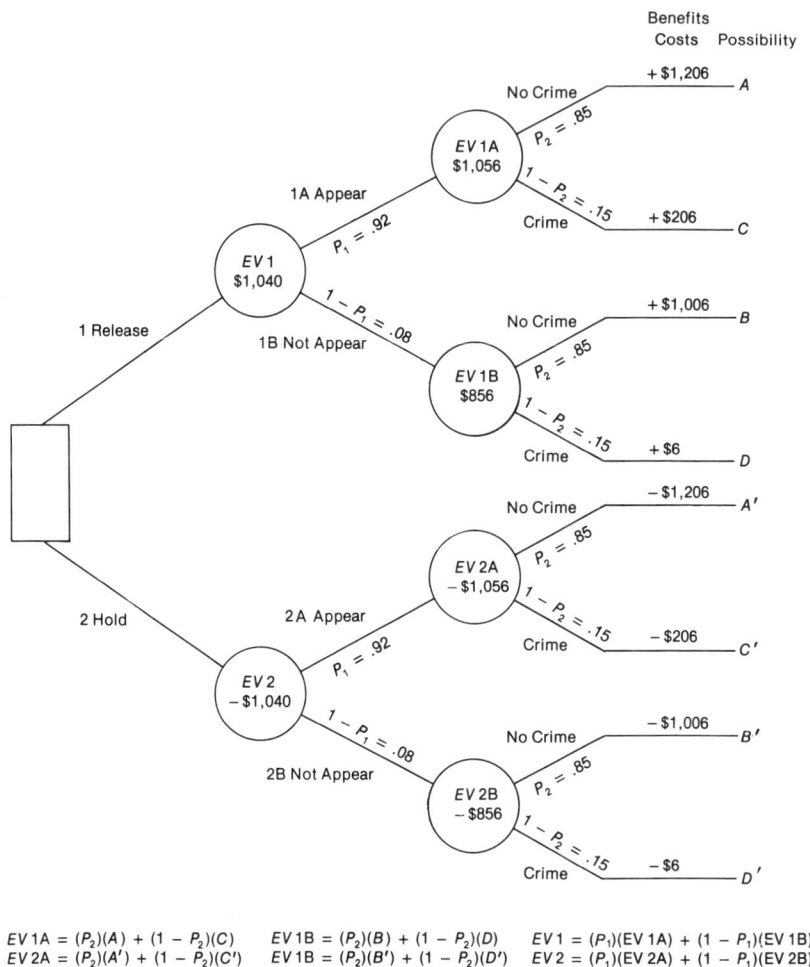

Figure 1-5. Decision Tree Involving Two Contingent Events and Monetary Values.

dant has a .92 probability of appearing, we assume he would have had that same probability of appearing if released regardless of whether he is actually released or held. Likewise, the model assumes that the benefits and costs are not affected by whether we hold someone. In other words, if an average defendant who commits a crime while released incurs $1,000 in social costs, he would incur the same $1,000 if he were to commit a crime while released regardless whether he is released or held. Often a decision tree perspective can be quite helpful in analyzing decisions that involve more than one contingent event, more than one decision-branching point, or more than dichotomous branches.

II. The Bond-Setting Decision

So far, we have been discussing the decision problem of whether to release or hold a defendant prior to trial. That, however, is how the pretrial release problem is usually stated in the courtroom context. In that context, usually the arraignment judge is faced with the decision of what bond to set for the defendant rather than the dichotomous decision of whether or not to release the defendant. Nevertheless, to a considerable extent, the bond-setting decision can be reduced to a release-hold decision if one equates release with a low bond (that is, a bond the defendant can and will meet) and hold with a high bond (that is, a bond the defendant cannot or will not meet). If an arraignment judge wants to release a defendant but the defendant is unexpectedly unable to meet the bond the judge has initially set, then the judge can lower it to arrive at a figure the defendant can meet. On the other hand, if an arraignment judge wants to hold a defendant and he sets a very high bond which the defendant unexpectedly can meet, then the judge cannot so easily raise the bond without some evidence of changed circumstances other than the fact that the defendant had more money than the judge imagined.

One interesting aspect about the bond-setting decision as contrasted to the releasing decision is that the decision itself can influence the probability of appearing in court, which is supposed to be the main criterion in arriving at the decision. Thus, a judge can increase the probability of a defendant appearing in court by setting a high bond, provided that the defendant can meet the bond. With a high bond, the defendant has more of an incentive to appear—in order to retrieve his bond—than he would with a low bond. A rational way to combine the bond-setting decision with the decision to release or hold might involve a five-step process. First, the judge involved can determine his own threshold probability of appearance (PA^*) through the payoff matrix approach discussed in section I or through whatever method the judge prefers. Second, the judge can determine whether the defendant's probability of appearing in court is greater than that threshold probability regardless of the bond set. Third, if the defendant's PA is greater than PA^*, then the defendant can be released on his own recognizance or on a nominal bond. Fourth, if the defendant's PA is less than PA^*, then the bond should be set just high enough to bring the defendant's PA above the threshold probability. Doing so involves the judge taking into consideration the defendant's ability to pay since a low bond will be more of an incentive for a poor person to appear in court than for a rich person.[21] Fifth, if no bond can bring the defendant's probability of appearing above the threshold, then the defendant may have to be held in jail pending a speedy trial. Likewise, if the bond that can bring PA above PA^* is too high for the defendant to meet, then he may also have to be held while awaiting trial. It is unfortunate that a defendant has to be held in jail pending trial when the holding costs usually are higher than the releasing costs. That fact, however, is implicitly taken into consideration in the lowness of the threshold probability which the judge uses as his criterion in determining which defendants to hold.

The bond-setting decision, like the releasing decision, can simultaneously consider the two contingent events of appearing in court and not committing a crime while released. In that decision situation, our five-step decision process would be adjusted as follows. First, the judge involved determines his PA^* threshold with the court-appearance contingency and then his probability-of-not-committing-a-crime threshold (PN^*) with the crime-committing contingency. Second, the judge determines whether the defendant's probability of appearance is greater than PA^* and whether the defendant's probability of not committing a crime (PN) is greater than PN^*. Third, if the defendant passes both tests, then he can be released on his own recognizance or on a nominal bond. Fourth, the judge can try to set a bond high enough to bring PA over PA^*. Doing so, however, may sometimes decrease PN since a high bond has been known to motivate a defendant to commit a crime in order to pay off the high bond loan or high bond premium. Fifth, the defendant may have to be detained in jail until his trial if the fourth step does not bring both his probabilities above the threshold cutoffs or if the only bond he can meet is one that provides an insufficient probability of appearance.

As an alternative to this five-step process, conceivably a judge could go through a kind of crude or implicit expected-value calculation with monetary values like those shown in figure 1-3. The only difference would be that instead of the alternative decisions being release or hold, they would be release on the highest bond that the defendant can meet versus hold. Thus the probabilities, with regard to appearing in court at the top of columns A and C, would be higher than if the choice were merely release or hold; and the probabilities with regard to failing to appear at the top of columns B and D would be lower. All the other calculations would be the same, and the defendant would be released if the expected value of releasing (EV_R) were greater than the expected value of holding (EV_H).

Perhaps we should emphasize that we are not saying that judges do or should prepare payoff matrices for each arraignment case. We are saying that the payoff matrix approach can provide an understanding of what may

The Bond-Setting Decision/Individual Cases 23

General Statement: Listed below are fifteen defendants appearing before you in an arraignment proceeding. For each defendant, indicate in what range you would generally set bond for an average defendant having those characteristics. The ranges we are using are as follows: (1) release on recognizance; (2) $0 to $99; (3) $100 to $499; (4) $500 to $999; (5) $1,000 to $1,999; (6) $2,000 to $4,999; (7) $5,000 to $9,999; (8) $10,000 to $19,999; (9) $20,000 to $49,999; (10) $50,000 to $99,999; (11) $100,000 or over; (12) no bond allowed.

Item	Charge	Probability of Appearing in Court	Other Characteristics	Bond Category (1 to 12)
1	Armed robbery	.90	None available	
.				
.				
4	Shoplifting	.20	Adult male	
.				
.				
7	Armed robbery	.15	None available	
.				
15	Shoplifting	.85	Adult male	

Figure 1-6. Some Questions for Obtaining a Judge's Propensities Regarding Bond-Setting Decisions.

be implicitly happening in an inexact way in a judge's mind. What we are also saying is that the payoff matrix or decision theory approach can provide a means for understanding the effects of various cost changes and probability changes on releasing and bond-setting decisions. That approach, when combined with a questionnaire or other data-gathering techniques, can also provide information relevant to encouraging more uniformity or more compliance with appropriate legal standards in releasing and bond-setting decisions.

A good set of questions to add to our questionnaire (figure 1-1) might especially include some short, hypothetical bond-setting problems. For example, the judges might be presented with fifteen hypothetical defendants and asked to place each one in about a dozen bond categories. Four such hypothetical case questions are shown in figure 1-6. That particular set is designed to determine the extent to which a responding judge is influenced by the severity of the crime committed irrespective of its relation to the probability of the defendant's appearing in court. Judges generally will admit that they set bond higher for more severe crimes—not in order to punish the defendant with pretrial detention, but rather in recognition of the relation between severity of crime and failure to appear in court.[22] If a judge gives a high bond in cases 4 and 7 and a low bond in cases 1 and 15, then he is more influenced by the probability of appearance than by the charge. If a judge gives a high bond in cases 1 and 7 and a low bond in cases

4 and 15, then he is more influenced by the charge than by the probability of appearance. If a judge is about equally high or low in all four cases, then he is not influenced by either the severity of the charge or PA. It might be interesting to know what explains those different propensities among different judges. It also might be interesting to point out their propensities to them in an unpublicized way, possibly as part of a judicial workshop, to see if doing so might change their subsequent bond-setting behavior in court. This questionnaire approach obviously works better than directly asking a judge what his propensities are, and it works better than trying to determine his propensities from a mass of cases in which the possibly influential variables cannot be separated out or controlled for. Other hypothetical defendants can be included to get at the role of the probability of crime committing and the effect of economic class, as well as to decrease the visibility to the respondent of the comparisons that are likely to be made.

III. Increasing the Expected Value of Releasing in Individual Cases

A. *The General Perspective*

In an arraignment proceeding, a judge must decide whether to release the defendant on his own recognizance or by way of a low bond, or whether to hold the defendant by refusing to set bond or by way of a high bond. Judges probably are more reluctant to make an error of releasing a defendant who would fail to appear (a type 2 error) than to make an error of holding a defendant who would appear if released (a type 1 error). Releasing errors are more avoided because they are more visible than holding errors since it is embarrassing to a judge if a defendant he released fails to appear, but no one knows for sure if a defendant the judge held would have appeared if he had been released. As a result, there may be much more pretrial holding than is necessary.

What is needed is to make the holding errors and the holding costs more visible in order to decrease the unnecessary and wrongful holding. What may be needed also is to decrease the releasing costs so that judges will be more inclined to release defendants. In addition, there is a need for raising and clarifying the probability that defendants will appear in court since much of the holding may be based on an unduly low actual or perceived probability of appearing, and also on an unduly vague probability of appearing plus an implicit strategy that prefers to hold rather than release when the situation is unclear. The tendency to hold when in doubt and the greater sensitivity to releasing errors rather than holding errors run contrary to the rule of law in pretrial release decisions which says the benefit of the

The Bond-Setting Decision/Individual Cases

doubt concerning appearance should go to the defendant as part of the general presumption of innocence and the presumption of appearing in court.[23] Thus, we are talking about promoting the rule of law in pretrial release decisions when we discuss this need for raising and clarifying the probability of appearance, making more visible the type 1 errors and costs of holding defendants who would appear, and when we talk about decreasing the costs of type 2 errors of releasing defendants who fail to appear.

In the top row of the four cells in figure 1-7, we show that the expected value of releasing (rather than holding) a defendant logically equals the

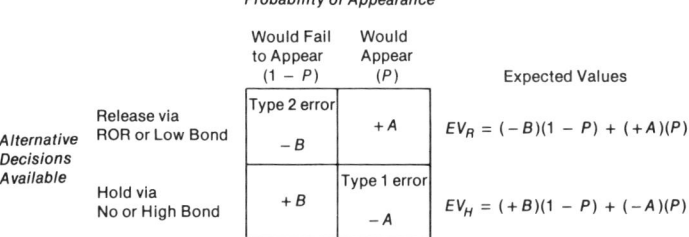

There are three general approaches to widening the positive difference between EV_R and EV_H:

I. Raise and clarify the probability of appearance (that is, increase P).
   1. Raise P through better screening and notification.
   2. Clarify P through statistical studies of what percentage of various types of released defendants appear in court.
   3. More vigorously prosecute those who fail to appear.

II. Make more visible the type 1 errors and costs of holding defendants who would appear (that is, increase A).

   1. Publicize for each judge the percentage of defendants he holds and the appearance percentage he attains. (Judges vary widely on percentage held, but appearance percentages tend to be about 90 percent.)
   2. Make more visible how much it costs to hold defendants in jail.
      a. Jail maintenance
      b. Lost income
      c. Bitterness from case dismissed after lengthy wait
      d. Families on welfare
      e. Increased conviction probability
      f. Jail riots from overcrowding

III. Decrease the costs of type 2 errors of releasing defendants who fail to appear (that is, decrease B).
   1. Make rearrest more easy through pretrial supervision.
   2. Decrease the time from arrest to trial.
      a. More personnel, more diversion, and shorter trial stage
      b. Better sequencing of cases
      c. Shorter path from arrest to trial
   3. Decrease pretrial crime committing.
      a. Increase probability of being arrested, convicted, and jailed
      b. Decrease benefits of successful crime committing
      c. Increase costs of unsuccessful crime committing

Figure 1-7. Increasing the Percentages of Defendants Released in the Pretrial Release Decision.

benefits of releasing minus the costs of releasing. The benefits are the positive value to the judge of having the released defendant appear in court (symbolized $+A$), and the costs are the negative value to the judge of having the released defendant fail to appear in court (symbolized $-B$). We cannot, however, merely determine $A - B$, because doing so would not take into consideration that those benefits and costs are contingent on the probability of the defendant appearing in court. Instead, the benefits have to be discounted by the probability of their occurring (that is, the value of A multiplied by P), and the costs have to be discounted by the probability of their occurring (that is, the value of B multiplied by $1 - P$).

Likewise, the expected value of holding a defendant in the bottom row of the table equals the discounted benefits of holding minus the discounted costs of holding. The benefits are the positive value to the judge of having held the defendant who would have failed to appear in court if released (symbolized $+B$), and the costs are the negative value to the judge of having held the defendant who would have appeared in court if released (symbolized $-A$). The expected value or discounted net benefits are thus equal to $(-A)(P) + (+B)(1 - P)$. Holding a defendant who would have appeared in court is a type 1 error (or an alpha error, which explains the use of the letter A), and releasing a defendant who would fail to appear is a type 2 error (or beta error, which explains the use of the letter B). A type 1 error rejects the hypothesis (or presumption that the defendant will appear) when it is true, and a type 2 error accepts the hypothesis (that the defendant will appear) when it is false.

As one can see by some simple algebraic manipulation, the expected value of releasing varies directly or positively with the values of P and A and inversely or negatively with the value of B. Likewise, the expected value of holding varies inversely with the values of P and A and directly with the value of B. Thus, if we want to increase the expected value of releasing relative to the expected value of holding, logically we should seek to increase P, increase A, and decrease B. In other words, we should seek to influence the awareness, perceptions, and facts which relate to (1) the probability of a defendant appearing in court, (2) the errors and costs of his being held when he would have appeared, and (3) the errors and costs of his failing to appear when released.[24]

B. Raise and Clarify the Probability of Appearance

An important way to increase the probability that released defendants will appear is through better screening and notification. Better screening might involve a combination of the subjective analysis of a defendant's probability of appearing and a more objective analysis like that used in the point system of the Vera Institute. Notifying the defendant by postcard or telephone the day before his court appearance may often prevent nonappearances, especially by low-income defendants who are not accustomed to middle-class procedures for appointment keeping.

To improve the effectiveness of pretrial release screening, more research is needed to determine what set of variables are the best predictors and what statistical procedure is the best way to weight the variables. A study in Rochester interestingly revealed that one can get better predictability from checking whether the defendant was telling the truth with regard to how long he has held his present job. This yes-no variable predicts better than the variable of whether the defendant has held his present job one month, six months, a year, or longer.[25]

These statistical techniques, by aiding in the screening process, improve the probability that released defendants will appear. They also clarify that the appearance rate is high for defendants in certain categories and for defendants in general. That clarification can increase the perceived probability of appearance even if it does not affect the actual probability of appearance. This is important since judges act on the basis of their perceptions of P, although that indirectly is influenced by what P actually is.

These statistical techniques also can decrease the gray area as to who will appear, which can be important in increasing the percentage of defendants released. This is so because many judges may be well aware that a high percentage of all defendants appear, say about 90 percent. They may, however, indicate that the problem which they do not know in advance is which released defendants would be likely to be in the 90 percent and which in the 10 percent. More specifically, a judge might say he releases about 70 percent of all defendants because those 70 percent are the ones he feels are likely to appear. Another 5 percent he feels are very unlikely to appear. The middle 25 percent he is not sure about either way, but he tends to hold them rather than risk the embarrassment of having them not appear. If the size of this gray or unpredicted 25 percent can be reduced, that should mean a substantial increase in the percentage of defendants released.

The probability of a defendant deliberately choosing not to appear in court also can be reduced by more vigorously prosecuting those who fail to appear without an adequate justification. Increasing the probability of such prosecution and the invocation of a substantial penalty raises the expected value of appearing relative to not appearing for the released defendant, thereby increasing the likelihood that he will choose to appear. The possibility of forfeiting one's bond can also encourage appearance for those released on bond, rather than on their own recognizance.[26]

C. Make More Visible the Errors and Costs of Holding Defendants Who Would Appear

The main reason judges are more sensitive to type 2 errors than type 1 errors is that the error of releasing someone who fails to appear is presently more visible than the error of holding someone who would appear. What needs to be done is to increase the visibility of the holding errors. One meaningful way to do that is to show for each judge serving in the same circuit both what percentage of defendants he holds in jail prior to trial and what percentage of his released defendants appear for their court dates. We would probably find a great deal of variation among the judges with regard to the percentage of defendants they hold. We would probably, however, not find so much variation among the judges with regard to the percentage of their released defendants who appear in court.[27]

If the judges were arranged on a list from the judge with the highest hold percentage to the judge with the lowest hold percentage, we might see that the highest hold judge (for example, about 70 percent hold) has an appearance rate of about 95 percent. The lowest hold judge (for example, about 20 percent) might have an appearance rate of about 90 percent. Thus, the highest hold judge could not justify his high holding rate on the grounds that he is getting a much better appearance rate than the judges with lower holding percentages. He also would find it difficult to argue that his sample of defendants is substantially different from the samples of fellow judges since there tends to be less shopping in arraignment proceedings than in trial proceedings. We are thus roughly indicating the number of errors of holding defendants who would appear through the use of these aggregate statistics, even though it is impossible to determine whether such an error has been made in an individual case where the defendant is held in jail prior to trial.[28]

The raw data for calculating hold percentages and appearance percentages for individual judges can be obtained from the docket sheets which are public information. Obtaining these data requires no special cooperation from the judges as having them answer hypothetical sentencing cases would. If these lists were made available periodically, it is likely that judges who are holding a high percentage of defendants would tend to move downward. They would be motivated partly by (1) embarrassment in comparison to their fellow judges, (2) lack of appearance rate justification for their high holding rates, (3) a respect for the norm of uniformity among judges, and (4) recognition of the high holding costs relative to releasing costs, to which we now turn.

In addition to publicizing the errors of holding defendants who would appear, the costs of such errors can be publicized. Many judges may be unaware of how high the holding costs are and how many different types of costs are involved. The most obvious is that of jail maintenance, which may be quite substantial when one considers the length of time the average defendant is held, and the fixed and variable costs needed to provide for him during that time. The costs also include the lost gross national product which can be attributed to defendants being unable to earn or produce anything while they are in jail. That cost may be substantial even if it is figured at only the minimum wage.

An additional cost that is hard to assess but should still be analyzed is the bitterness generated by being held in jail for a substantial time awaiting trial and then having one's case dismissed or acquitted for lack of sufficient evidence. It might be interesting to know what percentage of defendants held in jail prior to trial do have their cases dismissed or acquitted, or receive sentences shorter than the time they have already served awaiting trial. Another cost that can be more easily assessed is the number of families who are on welfare as the result of a breadwinner being held in jail prior to trial. Another cost from unnecessarily holding defendants is the cost of jail riots resulting from overcrowding. In recent years in New York, Washington, D.C., and elsewhere, some jail riots have been substantially attributed to the overcrowding from pretrial detention.

Still another important holding cost stems from the increased probability of an innocent defendant being convicted because he was unable to adequately prepare his case while being held in jail and because he made a substantially poorer impression on the judge or jury by being a pretrial detainee. Research by the Vera Institute does show that pretrial detention increases the probability of conviction even when all other relevant variables are held constant. Pretrial detainees who may be innocent or whose guilt may be quite difficult to prove also are quite vulnerable to prosecution offers to reduce the recommended sentence to the time served awaiting trial if the defendant will plead guilty. Released defendants are not vulnerable to that particular kind of pressure. Pretrial detainees may be more likely to be convicted regardless of their guilt because they get faster trials while the prosecution witnesses are still fresh. Some prosecutors may concentrate on prosecuting pretrial detainees to the neglect of released defendants out of a feeling that detainees should receive a priority or because speedy trial laws emphasize fast trials for detainees.

By publicizing for each judge the percentage of defendants he holds and the appearance percentage he attains, and by making more visible how much it costs to hold defendants in jail, in effect we are trying to make the ratio of each judge's individual holding costs to individual releasing costs approach the ratio of society's holding costs to society's releasing costs. As of now, these individual costs seem to produce a much lower ratio than the social costs. In other words, as an individual, a judge stands to lose more by releasing a no-show than by holding a defendant who would show, but society generally stands to lose more by a holding mistake than by a releasing mistake, given the relative social costs involved and the probabilities of their occurring.[29]

D. Decrease the Costs of Releasing Defendants Who Fail to Appear

Two main costs are involved in releasing a defendant who fails to appear. One is the cost of having to rearrest him. The other is the cost of any crime he might commit while released. That crime cost theoretically, however, is not supposed to be a major criterion in determining whether a defendant should be released, since regularly including it would amount to a constitutionally questionable system of preventive detention, as contrasted to including it in exceptional cases like those involving obviously dangerous defendants. The rearrest cost (and, incidentally, the crime-committing cost) can be reduced by having a better knowledge of where the defendant is through a system of pretrial parole. Such a system would involve releasing the defendant on the condition that he periodically report his whereabouts or be subject to rearrest for failure to do so. Heavy supervision in all cases, however, might be more costly than the incremental rearrest and crime-committing savings over an unsupervised system.

A way to substantially reduce both the nonappearance and crime-committing costs would be to reduce the time from arrest to trial. The longer the defendant is out, the more the probability increases that he will negligently or deliberately fail to appear, and the more time he has to become involved in a new criminal act. The defendant's ultimate nonappearance is especially increased if during that intervening period he is repeatedly told to come to court, which he does, and because of congestion and delay the court is unready to hear his case. Thus, the pretrial release problem is closely associated with the problem of reducing delay in the criminal justice system.[30]

Delay can be reduced by having more judicial personnel, diverting more cases away from the criminal justice system or at least away from trial, and attempting to shorten the trial stage through pretrial discovery and random jury selection. Delay can also be reduced by better sequencing and scheduling of cases. For example, if all the short cases were given a priority, the average waiting time would be reduced, although a maximum time constraint should be placed on all cases. Theoretically, by shortening the path from arrest to trial through the elimination of certain stages, delay could be substantially reduced, but doing so might violate federal or state constitutional constraints.

Releasing costs that relate to crime committing by released defendants can be reduced by the same methods which can be suggested for crime reduction in general. Basically they involve applying a model like that shown in figure 1-6 to reduce the expected value of crime committing and increase the expected value of engaging in legitimate alternate activities.

The Bond-Setting Decision/Individual Cases

By analogy to figure 1-6, these methods logically include increasing the probability of being arrested, convicted, and jailed which can come about through such means as more efficient criminal justice personnel or through less due process. The expected value of crime committing also is reduced by decreasing the benefits of successful crime committing by reducing the vulnerability of potential crime targets and reducing the peer group recognition that criminals often receive by trying to redirect gang orientations. The expected value of crime is further lessened by increasing the costs of unsuccessful crime committing, possibly through more severe punishments or by having criminals suffer the opportunity costs of missed occupational opportunities by first providing them with some meaningful opportunities to miss.

One method that would increase the probability of appearance and also decrease the cost of rearresting defendants who fail to appear is the method of high bond setting. If the bond is high and sure to be forfeited for nonappearance, the defendant is more likely to appear. Likewise, if the bond is high, or at least high enough to cover the rearrest costs, then if the defendant fails to appear, his bond forfeiture can be used to reduce those rearrest costs to zero in the average case. This makes bond setting like a pollution tax, which has often been proposed in environmental law. The tax on a given firm is to the total dollars desired to clean up the area as the firm's pollution is to the total pollution in the area. That kind of proportionate tax is designed to deter pollution, analogous to deterring nonappearance. If, however, a business firm cannot eliminate its pollution economically, then the tax it pays is used to clean up or reduce the damage its pollution has caused, analogous to paying the rearrest costs. This high-bond approach, though, has the undesirable effect of increasing the likelihood of holding defendants, unlike the other approaches which do not produce conflicting effects. However, this logically raises the question of how high the bond should be in order to increase the probability of appearance and decrease the releasing costs, without counterproductively increasing the occurrence of holding. That is the issue of devising optimum bond schedules to which we now turn.

Notes

Thanks are owed for comments on earlier drafts of chapters 1 and 2 to Leslie Wilkins of SUNY-Albany; Allan Goldman of the National Bureau of Standards; Herbert Miller and William McDonald of the Georgetown Law School; Paul Lermack of Bradley University; Daniel Fried of the Yale Law School; and Joseph Ebersole of the Federal Judicial Center.

1. Books on pretrial release, bond setting, and related matters include: Foote, ed., *Studies on Bail* (University of Pennsylvania Law School, 1966), especially pp. 4-15, 74-88; P. Wice, *Freedom for Sale: A National Study of Pre-Trial Release* (Lexington Books, 1974), especially pp. 25-34; D. Freed and P. Wald, *Bail in the United States* (U.S. Department of Justice, 1964); ABA, *Standards Relating to Pre-Trial Release* (American Bar Association, 1968); R. Goldfarb, *Ransom: A Critique of the Bail System* (Little, Brown, 1965); K. Bottomley, *Prison Before Trial: A Study of Remand Decisions in Magistrate Courts* (Ruthman, 1970); W. Thomas, *A Decade of Bail Reform* (University of California Press, 1976); B. Mahoney, *An Evaluation of Policy Related Research on the Effectiveness of Pretrial Release Programs* (National Center for State Courts, 1975); J. Mullen, *Pre-Trial Services: An Evaluation of Policy Related Research* (Abt Associates, 1975); W. Thomas et al., *Pre-Trial Release Programs* (Law Enforcement Assistance Administration, 1977); and Silverstein, "Bail in the States: A Field Study and Report," 50 *Minn. L. Rev.* 621 (1966).

2. The judge in figure 1-1a is more oriented toward avoiding a type 1 error than a type 2 error, whereas the judge in figure 1-1b is more oriented toward avoiding a type 2 error than a type 1 error. A type 1 error involves rejecting a true hypothesis whereas a type 2 error involves accepting a false hypothesis. The basic criminal justice system hypothesis or presumption is that the defendant is innocent and that he will appear in court. Rejecting that hypothesis when it is true (a type 1 error) means holding a defendant who would have appeared. Accepting that hypothesis when it is false (a type 2 error) means releasing a defendant who should have been held.

3. If one solves for PA in the equation which equalizes the expected value of releasing and the expected value of holding, then the solution is $PA^* = (a - c)/(a - b - c + d)$. The symbol PA is shown with a star to indicate this is the value of the probability of appearing when the expected values of releasing and holding are equal. The proof of this formula is as follows:

$$(1 - PA)(a) + (PA)(b) = (1 - PA)(c) + (PA)(d)$$

Removing the parentheses and substituting P for PA gives

$$a - Pa + Pb = c - Pc + Pd$$

Transposing yields

$$-Pa + Pb + pc - Pd = c - a$$

Factor out P:

$$P(-a + b + c - d) = c - a$$

Divide both sides by $(-a + b + c - d)$:

$$P = (c - a)/(-a + b + c - d)$$

Now multiply the numerator and denominator of the right side by -1:

$$PA^* = (a - c)/(a - b - c + d)$$

4. On various methodologies for obtaining payoff matrix data, see Huber, "Methods for Quantifying Subjective Probabilities and Multi-Attribute Utilities," 5 *Decision Sciences* 430 (1974); and P. Kotler, *Marketing Decision Making: A Model Building Approach* 583-595 (Holt, Rinehart & Winston, 1971).

5. As a variation on figure 1-2, instead of beginning by asking which of the four alternatives would give the most satisfaction, the questions can begin by saying, Which of these four alternatives would give you some satisfaction, and which would give you some dissatisfaction? Then the questions can ask, Of the satisfying alternatives, which is the most satisfying? The questionnaire could then determine a numerical value for the second most satisfying, as figure 1-2 does. Then one would ask, Of the dissatisfying alternatives, which is the most dissatisfying? and then likewise determine a numerical value for the second most dissatisfying. That procedure, in effect, partitions the decisions the respondent has to make into smaller, more manageable decisions of determining direction, rank within direction, and then relative numerical value for the lesser rank, rather than trying to determine the most satisfying alternative first (which is a question that combines both direction and rank). The respondent also might be more comfortable discussing the dissatisfying alternatives before the satisfying since people may tend to think more in terms of avoiding relatively bad errors in making decisions than in trying to maximize good results. In terms of figure 1-2, these questions involve determining (1) where to put a minus and where to put a plus, (2) which minus should be a double minus, and which plus should be a double plus, (3) how the single minus should be scored if the double minus is scored -100, and (4) how the single plus should be scored if the double plus is scored $+100$.

Another approach that has been used to assign payoff values to the alternative possibilities stemming from a decision theory problem is as follows: (1) rank the payoffs from the most desirable to the least desirable, (2) determine the relative distances between each payoff, (3) assign a value of 100 to the most desirable and a value of 0 to the least desirable, (4) determine which of the payoff outcomes has close to an indifferent value, meaning it produces neither satisfaction nor dissatisfaction, and (5) subtract the numerical value of that indifferent payoff from each of the other numerical values, giving positive values to payoffs above the indifferent payoff and negative values to those below. This method is used by Raymond Tanter,

"Evaluation and Anticipation of Choice in International Crisis Management" (unpublished paper available from the author at the University of Michigan Political Science Department, 1975). The results, however, become distorted if step 4 does not involve a truly indifferent payoff. Step 2 is difficult to execute if more than a pair of payoffs are being compared at once. Tanter also asks respondents to rank and distance the payoffs on separate dimensions rather than just on a dimension of overall satisfaction. He then weights the dimensions and combines the data through a form of geometric scaling.

6. As an alternative based on these four questions, the judge might find it helpful to indicate first which possibility is the most satisfying, most dissatisfying, next to the most satisfying, and next to the most dissatisfying. Then he would be asked, How many dollars of your own money would you be willing to pay to avoid the most dissatisfying possibility, to avoid the next most dissatisfying possibility, to receive the satisfaction of the most satisfying possibility, and to receive the satisfaction of the next to the most satisfying possibility? That two-stage approach (with four subparts to each stage) probably makes the evaluations easier, although it does sometimes mean referring to one's answers from the first stage in order to answer the second-stage questions.

7. 4 W. Blackstone, *Commentaries* *358.

8. Since Blackstone and others tend to express the relative undesirability of a type 1 error to a type 2 error as a ratio, the questions in either the four-alternative form or the two-alternative form should probably also do so. This would involve, for example, wording the second question in the two-alternative form to read as follows:

> 2. How many more times as bad is result A over result B? (This assumes A was the more undesirable of the two results. Reverse the wording if B was mentioned as the more undesirable result.) In other words, is result A twice as bad as result B, five times as bad, ten times as bad, or is A some other multiple as bad as B?

The researcher can then give the more undesirable result a score of -100 and the less undesirable result a score of $-100/M$, where M indicates how many times more undesirable the worse alternative is compared to the less worse one. For example, if the respondent says it is five times as bad to have result A as result B, then he is, in effect, saying result A gets a score of -100 and B gets a score of -100 and B gets a score of $-100/5$, or -20. He is also saying that his threshold probability is $20/(100 + 20)$, or .17.

9. This approach assumes that a logically consistent decision maker would get an amount of satisfaction from avoiding a type 1 error equal to the amount of dissatisfaction from making a type 1 error. This means if the value of cell d in figure 1-1 is found to be $-A$, then the value of cell b is

The Bond-Setting Decision/Individual Cases 35

assumed to be equal to $+A$. Likewise, this approach assumes that a logically consistent decision maker would get an amount of satisfaction from avoiding a type 2 error equal to the amount of dissatisfaction from making a type 2 error. This means that if the value of cell a in figure 1-1 is found to be equal to $-B$, then the value of cell c is assumed to be $+B$. Therefore, under the above approach, the expected value of releasing equals $(+A)(PA) + (-B)(1 - PA)$, and the expected value of holding equals $(-A)(PA) + (+B)(1 - PA)$. To find the threshold probability for a given judge involves setting those two expressions equal to each other and solving for PA. The result will be equivalent of the algebraically simplified formula $PA^* = B/(A + B)$. It is also the equivalent of solving for PA in the formula previously given:

$$(1 - PA)(a) + (PA)(b) = (1 - PA)(c) + (PA)(d)$$

by substituting d, b, a, and c for $-A$, $+A$, $-B$, and $+B$, respectively.

An even simpler approach to determining one's threshold probability would be to use the formula $PA^* = 1/(X + 1)$, where $X = A/B$. This approach merely involves determining the ratio between the amount of dissatisfaction from a type 1 error versus a type 2 error. It does not require determining the values of A and B but only the value of A/B. If that value is 10, as with Blackstone's standard of guilt, then $PA^* = 1/(10 + 1) = 1/11 = .09$. That approach is probably best for determining one's own threshold probability because of its simplicity. But it may not be a good approach to use in a questionnaire directed to judges or others because the respondents can too easily see what is involved and then give answers that they think are socially desirable rather than their true answers. The approaches which seek values for A and B, or for a, b, c, and d, are somewhat more complicated and time-comsuming, but those defects may be more than offset by the increased subtlety and validity of those approaches. One can prove algebraically that $1/(X + 1)$ is the equivalent of $B/(A + B)$ and $(a - c)/(a - b - c + d)$, given the definitions of the symbols.

10. In order for a judge to have a .50 threshold PA^* with $+100$ and -100 anchor points in the payoff cells, he would have to have the values of -100, $+100$, $+100$, and -100 in cells a, b, c, and d. No other combination of values could yield a .50 PA^* with $+100$ and -100 anchor points except having all four cells be $+100$ or all four cells be -100; but that would be psychologically inconsistent for all four cells to be equally satisfying or equally unsatisfying. If having all judges operating with a .50 PA^* were deemed desirable, then it would make sense to try to convince them that it is as desirable to hold a defendant who would fail to appear in court as to release a defendant who would appear in court. Then it would make sense to try to convince them that it is equally undesirable to release a defen-

dant who had failed to appear in court as to hold a defendant who would have appeared in court.

11. It might be difficult to devise a meaningful questionnaire or interviewing approach to determine in actual cases what a judge perceives to be the probability of appearing. This is so because it is quite possible that judges tend to reach an overall or holistic decision on whether to hold or release without making a determination (especially an explicit determination) of a defendant's probability of appearing. If judges were asked to write down what they perceived the *PA* to be in each case, they might have a tendency to say less than .50 when they had set a bond that resulted in holding the defendant and greater than .50 when they had set a bond that resulted in releasing the defendant. Perhaps some judges might be willing to record their perceived *PA* figures after observing and questioning the defendant, but before setting bond. This would be analogous to the cooperation the University of Chicago Jury Project received whereby judges agreed to indicate how they would decide a jury trial criminal case after the end of the evidence and the arguments, but before the jury reached its decision. H. Kalven and H. Zeisel, *The American Jury* 45-54 (1966). Another alternative research approach would be to present the judges with hypothetical situations like those discussed with regard to figure 1-6 and ask them to estimate the probability of appearing in each situation given the information available.

12. Given the above figures, the average holding cost per defendant held is $1,206. Of that total, $303 is jail maintenance cost ($4.43 per day times 30 days times 2.28 months); $821 is lost gross national product ($360 per month times 2.28 months); and $82 is bitterness cost ($300 per month times 2.28 months times 12 percent).

13. S. Nagel, P. Wice, and M. Neef, *The Policy Problem of Doing Too Much or Too Little: Pre-Trial Release as a Case in Point* (Sage Publications, 1976).

14. Just because 92 percent of the released defendants appear in court does not mean that 92 percent of all the defendants would appear in court since the 27 out of 100 defendants who are held do not get an opportunity to fail to appear. Assuming their failure rate is about double the 8 percent rate for those who are released, this means that if all the defendants were released, then the 92 percent appearance rate would drop to 90 percent. This figure is arrived at by weighting the .92 appearance rate by the fact that it covers .73 of the defendants and by weighting the .84 appearance rate (that is, 100 percent minus 16 percent) by the fact that it covers .27 of the defendants. In other words, the new .90 appearance rate equals (.73)(.92) + (.27)(.84). If we assume the failure rate for the detainees is triple the rate for those released, then we would calculate (.73)(.92) + (.27)(.76), which yields an appearance rate of .88. If we go so far as to assume none of the detainees

would appear if released, then the overall appearance rate would still be .67, or two-thirds, since $(.73)(.92) + (.27)(0) = .67$.

The reason the appearance rate is not drastically changed by figuring in those who are not released is that (1) almost three-fourths of the defendants are released, (2) only a low 8 percent are known to fail to appear, and (3) many defendants who are not released may be good risks, but they lack the funds to pay the bond or they are possibly misperceived as being bad risks. Thus with these data, each doubling of the failure-to-appear rate of those not released only results in a reduction of 2 percent in the general appearance rate since $(.73)(.08) = .02$. Even if a substantially lowered appearance rate figure were used, the general conclusions of this section would not be changed—that the expected value of releasing the average defendant is substantially greater than the expected value of holding the average defendant. Another useful aspect of this kind of analysis is that one can easily change the probabilities (or the costs) and see how the results would change with regard to which of the alternative decisions is the best decision in benefit-cost terms, as in note 20. The same above considerations apply to the .85 tentative probability which is used to indicate the percentage of the released defendants who are not known to have committed a crime while released.

15. If we had 100 cases of defendants who were released, the following four-cell table would be consistent with our data which show that 92 percent of the released defendants appear in court and 85 percent of the released defendants do not commit crimes.

		Appearance		
		Fail	Appear	
	No Crime	B 5	A 80	85
Crime Committing	Crime	D 3	C 12	15
		8	92	100 cases

With these hypothetical data, the probabilities of occurrences A, B, C, and D are .80, .05, .12, and .03, respectively, all of which are consistent with the ranges given in figure 1-3b. These are referred to as empirical combined probabilities, rather than empirical single probabilities like the .92 probability of appearing, or a priori combined probabilities like the .92 times .85 probabilty of appearing and not committing a crime. With those hypothetical data, one can also say that if a defendant appears, the probability that he did not commit a crime is 80/92, or .87. Likewise, if a defendant does not commit a crime, the probability that he will appear is 80/85, or .94. Knowing any one of the four categories on the columns or rows, we can give a probability for any of the other categories. These are referred to as *conditional,* or *Bayesian,* probabilities. If we know with 1.00 accuracy that a defendant failed to appear, then we know, of course, that there is a zero probability that he appeared since those are complementary probabilities.

16. Essentially the same information presented by the eight-cell tables of figure 1-3 could be presented by a decision tree that ends in eight branches. It begins with the decision fork of releasing or holding, with each of those two forks going into an appearing versus a failing-to-appear fork, and each of those forks going into a no-crime versus a crime fork. A decision tree approach, however, consumes more space to present, conveys less detail, contains more repetitive labels, has extra arithmetic steps by not working with combined probabilities, and is probably not so easy to read. A decision tree approach is also arbitrary in whether it presents the appearance contingency before or after the crime-committing contingency since they are not sequential events. The results, however, should be identical between the tabular approach and the decision tree approach since these are basically just different methods of visual presentation, not differences in substance.

17. Prediction techniques which consider the characteristics of the defendant and his crime can be useful in predicting his probabilities and costs. The most widely known prediction scheme for predicting the probability of appearing was developed by the Vera Institute of New York City. See Ares, Rankin, and Sturz, "The Manhattan Bail Project: An Interim Report on the Use of Pre-Trial Parole," 38 *N.Y.U.L. Rev.* 67 (1963). For predicting the probability of crime committing while released, see J. Locke et al., *Compilation and Use of Criminal Court Data in Relation to Pre-Trial Release of Defendants: Pilot Study* 112-115 (National Bureau of Standards, 1970). On the use of subjective probabilities rather than probabilities based on statistical data, see Huber, "Methods for Quantifying Subjective Probabilities," and Kotler, *Marketing Decision Making.* On the use of statistical techniques for arriving at probabilities, see S. Nagel, *The Legal Process from a Behavioral Perspective* 144-172 (Dorsey, 1969) and D. Finney, *Probit Analysis* (Cambridge University Press, 1971). For a recent example of the application of probit analysis (which involves using statistical techniques to arrive at probabilities), Warren Hausman and Richard Thaler of the University of Rochester School of Management have been experimenting with the application of probit analysis for obtaining pretrial release prediction probabilities.

18. It is *not* meaningful to say that someone released who appears in court without committing a crime has provided the system with $200 in

The Bond-Setting Decision/Individual Cases 39

benefits by not having to be rearrested or with $1,000 in benefits by not having committed a crime. All one can say is that such a person has not caused the system to incur $200 in rearrest costs ($RC_1$) and has not caused the system to incur $1,000 in crime-committing costs (RC_2).

19. A related conclusion is reached in Friedman, "The Evolution of a Bail Reform," 7 *Policy Sciences* 281 (1976). In his appendix, Friedman shows that the benefits of releasing on recognizance are greater than the costs of releasing on recognizance, at least in New York City. He does so by working with monetary values *not* for all the benefits and costs involved, but only for those that are relatively easy to assign a monetary value to. The only holding cost he deals with is the jail maintenance cost, which he figures at $3 a day for an average of 30 days per defendant held. The only ROR releasing cost he deals with is the cost of interviewing, verifying, and following up on released defendants, which he figures at $45 per defendant released. Thus, the problem for him is whether $90 + V is greater than $90 + .016C$. The V represents the benefits from releasing other than the $45 saved in jail maintenance. The C represents the costs of releasing other than the $45 spent as part of the ROR processing. The .016 indicates that those costs are only incurred in the 1.6 percent of the cases where the ROR defendant fails to appear.

He establishes that $90 + V must be greater than $45 + .016C$ by the following steps:

1. Since the average defendant is released rather than held, this means $90 + V$ must be more than $.04 C$, where .04 indicates that 4 percent of the released defendants failed to appear (but not released ROR).
2. The $C < 2,250 + 25V$, by interchanging both sides of the inequality and dividing both sides by .04.
3. Then $45 + .016C < 45 + .016(2,250 + 25V)$, by substituting $2,250 + 25V$ as a value greater than C.
4. Then $45 + .016C < 81 + .4V$, by simplifying the right side of the inequality through the removal of the parentheses.
5. Therefore, the costs of ROR (that is, $45 + .016C$) are less than the benefits of ROR (that is, $90 + V$) since $81 + .4V$ is less than $90 + V$. If $d < e$ and $e < f$, then $d < f$ and $f > d$.

In other words, basically Friedman is saying that society must consider releasing to be more valuable than holding since society does more releasing than holding, and therefore it must consider ROR to be more valuable than holding since ROR is a form of releasing that has a better appearance rate than releasing in general. The big defect in his analysis is that he does not show that releasing or ROR is actually more profitable than holding; rather he shows only that society must perceive releasing or ROR as being more profitable if one operates on the assumption that society or an individual decides in favor of the alternative activity that is perceived to be the most profitable.

20. The same analysis based on figure 1-3a and 1-3b and the above calculations could be applied to determining the sensitivity of the outcome to changes in the inputs. In other words, how much would the inputs have to be changed in order to reverse the decision from favoring the release of the defendant to favoring his being held? More specifically, how much would the .92 appearance rate have to drop before the expected value of releasing would fall below the expected value of holding? If we were concerned only with one holding cost and one releasing cost and only with the probability of appearing rather than the probability of crime committing, then the formula for the expected value of releasing would be $(1 - PA)(RB - RC) + (PA)(RB)$. In other words, the value of cell a in figure 1-1 is the releasing benefits minus the releasing costs, or $RB - RC$, and the value of cell b is RB, as is shown below. Likewise, the formula for the expected value of holding would be $(1 - PA)(HB - HC) + (PA)(HC)$, which means the value of cell c in figure 1-1 is $HB - HC$ and the value of cell d is HC. Now all we have to do to answer this question—how low does PA have to drop to make the expected value of holding greater than the expected value of releasing?—is (1) substitute monetary values for RB, RC, HB, and HC, (2) set those two formulas equal to one another, and (3) solve for the value of PA. Any probability lower than that value would make it more worthwhile to hold the defendant. Actually, with the releasing and holding cost data for the average defendant from figure 1-3, it would always be more profitable to release such a defendant, no matter how low the value of PA is. This is so because all the cell values on the releasing row are higher than the corresponding cell values on the holding row, which they would not be if the holding costs were lower or the releasing costs were higher. By using the data in figure 1-3 and solving for PA^* by the above approach or the formulas given in note 3 or 9, one obtains a PA^* that is negative but rounds off to zero, which is the nearest possible PA.

	Fail to Appear $(1 - PA)$	Appear (PA)	Expected Value
Release	$RB - RC$	RB	$(1 - PA)(RB - RC) + (PA)(RB)$
Hold	$HB - HC$	HC	$(1 - PA)(HB - HC) + (PA)(HC)$

One could similarly answer the question, How much would the holding costs have to decrease (or the releasing costs have to increase) in order to make the expected value of holding greater than the expected value of releasing? To answer that question about *HC*, one would substitute numerical values for *PA* and *RC*. This would also give the numerical value of *HB* since holding benefits are simply the positive sign of the minus releasing costs. We could then use $-X$ to label *HC* and X to label *RB*. The next step would be to set those two formulas equal as we previously did, but this time solve for X rather than for *PA*. If the holding costs decrease $1 below the value of X, then it is more worthwhile to hold the defendant than to release him, assuming everything else is held constant. With the partial data from figure 1-3, the value of X is only $16 since the expected value of releasing is $(.08)(X - 200) + (.92)(X)$ and the expected value of holding is $(.08)(-X + 200) + (.92)(-X)$. Thus the holding cost would have to be drastically reduced (or the releasing cost drastically raised) in general or in a specific case to make holding more worthwhile than releasing if one considers only the probability and cost given of rearresting for nonappearance. One could easily extend this sensitivity analysis (that is, the sensitivity of the result to changes in the inputs) by expanding the formulas to include more kinds of holding and releasing costs and more kinds of contingent probabilities analogous to those in figure 1-3.

21. Somewhat contrary to this rational scheme, however, is the fact that bond tends to be set lower for nonindigent defendants than for indigent ones if we count release on recognizance as a zero bond. The median or middlemost bond for a nationwide sample of 246 indigent defendants charged with grand larceny was $2,328, whereas the median bond for a similar sample of 354 nonindigents was only $1,850. Further details are given in Nagel, "Effects of Alternative Types of Counsel on Criminal Procedure Treatment," 48 *Ind. L. J.* 404 (1973), especially notes 15 and 28 and the accompanying text. That seeming discrepancy can, though, be partly explained by the possible fact that nonindigent defendants have a greater probability of appearing in court than indigent defendants do, especially if there is no trial-day notification system.

22. Wice, *Freedom for Sale*, pp. 25-34.

23. The ABA *Minimum Standards for Criminal Justice Relative to Pre-Trial Release* provides at section 1.1, "The law favors the release of defendants pending determination of guilt or innocence," and at section 5.1, "It should be presumed that the defendant is entitled to be released in order to appear on his own recognizance." The *Illinois Criminal Code,* ch. 38, art. 110-2, provides, "When from all the circumstances the court is of the opinion that the accused will appear as required either before or after conviction, the accused may be released on his own recognizance. . . . This Section shall be liberally construed to effectuate the purpose of relying upon

criminal sanctions instead of financial loss to assure the appearance of the accused." *The Federal Rules of Criminal Procedure*, Rule 46, provides, "A person arrested for an offense not punishable by death shall be admitted to bail. . . . the amount thereof shall be such as in the judgment of the commissioner or court or judge or justice will insure the presence of the defendant, having regard to the nature and circumstances of the offense charged, the weight of the evidence against him, the financial ability of the defendant to give bail, and the character of the defendant."

24. An alternative way to categorize what needs to be done to increase the expected value of releasing relative to the expected value of holding might involve thinking in terms of four separate cells, rather than two key cells where those two cells determine the values of the other two cells although they are opposite in sign. More specifically, if releasing is considered the more desired behavior and holding the less desired behavior, then what needs to be done is to (1) increase the (perceived) benefits of releasing, (2) decrease the costs of releasing, (3) decrease the benefits of holding, and (4) increase the costs of holding. Item 2 in this list corresponds to decreasing B, and item 4 corresponds to increasing A. Item 1 mainly involves increasing the satisfaction that comes from saving the holding costs, which is the equivalent of making more visible the value of A. Item 3 mainly involves decreasing the satisfaction that comes from saving the releasing costs, which is the equivalent of decreasing the value of B. Thus, with this subject matter, the four-cell approach tends to reduce to two cells. Either approach to encouraging socially desired behavior could be used where a choice is present that does *not* involve a contingent event. In such a situation, one would concentrate on changing the values of A and B or of $a, b, c,$ and d without one or more P's or probabilities to be concerned with.

25. See the reference to Hausman and Thaler, in note 17.

26. The problem of how to increase the probability of a defendant appearing in court can be thought of as a decision theory problem. The released defendant has basically two choices, to appear or not. He will appear if he perceives the expected value of appearing to be greater than the expected value of not appearing. The expected value of appearing equals the benefits of appearing (for example, getting one's bond back and avoiding prosecution) minus the costs of appearing (for example, being subjected to a trial or wasting time if there is no trial) with those benefits and costs discounted by the probability of their occurring. The expected value of not appearing equals the benefits of not appearing (for example, temporarily avoiding either a trial or waiting at the courthouse) minus the costs of not appearing (for example, losing one's bond and getting prosecuted for bond jumping) with those benefits and costs discounted by the probability of their occurring. Thus, defendants are more likely to appear if those perceived benefits and costs can be changed so that the expected value of appearing will be perceived more often as being the greater value. Notifica-

tion systems have the effect of reminding defendants of the costs of not appearing and the benefits of appearing. Screening systems have the effect of finding defendants who are more likely to perceive the expected value of appearing to be greater than the expected value of not appearing.

27. Variation among the judges in holding rates is partly indicated by substantial variations in holding rates across cities. See W. Thomas, *Bail Reform in America* 37-64 (1976), and Nagel, Wice, and Neef, *The Example of Pretrial Release* (Sage, 1977). Lower variation among judges on appearance rates and crime-committing rates is indicated partly by the lower variation in those rates across cities. See Thomas, pp. 87-109, and Nagel, Wice, and Neef. The Thomas study showed that when felony holding rates dropped from 52 percent in 1962 to 33 percent in 1971, and misdemeanor holding rates dropped from 40 percent in 1962 to 28 percent in 1971, the appearance rates of the increasingly large number of defendants released only dropped from 94 to 91 percent.

28. If, contrary to our predictions, we find that the low holding judges on a court have a substantially worse appearance rate (rather than about the same appearance rate) than the high holding judges, then revealing those differences should encourage the low holding judges to do more holding. Likewise, if, contrary to our predictions, we find the judges have about the same holding rates (rather than substantial variation in their holding rates) and different appearance rates, then revealing those differences should stimulate the judges with lower appearance rates to be more selective in whom they release and possibly to raise their holding rates. If the judges have about the same holding rates and about the same appearance rates, that revelation is not likely to change any behavior, even though lowering their holding rates might save holding costs without a commensurate increase in releasing costs, and even though raising their holding rates might save releasing costs without a commensurate increase in holding costs.

29. Some judges or legislators may have a more narrow or different concept of social costs than others. For example, making more visible the holding cost of lost gross national product may be less impressive to some judges than to others as compared to the extra jail maintenance costs even if both dollar amounts are equal. Likewise, some judges may be relatively unconcerned with jail maintenance costs if they are borne by the state government rather than by their own local government. This further illustrates the value of working with nonmonetary measures which tend to express the relative perceived utility of alternative possibilities to the decision makers rather than the more superficial, but often more measurable, monetary measures.

30. One benefit from delaying the trial of released defendants is that while on bond, they may feel constrained to be more law-abiding in order to avoid having their bond and release revoked, and especially to avoid more severe treatment from the prosecutor and the court when the case

eventually does come up. Such a deliberate or negligent use of delay might, however, violate speedy trial laws and the speedy trial clause of the Constitution; and the longer the delay, the greater the probability of crimes being committed by persons released on bond. Release on bond in some cases may encourage crimes that would not otherwise have occurred if the defendant engages in illegal behavior in order to pay a bondsman. That effect could occur with a short delay between arrest and trial, but a long delay by providing more time makes the occurrence more possible.

2

The Bond-Setting Decision Across Cases

I. Nondiscretionary Bond Schedules

A. The Problem

Thus far we have been discussing the releasing and bond-setting decision on an individual, case-by-case basis although we used illustrative data representing an average defendant rather than a specific defendant. Now, however, we will discuss the problem of developing rules to cut across cases of a given type, as is done in nondiscretionary bond schedules which specify, for example, that bond for nonaggravated battery shall be $1,000.[1] Bond schedules like that increasingly are being used to set bond by the police when judges are not available at night or on weekends in misdemeanor cases. Bond that is determined by such a schedule can be lowered or raised subsequently in a judicial proceeding initiated by the defendant or the prosecutor. There also may be an increase in the use of such schedules by arraignment judges in view of their advocacy by various legal scholars.[2] At the turn of the century, judicial reformers advocated indeterminate sentences in hopes of obtaining enlightened, individualized discretion in criminal cases. By mid-century, judicial reformers had become somewhat disillusioned with the feasibility of obtaining such enlightened discretion, especially in view of various studies which show how arbitrary sentencing and other forms of judicial discretion have become.[3] As a result, there is an increasing tendency to return to more objective, though automatic, standards as being preferable to arbitrary discretion and as being much more feasible than enlightened discretion.[4]

The problem here is one of scientifically determining what bond should be set for each crime and for different types of defendants where the characteristics of the defendant can be legally considered. It would be unconstitutional to have one bond schedule for blacks and one for whites, regardless what might be shown scientifically about the relation between race and appearance rates. So long as the correlation is substantially short of a perfect correlation (for example, where no blacks appear and all whites do), we do not want to use such a correlation because it would result in too many type 2 errors of releasing white persons who should be held and especially too many type 1 errors of holding black persons who should be released. It would not, however, be unconstitutional to provide lower bonds for teenagers than for adults, so as to facilitate the release of teenagers for whom

45

the holding costs to society may be greater in terms of creating increased criminal behavior. A bond schedule that takes into consideration ability to pay probably would be constitutional, although it might be easier to administer such a schedule if ability to pay were dichotomized into indigent and nonindigent with indigency determined as part of the proceeding associated with appointing the public defender or assigned counsel. Just as bond schedules can vary from state to state, they can also probably vary by size of city within a state in view of the different relation between bond and the probability of appearing in rural, urban, and metropolitan areas.

B. *The Goal and a Solution*

The ideal or optimum bond for a given crime and type of defendant would be the bond that maximizes the probability of the defendant appearing in court (PA) while minimizing the probability of his being held in jail (PH). A major defect in this statement is that it fails to consider that as the bond goes up, the probability of appearing goes up (which is desirable), but the probability of being held in jail also goes up (which is undesirable). Thus, we cannot simultaneously maximize PA and minimize PH.

Thus a better statement of the optimum bond for a given crime would be that the optimum nondiscretionary bond is the bond that maximizes the difference between the probability of appearing and the probability of being held, or that maximizes $PA - PH$. For the average defendant in the data on which figure 1-3 is based, the probability of appearance is .92 and the probability of being held in jail is .27. Thus, in the average case, the bond is being set at such a level that $PA - PH = .65$. Perhaps through a scientifically determined bond schedule, that difference could be made even greater, partly by raising PA, but mainly by lowering PH. Even if the bond schedule did not increase the .65 difference, still it might be an improvement over the prevailing system if it substantially decreases arbitrary and discriminatory bond setting, particularly if there is a system for adjudicating cases where the defendant can show that the automatic bond is especially unreasonable in his specific case. Too easy a system for adjudicating the automatic bond, however, would lead to disparities that favor those who have access to expensive lawyers who could obtain a lower bond.[5]

To set a bond figure that maximizes $PA - PH$, one could simply determine for a large set of past cases what was the average bond set for the disorderly conduct cases, the shoplifting cases, and so on. Thus the past average would become the future automatic bond. This may be the way some bond schedules are established. That would be more scientific (that is, based more on empirical data) and possibly more rational (that is, more likely to maximize $PA - PH$) than a kind of gut reaction attempt to create a bond schedule. That average-bond method, however, presumes that past practice has been as rational as one can get. Such a presumption may be quite faulty.

The Bond-Setting Decision Across Cases

A possibly more goal-effective alternative would be to take that large set of past disorderly conduct cases, shoplifting cases, and so on and then group the cases for a given crime into various bond catagories somewhat like those used in the questionnaire in figure 1-6. The set of approximately ten categories used should vary with the crime, and they should be set up so that each category has approximately the same number of cases.[6] For each bond category in the disorderly conduct cases, we would then determine what percentage of the defendants appeared in court (that is, *PA* for that category on that crime), and we would determine what percentage of the defendants were held in jail (that is, *PH* for that category on that crime).

That information could easily be plotted on a figure like figure 2-1. For each bond category, there is a dot corresponding to the percentage of appearance for that category (*PA*) and an X corresponding to the percent-

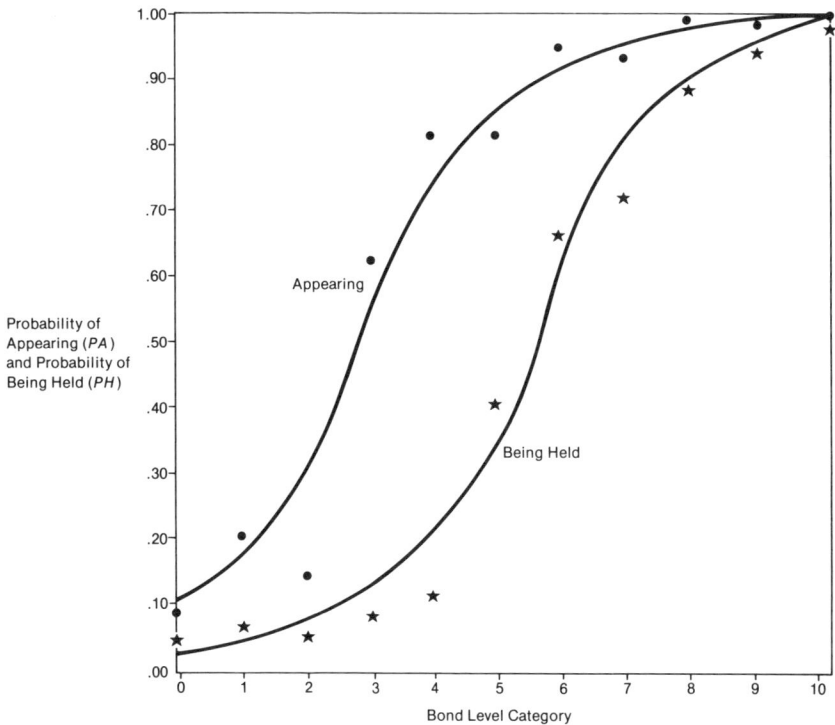

(Hypothetical data for the crime of disorderly conduct in medium-sized cities in the state of Illinois.)

Figure 2-1. The Relation between Level of Bond and Both the Probability of Appearing in Court and the Probability of Being Held in Jail.

age of being held for that category (*PH*).⁷ There are thus ten pairs of dots and X's. To find the pair where *PA* − *PH* is greatest, all we have to do is subtract each *PH* from its corresponding *PA*. Doing so will possibly tell us with these hypothetical data that bond category 4 involves the biggest difference between *PA* and *PH*. Therefore, we could specify that the midpoint of the interval for category 4, or the range for category 4, shall be the fixed bond for disorderly conduct in medium-size cities in the state of Illinois (that is, in cities between 100,000 and 1 million population).⁸ In other words, in effect, we have treated the probability of appearing as being like income, and the probability of being held as being like expenses, and we are trying to find the optimum price or quantity to produce that will maximize income minus expenses.⁹

C. Variations on the Solution

With these data, however, we could try to fit a smooth curve to the *PA* dots and another smooth curve to the *PH* X's. We could then geometrically or algebraically determine where the greatest separation exists between those two curves. Doing so might reveal that the optimum bond category is 4.6, and by simple interpolation we could translate that into a dollar figure. The type of smooth curve that is likely to nicely fit our dots and X's is a third-degree polynomial or cube law or S-shaped curve of the form

$$PA \text{ or } PH = a + b_1 C + b_2 C^2 + b_3 C^3$$

where *C* stands for category number. The *a*, b_1, b_2, and b_3 are coefficients whose values can easily be determined by feeding into a computer the ten *PA*'s, the ten *C* numbers from 1 to 10, their squares, and their cubes, along with a linear regression program, and then doing the same thing for the ten *PH*'s.¹⁰ Once we have those numerical coefficients, then we want to find the slope of *PA* − *PH* relative to *C*. After we find that slope, we want to set that slope equal to zero and then solve for *C* in terms of the numerical coefficients. Where the slope of *PA* − *PH* relative to *C* becomes zero after rising up and before starting down is where *PA* − *PH* is at a maximum. Solving for *C* at that point involves solving a high school quadratic equation. Doing so and then interpolating will give us a more precise bond figure than merely finding the percentage of appearance and corresponding percentage of being held that have the biggest difference.¹¹ Finding a precise point within a bond category or interval (rather than simply using the range of the category or a range around the precise point), however, might not be desirable because an optimum bond schedule probably should provide ranges for each crime which allow some discretion rather than a precise point or dollar figure which allows no discretion.¹²

The Bond-Setting Decision Across Cases

If a legislature considers promoting appearance to be twice as important as promoting release, then the goal to maximize might be expressed as $2(PA) - PH$, and the optimum bond interval would be the one that is highest on that goal. In more general terms, one could say the goal to be maximized is $W(PA) - PH$, where W is the desirability weight of PA relative to PH. The value of W could be less than 1 if PH is valued more highly than PA. For example, the value of W could be .5 if PH is considered twice as important as PA.

For a still more realistic way to express the goal for determining an optimum bond interval, one might use the expression $(PA)^W/PH$. Doing so takes into consideration that as the probability of appearing increases, community satisfaction increases, but not as a constant rate in view of the fact that the first unit of a good thing normally produces more incremental satisfaction than the second unit. Likewise, the dividing takes into consideration that as the probability of holding increases, community satisfaction decreases, but not at a constant rate in view of the fact that the first unit of a bad thing normally produces more incremental dissatisfaction than the second unit. The W still represents the desirability weight of PA relative to PH, but it is now an exponent of PA rather than a multiplier. This goal is, in effect, like a weighted benefit-cost ratio to be maximized by finding the optimum, or highest-scoring, bond interval for each type of crime in each geographical area.

In addition to being useful for determining an optimum bond level for each type of crime, the kind of data shown in figure 2-1 can also be helpful for obtaining a better understanding of the relation between bond setting and other variables. If the hypothetical data shown in figure 2-1 are reasonably accurate, that means at the lower bond levels, the probability of being held is continuously quite low; and at the higher bond levels, the probability is continuously quite high. Only in the middle levels is there a substantial variation between bond level and the probability of being held, or for that matter the probability of appearing in court. In other words, the average individual can equally meet a bond of $10, $20, $30, and so on at the low levels; and he will equally fail to meet a bond of $100,000, $200,000, $300,000, and so on at the high levels. The probability of appearing may drop and stay especially low when the bond is low and a bond forfeiture is treated as a fine with little or no likelihood of prosecution for bond jumping. If our data are reasonably accurate, we can predict PA and PH at various bond categories for the average disorderly conduct case in medium-size Illinois cities or whatever our data base is. That kind of predictive power could be helpful to judges in discretionary bond-setting cases either done geometrically with figures like figure 2-1 or done algebraically with a third-degree polynomial equation. Thus, the kind of analysis represented by figure 1-7 can be helpful in both the making of bond-setting statutes and the resolving of specific bond-setting cases.[13]

II. The Optimum Percentage to Release

Another pretrial release problem that cuts across cases is that of trying to decide approximately what should be the optimum percentage of defendants to release prior to trial. If too few are released, there will be excessive holding costs, although releasing costs will be down. If too many defendants are released, there will be excessive releasing costs, although holding costs will be down. An optimum percentage to release can be found in a manner similar to the approach in figure 1-7 to finding an optimum bond level. We can, in effect, plot total holding costs and total releasing costs for different releasing percentages in the same city at different points in time, in different cities at the same point in time, or a combination of both. The optimum percentage is the percentage where the sum of the holding costs plus the releasing costs is at a minimum, or where the sum of the holding benefits plus the releasing benefits is at a maximum.

That kind of analysis is the subject of a separate work.[14] What we want to discuss briefly here is how that kind of analysis relates to pretrial release decisions in individual cases and in nondiscretionary bond schedules. All three kinds of analysis will be reconcilable if they all consider the same values in the same cases. Thus, when that occurs, if the optimum percentage analysis indicates that total costs are minimized when 96 percent of the defendants are released, then the bond schedule approach will also result in releasing 96 percent of the defendants, as will the individual case approach. We cannot, however, be sure that the judges in the nonmonetary, individual case analysis are operating under the same values as we included in the monetary case analysis. We know that in our bond schedule analysis, we did not use the same values as in the monetary, individual case analysis (because of the need to simplify when one is working across cases rather than in an individual case). We know further that the optimum percentage to hold is not the same as the actual percentage held.[15]

These variations inform us that our models are not completely capturing empirical reality with regard to what goes on in pretrial release. Those discrepancies could be remedied possibly by gathering more questionnaire and other data in order to make our models fit reality better. Those discrepancies could also be remedied possibly by trying to get judges and legislators to move closer to the models if the models have some aspects that are more rational and objective than may be present in the prevailing decision making. Perhaps what is needed is more realistic social science and more rationalistic governmental decision making, both at the same time.

III. Some Tentative Conclusions

In addition to our general statement on the need for realism and rationalism, it seems appropriate to conclude by stating what specific hypotheses our deductive analysis has implicitly generated that might now be explicitly tested with additional data. One set of hypotheses is largely methodological in nature and relates to the measuring tools presented. In effect, we hypothesized that the questionnaire approach included in figure 1-2 would be a meaningful way to determine the satisfaction and dissatisfaction received by an arraignment judge from releasing a defendant who would or would not appear or from holding a defendant who would or would not appear. The same kind of measuring instrument involving rank ordering, anchoring, and then relative numerical measures could also be applied to other decision makers in the criminal justice process. The second measuring tool presented involved multiple sets of hypothetical situations like the set included in figure 1-6. We implicitly hypothesized that such an approach would be a meaningful way to determine the relative importance of various criteria in bond-setting and other decisions more so than an approach directly asking decision makers what criteria they use. Likewise, the decision theory questionnaire of figure 1-2 seems to be a more meaningful way of determining threshold probabilities for releasing defendants than directly asking a judge what his threshold probability is.

In addition to the measuring instruments, our analysis has implicitly stated a number of substantive hypotheses that might merit further testing. They include such statements as these: (1) Some arraignment judges are mainly oriented toward avoiding the release of bad-risk defendants and a probably smaller group of other judges are mainly oriented toward avoiding the holding of good-risk defendants. (2) There are substantial relations between the background and attitudinal characteristics of arraignment judges and their orientations toward avoiding type 1 and type 2 errors. (3) There are substantial relations between the characteristics of the defendants and their crimes and the threshold probabilities indicated by the responding judges to the decision theory situations. (4) There are substantial relations between the characteristics of the cities, particularly regarding holding and releasing costs, and the threshold probabilities indicated by the responding judges. (5) Judges who tend to perceive the probability of appearing as being low are judges who demand a high probability of appearing before they will release. (6) In these five hypotheses, one could substitute probability of not committing a crime for the probability of appearing in order to test the role of both probabilities in pretrial release decisions. (7) Arraignment judges tend to set bond in terms of past average bonds for certain crimes rather than in terms of an analysis of the defendant's probability of appearing in court at various bond levels. (8) The probability of appearing and the probability of being held in jail bear a positively sloped, S-shaped relation with bond levels like that shown in figure 2-1.

In addition to the substantive hypotheses listed which emphasize understanding why variations occur in pretrial release, the analysis also generates hypotheses on how to improve the pretrial release system in light of given goals. Take these examples: (1) If judges are informed how their threshold probabilities, holding percentages, and appearance percentages compare to those of their fellow judges, then those judges who are relatively more different will tend to change their attitudes and behavior more toward the average. (2) If data are obtained on holding costs and releasing costs from various cities, one will find that the expected value or cost of releasing is substantially less than the expected value or cost of holding for the average defendant; this supports the rationality of releasing the average defendant although the costs may exceed the benefits for certain types of defendants. (3) If arraignment judges want to maximize the benefits minus the costs in a bond-setting decision, they should decide in terms of an analysis of the defendant's probability of appearing in court at various bond levels. (4) If legislators, state supreme courts, or other bond-schedule makers want to maximize the probability of appearing minus the probability of being held, they should adopt the bond level for each crime where (in the past) the separation between those two probabilities or percentages has been greatest. (5) If arraignment judges want to minimize the sum of the holding costs and releasing costs, they should hold only about 5 percent of all defendants. (6) To more accurately determine the probability of a defendant appearing in court, an arraignment judge should make some use of the multiple-variable prediction schemes developed by such sociolegal programs as the Vera Institute.

In light of the implications raised by this analysis, one can reach the overall conclusion that decision theory is a useful approach for generating some insights, hypotheses, and explanations with regard to pretrial release decisions. One might also be able to see how decision theory can be a similarly useful approach with regard to other decisions in the criminal justice process that relate to contingent events, such as the decision by (1) a police officer to arrest rather than issue a summons, (2) a prosecutor or defense counsel to go to trial rather than accept an out-of-court settlement, (3) a sentencing judge or parole board to incarcerate or continue incarceration, (4) a jury to find liability or convict, and (5) a lawyer to appeal. Decision theory is a provocative way to conceptualize what is and what ought to be involved in decision making. The approach is a provocative way of conceptualizing what is and ought to be involved in decision making. The approach in itself does not provide hard data answers, but it may serve a useful function by providing many questions and a means for integrating the answers being developed.[16]

Notes:

1. *Ill. Rev. Stats.*, ch. 110A, § 528c (1969). "Bail for misdemeanors (other than traffic or conservation offenses) punishable by fine or imprisonment in a penal institution other than a penitentiary, shall be $1,000."

The Bond-Setting Decision Across Cases 53

2. M. Kelly, "Social Science Evaluation and Criminal Justice Policy-Making: The Case of Pre-Trial Release," in *Public Policy Evaluation*, ed. Dolbeare (Sage Publications, 1975); Wisotsky, "Use of a Master Bond Schedule: Equal Justice Under Law?" 24 *Miami L. Rev.* 808 (1970); W. Thomas, *A Decade of Bail Reform* 211-213, 258-259 (University of California Press, 1976); and R. Hand and R. Singer, *Sentencing Computations Laws and Practice* 2-39 (American Bar Association, 1974).

3. M. Frankel, *Criminal Sentences: Law without Order* (Basic Books, 1973); R. Dawson, *Sentencing: The Decision as to Type, Length, and Conditions of Sentence* (Little, Brown, 1969); A. Trebach, *The Rationing of Justice: Constitutional Rights and the Criminal Process* (Rutgers University Press, 1964); Nagel, "Disparties in Criminal Procedure," 14 *UCLA L. Rev.* 1272 (1967); and D. Fogel, ". . . We Are the Living Proof . . .," *The Justice Model for Corrections* (Anderson, 1975).

4. The Illinois legislature is currently considering the adoption of a sentencing system in which all sentences are fixed rather than indeterminate. The fixed terms are specified for certain types of crimes and defendants by statute with no judicial or parole board discretion, although discretion in the charging process is still available to the prosecutor. The fixed term can be reduced one day for each day of good time in prison, but the good time cannot be retroactively taken away if the defendant subsequently misbehaves. See J. Foster et al., *Definite Sentencing: An Examination of Proposals in Four States* (Council of State Governments, 1976).

5. Usually if a defendant can afford an expensive lawyer, he can also afford a high bond. Thus, easy adjudication of the automatic bond probably would favor not the rich but rather middle-income defendants who are not rich enough to meet the high bond but not poor enough to have to rely on the public defender. In other words, the rich defendant does not need an easy system for arguing that the automatic bond is unreasonable, and the poor defendant may have a lawyer who lacks the time and assistance to be able to effectively argue for a bond reduction. This kind of discriminatory pattern against the poor may, however, not be as great under automatic bond schedules as under traditional bond-setting systems if the bond schedules tend to involve lower bonds in recognition of the fact that those bonds produce the best $PA - PH$ values.

6. Although somewhat more difficult to handle, the subsequent interpolation and curve fitting would be more meaningful if each bond category involved an equal interval in the sense of covering an equal number of dollars rather than covering an equal number of cases. Equal-distance intervals (that is, equal dollars) are more difficult to work with than equal-frequency intervals (that is, equal cases) in the analysis which follows because the base of the percentages (that is, the number of cases) for each equal-distance interval may sometimes be too small to produce reliable percentages. A good compromise in the bond-setting context might involve seven or so

equal-distance intervals or categories, with a zero category added saying "less than $1" and a last category added saying "more than D dollars." The "less than $1" category refers to release on recognizance, someone else's assurance of appearance, a specified cash bond which is not collected but which would be collected and forfeited if nonappearance occurs, or other release not involving a cash or property deposit. "D dollars" is the highest figure one can have and still have seven equal-distance intervals between category zero and the last category, given the nature of the crime and the bond-setting data that relate to it.

7. Figure 2-1 is drawn rather roughly to illustrate the hypothesized general relations between PA and the bond level categories, and between PH and the bond level categories. A more exactly drawn PH curve would end at the zero point in the lower left-hand corner of the graph if the zero-level category meant release on one's own recognizance, since there would then be zero probability of being held. Likewise, a more exactly drawn PA curve would curve upward at the zero-bond-level category because those who are released on their own recognizance usually have a high probability of appearing by virtue of their background characteristics, not because of the incentive to retrieve their bond. Thus, to make figure 2-1 more meaningful for bond-setting purposes, the zero-level, or ROR, category should probably not be included in the analysis.

8. This approach of trying to find a bond level for each crime that maximizes the probability of appearing minus the probability of being held can be contrasted with both the prevailing highly discretionary bond setting and nondiscretionary schedules that merely codify previous average bond levels for given crimes or that use arbitrary bond levels to achieve objectivity but fail to adequately achieve pretrial release goals. By seeking bond levels that maximize $PA - PH$, objectivity is likely to be increased. There is also likely to be a small increase or no change in appearance rates, and a substantial decrease in holding rates, since optimum bond levels in light of that $PA - PH$ criterion are likely to be quite low, but without lowering the probability of appearing. A pretrial release system in which there are no money bonds at all might, at first glance, seem fairer in not discriminating against the poor. If, however, such a system allows considerable judicial discretion as to who will be held rather than released on one's own recognizance, then stereotypes and prejudices may result in more, not less, discrimination and more ineffectiveness in achieving the goal of maximizing appearance rates minus holding rates. A pretrial release system that abolishes money bonds is also not likely to be adopted.

9. As an alternative to figure 2-1 where we plot PA and PH separately, we could plot one curve showing $PA - PH$ at each bond level category. Such a curve would tend to be relatively low at both the lowest and the highest bond level categories. It would be relatively high at a low to middling bond level category, where in figure 2-1 the gap between PA and PH is greatest. Such a hill-shaped curve could be adequately expressed by the

equation $PA - PH = a + b_1 C + b_2 C^2$, where C represents the bond level category for say ten categories. The values of b_1 and b_2 are determined by a computerized regression analysis which involves providing the computer with ten sets of values for C (from 1 to 10), C^2 (from 1 to 100), and the corresponding $PA - PH$ from the data gathered. The optimum C (or C corresponding to the maximum $PA - PH$) is equal to $-b_1/(2b_2)$ by virtue of the high school algebra rules for finding the value of X where Y is a maximum, when Y has a quadratic relation with X.

10. On fitting curves like third-degree polynomials to data like those shown in figure 2-1, see H. Blalock, Jr., *Social Statistics* 459-62 (McGraw-Hill, 1972); and E. Tufte, *Data Analysis for Politics and Policy* 108-134 (prentice-Hall, 1974).

11. On finding the slope of a difference between two polynomials, setting the slope to zero, and then solving for the independant variable, see S. Richmond, *Operations Research for Management Decisions* 40-86 (Ronald, 1968); or M. Brennan, *Preface to Econometrics* 111-79 (Southwestern, 1973). If the equation for the *PA* curve is

$$PA = a + b_1 C + b_2 C^2 + b_3 C^3$$

and the equation for the *PH* curve is

$$PH = a' + b'_1 C + b'_2 C^2 + b'_3 C^3$$

then

$$PA - PH = (a - a') + (b_1 - b'_1)C + (b_2 - b'_2)C^2 + (b_3 - b'_3)C^3$$

That equation simplifies to

$$PA - PH = A + B_1 C + B_2 C^2 + B_3 C^3$$

where $A = a - a'$, $B_1 = b_1 - b'_1$, $B_2 = b_2 - b'_2$, and $B_3 = b_3 - b'_3$. Given that equation, the slope of $PA - PH$ relative to C is $B_1 + 2B_2 C + 3B_3 C^2$. Setting that slope equal to 0 and solving for the value of C involves solving the quadratic equation

$$C^* = \frac{-2B_2 + \sqrt{2B_2^2 - 12B_1 b_3}}{6B_3}$$

since if $c + bX + aX^2 = 0$, then $X = \left(-b + \sqrt{b^2 - 4ac}\right)/(2a)$.

12. The most meaningful way to relate bond level to either the probability of appearing or the probability of being held might be to plot each case individually rather than by groups, categories, or intervals which are subjectively arrived at. If each case is plotted individually, the dot plotted

for *PA* would be at either 1.00 or 0 since the defendant would have either appeared or not. With that set of data for a large number of cases, one can fit an S-shaped curve to the *PA* data by using the method described in note 11 and the accompanying text, except that each *C* would correspond not to a bond category number, but rather to the exact amount of the bond for each case. One can do likewise with the *PH* data. One can then find the exact bond level where *PA* − *PH* is at a maximum by using the method described in note 11 or 9 and the accompanying text. This more exact approach, however, may not be as simple to work with as the approach that involves grouped data, as described in note 6 and the accompanying text.

13. An unpublished paper entitled "Bail and Parole Jumping in Manhattan in 1967" by S. Andrew Schaffer of the New York Vera Institute of Justice provides some empirical data on the relation between bond levels and both the probability of appearance and the probability of being held, which reinforce the general nature of the hypothetical curves shown in figure 2-1. With regard to *PA*, his data show at p. 29:

Bond Level	Probability of Appearance	Bond Level	Probability of Appearance
$1– $25	.76	$251– $500	.95
$26– $50	.82	$501–$1,000	.93
$51–$100	.81	$1,001–$2,500	.89
$101–$250	.84	Over $2,500	(1.00)

Probabilities in parentheses indicate that the number of cases was between 11 and 50, whereas probabilities not in parentheses indicate the number of cases was over 50.

The general pattern shown here is that the probability of appearance generally does increase as the bond level increases, although that pattern might have been clearer if separate charts were shown for each crime rather than combining all cases. One would expect higher bonds for more severe crimes and generally a lower probability of appearance for more severe crimes, which means crime severity should be held constant in order to determine the relation between the bond level and probability of appearance.

With regard to *PH*, Shaffer's data show at p. 23:

Bond Level	Probability of Being Held	Bond Level	Probability of Being Held
Under $100	.03	$1,001–$2,500	.80
$101– $500	.57	Over $2,500	.96
$501–$1,000	.65		

The general pattern shown here is that the probability of being held does clearly increase as the bond level increases. That is probably true regardless of the crime although some crimes are disproportionately committed by poorer people who are less able to meet a given bond level. Note that (as in figure 2-1) *PA* tends to be above *PH* for a given bond level. They come close together at very high bond levels and seem to be farthest apart in the second category of $26 to $50. The fact that Schaffer uses different bond level categories for the two sets of relations complicates the analysis and illustrates the subjectivity of arriving at appropriate bond level categories as mentioned in notes 12 and 6.

14. S. Nagel, P. Wice, and M. Neef, *The Policy Problem of Doing Too Much or Too Little: Pre-Trial Release as a Case in Point* (Sage, 1976).

15. The 96 percent optimum release level arrived at in S. Nagel, ibid., and the optimum bond amount of $26 to $50 arrived at in note 13 would be equal in their results if they were based on the same empirical data and the same normative values. The 96 percent optimum release figure, however, is based on data from a sample of 23 cities, whereas the $26 to $50 optimum bond figure is based on data from New York City, although both figures are for about 1969. Likewise, the 96 percent optimum release figure is based on more considerations than just maximizing *PA* − *PH*. Those additional considerations include minimizing pretrial crime committing and having monetary weights associated with *PA* and *PH*.

16. The measuring instruments, the substantive or causal hypotheses, and the means-ends or prescriptive hypotheses mentioned are the subject of an empirical research design proposal which has been submitted by Nagel and Neef to the National Science Foundation and other funding agencies under the title "Decision Theory and the Criminal Justice System." The research design basically involves working with twenty federal and state court systems to (1) increase the sensitivity of criminal justice decision makers to avoiding type 1 errors, (2) develop more objective and effective decision-making guidelines for criminal justice decision makers, and to (3) understand better the threshold probabilities of criminal justice decision makers. A copy of the proposal is available from the authors on request.

Appendix 2A.
Glossary of Symbols

Symbol	Represents	First Appearing
Errors:		
Type 1	An error of holding a defendant who would appear or who should be released (rejecting a true hypothesis or presumption)	I-A, Ch. 1
Type 2	An error of releasing a defendant who would fail to appear or who should be held (accepting a false hypothesis or presumption)	I-A, Ch. 1
Expected Values:		
EV_H	Expected value of holding a defendant	II, Ch. 2
EV_R	Expected value of releasing a defendant	II, Ch. 2
Holding Costs and Benefits:		
HC	Holding costs in keeping a defendant in jail pending trial	I-C, Ch. 1
HB_1	Holding benefits which result from rearresting releasing costs being saved when defendant is held	I-C, Ch. 1
HB_2	Holding benefits which result from crime-committing releasing costs being saved when defendant is held	I-C, Ch. 1
Judges, Type of:		
Judge a	Judge who is more worried about holding a good-risk defendant than releasing a bad-risk defendant	I-A, Ch. 1
Judge b	Judge who is more worried about releasing a bad-risk defendant than holding a good-risk defendant	I-A, Ch. 1
Probabilities, Separate:		
PA, or just P	Probability that defendant will appear or percentage of defendants who have appeared for a given bondsetting category	I-A, Ch. 1
PA^*, or P^*	Threshold probability of appearance that has to be met before judge will release a defendant in a given situation	I-A, Ch. 1
PC	Probability or percentage of defendants committing a serious crime	I-C, Ch. 1
PF, or $1 - P$	Probability or percentage of defendants failing to appear in court	I-C, Ch. 1
PH	Probability of defendant being held in jail or percentage of defendants held for a given bond setting category	II, Ch. 2
PN	Probability of defendant not committing a serious crime if released	I-B, Ch. 1

Decision Theory and the Legal Process

Symbol	Represents	*First Appearing*
PN^*	Threshold probability of defendant not committing a crime that has to be met before judge will release a defendant in a given situation	I-C, Ch. 1
Probabilities, Combination:		
A	Probability of appearing in court and not committing a crime while released	I-C, Ch. 1
B	Probability of failing to appear in court and not committing a crime while released	I-C, Ch. 1
C	Probability of appearing in court and committing a crime when released	I-C, Ch. 1
D	Probability of failing to appear in court and committing a crime while released	I-C, Ch. 1
Relating PA and PH to Bond Level:		
a	Value of PA or PH when bond-setting category C or level equals zero	II, Ch. 2
b_1, b_2, b_3	Ratio between a change in PA or PH and a change in C, C_2, or C_3	II, Ch. 2
C	Bond-setting category number from 1 to 10 that was used in specific cases to be fed into a computerized regression analysis to obtain values for a, b_1, b_2, and b_3	II, Ch. 2
Releasing Costs and Benefits:		
RB	Releasing benefits, or the holding costs saved by releasing a defendant	I-C, Ch. 1
RC_1	Releasing cost of rearresting an average defendant, estimated at $200	I-C, Ch. 1
RC_2	Releasing cost of a crime committed by an average defendant while released, estimated at $1,000 each	I-C, Ch. 1
Satisfaction Associated with Different Occurrences:		
Cell a, or $-B$	Relative dissatisfaction received by a judge if defendant fails to appear after being released	I-A, Ch. 1
Cell b, or $+B$	Relative satisfaction received by a judge if defendant appears after being released	I-A, Ch. 1
Cell c, or $-A$	Relative satisfaction received by a judge if he holds a defendant who would have failed to appear if released	I-A, Ch. 1
Cell d, or $+A$	Relative dissatisfaction received by a judge if he holds a defendant who would have appeared if released	I-A, Ch. 1
Miscellaneous Symbols:		
ROR	Release of the defendant on his own recognizance without any bond	I-A, Ch. 1

Appendix 2B.
Basic Formulas Used

1. Expected value of releasing, nonmonetary values:

$$EV_R = a(1 - PA) + b(PA)$$

2. Expected value of holding, nonmonetary values:

$$EV_H = c(1 - PA) + d(PA)$$

3. Threshold probability for releasing, nonmonetary values:

$$PA^* = \frac{a - c}{a - b - c + d}$$

$$PA^* = \frac{B}{A + B} \text{ in simplified version}$$

$$PA^* = \frac{1}{X + 1} \text{ in a further simplified version where } X = A/B$$

4. Expected value of releasing, monetary values:

$$EV_R = (RB + RC)(1 - PA) + (RB + RC)(PA)$$

where RC is a negative number and there are no releasing costs when the defendant appears

5. Expected value of holding, monetary values:

$$EV_H = (HB + HC)(1 - PA) + (HB + HC)(PA)$$

where HC is a negative number and there are no holding benefits when the defendant would have appeared

6. Threshold probability for releasing, monetary values:

$$PA^* = \frac{(RB + RC) - (HB + HC)}{RC - HB}$$

where a negative number divided by a negative number is a positive number, which as a probability should be between 0 and 1, unless releasing (or holding) always produces more net benefits $(B - C)$ than holding (or releasing) regardless of PA

61

7. Decision rule on releasing or holding:

   Release if $\quad EV_R > EV_H \quad$ (that is, if $PA > PA^*$)

   Hold if $\quad EV_H > EV_R \quad$ (that is, if $PA^* > PA$)

8. Combined probabilities:

$$A = (PA)(PN) \quad B = (PF)(PN)$$

$$C = (PA)(PC) \quad D = (PF)(PC)$$

9. Relating PA and PH to bond level category:

$$PA = a + b_1 C + b_2 C^2 + b_3 C^3$$

$$PH = a' + b'_1 C + b'_2 C^2 + b'_3 C^3$$

10. Optimum bond level category:

    $C^* = C \quad$ where $PA - PH$ is a maximum positive difference

$$C^* = \frac{-2B_2 \pm \sqrt{2B_2^2 - 12B_1 B_3}}{6B_3}$$

11. Probability of appearing for all defendants:

$$PA' = (1 - PH)(PA) + (PH)(1 - X \cdot PF)$$

where PA and PF apply to released defendants and X equals how many times greater than PF is the probability of a held defendant failing to appear if he were released

---

Note: See Appendix 2A for definition of symbols in the context of the formula presented.

**Part II
The Two-Person
Bargaining Situation:
Plea Bargaining**

Introduction to Part II

Plea bargaining refers to the negotiations between a prosecutor and a defense lawyer or defendant over the prosecutor's charge or over the sentence which the prosecutor will recommend to the judge in return for a plea of guilty. A high percentage of the disputes that enter into the judicial process at either the criminal or the civil complaint stage are resolved by bargaining among the lawyers or litigants rather than by a trial.[1]

Most of the literature on plea bargaining has been descriptions or evaluations of the legal rules governing the relation between prosecutors and defendants[2] or anecdotal descriptions of plea bargaining incidents.[3] The legal evaluative literature emphasizes that if a prosecutor promises a defendant a lighter sentence for pleading guilty, then a guilty plea under those circumstances does not constitute an involuntary confession, but rather a generally useful method for reducing court congestion. The anecdotal literature often mentions instances where the system is used to take advantage of hard-pressed defendants or prosecutors or where other socially undesirable results occur.

It is the purpose of these chapters to discuss plea bargaining mainly from the perspective of what actually tends to occur, rather than from what the law or other evaluators say should occur. This empirical perspective avoids human interest anecdotes in order to concentrate on the general essence of the plea bargaining transaction. By doing so, a descriptive model of plea bargaining will be developed that has enough empirical validity and generality to answer questions about the effects of judicial system changes on the likelihood and the level of plea bargaining settlements.

System changes, in this context, refer to the effects of changes in the degree of pretrial release, provision of counsel to the indigent, judicial delay, mutual discovery, exclusion of illegally seized evidence, abolition of capital punishment, or other changes that affect the litigation or settlement costs of the parties, the probability of conviction, or the severity of sentences. A model that is capable of predicting the effects of changes like those in the criminal justice system seems worth pursuing in order to better plan and understand the operations of the criminal justice process.

For example, in the early 1960s, partly as a result of studies by the Vera Institute, the New York criminal courts increased the extent to which defendants were released prior to trial. This policy, administered under a system of quantitative screening and pretrial notification, simultaneously kept the costs of rearresting nonappearing defendants at the former cost levels in spite of the higher release rate, while reducing the costs of imprisonment to the defendant and society.[4] However, the planners did not anticipate that pretrial release would increase court backlog and delay by reducing the incentive of many defendants to accept a plea-bargained settlement. The incentive to settle was reduced since many defendants were now no longer suffering the high litigation cost of being held in jail prior to trial if they refused to settle.[5] If the new congestion causes those who are in jail to be subjected to longer delay to have their cases tried, then the number of pretrial jail inmates actually may increase even though the percentage being sent to jail to await trial has decreased. If the system had a better model of its operations, that effect could have been anticipated and prepared for—mainly by having the prosecutors offer a greater discount on their settlement offers.

A model designed to describe a social process like plea bargaining consists of a set of statements about the relations between certain inputs, causes, or predictor variables, on the one hand, and certain outputs, effects, or predicted variables, on the other. A good descriptive model is one in which (1) the conclusions logically follow from the premises; (2) the premises conform to empirical reality; (3) the conclusions have broadness in time, geography, and abstractness; (4) the conclusions help explain why things happen and how one might more effectively achieve given goals; (5) the relations between the variables are capable of being expressed with some measurability so the model can be objectively applied; and (6) the total structure is simple and understandable but captures the essence of a complex phenomenon.[6]

The plea bargaining model presented in these chapters tries to achieve those goals. The only assumption of the model are that defendants normally want to minimize their sentences and their likelihood of being convicted and that prosecutors normally want to maximize the sentences (within legal and ethical constraints) and the likelihood of obtaining a conviction. The model is based largely on the concepts and methods of decision theory and equilibrium modeling which have been used by economists and operations researchers to study bargaining and exchange relations among buyers and sellers, unions and management, and among competing business firms.

Decision theory is the mathematical tool that determines which combination of various available decisions should be reached in order to maximize given goals in light of probabilistic or uncertain events. If those uncertain events are the actions of decision makers with conflicting interests, a gaming type of decision theory may be involved. If those uncertain events are the actions of nature or a nonperson (for example, the weather) or the actions of some person or group who is not in conflict with the decision maker (for example, the jury or bench trial in plea bargaining), then the kind of decision theory involved often is referred to as a game against nature, or simply as decision theory.[7]

An *equilibrium model* can be defined as a set of quantitative statements that describe the behavior of objects such that if the statements are true, the objects will tend to move toward a given equilibrium whenever they are displaced from it.[8] Equilibrium models can be either static or dynamic. With a static model, one can say, given certain assumptions and starting data, where the objects will end. With a dynamic model, one can also say what steps will be involved in moving over time from the starting point to the equilibrium point.

In addition to presenting a mathematical model that captures the essence of the plea bargaining process for testing hypotheses and integrating findings, these chapters also will develop a model that can provide insights to legal practitioners for improving their bargaining techniques and, especially, that can provide insights to legal policy makers for improving the operations of the criminal justice system.[9] In addition, it is hoped that these chapters will clarify the process of applying decision theory and equilibrium models to certain aspects of law and the legal process so that others will be better able to use those concepts and methods in studying other aspects of law, policy, politics, and the legal process.

Notes

1. In the Wisconsin county studied by Newman, he found: only 6 percent of all felonies went to trial; 40 percent involved cases where the defendant originally entered a not-guilty plea which he subsequently changed to a guilty plea largely because of plea bargaining; and 54 percent involved cases where the defendant originally entered a guilty plea which may or may not have been a negotiated guilty plea. Of the 94 percent who pleaded guilty, 60 percent did so with bargaining and 40 percent without bargaining. Newman, "Pleading Guilty for Considerations: A Study of Bargain Justice," 46 *J. Crim. L.C. & P.S.* 780 (1956). In New York City, only 2 percent of all negligence claims are terminated by trial, with 98 percent terminated by out-of-court settlements or withdrawals. Franklin, Chanin, and Mark, "Accidents, Money and the Law: A Study of the Economics of Personal Injury Litigation," in *Dollars, Delay and the Automobile Victim: Studies in Preparation for Highway Injuries and Related Court Problems* (Walter E. Meyer Research Institute of Law, 1968), pp. 39-40.

2. See, for example, American Bar Association Project on Minimum Standards for Criminal Justice, *Standards Relating to Pleas of Guilty* (ABA, 1967) and the references cited therein.

3. See, for example, J. Bond, *Plea Bargaining and Guilty Pleas* (Mathew: Bender, 1975); M. Marcus and R. Wheaton, *Plea Bargaining: A Selected Bibliography* (Law Enforcement Assistance Administration, 1976); D. Newman, *Conviction: The Determination of Guilt or Innocence without Trial* (Little, Brown, 1966); A. Rossett and D. Cressey, *Justice by Consent:*

Plea Bargains in the American Courthouse (Lippincott, 1976); Alschuler, "The Prosecutor's Role in Plea Bargaining," 36 *U. Chi. L. Rev.* 50 (1968); and Alschuler, "The Defense Attorney's Role in Plea Bargaining," 84 *Yale L. J.* 1179 (1975).

4. The costs that were reduced included jail maintenance, lost gross national product, and bitterness generated by imprisonment for a complaint that is eventually dismissed or withdrawn, at least for those released who would have formerly been held.

5. See R. Goldfarb, *Ransom: A Critique of the American Bail System,* 161 (Little, Brown, 1965); Kelly, "Social Science Evaluation and Criminal Justice Policy Making: The Case of Pretrial Release," in *Public Policy Evaluation,* 273 ed. Dolbeare (Sage, 1975); and Nagel and Neef, "Unintended Consequences: Two Examples from the Legal Process," 2 *Policy Analysis* 356 (1976).

6. On social science models in general, especially those that can be mathematically formulated, see H. Blalock, *Theory Construction: From Verbal to Mathematical Formulations* (Prentice-Hall, 1969); S. Gass and R. Sisson, eds., *A Guide to Models in Governmental Planning and Operations* (Environmental Protection Agency, 1973); M. Greenberger, *Models in the Policy Process* (Russell Sage, 1976); C. Lave and J. March, *An Introduction to Models in the Social Sciences* (Harper & Row, 1975); R. Singleton and W. Tyndall, *Games and Programs: Mathematics for Modeling* (Freeman, 1974).

7. For further literature on interactive decision theory and related game theory, see A. Rappaport, *Two-Person Game Theory: The Essential Ideas* (1966); S. Richmond, *Operations Research for Management Decisions* 501-560 (1968); M. Davis, *Game Theory: A Nontechnical Introduction* (Basic Books, 1970); R. Luce and H. Raiffa, *Games and Decisions* (Wiley, 1957); J. Cross, *The Economics of Bargaining* (Basic Books, 1969); J. Williams, *The Complete Strategyst* (McGraw-Hill, 1954); M. Shubik, *Games for Society, Business and War: Towards a Theory of Gaming* (Wiley, 1975); and S. Brams, *Game Theory and Politics* (Free Press, 1974).

8. For further literature on equilibrium models, see M. Brennan, *Preface to Econometrics* 199-250 (Southwestern, 1973); J. Cross, *Economics of Bargaining* (Basic Books, 1969); P. Newman, *The Theory of Exchange* (Prentice-Hall, 1965).

9. Numerous concrete examples could be given of other applications of mathematical models to the legal process. Those applications include probabilistic decision theory applications (for example, where an arraignment judge is trying to decide whether to release a defendant prior to trial contingent on the probability of the defendant appearing in court) and bargaining applications (for example, where two contract negotiators are trying to decide on contract terms). Those applications also include equilibrium

models with an optimum-mix orientation (for example, finding an optimum mix between law reform and case handling in the OEO Legal Services Program) and equilibrium models with an optimum-level orientation (for example, the optimum jury size problem). Before one can understand or appreciate the variety of applications, it is probably best to master at least roughly one mathematical model problem such as that of the plea bargaining model.

3

Decision Theory Applied to the Defendant and the Prosecutor

The quantitative statements that serve as the basis for the static and dynamic equilibrium models of the plea bargaining process utilized in this chapter are derived from decision theory. Therefore we should begin by presenting the decision theory under which a defendant is likely to operate in dealing with a prosecutor if the defendant wants to minimize his sentence. We also should present the decision theory under which a prosecutor is likely to operate in dealing with the defendant if the prosecutor wants to maximize the defendant's sentence within the constraints of the criminal statutes and the prosecutor's notion of what constitutes a fair maximum sentence. In presenting the defendant's and the prosecutor's perspective of the decision-making process, hypothetical but realistic cases will be used. Throughout the chapter, methods of obtaining survey and other data will be mentioned, as well as methods of applying such data to test the theories presented.

I. The Payoff Matrices as Perceived by the Bargainers

A. Interpreting the Matrices

Table 3-1 shows how a defendant and a prosecutor in a hypothetical case each views the most likely sentence if (1) the defendant pleads guilty before a judge in a nonnegotiated plea when his probability of being convicted (or *PC*) is zero or extremely low, (2) the defendant pleads guilty before a judge when in a nonnegotiated plea the probability of his being convicted is 1.0 or extremely high, (3) the defendant goes to trial when his probability of conviction is zero, and (4) the defendant goes to trial when his probability of conviction is 1.0. The cell entries show likely sentences in terms of years for a crime that allows for at least as much as 10 years in prison, which would mean a major felony case.[1] The prosecutor and the defense more often bargain over the crime with which the defendant should be charged rather than what sentence the prosecutor should recommend, since the prosecutor has more control over the charge than over the sentence. Different charges, however, can be translated into sentences by thinking in terms of the average, maximum, or minimum sentence for the charge or a range of sentences on the charge.[2]

Table 3-1 shows that both the defendant and the prosecutor perceive the most severe sentence of the four payoff categories as likely to be received if the defendant goes to trial when the probability of conviction is

Table 3-1
The Payoff Matrices as Perceived by a Defendant and a Prosecutor

a. A Defendant's Payoff Matrix

	Probability of D Being Convicted (PC)	
	0	1.0
D Pleads Guilty before a Judge without Bargain (Alternative 2)	a 4	b 7
D Goes to Trial (Alternative 1)	c 0	d 10

b. A Prosecutor's Payoff Matrix

	Probability of D Being Convicted (PC)	
	0	1.0
D Pleads Guilty before a Judge without Bargain (Alternative 2)	a 3	b 6
D Goes to Trial (Alternative 1)	c 0	d 8

Cells indicate likely sentences (LS) in years as perceived by a hypothetical prosecutor (P) or defendant (D).

high, and the least severe sentence to be received when the defendant goes to trial with a low probability of conviction. Thus in comparing row *ab* and row *cd*, the defendant has more to lose and more to gain by going to trial than by a nonnegotiated guilty plea before a judge. If the conviction probability is zero, the defendant receives the longer sentence by pleading guilty than by going to trial when he thinks he will be acquitted. The judge, in taking a guilty plea, will assume the defendant is guilty, even if the probability of conviction is low due to the weakness of the evidence. If the conviction probability is 1.0, the defendant receives a shorter sentence by pleading guilty than by going to trial when he thinks he will be convicted. The judge, in effect, rewards the defendant for (1) saving the court time and money by not going to trial, (2) showing contriteness through a guilty plea, and (3) saving the victim and the witnesses from having to testify. It is an exceptional situation for a jury on conviction to give a lower sentence than the judge taking a plea gives, since few states allow juries to participate in sentencing.[3]

Table 3-1 also shows that both the defendant and the prosecutor perceive that when the conviction probability is low, the defendant will receive a lower sentence on a guilty plea before a judge than when the conviction probability is high. This is so because the stronger the evidence is against a defendant, the more confident the judge will be about the defendant's guilt and the more severe the judge is likely to be.[4] Thus, in comparing column *ac* and column *bd*, the defendant will receive a more severe sentence if his probability of conviction is high rather than low regardless whether he pleads guilty or goes to trial.[5]

Comparing table 3-1*a* and table 3-1*b*, our hypothetical defendant perceives his likely payoff sentences as generally being more severe than the prosecutor perceives them. This may be because the defendant is more aware than the prosecutor of his own guilt or of aggravating circumstances, and defendants usually are guilty, as indicated by high conviction rates. On the other hand, the defendant may perceive lower payoff sentences than the prosecutor because of wishful thinking or because the defendant is aware of his own innocence, or he is aware of mitigating circumstances.[6] The decision theory equilibrium model, however, need not presuppose anything with regard to the relative perceptions of the defendant and the prosecutor[7] in order to be meaningfully applied.[8]

To clarify the terminology, four kinds of payoff cells must be distinguished. In this context, the reference is not to the fact that there are four payoff cells, namely *a, b, c,* and *d* in table 3-1. Rather, the reference is to the fact that the payoff cells can be those perceived by the defendant, by the prosecutor, by an omniscient being, or by an omnibenevolent being. Table 3-1*a* and table 3-1*b* show the payoff cells as perceived by the defendant and the prosecutor, respectively. To the extent that both sides are represented by experienced, knowledgeable attorneys, those payoff cells should be reasonably accurate. The true payoff cells, which are unknowable, indicate exactly what sentence the defendant will receive. Those true payoff values are known with certainty only by one with omniscient powers, although the next section will deal with how prosecutors, defendants, and social scientists can try to estimate the true payoff cells. The fourth set of payoff cells are those which indicate what sentences the defendant deserves to receive in situations *a, b, c,* and *d*. Those "just" payoff values are quite subjective and known, if at all, only by an omnibenevolent being who has a set of values that represent the right set of values, assuming, of course, that some right set of values exists. Our mathematical model, however, does not require the user to know what the empirically true or the normatively just payoff cells actually are in order to apply the model, regardless whether the user is a practicing lawyer, a legal scholar, a policy maker, or some other type of user.

B. Deriving the Matrices

A defendant, prosecutor, or social scientist must be able to determine what the sentences are likely to be for each of the four payoff cells. Cell *c* is logically always 0 if the cells are expressed exclusively in sentence time units. If stigma and money costs are also included, the defendant might suffer some adverse payoffs even if acquitted on trial.[9]

Cell *d* can be figured by determining the average sentence received in all or a sample of the cases known to the defense lawyer, the prosecutor, or the docket files in which the defendant went to trial and was convicted of a charge similar to the one in our hypothetical case. If the defendant was convicted, then the evidence must have indicated close to a 1.0 probability of conviction, because theoretically defendants can be convicted only when there is no reasonable doubt, which means roughly more than a .95 conviction probability. Cell *d* will be close to the statutory maximum, but probably beneath it, since convicted felons seldom receive the maximum possible sentence.

The values for cells *a* and *b* are harder to determine. If the average sentence is used for all cases in which the defendant did plead guilty on a charge similar to one in the hypothetical case, then both cell *a* and cell *b* would have the same value, probably contrary to empirical reality. As a rule of thumb, one-third of the average trial conviction figure of cell *d* could be used in cell *a*, and two-thirds of cell *d* could be used in cell *b*.[10] To avoid rules of thumb, knowledgeable prosecutors and defense attorneys could be asked (as part of a mailed questionnaire or selective interviewing) for how long would judges be likely to sentence the defendant when the probability of conviction is extremely low but the defendant pleads guilty and the judge believes him to be guilty. Likewise, they also could be asked how long will the sentence run when the probability of conviction is extremely high and the defendant pleads guilty. Through such a questionnaire or interviewing approach, a rule of thumb might be refined by asking those knowledgeable persons what percentage of cell *d* the cell *a* sentence and the cell *b* sentence tend to represent, and then averaging those responses to get mean responses for cell *a* and for cell *b*.[11] As a more statistically sophisticated approach to determining the likely sentences of cells *a, b,* and *d,* a regression analysis could be used to predict sentences from the probability of conviction.[12]

C. Translating the Matrices into Satisfaction Units

The likely sentences shown in table 3-1 can be translated into dissatisfaction or satisfaction units to reflect the principles of diminishing disutility and utility. It is reasonable to assume that the defendant receives dissatisfaction from being sentenced, although the model can be modified to include an unusual defendant who wants to be martyred, is masochistic, or has other reasons for wanting a longer sentence. If it is assumed that defendants receive dissatisfaction from being sentenced, it is also reasonable to assume that the incremental dissatisfaction increases at a decreasing rate with each incremental year received as part of the sentence. This is likely to be so by virtue of the general principle of diminishing marginal disutility, which says that the more of a bad thing one has, the less dissatisfaction one gets out of each incremental unit.

Likewise, it is reasonable to assume that that prosecutor receives satisfaction from obtaining a sentence of a defendant that he believes is guilty, although the model can be modified to include the behavior of an unusual prosecutor who is seeking to enable a given defendant to receive as light a sentence as possible. Presumably, no ethical prosecutor seeks to obtain a sentence or to plea-bargain with a defendant whom he believes is innocent. It is also reasonable to assume that the incremental satisfaction to the prosecutor increases at a decreasing rate with each incremental year he obtains as part of the sentence to the point where diminishing absolute, not just marginal, utility sets in when the prosecutor's threshold of a maximum fair sentence is exceeded. The decreasing rate is due to the general principle of diminishing marginal utility, which says the more of a good thing one has, the less satisfaction one gets out of each incremental unit.

The principles of diminishing disutility and utility in the sentencing context can be expressed in terms of equations which translate likely sentences into dissatisfaction or satisfaction units. For the average defendant, the equation would probably take the form

$$DIS = A(LS)^B$$

where *DIS* is dissatisfaction units, *LS* is likely sentence expressed in years or other time units, *A* is the amount of dissatisfaction received if *LS* is only one time unit, and *B* equals a positive exponent less than 1 to which *LS* is raised to show the degree of increasing dissatisfaction from additional time units. For the average prosecutor, the equation would take the form

$$SAT = A(LS)^B$$

where *SAT* is satisfaction units and the other symbols have meanings like those in the defendants' equation.

If no better data are available, it could be assumed that the *A* multiplier in both equations equals 1 and the *B* exponent in both equations equals .5. This means that for the defendant, dissatisfaction, or more accurately, relative dissatisfaction, is $\sqrt{LS}$. In more concrete terms, if table 3-1a were to reflect the principle of diminishing disutility and show relative dissatisfaction scores, then the cells would be cell $c = 0$, $a = 2$, $b = 2.6$, and $d = 3.2$.[13] Likewise, the prosecutor's payoff matrix would be cell $c = 0$, $a = 1.7$, $b = 2.4$, and $d = 2.8$. To determine more precise values for *A* and *B* in the above equations requires feeding data for some defendants and some prosecutors into a computerized linear regression analysis, which then determines the A and B in each equation that best fits the data.[14]

For the sake of simplicity, the rest of this chapter will work with the likely sentence payoffs shown in table 3-1a and 3-1b which are stated in time units rather than the above translated satisfaction units. Doing so is also justifiable partly on the grounds that over short distances there is probably a linear relation, rather than a diminishing-rate relation, between sentence years and satisfaction such that the diminishing utility phenomenon does not significantly affect the defendant's or prosecutor's optimum strategy or their equilibrium point. Perhaps the bargaining area between defendants and prosecutors generally covers only such short distances. The average distance covered by plea bargaining can be determined by the same questionnaire approach designed to develop more precise satisfaction translation equations.[15] Regardless of whether one uses the payoff units shown in table 3-1 or the translated payoff units, the subsequent arithmetic manipulation is the same for deriving optimum strategies and equilibrium points.[16] In turning now to the subject of optimum strategies or bargaining limits, the role of benefits and costs other than sentence years such as the saving of time, money, and reputation will be discussed.

II. The Bargaining Limits of the Bargainers

In plea bargaining, the defendant is like a buyer seeking the lowest price possible. The prosecutor is like a seller seeking the highest price possible, although like some sellers, he is subjected to statutory maximum price control. In fact, the plea bargaining process is like an old-fashioned marketplace where there are no fixed prices on the products and the potential buyer and potential seller haggle over the price upon which they ultimately settle. The buyer knows the maximum price that he is willing to pay, but the buyer tries to convince the seller that his limit is much lower than it really is. Likewise, the seller knows the minimum price which he is willing to accept, but the seller tries to make the buyer think that his limit is much higher than it is. If the buyer-defendant's upper limit and the seller-prosecutor's lower limit can be determined, a more realistic assessment may be made about whether and at what point an equilibrium price will be reached.

A. Determining the Likely Sentences at Varying Conviction Probabilities

To obtain a better understanding of the bargaining limits of the bargainers, it is helpful to convert table 3-1 into a graph that will indicate the likely sen-

Decision Theory Defendant/Prosecutor 77

tences at all possible conviction probabilities between 0 and 1.0 rather than just at 0 and at 1.0. Such a graph involves showing the perceived probability of conviction (*PC*) along the horizontal axis and the likely sentence (*LS*) along the two vertical axes, as in figure 3-1. The defendant's trial payoff line can be expressed by the equation $LS_1 = 0 + 10(PC)$.[17] The subscript 1 indicates the likely sentence from going to trial as contrasted to the subscript 2 which indicates the likely sentence of a nonnegotiated plea.[18] By applying the same logic, the defendant's plead line, that is, what his sentence will likely be from a guilty plea, can be expressed as the equation $LS_2 = 4 + (7 - 4)PC$, or $LS_2 = 4 + 3(PC)$.[19] With the equations for LS_1 and LS_2, the defendant's perceived likely sentence may be determined for any *PC*. For example, if the defendant perceives his *PC* to be .5, he would logically perceive his likely sentence on going to trial to be 5 years, or ten times

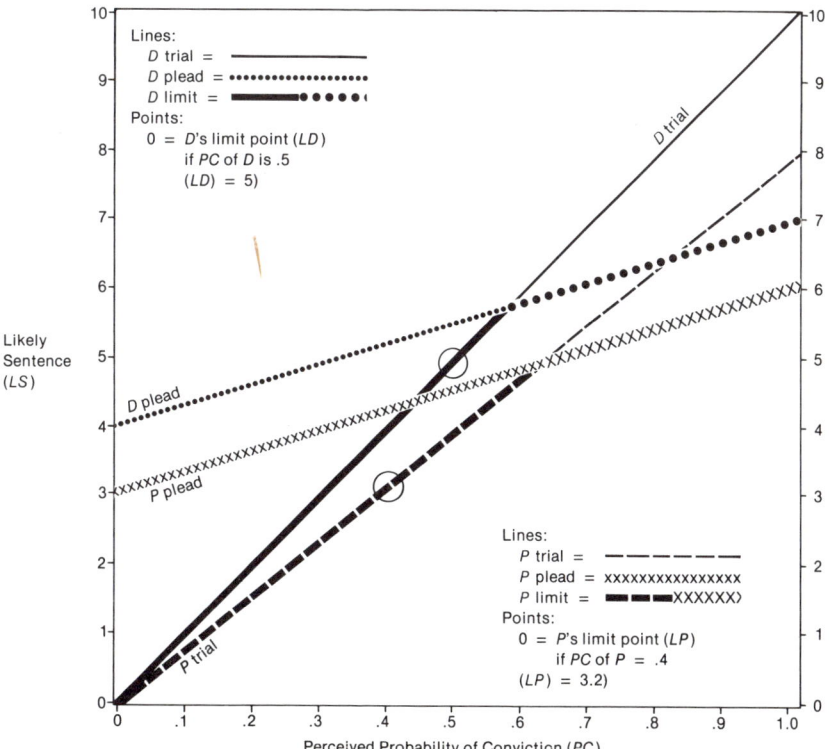

Figure 3-1. The Likely Sentences which Correspond to Various Conviction Probabilities (Strategies Graph).

.5, and he would perceive his likely sentence on pleading guilty to be 5.5 years, or 4 + 3(.5). These two predictions could be arrived at algebraically as above, or geometrically by reading up from the .5 on the horizontal axis of figure 3-1 to the D trial line and then up to the D plead line.

The prosecutor's perceptions of the payoffs can also be similarly graphed. When so graphed, the P trial line, the dashed line in figure 3-1, yields a prediction equation of $LS_1 = 0 + 8(PC)$. The P plead line, the X line, yields a prediction equation of $LS_2 = 3 + (6 - 3)PC$, or $LS_2 = 3 + 3$ (PC). This means that if the prosecutor perceives the case as being a .4 probability, then the prosecutor will tend to predict that the defendant will receive a sentence of 8(.4), or 3.2, years if he goes to trial and 4.2 years if he pleads guilty before a judge.[20]

B. Determining the Bargaining Limits from the Likely Sentences

1. Numerical and Graphical Interpretation. Once the likely sentences that correspond to any conviction probability have been calculated, they may be used to determine the bargaining limits for the buyer-defendant and the seller-prosecutor. From the above calculations, the defendant with a PC of .5 would prefer to go to trial rather than plead guilty before a judge since he thinks he will get 5½ years from a guilty plea but only an average of 5 years from going to trial. The defendant, however, will be willing to work out a bargain with the prosecutor if the prosecutor will offer him anything less than 5 years. Likewise, from these calculations the prosecutor with a PC of .4 would prefer to have the defendant plead guilty before a judge rather than go to trial since the prosecutor thinks the defendant will average only 3.2 years by going to trial rather than 4.2 years by pleading guilty. The prosecutor, however, will be willing to work out a bargain with the defendant if the defendant will accept anything over 3.2 years. In this simple example, the defendant's upper limit, or fall-back position, is 5 years, and the prosecutor's lower limit, or fall-back position, is 3.2 years. The defendant has no lower limit except for the fact that he cannot receive a sentence lower than 0. Likewise, the prosecutor has no upper limit except for the fact that he cannot obtain a sentence greater than the statutory or ethical maximum.

What is now needed is a more general method of calculating the defendant's upper limit and the prosecutor's lower limit. A method is required which will apply regardless of how each party numerically perceives the probability of conviction or regardless even of how each perceives the cell payoffs. Figure 3-1 provides a simple graphic or geometric method for doing that. The defendant's upper limit is along the D trial line until that line intersects with the D plead line and then along the thickened dotted line. The defendant will always select the lower of the two values. At any given conviction probability, the defendant would, of course, accept an offer from the prosecutor that is *below* that thickened, kinked, positive concave line because that line represents the best set of likely sentences the defendant can achieve by either going to trial or pleading guilty before a judge. Likewise, the defendant should reject any final offer from the prosecutor that is *above* that thickened line at any given perceived conviction probability because the defendant can do better than such an offer by either going to trial or pleading guilty before a judge.

By similar reasoning, the prosecutor's lower limit line is the thickened, dashed P trial line up to the intersection with the P plead line and then along the thickened P plead line of X's. The prosecutor should be willing to accept any offer the defendant makes *above* that thickened line because the prosecutor logically reasons that if the defendant wants to minimize his sentence and is as knowledgeable as the prosecutor, then the defendant by going to trial or pleading guilty before a judge can bring his sentence down to the prosecutor's thickened line level or limit. Likewise, the prosecutor should reject any final offer from the defendant that is *below* that thickened line at a given perceived conviction probability. The prosecutor should reason that such a rejection would force the defendant to either go to trial or plead guilty before a judge, thereby resulting in a higher sentence than the point below the prosecutor's thickened line would mean at that perceived PC.

Figure 3-1 indicates the upper limit for the defendant and the lower limit of the prosecutor at any conviction probability, given each party's perceived cell payoffs from table 3-1. By following the same reasoning used to derive figure 3-1 from table 3-1, a similar figure or graph for any set of defendant cell payoffs and prosecutor cell payoffs could be derived.[21] The defendant's upper limit thickened line will always be the combination of his two lines which produces the lowest thickened line that can be made. Likewise, the prosecutor's lower limit thickened line will always be the combination of his two lines that also produces the lowest thickened line.

2. Limits Based on Only One Alternative to Plea Bargaining. This scheme presents, in effect, a buyer-defendant haggling with a seller-prosecutor while operating in an oligopolistic market, that is, a market with only a few sellers. If the buyer-defendant cannot bring the seller-prosecutor down below the buyer-defendant's maximum price level, the defendant can turn to the two other sellers whose anticipated prices determine the defendant's bargaining limit. The other sellers are a judge in an unbargained guilty plea situation and a judge or a jury in a bench or a jury trial.

If the first alternative seller, that is, the judge in a guilty plea situation, is too cooperative with the prosecutor, in effect they have the equivalent of a price conspiracy and both will offer the same sentence. The buyer-defendant then has only one alternative seller from whom he can buy, namely the bench or jury trial or possibly just the jury trial. In the case of the one alternative seller, the defendant's limit line is the same as the defendant's trial line, and likewise the prosecutor's limit line is the same as the prosecutor's trial line.[22]

In certain cases the opposite situation may exist where the defendant only sees the plead line because going to trial is not a meaningful alternative given the trivial nature of the sentences involved even if the defendant is certain he would be acquitted. This is often true for defendants in traffic violation cases and especially parking meter violation cases. The maximum fine involved in a parking meter violation is so small relative to the cost of either a bench trial or a jury trial that many innocent automobile drivers will simply sign the parking ticket, thereby pleading guilty, even though they know that if they wanted to go to the trouble, they could be acquitted.[23]

There are two other related situations where the buyer-defendant or the seller-prosecutor may have his thickened limit line determined by only one of his two lines rather than both. First, a defendant who has a "maximax" strategy toward risk is one who will always go for the alternative decision that holds out the possibility of a maximum gain.[24] This means that if the lowest sentence is in cell c, as one would expect it to be, the maximax, or go-for-broke, defendant in effect will be blind to the D plead line and see only the D trial line. If the prosecutor is aware that the defendant is a maximax strategist, the prosecutor's lower limit line would just be the P trial line. An extreme maximax defendant is one who sees only the D trial line and who is certain he will be acquitted. His maximum limit would be zero, and he is obviously a difficult target for the plea bargaining process. The uncertain maximax defendant can, however, be bargained with since he is not certain that he will be acquitted on trial.

Second, a defendant who has a "minimax" strategy toward risk is one who will always go for the alternative decision that holds out the possibility of a minimum loss. This means that is cell b is less than cell d, as one would expect, then the minimax, or cautious, defendant will be blind to the D trial line and see only the D plead line. An extreme minimax defendant is one who sees only the D plead line and is certain he will be convicted. His maximum limit would be whatever is in cell d, and he is obviously an easy target for the plea bargaining process. The uncertain minimax defendant can, however, break off negotiations if the prosecutor is seeking the maximum cell d sentence since such a defendant is uncertain that he will be convicted.

Most defendants probably do not follow a pure strategy of considering trial as the only alternative to plea bargaining or of considering pleading before a judge as the only alternative. Instead, they recognize both payoff rows and will either go to trial or plead guilty depending on which of those two alternatives will give them the lowest likely sentence at their perceived probability of conviction. Thus they will follow a mixed strategy of sometimes going to trial and sometimes pleading guilty as an alternative to unsuccessful plea bargaining, depending on what their perception of *PC*.

Closely related to the situation where the defendant sees only going to trial or only pleading before a judge as the alternative to plea bargaining is the situation where plea bargaining is not a meaningful alternative. In other words, the defendant-buyer typically has three sellers from which he can buy—the trial court, the pleading judge, or the bargaining prosecutor. In nontypical situations, one or two of these sellers are eliminated as alternatives. The plea bargaining alternative may be eliminated because the defendant, the judge, or the prosecutor rejects plea bargaining under the circumstances. The defendant may reject the idea of having anything to do with plea bargaining when the transaction or settlement costs in terms of time or money, especially if defense counsel has to be hired, are simply too high relative to the incremental benefits that can be obtained by plea bargaining rather than by simply pleading guilty to the maximum penalty. As mentioned earlier, parking violations and other minor traffic matters are instances where defendants rarely resort to plea bargaining. A similar situation exists if the judge refuses to accept a plea bargain negotiated by the prosecutor and defendant. In that situation, the parties have to either rebargain in light of the constraints imposed by the judge or consider plea bargaining as an unavailable alternative. Such a situation may be fairly common with regard to bargaining over sentences, although not with regard to bargaining over what the charge should be.[25] The third and possibly least common situation is where the prosecutor refuses to have any dealings with the defendant because of the nature of the defendant's crime, the defendant's character, or the custom in that area. In all the situations where plea bargaining is eliminated as an alternative, the defendant is faced with a decision theory problem where he must decide between going to trial or pleading guilty before a judge. This decision must be based on the defendant's perception of which alternative will produce the lowest likely sentence or the lowest disutility.

3. Algebraic Interpretation. Algebraically, the defendant's bargaining limit can be calculated from this rule: LD, the limit of the defendant, equals the lower of LS_1 or LS_2, where LS_1 is the likely sentence from going to trial and LS_2 is the likely sentence from pleading guilty before a judge in light of the perceived payoff cells and conviction probability of the defendant.[26] Similarly, the prosecutor's bargaining limit can be calculated from this rule: LP, the limit of the prosecutor, equals the higher of LS_1 or LS_2, where LS_1 is the likely sentence from going to trial and LS_2 is the likely sentence from pleading guilty before a judge in light of the perceived payoff cells and conviction probability of the prosecutor.[27] Although the defendant and the prosecutor calculate their bargaining limits in a similar manner, the defendant will accept only an offer that is below his bargaining limit, and the prosecutor will accept only an offer that is above his bargaining limit. The conviction probability at which the likely sentence from pleading before a judge becomes lower than the likely sentence from going to trial can be easily determined. To do so for the defendant with the data available involves determining the *PC* at the point where LS_1 equals LS_2, that is, where *PC* = .57.[28] This means that if the defendant perceives *PC* to be less than .57, he should calculate his maximum limit by using the LS_1, or trial, formula. If instead he perceives *PC* to be greater than .57, he should calculate his maximum limit by using the LS_2, or plead, formula. If *PC* is perceived to be exactly .57 (or, more precisely, .5714), the defendant is indifferent between the trial and plead alternatives. Conviction probabilities, however, are not likely to be perceived that precisely, and a defendant is not likely to be concerned only with sentence minimization.[29]

A similar algebraic operation may be performed on the prosecutor's payoff data. The result for the data used above is *PC* = .60.[30] Thus if the prosecutor perceives *PC* to be less than .60, he would calculate his minimum limit by using his LS_1 trial formula. If instead he perceives *PC* to be greater than .60, he would calculate his minimum limit by using his LS_2, or plead, formula.

Furthermore, at the point where the trial line crosses the plead line (that is, where $LS_1 = LS_2$), then that probability of conviction (*PC**) equals $(a - c)/(a - b - c + d)$.[31] Also where $LS_1 = LS_2$, then that likely sentence (*LS**) equals $(ad - b - c)/(a - b - c + d)$.[32] By applying this formula to the hypothetical defendant, his *PC** is .57 probability, and his *LS** is 5.71 years. This means that if the defendant's limit (*LD*) is *less* than 5.71 years and the prosecutor will not come down to the *LD*, then the defendant will go to trial. If the defendant's limit is *more* than 5.71 years at his perceived *PC* and the prosecutor will not come down to the *LD*, then the defendant will plead guilty before the judge in order to minimize his sentence.

C. Determining the Conviction Probabilities

1. PC in General. As the previous discussion of figure 3-1 indicates, perceived probability of conviction is quite important in determining the defendant's upper bargaining limit and the prosecutor's lower bargaining limit. This is so because those limits differ for every perceived probability of conviction since they are not horizontal lines. They rise positively with increases in *PC* since the greater the *PC*, the greater the *LS*. They kink where the trial line intersects the plead line, since at that *PC* point the defendant is better off pleading guilty than going to trial. Given the importance of *PC*, it is appropriate to say something about how defense counsel, prosecutors, or social scientists might determine the conviction probabilities for various types of cases.

The methods available for determining *PC* are somewhat similar to those discussed previously in regard to determining the likely sentence in each cell of the payoff matrices.³³ The most common method is for a prosecutor or defense attorney to rely on his own unquantified experience. Another method is for the researcher to ask persons knowledgeable in a given area about specific cases or types of cases. Their responses would then be averaged in order to arrive at a consensus *PC* or guideline *PC*'s. As alternatives to simply averaging the *PC* or cell payoff estimates of experts, the researcher might (1) bring them together for a group discussion before they answer individually or collectively; (2) prod them to reveal the assumptions behind their estimates in order to recycle those estimates and assumptions to obtain consensus and further clarification; or (3) weight the estimates, if they are diverse, before averaging them, with weights proportionate to subjective ranking or rating of the experts, their own self ratings, or their past predictive accuracy.

In the questions about *PC*'s for a given type of case, each respondent can be asked to give a most likely *PC,* a low but still reasonable *PC,* and a high but still reasonable *PC*. If those estimates tend to have symmetrical distribution, each respondent's high and low estimates may simply be averaged to get his best or mean estimate rather than using his most likely or modal *PC,* although the mean and mode should be nearly equivalent were symmetry tends to be present. If the high and low estimates are not equidistant from the most likely, or mode, estimate, then the best or mean estimate can be obtained by adding the low estimate plus the high estimate to four times the most likely estimate and dividing that sum by 6. This same approach of getting three estimates for each point can also be used in estimating the payoff cells as well as the conviction probability.³⁴

More sophisticated and less obstrusive but harder to apply methods involve gathering data concerning relevant variables for a large sample of cases. One computer card could be used for each case to indicate how the case was positioned on each of the relevant variables and whether the defendant or prosecutor won. Relevant variables might include characteristics of the defendant, victim, witnesses, judge, jury, and lawyers. Characteristics of the evidence such as the presence of eyewitnesses, confessions, fingerprints, ballistics tests, and other matters may be more relevant but harder to categorize. The nature of the crime may also bear some relation to the probability of conviction.

These computer cards can then be processed to generate regression or discriminant equations of the form $Y = b_1X_1 + b_2X_2 + \cdots + b_nX_n$, where the b's represent regression or discriminant weights determined by the computer in order to obtain an equation that represents the best fit to the data. The Y indicates the predicted case outcome which can range from 1, meaning defendant is convicted, to 0, meaning defendant is acquitted. The X's represent the scores in the case to be predicted for the characteristics of the personnel, the evidence, and the crime. Applying the above equation to a given case will yield a score that can be treated like a probability; or better yet, for each .10 interval from 0 to 1, the percentage of cases in the interval which were lost by the defendant may be determined. That percentage can then be used as a more meaningful indication of the probability of conviction when the interval in which the case being predicted falls is known.[35]

To clarify the terminology, four concepts related to conviction probabilities need to be distinguished and emphasized. The first is *PC* as perceived by the defendant. The second is *PC* as perceived by the prosecutor, which may be similar to that perceived by the defendant or by his lawyer if both the prosecutor and defense counsel are relying on similar information. The third is the true *PC*, or the *PC* perceived by an omniscient being. It is always 1.0 or 0.0 since an omniscient being would know with certainty whether the defendant will be convicted or acquitted. Although the defendant or the prosecutor may sometimes think he knows with certainty that *PC* is 1.0 or 0.0, he obviously cannot know with the absolute certainty what an omniscient being could. The *PC* of both the defendant and the prosecutor should move closer to 1.0 or 0.0, depending on whether the defendant will be convicted or acquitted, as the case gets closer to trial, closer to a verdict, or as the defendant and prosecutor acquire additional information. The fourth concept is not the probability of the defendant being convicted, but rather the probability of whether he is actually guilty. In seeking a plea bargain the prosecutor generally thinks the defendant is guilty, although the prosecutor may recognize that the probability of getting a conviction is substantially less than 1.0, especially where incriminating but nonadmissible evidence is involved. By plea bargaining the defendant is not necessarily admitting his guilt, and in some cases he may strike a plea bargain when he believes he is innocent but feels that the probability of conviction is too high to risk going to trial. These four concepts can be symbolized *PCD, PCP, PC', and PG* respectively, although usually they are referred to verbally rather than symbolically.

Knowing what the probability of conviction is between 0 and 1.0 is essential in determining the defendant's upper limit or the prosecutor's lower limit in figure 3-1. The following sections deal with the problems raised when *PC* is known to be either 0 or 1.0, when *PC* is known to be within a range between one probability and another, or when *PC* is totally unknown.

2. *PC* under Certainty of Conviction or Acquittal. The certainty situation is relatively easy. Since *PC* is either 0 or 1.0, this situation involves working with only the original payoff matrices of table 3-1 rather than the strategies graph of figure 3-1. If the defendant is certain that he will be acquitted, that is, that *PC* is 0, he should reject any prosecutor's offer other than one to dismiss the charges. Even an offer of probation or a suspended sentence would be too high. Likewise, if the prosecutor is certain the defendant will be acquitted and the defendant knows it, the prosecutor should dismiss the charges rather than seek to plea-bargain. Even if the prosecutor thinks, in spite of the lack of convincing evidence, that the defendant is guilty, he should dismiss the charges, unless the prosecutor knows that the defendant is unaware that PC is 0.

If the defendant is certain that he will be convicted, that is, that PC is 1.0, he should accept any prosecutor's offer of a sentence less than his cell d perceived maximum. In order to save his time and money, he should even accept an offer from the prosecutor as high as the cell d maximum if he is truly convinced that PC equals 1.0. Likewise, the prosecutor can hold out for his cell d maximum if he thinks PC is 1.0, although later a prosecutor's discount factor will be discussed whereby the prosecutor may be willing to discount the likely sentence in order to save time and money.[36] However, there are few, if any, realistic situations where either the defendant or the prosecutor is absolutely certain that the defendant will be acquitted or convicted if the case goes to trial.

3. PC within a Range between 1.0 and 0.0. The second situation regarding the PC perceptions of the defendant and the prosecutor is where one does not feel confident that the conviction probability is at a given point. The litigant instead feels that it is within a range between two points. The defendant's bargaining limit under those circumstances depends on his degree of optimism or pessimism. For example, if the defendant perceives his probability of conviction as being between .2 and .5, he would act as if PC were .2 if he were optimistic. On the other hand, he would act as if PC were .5 if he were pessimistic. If he is neither an optimist nor a pessimist, but rather has a middling attitude toward his probability of conviction, then he would probably act as if his PC were 3.5, or $(.5 + .2)/2$. On the other side, if we had an optimistic prosecutor who perceived PC as being between .2 and .5, then he would act as if PC were more like .5 than .2 since the optimistic prosecutor perceives PC as being high when the optimistic defendant perceives PC as being low. Likewise, the pessimistic prosecutor in this hypothetical situation would act as if PC were .2, and the middling prosecutor would act as if PC were 3.5.

The notion of optimism-pessimism can be applied to the payoff cells in table 3-1 as well as to the conviction probabilities. Thus, a defendant or defense counsel may be quite unsure that cell a involves a likely sentence of 4 years, but may feel reasonably confident that it involves a sentence somewhere between 3 and 6 years. If such a defendant is optimistic, he will act as if that cell means a likely sentence of 3 years, while he might act as if that cell means a likely sentence of 6 years if he is pessimistic. The middling defendant would assume a sentence of about 4.5 years. Likewise, an optimistic prosecutor would tend to assume the maximum sentence within his perceived range, and a pessimistic prosecutor would tend to assume the minimum sentence within that range.

To determine an individual's optimism-pessimism coefficient, one could refer first to table 3-a with its a, b, c, and d cells of 4, 7, 0, and 10, respectively. Now determine how cell a would have to be changed—upward or downward—in order to make going to trial as appealing as pleading guilty or vice versa. For example, a defendant may decide that going to trial is as appealing as pleading guilty when the cells are changed to 2, 7, 0, and 10, respectively. Given these data, the optimism-pessimism (O-P) coefficient may be calculated. What the individual defendant has said, in effect, is that when the cells are 2, 7, 0, and 10, then LS_1 will equal LS_2. This is the same as saying that $0 + (10 - 0)(PC) = 2 + (7 - 2)(PC)$. Thus, in solving for PC in that equation, the measure of his degree of optimism-pessimism is determined. This yields a PC coefficient of 2/5, or .40, which is fairly optimistic as compared to .50, but not as optimistic as .30.[37]

After the defendant's optimism-pessimism coefficient is determined by this method, the coefficient can be applied to finding a point within the estimated range of a payoff cell or a conviction probability. For example, if the perceived range in a payoff cell of the defendant is 3 to 6 and the O-P coefficient is .5, then the difference between 3 and 6 should be split, yielding the point 4.5. If the O-P coefficient is .6, then take .6 of the difference, that is, .6(3), which equals 1.8. This yields a working value or point estimate for the defendant's cell of 4.8 (or 3 + 1.8). A similar approach can be used to find a working value for PC between .2 and .5: that is, multiply the .3 difference between .2 and .5 by the O-P coefficient and add that product to .2. A similar procedure can be followed to reduce the prosecutor's perception of PC from a range to a point. The only difference is that when the range is multiplied by the O-P coefficient, the product is subtracted from the top of the range for the prosecutor, whereas it is added to the bottom of the range to obtain a meaningful point for the defendant.[38]

4. *PC* Totally Unknown. The third problem of a totally unknown *PC* presents the extreme version of the defendant or the prosecutor who thinks of *PC* in terms of a range. In this situation, the defendant or the prosecutor thinks *PC* could just as easily be 0 or 1.0. The point on that complete range at which the defendant or the prosecutor will operate depends on his degree of optimism-pessimism. If the defendant is highly optimistic, he will act on the assumption that *PC* is 0 or close to 0. If he is highly pessimistic, he will act on the assumption that *PC* is 1.0 or close to 1.0. Likewise, if the prosecutor is highly optimistic, he will act as if *PC* is about 1.0; and if he is highly pessimistic, he will act as if *PC* is about 0. If, however, either the defendant or the prosecutor has a middling degree of optimism, he will act as if *PC* is about .5. In the hypothetical case previously discussed, such a defendant would have an upper bargaining limit of 5 years since figure 3-1 and the algebraic formulas indicate that a bargaining limit of 5 years corresponds to a PC of .5.

A defendant who is unknowledgeable as to PC and middling on optimism-pessimism might flip a coin to determine whether he prefers to go to trial or to plead guilty before a judge. If he flips a coin between trial and pleading, the defendant is saying that he is indifferent in terms of his perceptions and values between trial or pleading guilty. Such a defendant is acting as if PC were PC^*. In other words, he is acting as if the likely sentence from going to trial is the same as the likely sentence from pleading guilty before a judge. In the hypothetical example, such a defendant would be acting as if PC were .57 rather than acting as if PC were .5. His limit would thus be 5.7 years rather than 5 years since he could fall back on an expected 5.7-year sentence by going to trial or pleading guilty before a judge if negotiations with the prosecutor break down.

The better of these two alternatives for our unknowledgeable defendant with middling optimism-pessimism is that which assumes PC equals .5, rather than flipping a coin which implicitly assumes PC equals .5. It is the better alternative because we are trying to capture what is really likely to happen in the rare situation of a defendant who is completely unknowledgeable as to PC. It is also a simple method that provides an estimation of PC with a minimum of effort, whereas assuming PC equals .57 involves a somewhat complicated chain of thinking which runs from (1) flipping a coin between going to trial and pleading guilty before a judge to (2) thinking that doing so means LS_1 equals LS_2 and to (3) thinking this means PC equals .57. Therefore, to avoid this complicated chain of thinking, the PC equals .5 approach will be used elsewhere in this book.[39]

To clarify further the specific terminology, it should be pointed out that the optimistic defendant is not necessarily the same as the maximax defendant. The optimistic defendant is one who sees PC or a cell payoff as being at the lower end of the range of realistic possibilities. The maximax defendant is the one who seeks the alternative between going to trial or pleading guilty before a judge that can lead to the best possible payoff regardless of the probability of conviction. Most maximax defendants are also likely to be optimistic defendants, although most optimistic defendants are not necessarily also maximax defendants. Likewise, most minimax defendants are also likely to be pessimistic defendants, although most pessimistic defendants are not necessarily also minimax defendants. Regardless of the correlation between strategy toward the alternatives and optimism-pessimism, it is helpful to keep these concepts separate in order to allow the model to recognize more types of defendants and prosecutors. The separate concepts of risk preferrer and risk avoider will also be introduced later to refer to defendants and prosecutors who enjoy or abhor risk as a nonsentence goal or antigoal separate in itself, from the basic goal of sentence minimization for the defendant and sentence maximization for the prosecutor.

D. Determining the Bargaining Limits where Nonsentence Goals are Involved

1. What the Other Goals Are. Thus far, only the defendant's goal of sentence minimization and the prosecutor's goal of sentence maximization, within the constraints of the law and the prosecutor's notions of fairness, have been discussed. Other goals, however, have been mentioned, such as when the certainty probability was discussed in section II-C-2. Now is an appropriate time to discuss the other goals since they particularly influence the bargaining limits of the parties (*LD* and *LP*) rather than the likely sentence payoff cells: *a, b, c,* and *d*. Although it is generally more difficult to quantify goals other than sentence minimization and sentence maximization, it is possible to identify some of the goals and to determine how they tend to influence the limits of the defendant-buyer and the prosecutor-seller.

Other goals of the defendant might include (1) getting out of jail as quickly as possible if he is unable to make bond pending trial, (2) saving the costs of hiring an attorney, or of the additional attorney fees required in going to trial without a court-appointed lawyer, (3) saving the time involved in preparing his case and appearing in court, (4) saving his reputation from the bad publicity often associated with a contested trial even if he is acquitted, and (5) saving himself the anxieties associated with prolonging the outcome of the case. These five goals are all likely to cause the defendant to accept a higher bargaining limit, thereby increasing the likelihood of the pretrial settlement. He may have still other goals that push him in the opposite direction, thereby making it more difficult for the prosecutor to deal with him. These goals might include (1) seeking to delay the outcome of the case in order to prolong his freedom if he is likely to be convicted, (2) seeking the publicity of a trial in those cases where publicity is desired, (3) seeking delay in hopes that the prosecution's case will weaken through the increased forgetfulness and unavailability of witnesses, and (4) seeking the safeguards for the innocent, which also benefit the guilty, that are only associated with trial, such as requiring conviction by a unanimous twelve-person jury.

The main goals of the prosecutor, other than sentence maximization, include (1) saving the costs of preparing for a trial and appearing in court, (2) reducing the backlog of cases awaiting trial, thus reducing court congestion and delay, (3) increasing the percentage of convictions,[40] and (4) obtaining cooperation from the defendant as a witness or informer in other cases. These four goals encourage the prosecutor to decrease his bargaining limit, thereby tending to avoid trial. Other nonsentence goals, however, might have a partially offsetting effect on these four goals. Such other and opposite goals include (1) seeking the publicity of a trial where the prosecutor may be politically motivated or (2) seeking the publicity of a trial in order to use the defendant as an example to others even though the likely sentence from the trial might be less than what the prosecutor could achieve through plea bargaining.

A nonsentence goal is not involved if the defendant wants to avoid trial because he thinks a trial will get him a longer sentence or wants to go to trial because he thinks a trial will get him a shorter sentence. That kind of goal is included in the table 3-1 payoff matrix and the figure 3-1 bargaining limits. Likewise, the table and figure do take into consideration the prosecutor who avoids trial because he thinks he can get as long a sentence through plea bargaining. This concept of "other goals" includes only those goals which do not relate to either party's perception of either the conviction probability or the likely sentences of the payoff cells.

2. Figuring Other Goals and Their Determinants into the Calculations. In light of the analogy of the defendant to a buyer and the prosecutor to a seller, it can be said that the defendant-buyer is willing to add a bonus to his price or bargaining limit in order to achieve his other goals, assuming, as is generally the case, that his other goals tend more to raise his willingness to pay than to lower it. If they tend to lower his willingness to pay, then he adds a negative bonus. Likewise, the prosecutor-seller is willing to subtract a discount from his price or bargaining limit in order to achieve his other goals, assuming, as in generally the case, that his other goals tend more to lower the price he demands than to raise it.

In more quantitative terms, it can be said that the defendant's adjusted limit, that is, his bargaining limit adjusted for his nonsentence goals, equals *LD* + *XD*, where *LD* is his unadjusted limit and *XD* is his bonus factor. For example, if the defendant, in accordance with figure 3-1, which is based on table 3-1, has a 5-year limit at his *PC* of .5 and he is willing to provide a 10 percent bonus, then his adjusted limit is 5.5 years and his bonus factor is .5 year. This is comparable to a municipality giving a 10 percent bonus for early construction of a needed bridge. The defendant-buyer is, in effect, seeking early delivery of his purchase or early pretrial resolution of this case.[41]

The prosecutor's adjusted limit equals *LP* + *XP*, where *LP* is his unadjusted limit and *XP* is his discount factor. For example, if the prosecutor, in accordance with table 3-1 and figure 3-1, has a 3.2-year limit at his *PC* of .4 and he is willing to provide a 15 percent discount, then his adjusted limit is 2.7 years and his discount factor is a little less than .5 year. This is comparable to a business firm giving a 15 percent discount for early payment on an invoice.[42] The prosecutor-seller is, in effect, seeking early payment on his sale or early pretrial resolution of his case.[43]

Both the defendant's bonus factor and the prosecutor's discount factor are probably closely related to the severity of the case, although in opposite directions.[44] Other general factors that help explain the level of XD and XP are the attitudes of the defendant and the prosecutor toward risk. If the defendant is a risk avoider, irrespective of his perception of the payoff cells and his conviction probability, he is likely to be willing to give a higher bonus than if he were a risk preferrer. Likewise, if the prosecutor is a risk avoider, meaning he has risk aversion as one of his additional goals, he is likely to be willing to give a higher discount than he would if he were a risk preferrer.[45]

Still another general variable that shapes the defendant's bonus factor and the prosecutor's discount factor is the amount of resources available to both sides. If the defendant is rich, the costs of hiring an attorney will mean less than if he is a lower-middle-class defendant. Likewise, if the prosecutor or the public defender has abundant resources, he will not be so concerned about the costs of preparing for a trial and appearing in court. Some models that have been developed to explain certain aspects of plea bargaining, especially those dealing with the behavior of prosecutors, include the litigants' resources as an important component.[46] The resources available to each side can also affect the probability of conviction regardless of how guilty or innocent the defendant actually may be. Given the possible tendency of some judges to favor those defendants who contribute more to the gross national product, the resources of the defendant may enable him to obtain a shorter sentence than other defendants. Still, a high-income defendant may suffer more disutility stigma and economic loss from a shorter sentence than a lower-income defendant would.[47]

By way of algebraic summary, it can be said that where ALD is the adjusted limit of the defendant, $ALD = LD + XD$. If XD can also be expressed as a percentage ($\%XD$), then we can say $ALD = LD + (\%XD \cdot LD)$. This equation can also be written as $ALD = LD(1 + \%XD)$, with $\%XD$ expressed as a decimal. Similarly, it can be stated for the prosecutor that, where ALP is the prosecutor's adjusted limit, $ALP = LP - XP$, or $ALP = LP(1 - \%X)$. For the sake of simplicity, however, only the terms LD and LP will be used in the further portions of this book dealing with the determination of the equilibrium point toward which the defendant and prosecutor tend to move. The equilibrium models presented, however, would apply equally well even if the ALD and ALP approach were used.

At the simplest level, the defendant is seeking to minimize his sentence subject to the constraint that the sentence cannot be a negative value less than zero. The prosecutor in that context is seeking to maximize the defendant's sentence subject to the constraint that the sentence cannot be greater than the maximum provided for in the statutes or the maximum which the prosecutor considers appropriate to the circumstances of the case. At a more complete level of analysis, the defendant is seeking to minimize both his sentence and his nonsentence costs and to maximize his nonsentence benefits. Likewise, the prosecutor is seeking to maximize both the defendant's sentence and the prosecutor's nonsentence benefits and to minimize his nonsentence costs. These nonsentence goals are taken into consideration in calculating the adjusted limit of the defendant and the adjusted limit of the prosecutor. At a still more complete level of analysis, both the defendant and the prosecutor are seeking to maximize their respective satisfaction units. That concept requires arithmetically transforming both the sentence payoff cells and the non-sentence considerations,[48] so as to reflect the principles of diminishing incremental satisfaction and dissatisfaction. Fortunately for the sake of simplicity, such a transformation is probably unnecessary over the short ranges that are the subject of plea bargaining. The next analysis must be of when and how that range is narrowed to a settlement point.

Notes

The authors would like to thank Albert Alschuler of the University of Colorado Law School, Raymond Nimmer of the American Bar Foundation, Jon Bond of Texas A&M, and Cary Covington of the University of Illinois for their helpful comments concerning chapters 3, 4, and 5.

1. One advantage of working with a major felony case is that all the payoff cells can be measured in years in prison. With a lesser crime, cell *a* might yield probation for a long time, probation for a short time, a suspended sentence, or a fine. If all four cells cannot be measured in the same units, like years or portions of years, then one may have to express the cell payoffs in relative units or rank orders rather than in absolute units. It would, however, be arbitrary to equate guilty plea probation with the zero years from acquittal associated with cell *c*. See note 16 and note 41 in chapter 5 on handling a relative units payoff matrix.

In order to measure all four cells in the same units where one is dealing with payoffs that relate to probation, fines, and jail sentences, one can resort to asking a defendant, defense counsel, or prosecutor the following type of questions: How much would you have to be offered to make it worth your while to plead guilty and receive a 1-year sentence for a certain crime that you did not commit? How much would you have to be offered to make it worth your while to plead guilty and receive 2 years' probation for a certain crime that you did not commit? The questions could be extended to any crime and any type of sentence. The answers would indicate in dollars rather than index numbers how the respondent values the sentences relative to each other. The method, however, does not provide for an interpersonal unit or measure of satisfaction since the value of a dollar varies from individual to individual depending partly on how many dollars he already has.

2. An attempt has been made to use realistic numbers in the cell entries, but the relative size or even rank order of the cells has no essential bearing on the meaningfulness of the decision theory equilibrium model. See section I-B for a discussion of various methods for predicting likely sentences or cell payoffs in given cases. These methods can also be used to translate charges into likely sentences while considering other circumstances in the case.

3. For the sake of simplicity, the table does not make any distinction between going to a bench trial or going to a jury trial. Likewise, it does not distinguish between pleading guilty before one judge or another judge. The trial row of the payoff matrix should show the payoff of whichever is lower between a bench trial and jury trial. Likewise, the pleading row should show the payoff for whichever judge is likely to give the lowest sentence where "judge shopping" is possible or the mean sentence where random assignment is used. Otherwise, it should show the likely payoffs for the judge who has been assigned to the case. Additional rows could be added to distinguish between bench trial and jury trial and between pleading before one judge or another judge, but doing so in this context would serve no useful purpose although a decision theory payoff matrix often has more than two rows or two alternative decisions.

The defendant should work with the lowest payoffs available to him in implicitly preparing his payoff matrix, since the payoff matrix is designed to determine the defendant's fall-back position or best alternative position if plea bargaining breaks down. To be more exact, the defendant should work with the combination of conviction probabilities *and* payoffs that are the lowest. Thus, a bench trial row should be used rather than a jury trial row if the combination of bench trial conviction probabilities and sentencing payoffs is lower than the combination of jury trial conviction probabilities and sentencing payoffs. The prosecutor should do likewise since the prosecutor's payoff matrix is designed to determine the worst thing that can happen to the prosecutor if he fails to give in to the defendant and the plea bargaining breaks down.

4. If the defendant perceives the sentence imposed by the judge without a bargain as not being influenced by the probability of the defendant's being convicted, then cells *a* and *b* would have the same sentence in them, and not be discounted by the probability of conviction. The defendant

might, however, perceive the sentence as being influenced by the contingent probability of getting a harsh rather than a lenient judge. For example, if 70 percent of the judges on the bench are considered harsh and likely to give 9-year sentences and 30 percent are considered lenient and likely to give 2-year sentences, and if the defendant has no knowledge of which judge he would plead guilty before, then the expected value or likely sentence would be 7 years, which equals .70(9 years) + .30(2 years), or 6.4 + .6 years. That approach to calculating the likely sentence of pleading guilty without a bargain, however, is more complicated and less realistic than assuming defense counsel does have some knowledge before which judge he would be pleading guilty without a bargain and what sentence that judge is likely to render.

5. An alternative way to view a payoff matrix would be as a Markov probability chain. Such a perspective would show table 3-1a as an arrow diagram like the following:

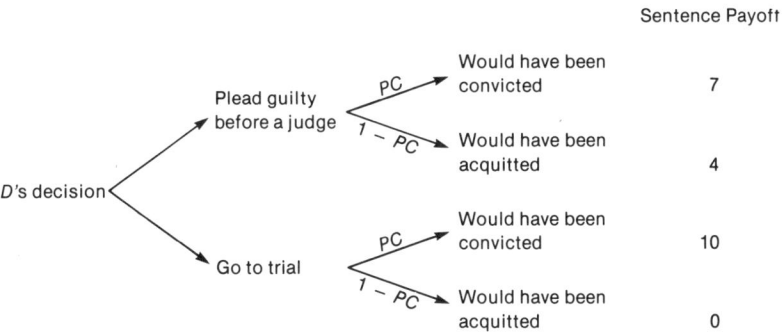

This decision tree perspective, however, adds nothing to our matrix approach, although Markov chain analysis and decision trees are quite useful in analyzing a problem involving more sequences or links in a decision or behavior chain than that with which we are working. For an example of this type of approach applied to plea bargaining, see Fried, "A Decision Theoretic Model of Plea Bargaining" (Mimeographed paper presented at the Midwest Political Science Association convention, 1974).

6. Some of these same considerations affect the relative perceptions of the defendant and the prosecutor of the conviction probabilities, as well as the payoff cells.

7. In most of this chapter, the plea bargaining process is referred to as involving basically two bargainers—the prosecutor and the defendant. However, occasionally it will be recognized that the prosecutor may not be a single individual, but rather a number of assistant prosecuting attorneys

who have differing perceptions of the probability of conviction and the sentencing payoffs. When the prosecutor's perception is discussed, sometimes it will be in reference to a collective perception of the prosecuting attorneys involved in the case.

Likewise, the defense does not always consist of one mind, but rather of a defendant and sometimes more than one defense attorney. Thus, the defense bargainer is also a collective entity where the perceptions of the defense attorney normally count for substantially more than the perceptions of the defendant, although how their input varies is an empirical question. Sometimes their goals may even conflict (or at least not be the same) with regard to the importance of minimizing the sentence and the litigation costs. There may thus be a separate bargaining game occurring between the defendant and his attorney, but modeling that bargaining process is a subject for a separate article.

On the defense side, there may be not only multiple players in the form of defense attorneys and the defendant, but also multiple defendants in the case at bar and in other cases which the defense attorney is simultaneously handling. That kind of multiple representation may result in trade-offs among the defendants which is analogous to a resource allocation model, whereby the defense attorney decides how he can optimally allocate his scarce bargaining resources among a set of defendants. That, too, might be included in an expanded decision theory analysis of the criminal and civil legal process.

8. As another alternative to using the sentence-years approach in table 3-1, one could determine for each cell how much it differs from the worst cell as a measure of benefits, and subtract from each cell the opposite cell in the same column as a measure of opportunity costs. One could likewise determine for each cell how much it differs from the best cell as a measure of costs, and subtract each cell from the opposite cell in the same column as a measure of opportunity benefits. Opportunity costs indicate what one is sacrificing by choosing an alternative decision at a given probability of conviction, whereas opportunity benefits indicate what one is gaining.

These kinds of benefit minus cost calculations, however, result in units that have no meaning in the real-world context of plea bargaining. In that real world, the defendant sees no benefits from being sentenced, only costs which he wants to minimize. Likewise, the prosecutor sees no costs from the *issuance* of a sentence, only benefits which he wants to maximize subject to constraints. There may be costs to the prosecutor involved in obtaining or enforcing the sentence, but not in the sentence itself. The prosecutor is like a seller seeking as high a price as possible, and the defendant is like a buyer, seeking as low a price as possible.

9. Likewise, the prosecutor might gain some positive payoffs from an acquittal if the trial serves to frighten other perceived social deviants. The

prosecutor might also suffer adverse payoffs from a conviction via lost office resources which were devoted to the trial.

10. There is now available in the archives of the Inter-University Consortium for Political Research at Ann Arbor, Michigan, a sample of 11,256 criminal cases from across the country for the early 1960s from which one can derive average sentences to various crimes when the defendant (1) pleads guilty to a lesser charge, implying a negotiated plea; (2) pleads guilty to the original charge, implying a nonnegotiated plea, or (3) has a trial and is found guilty. For example, in the subset of murder cases, when the defendants pleaded guilty to a lesser degree of murder, they averaged 7 years, figuring a life sentence at 20 years. When the murder defendants pleaded guilty to the original charge, their sentences averaged 17 years. When the murder defendants were found guilty in a trial, they averaged 14 years.

One obvious defect in this approach to obtaining real rather than hypothetical numbers for the payoff cells is the fact that the cases involving a guilty plea to the original charge may be more (or less) heinous than the cases which go to trial, and thus the unbargained guilty plea cases should involve a higher (or lower) average sentence than the guilty verdict cases because they are different cases. What is needed is to determine from knowledgeable experts how a case or case type is likely to be sentenced if it goes to trial, as well as how the *same* case is likely to be sentenced if the defendant pleads guilty without a bargain. If we apply the rule-of-thumb approach, we can say the average murder case in the United States gets a sentence of (1) 14 years if tried to conviction, (2) two-thirds of that, or 9 years, if pleaded guilty when a guilty verdict would have been received, and (3) 5 years, or one-third of the 14, if pleaded guilty when an acquittal verdict would have been received.

11. For a discussion of some of the methodological problems involved in getting knowledgeable persons to be more accurate than they otherwise would be in responding to questionnaires about payoffs or contingent probabilities, see P. Kotler, *Marketing Decision Making: A Model Building Approach* 583-95 (1971) and Huber, "Methods for Quantifying Subjective Probabilities and Multi-Attribute Utilities," 5 *Decision Sciences* 430 (1974). See also text accompanying note 34, discussion of how to average the estimates of a group of knowledgeable persons and how to manipulate multiple estimates from each person to obtain a more accurate estimate per person. For a discussion specifically directed at how a prosecutor should evaluate the importance or utility of cases, see J. Jacoby, *A System for Manual Evaluation of Case Processing in the Prosecutor's Office* (1972); National Center for Prosecution Management, *Report to the Bronx District Attorney on the Case Evaluation System* (1974). The information emphasized indirectly relates to both sentencing payoffs and the probability of conviction.

12. A regression analysis might involve a linear prediction equation of the form $LS = A + B(PC)$, where $A = 0$ since that is the likely sentence when $PC = 0$, and B is the number of units that LS changes when PC changes 1 unit. One such prediction equation would be needed for all trial cases for each crime category and for all guilty plea cases for each crime category. An alternative prediction equation might be $LS = A + B_1(PC) + B_2(CS) + B_3(MR)$, subject to the condition that when $PC = 0$, $LS = 0$. In this equation, CS is a measure of crime severity based on the sentences provided in the statutes, MR refers to the method of resolution with a 1 for going to trial and a 2 for pleading guilty, and the B's represent the weights by which the variables have to be multiplied to have the equation best fit the case data gathered for generating the equation. In section II-C, there is a discussion of how to determine the conviction probability of a case from the characteristics of that case. The regression method for determining likely sentences is obviously much more cumbersome and may produce less accurate predictions than the knowledgeable-persons method or even the rule-of-thumb method, although it may generate insights as to what causes sentences to vary.

The symbols A and B (rather than a and b) are used throughout this chapter to represent regression coefficients so as to avoid confusion with the cell payoffs. Perhaps the cell payoffs should have been designated with capital letters since it is customary to designate unstandardized regression coefficients with lowercase letters. For further detail on using linear regression analysis to predict sentences or other case outcomes, see Nagel, "Predicting Court Cases Quantitatively," 63 *Mich. L. Rev.* 411 (1965); Tanenhaus et al., "The Supreme Court's Certiorari Jurisdiction: Cue Theory," in *Judicial Decision Making*, ed. G. Schubert (1963). As the probability of conviction goes up, the likely sentence also goes up at what is probably a fairly constant rate, although empirical data would be useful to confirm that. As crime severity goes up, however, the likely sentence may go up, but at a decreasing rate. The best-fitting curve thus might involve using the logarithm of CS instead of CS in the above equation. On nonlinear regression analysis, see J. Guilford, *Psychometric Methods* 43-78 (1954). The nonlinear, diminishing-returns relation between likely sentence and a measure of utility or satisfaction is discussed in section I-C. Instead of trying to determine a single likely sentence or sentencing point for each of the four cells, one might feel more comfortable determining a range of sentences for one or more cells, especially where bargaining is over the charge and thus only indirectly over the sentence. For a discussion of the range approach in determining cell payoffs and conviction probabilities, see section II-C.

13. Note that although 10 years is 2½ times 4 years in table 3-1*a*, 3.2 dissatisfaction units is less than 2½ times 2 dissatisfaction units for the corresponding cells, illustrating the principle of diminishing disutility.

14. The most meaningful kind of utility data to obtain involves asking the respondents a series of questions designed to determine the relative number of satisfaction or dissatisfaction units associated with a 2-year sentence, a 4-year sentence, and other time units. The questions for the prosecutor can have the form, Which choice would you prefer: (1) obtaining a *2-year* jail sentence for a crime that has a 10-year maximum, or (2) having a lottery ticket that gives you a 90 percent chance to get a $1,000 raise in salary and a 10 percent chance to get a $1,000 reduction in salary? The next question provides for an 80 percent-20 percent split on alternative 2, and the next question after that might provide for a 70 percent-30 percent split until the split is obtained where the respondent says he is indifferent between choices 1 and 2. We then ask a series of questions in which choice 1 involves a *4-year* jail sentence. With the answers to these kinds of questions for a group of prosecutors, we can then roughly determine through some simple arithmetic manipulation how many relative satisfaction units a 2-year sentence, a 4-year sentence, and so on has for the average prosecutor. By an analogous approach, we can make a similar determination for the average defendant. For further detail on translating absolute numbers into relative satisfaction units, see W. Baumol, *Economic Theory and Operations Analysis* 512-28 (1965); D Miller and M. Starr, *Executive Decisions and Operations Research* 55-78 (1960).

15. See note 14.

16. As an alternative to using the satisfaction units approach in table 3-1, one could try an index number approach whereby the worst cell is assigned a -100, the best cell is assigned a $+100$, and the other two cells receive numbers between -100 and $+100$, depending on how close they are viewed to the worst or best cell. Such an approach is highly subjective, and it involves units that are not actually used by defendants or prosecutors in plea bargaining (unlike sentencing time units) or even present at a subconscious level (unlike satisfaction units). If no better measuring units were available, however, that index number approach could produce adequate results. See note 41 to chapter 5.

17. Any straight line can be written in the general form $Y = A + BX$. A is the value of Y when $X = 0$; B is the number of units of change in Y per 1-unit change in X. The X in this example is PC; the Y is LS_1, where the subscript 1 indicates that LS_1 is the likely sentence from going to trial. When $PC = 0$, then $LS_1 = 0$, the amount in cell *c*. Similarly, when $PC = 1.0$, then $LS_1 = 10$, the amount in cell *d*. Therefore, $LS_1 = 0 + 10(PC)$, which may be graphed by connecting the 0 point on the left vertical axis with the 10 on the right vertical axis. See note 12 on the use of A and B, rather than *a* and *b*, to represent regression coefficients.

18. Instead of connecting the 0 and the 10 by a straight line of the form $LS = A + B(PC)$, we could have connected them by a decreasing rate line

of the form $LS = A(PC)^B$, where $A = 10$ and B is any positive number less than 1 (for example, .5), or by an increasing rate line of the form $LS = A(PC)^B$, where $A = 10$ and B is a positive number greater than 1 (for example, 1.5). The same thing could be done with any of the four straight lines shown in figure 3-1, but there are no data or theoretical reason for suspecting these relations are nonlinear. See note 12. Payoff matrices could show the payoffs when *PC* or another contingent probability is .5 as well as 0.0 and 1.0, giving us a payoff matrix with three columns rather than two. Doing so would be useful if the payoffs rise in the middle and then fall, or fall in the middle and then rise. One cannot, however, have a payoff matrix with only one probability column, although (as discussed in section II-B-2-b and I-A of chapter 5) a payoff matrix with only one row or one decisional alternative is possible. As a minimum, the payoff for a 0.0 probability column (that is, what would happen if the contingent event would not occur?) and a 1.0 probability column (that is, what would happen if the contingent event would occur?) must be determined.

19. By using the same logic as was used in note 17, the likely sentence from a guilty plea is 4 when $PC = 0$, and it is 7 when $PC = 1.0$, which are the amounts in cells *a* and *b*. The equation of the plead line is then $LS_2 = 4 + (7 - 4)PC$. Moreover, the graph or slope of the line is established by connecting the 4 on the left vertical axis with the 7 on the right.

20. An alternative to the regression approach for relating *LS* to *PC* is a weighted average approach. A weighted average approach involves saying that $LS_1 = (1 - PC)(c) + (PC)(d)$. Thus, if the prosecutor perceives that $PC = .4$, then by this equation $LS_1 = (1 - .4)(0) + (.4)(8) = 3.2$ years. What we are, in effect, saying is that a good way to determine the likely sentence upon going to trial of a case with a .4 *PC* is to calculate a weighted average of all the payoffs in which each payoff is weighted by the probability of its occurrence. The formula for a weighted average or mean equals (1) the sum of the weights times the associated scores divided by (2) the sum of the weights. In this context we substitute the probabilities $1 - PC$ and PC for the weights and *c* and *d* for the scores. Since the sum of $1 - PC$ and PC equals 1, the average or the best expectation is simply the sum $(1 - PC)(c) + (PC)(d)$. Likewise, the weighted average formula for LS_2 is $LS_2 = (1 - PC)(a) + (PC)(b)$, where *a* and *b* refer to cells *a* and *b* rather than to the regression coefficients. If the regression approach is expressed in terms of cell letters, then $LS_1 = c + (d - c)(PC)$, and $LS_2 = a + (b - a)(PC)$. The weighted average approach and the regression approach produce identical results because they are algebraically equivalent when they are both simplified by removing the parentheses.

When we use the weighted average approach, in effect we are using the mean of the population or universe of cases like the case at bar (as perceived by the defendant or prosecutor) in order to estimate the likely sentence score of the case at bar. In other words, we are using the mean of the universe to predict the mean of a sample where the sample size is 1. The mean provides the best estimation because it tends (in the usual statistical usage) to minimize deviations from the actual score of the sample to the estimated score of the universe, or because it tends (in our decision theory usage) to minimize deviations from the perceived score of the universe (or set of cases) to the estimated score of the sample (or immediate case). Likewise, when we use the regression line approach, we are using a regression equation for the perceived universe in order to estimate the likely sentence score of the case at bar. The regression line provides the best estimation because it tends (in the statistical usage) to minimize deviations from the actual cases to the estimated regression line, or because it tends (in decision theory) to minimize deviations from the perceived regression line to the case at bar whose likely sentence is being estimated.

Predicting the mode, the most common occurrence, or the cell which has the highest frequency on a row is more accurate than predicting from the mean in the sense of minimizing the average difference from the actual scores to the predicted scores. Predicting from the mean minimizes the average squared difference from the actual scores to the predicted scores. However, one would not want to predict or obtain expected values by simply assuming that the most frequent occurrence will occur in the case under consideration, because doing so does not take into consideration the degree of probability of a conviction. As a result, modal prediction (rather than mean prediction) would cause defense counsel to engage in settlement behavior that would not minimize the sentences received, and it would cause the prosecutor to engage in settlement behavior that would not maximize the sentences received. Throughout this analysis, we assume the defense side wants to minimize expected sentences and the prosecutor wants to maximize them, rather than assume that they are both trying to maximize accuracy of prediction. On measuring prediction accuracy and achieving it, see Nagel and Neef, *Policy Analysis and Social Science Research* (1978).

21. Regardless of what the cell payoffs are, the *Y-intercept* or left vertical axis intersection of (1) the defendant's D trial line will be the payoff in his cell c, (2) the defendant's D plead line will be the payoff in his cell a, (3) the prosecutor's P trial line will be the payoff in his cell c, and (4) the prosecutor's P plead line will be the payoff in his cell a. Likewise, regardless of the cell payoffs, the *slope* of (1) the defendant's D trial line will be his cell d minus cell c, (2) the defendant's D plead line will be his cell b minus cell a, (3) the prosecutor's P trial line will be his cell d minus cell c, and (4) the prosecutor's P plead line will be his cell b minus cell a.

22. The questionnaire or interviewing survey will possibly throw some light on the extent to which pleading guilty before a judge provides a meaningful alternative to plea bargaining with the prosecutor. Trial judges have

been found to play a substantial role in plea bargaining, as indicated in Alschuler, "The Trial Judge's Role in Plea Bargaining," 76 *Col. L. Rev.* 1059 (1976).

23. Where the defendant sees only the pleading line as a possibility, it may be due to the fact that his perceptions of the cell payoffs are such that the adverse payoff in cell c is greater than the adverse payoff in cell a, and likewise cell d is greater than cell b. In such a situation, the pleading line is said to *dominate* the trial line as an alternative. In the plea bargaining context, this means at all points the pleading line is below the trial line. Such a situation, however, would be likely to occur only if the defendant were considering goals other than sentence minimization. Where the defendant sees only the trial line as a possibility, this may likewise be due to the fact that the trial line dominates or is always better than the pleading line, as indicated by the trial cells being always higher than the corresponding pleading cells.

Another type of defendant who sees only the trial line as a possible alternative is one for whom any conviction regardless of the length of the jail sentence would be devastating. Thus no matter how high he perceives PC (so long as it is short of 1.0), he will hold out for a trial. In other words, such a defendant perceives the payoffs in cells a, b, and d to be infinitely bad or equally horrible in terms of satisfaction units, and only cell c offers any hope.

24. A *maximax* strategist is literally one seeking to maximize his maximum possible gain, as contrasted to a *minimax* strategist who is literally one seeking to minimize his maximum possible loss. The maximax strategist will choose the alternative that will give him the biggest gain when the contingent probability is favorable, even though it may also give him the biggest loss when the contingent probability is unfavorable. The minimax strategist will choose the alternative that will give him the smallest loss when the contingent probability is unfavorable, even though it may also give him the smallest gain when the contingent probability is favorable. For further details on these two general types of decision makers in a context broader and more abstract than plea bargaining, see S. Richmond, *Operations Research for Management Decisions* 32–38, 504 (1968).

25. If the defendant pleads guilty in reliance on the prosecutor's promise that the judge will give a certain sentence and the judge fails to do so, the defendant normally cannot withdraw his guilty plea. This, however, is usually known to defense counsel and experienced defendants, and they will not plead guilty as part of a plea bargain unless they feel almost sure the judge will abide by the prosecutor's recommendation. If the prosecutor or his successor breaks his promise concerning a recommended sentence, then the guilty plea can be withdrawn. *Santobello* v. *New York*, 404 U.S. 257 (1971). No matter how intimidating the likely sentence may appear to be, a defendant's plea of guilty as part of a plea bargain will not be considered a coerced confession. *Brady* v. *United States*, 397 U.S. 742 (1970).

Decision Theory Defendant/Prosecutor   101

26. As previously described, $LS_1 = c + (d - c)(PC)$, using the regression approach, or $LS_1 = (1 - PC)(c) + (PC)(d)$, using the weighted average approach. Likewise, $LS_2 = a + (b - a)(PC)$, using the regression approach, or $LS_2 = (1 - PC)(a) + (PC)(b)$, using the weighted average approach.

27. The formulas for calculating LS_1 and LS_2 for the prosecutor are the same as those for the defendant except one inserts the prosecutor's perceptions of the cell payoffs from his payoff matrix, and the other inserts his perception of the probability of conviction.

28. Since $LS_1 = 0 + 10(PC)$ and $LS_2 = 4 + (7 - 4)(PC)$, therefore PC^*, or the intersection PC, is found by solving for PC in the equation $0 + 10(PC) = 4 + (7 - 4)(PC)$. That equation simplifies to $10(PC) - 3(PC) = 4$, which means $7(PC) = 4$, or $PC = 4/7 = .57$.

29. Although a probability cannot be greater than 1.00, PC^* can be greater than 1.00 if in a given situation, pleading guilty without a bargain were always better than or dominant to going to trial, that is, if cell a involved a lower sentence than cell c, and cell b involved a lower sentence than cell d. Likewise, although a probability cannot be less than 0, PC^* can be less than 0 if in a given situation going to trial were always better than or dominant to pleading, that is, if cell c involved a lower sentence than cell a, and cell d involved a lower sentence than cell b. In either situation, one would always choose to plead, or always choose to go to trial by, in effect, rounding PC^* down to 1.00 if it is greater than 1.00 or rounding PC^* up to 0 if it is less than 0.

30. If $LS_1 = LS_2$, then $0 + 8(PC) = 3 + (6 - 3)(PC)$. The solution produces $PC = .60$.

31. This equation may be proved since we know $LS_1 = c + (d - c)(PC)$, and $LS_2 = a + (b - a)(PC)$. At PC^*, $LS_1 = LS_2$. Therefore, PC^* may be algebraically determined by solving for PC in the equation $c + (d - c)(PC) = a + (b - a)(PC)$. Doing so reveals that $PC^* = (a - c)/(a - b - c + d)$. The algebraic solution for PC^* is:

$$LS_1 = LS_2$$

$$c + (d - c)(PC) = a + (b - a)(PC)$$

$$(d - c)(PC) - (b - a)(PC) = a - c$$

$$PC\left[(d - c) - (b - a)\right] = a - c$$

$$PC^* = \frac{a - c}{a - b - c + d}$$

32. The algebraic solution for LS^* is

$$LS^* = c + (d - c)(PC^*)$$

By substituting value of PC^* we get

$$LS^* = \frac{c + (d - c)(a - c)}{a - b - c + d}$$

Multiply the two numerator terms:

$$LS^* = \frac{c + ad - ac - cd + c^2}{a - b - c + d}$$

Express both addends in terms of a common denominator:

$$LS^* = \frac{(a - b - c + d)(c) + ad - ac - cd + c^2}{a - b - c + d}$$

By removing parentheses in the numerator we have

$$LS^* = \frac{ac - bc - c^2 + cd + ad - ac - cd + c^2}{a - b - c + d}$$

By eliminating pairs of terms in the numerator with opposite signs we have finally

$$LS^* = \frac{ad - bc}{a - b - c + d}$$

33. See section I-B.

34. On the use of survey data to determine outcome probabilities, see Kotler, *Marketing Decision Making*, and Huber, "Methods for Quantifying Subjective Probabilities." For a further discussion of the how and why of handling symmetrical estimates, see Richmond, *Operations Research for Management Decisions*, pp. 487–491, 220–224. Three estimates for each point can be meaningfully obtained for a payoff cell by asking for an estimate below the most likely estimate that is likely to occur less than a certain percentage of the time with the given type of case being considered. Likewise, a high estimate may be explained as an estimate above the most likely estimate that is also likely to occur less than the same certain percentage of the time with the given type of case being considered.

35. For a discussion of various methods designed to obtain case outcome probabilities from case data, see Nagel, "Judicial Prediction and Analysis from Empirical Probability Tables," 41 *Ind. L. J.* 403 (1966). Those methods include regression analysis, discriminant analysis, Bayesian probability, and the Sonquist-Morgan automatic interaction detector.

By using the same nationwide sample of 11,256 criminal cases mentioned in note 10, an average probability conviction for each major crime may be obtained by simply observing, for any given crime, how many of the cases involving that crime resulted in a conviction on trial. For example, in looking at the murder cases, of the 86 cases that went to trial for which information was available, 70 resulted in guilty verdicts and 16 resulted in acquittal. This means that the empirical probability of conviction in that nationwide sample of murder cases was .81. With the same data, a probability may be deduced by trying to predict whether the defendant will be convicted from various characteristics of his case plus the crime with which he has been charged. Thus, if the crime is known to be murder and the defendant is known to be indigent, by using the Bayes method of determining probabilities, it can be said that the conviction probability in light of the data and those two circumstances is .84. This estimated *PC* is derived from these facts: (1) .81 of the murder trial cases result in convictions and .19 in acquittals; (2) about .31 of those 70 in the sample convicted of murder in a trial were indigent enough to have court-appointed counsel; (3) about .25 of those 16 in the sample acquitted of murder were indigent; and (4) .84 = (.81)(.31)/ [(.19)(.25) + (.81)(.31)]. For further details on Bayesian empirical probabilities, see Richmond, *Operations Research for Management Decisions*, pp. 145-152, 541-550.

36. The statements concerning defendants and prosecutors operating under conditions of certainty assume that both the trial line and the plead line are being used. See the discussion of the certainty part of table 4-2 in section I-A2, chapter 4, and section II-B-2, of this chapter for the highly unusual defendant who is certain he will be acquitted but still pleads guilty or who is certain he will be convicted but still goes to trial.

37. A defendant's optimism coefficient is equal to *PC** when the cell payoffs are adjusted so that the expected value or likely sentence of going to trial is perceived as about equal to the likely sentence of pleading guilty before a judge. This method for calculating an optimism-pessimism coefficient or a *PC* value designed to reflect one's optimism-pessimism was developed by Leonid Hurwicz. See Richmond, *Operations Research for Management Decisions*, pp. 33-34.

38. An alternative approach to handling the problem of the *PC* range is to think in terms of a vertical probability band in figure 3-1 rather than a probability point. For example, a defendant with a perceived *PC* range between .2 and .5 in figure 3-1 would have a limit between 2 and 5 years. This would mean that the prosecutor would have to make an offer below 2 years in order for the defendant to accept it if the defendant accepts only offers below his limit. Thus, the probability band approach would arrive at the same result as the optimistic defendant concept. Likewise, the probability band approach applied to the prosecutor would produce the same result as the optimistic prosecutor concept. Since not all defendants and prosecu-

tors are optimistic, this probability band approach is less likely to reflect empirical reality than thinking in terms of three types of defendants and three types of prosecutors on an optimism-pessimism scale.

If the defendant's cell a in table 3-1 ranged from 3 to 6 years instead of being exactly 4, a limit band approach applied to figure 3-1 would result in an elongated triangle lying on its side with the base extending from the 3 to the 6 on the left vertical axis over to the apex 7 on the right vertical axis. This elongated triangle would constitute the defendant's new D plead band. The defendant, under these circumstances, would reject all offers by the prosecutor which are not below a line from 5 to 7 years when the defendant's PC is between .5 and 1.0 instead of the higher former D plead line in figure 3-1. The limit band approach has the effect of generating a limit for the defendant which is the same limit as the one for the optimistic defendant who perceives the likely sentence of cell a to be between 3 and 6 years and who therefore has a D plead line extending from 3 when $PC = 0$ to 7 when $PC = 1.0$. As contrasted to the more realistic approach of using the three-point optimism-pessimism scale, the limit band approach is as inapplicable as the probability band approach to a defendant or a prosecutor who thinks in terms of a PC range or a payoff-cell range. The combination of a limit band and a probability band can create a shaded region that the prosecutor must go below if the defendant is going to accept the prosecutor's offer. The lowest point on that shaded region thus determines the defendant's limit, and the lowest point is the most optimistic point with regard to both PC and the payoff cells. The three-point approach, on the other hand, allows the prosecutor to go below any one of those points depending on the defendant's optimism-pessimism attitude.

39. On the other hand, assuming that $PC = .57$ comes closer to satisfying the technical criterion which is used in formal decision theory to make decisions when the contingent probabilities are totally unknown. That technical criterion says to mix decisions between the alternatives of trial and pleading in such proportions as to equalize (1) the average return which will be received when the contingency, that is, being convicted, does not occur and (2) the average return which will be received when the contingency does occur.

By applying this technical criterion to the hypothetical data in table 3-1a and figure 3-1, it is found that if the defendant operates on the assumption that $PC = .5$, then 0 percent of the time he will plead guilty and 100 percent of the time he will go to trial, given these data and those alternatives. This means that when he would have been acquitted, his average sentence would be 0 times 4 *plus* 1 times 0, or the proportion allocated to pleading (which is 0) times cell a (which is 4) *plus* the proportion allocated to trial times cell c. When he would have been convicted, his average sentence would be 0 times 7 *plus* 1 times 10. The first sum equals 0, and the second sum equals 10, for a difference of 10 years. On the other hand, if the defendant operates on the assumption that $PC = .57$, then 50 percent of the time he will plead guilty and 50 percent of the time he will go to trial. When he would have been acquitted, his average sentence would then be .5 times 4 *plus* .5 times 0, or 2 years. When he would have been convicted, his average sentence would be .5 times 7 *plus* .5 times 10, or 8½ years. The difference between 8½ years and 2 years under the .57 assumption is smaller than the difference of 10 years under the .5 assumption.

Actually, the smallest difference which could be created between those two averages with the data given would involve pleading guilty 100 percent of the time and never going to trial as if PC were 1.0. Then the difference between those two averages is 7 − 4 years, or just 3 years. This same result would occur if the unknowledgeable defendant acted in the most pessimistic way possible by assuming that his conviction probability equaled 1.0. By using the technical criterion, this would be the best thing for the defendant to do. This, however, illustrates how conservative or pessimistic and probably unrealistic that technical criterion or minimax criterion is.

If the minimax or other criterion had indicated that the best strategy when operating under ignorance is to go to trial 65 percent of the time and plead guilty 35 percent of the time, then what would one do if he were involved in only a single case? At a superficial level, it might be said to go to trial since that is what one is supposed to do most of the time. At a more sophisticated level that in the long run will lead to more satisfaction, the answer is to draw the first two-digit number from a random numbers table. If the two-digit number is less than 65, go to trial; if the two-digit number is more than 65, plead guilty before a judge. In game theory, such a randomized strategy is often the optimum strategy on the assumption that the player being advised is totally ignorant of the other player's likely moves. Seldom, if ever, will a real-world decision maker admit to such ignorance that he has to draw random numbers to make important litigation or business decisions. For further discussion of decision making when one is ignorant of the contingent probabilities, see Richmond, *Operations Research for Management Decisions*, pp. 32-38, 535-538.

40. Prosecutors want to maximize the percentage of convictions as well as the sentences received by convicted defendants. To take into consideration that nonsentence goal of maximizing conviction percentages, prosecutors probably are willing to allow an extra discount when PC falls below .50. In fact, that portion of the discount may go up at a roughly linear rate as PC goes down from 1.00 to 0.

Defendants, however, who want to minimize their conviction probabilities will not plead guilty as a bonus since a guilty plea is a conviction. Through the bargaining process, a prosecutor can minimize the number of low PC cases that go to trial. Likewise, through the bargaining process, a defense counsel who has many cases can minimize the number of high PC cases that go to trial. The defendant with one case, however, can only minimize *PC* by getting better witnesses or evidence on his behalf, not through bargaining whereby he agrees to plead guilty to a reduced charge or recommended sentence.

41. In terms of the graph shown in figure 3-1, adding a 10 percent defendant's bonus to avoid the defendant's litigation costs over his settlement costs has the effect of raising the defendant's limit line by 10 percent. Without the bonus, *LD,* the defendant's unadjusted limit, is $LD = c + (d - c)(PC)$ below *LS**, or $LD = 0 + (10 - 0)(PC)$ below 5.7; and $LD = a + (b - a)(PC)$ above *LS**, or $LD = 4 + (7 - 4)(PC)$ above 5.7. With the bonus, the kinked *LD* line, the defendant's limit line, equals *LD* plus 10 percent of *LD*. That new kinked line would run parallel and above the old *LD* line, and it is symbolized *ALD* (adjusted limit of the defendant). In terms of figure 4-1, the dashed *ALD* line is 10 percent above the unshown *LD* line, so long as the bonus factor remains at 10 percent for the defendant throughout the plea bargaining time points, although it can change.

42. In terms of the graph shown in figure 3-1, deducting a 15 percent prosecutor's bonus to avoid the prosecutor's litigation costs over his settlement costs lowers the prosecutor's limit line by 15 percent. Without the discount, *LP,* the prosecutor's unadjusted limit, is $LP = c + (d - c)(PC)$ below *LS**, or $LP = 0 + (8 - 0\,PC)$ below 4.8; and $LP - a + (b\ \ a)(PC)$ above *LS**, or $LP = 3 + (6 - 3)(PC)$ above 4.8. With the bonus, the kinked *LP* line, the prosecutor's limit line, equals *LP* minus 15 percent of *LP*. That new kinked line would run parallel and below the old *LP* line, and it is symbolized *ALP* (adjusted limit of the prosecutor). In terms of figure 4-1, the dotted *ALP* line is 15 percent below the unshown *LP* line, so long as the discount factor remains at 15 percent for the prosecutor throughout the plea bargaining time points, although it can change.

43. References to a percentage bonus for the defendant to cover his nonsentence goals and a percentage discount for the prosecutor to cover his nonsentence goals could be avoided if sentences and nonsentence goals could be translated into a common unit of measurement like dollars or satisfaction units. This is, in effect, what is done in G. Tullock, *The Logic of the Law* 176-186 (1971); Landes, "An Economic Analysis of the Courts," 14 *J. L. & Econ.* 61-107 (April 1971). However, they work only with algebraic symbols. In the real world, it may be virtually impossible to translate all the goals into dollars and especially into satisfaction units, but it may not be so difficult to deal with sentence years and a percentage bonus or a percentage discount.

44. The more severe a case is, the less willing a defendant might be to plea-bargain and thus plead guilty, especially when he is innocent or has a low perceived conviction probability. Thus a higher percentage of plea bargains and guilty pleas probably exist in misdemeanor violations than in murder cases. The severity of the case as perceived by the defendant can be

measured by looking to the value in the defendant's payoff cell d. It can then be said that $XD = A - B(d)$, assuming a negative linear regression relation between XD and d. A is the value of XD when cell d is 0, and B indicates how many units XD changes when d changes 1 unit. Perhaps through appropriate interviews and questionnaires of defense attorneys, some data could be obtained to establish numerical values for A and B.

The more severe a case is, the more willing a prosecutor might be to plea-bargain since the more severe cases involve more time and other costs which the prosecutor is seeking to avoid. Therefore, his XP regression equation might take the form $XP = A + B(d)$, assuming a positive linear regression relation between XP and cell d. Alternatively, prosecutors might prefer to take big cases to trial because of the possibly favorable publicity from obtaining a conviction and because of an unwillingness to be blamed for having reduced the charge. Mather, "Some Determinants of the Method of Case Disposition: Decision-Making by Public Defenders in Los Angeles," 8 *Law & Society Rev.* 187-216 (1974). Perhaps interviews and questionnaires of prosecutors could establish numerical values for A and B, and perhaps such data would indicate the degree to which XD differs from XP and why.

45. Suppose a defendant is offered 2 years in prison for a guilty plea and the defendant perceives the sentence upon conviction would be 5 years with a .20 probability of conviction. If the defendant accepts the 2-year offer, then he is a risk avoider, since he is accepting a certain offer that has a worse expected value than the expected value of the risky outcome. More precisely, the defendant would be a risk avoider in this situation if he accepted any prosecutor's offer greater than 1 year in prison, assuming the only relevant consideration is minimizing the sentence. Likewise, the defendant would be a risk preferrer if he were willing to go to trial when the prosecutor, under these circumstances, offered less than 1 year. He would be risk-neutral if his threshold offer to accept were exactly 1 year; or, stated differently, he would be risk-neutral if his threshold probability in responding to a 2-year offer were .40 (with a 5-year perceived sentence) or if his threshold perceived sentence is 10 years (with a .20 probability of conviction).

Likewise, a prosecutor is a risk avoider if he accepts a defendant's offer which involves a lower sentence or a worse expected value than the perceived expected value of going to trial. A prosecutor is a risk preferrer if he rejects a defendant's offer which involves a higher sentence or better expected value than the perceived expected value of going to trial. A prosecutor is risk-neutral if the threshold offer between those he will accept or reject is exactly equal to the expected value of going to trial. A prosecutor is also risk-neutral if his threshold probability between accepting a defendant's offer and going to trial exactly equalizes the expected value of going to trial and the defendant's offer. In other words, the risk avoider takes the alternative that has certainty, even when the alternative that lacks certainty has a higher expected value. The risk preferrer takes the alternative that lacks certainty even when that alternative has a lower expected value than the offer with no risk. Where two risky choices are available from trial and pleading, compare the nonrisky offer from the other side with both of the risky alternatives.

46. Landes, "An Economic Analysis of the Courts"; Lachman, "The Prosecutor's Decision to Plea Bargain: An economic Perspective" (unpublished Ph.D. dissertation written at Michigan State University, 1975).

47. A perspective that concentrates on the prosecutor's resources may lead one into an alternative model that involves explaining the prosecutor's behavior in terms of his trying to find an optimum mix of his resources among his cases in terms of their respective probabilities of conviction and their sentences if conviction occurs. That type of behavior is analogous to an investment company manager trying to develop an optimum portfolio of stocks for a client, given (1) the client's resources, (2) the probabilities of certain contingent events that can result in stock increases or decreases, and (3) the amount of increase or decrease if the contingencies occur. W. Baumol, *Portfolio Theory: The Selection of Asset-Combinations* (1974). Michael Fried, in a forthcoming expansion of his paper, is experimenting with the application of portfolio analysis to the behavior of prosecutors using empirical data from Detroit, Michigan. See Fried, "A Decision Theoretic Model of Plea Bargaining." The situation is relatively simple if the prosecutor has only two cases between which his resources must be allocated and the only defense attorney is the public defender who has the same two cases. Then the problem becomes one of developing an indifference curve for the prosecutor showing what combinations of resources between those two cases would provide him with equal satisfaction at a given level of satisfaction. A similar set of indifference curves could then be developed for the public defender, and both sets of indifference curves could be placed in an Edgeworth box format roughly related to that described in note 18 to chapter 4. That approach would enable a determination of whether the bargainers would be likely to arrive at a settlement and within what range such a settlement might occur. E. Mansfield, *Microeconomics: Theory and Applications* 20-49 (1970)) Birmingham, "Damage Measures and Economic Rationality: The Geometry of Contract Law," 1969 *Duke L. J.* 49-71 (1969); and Lachman, "The Prosecutor's Decision to Plea Bargain." The situation, however, becomes quite complicated if the number of cases is increased beyond two, the number of defense attorneys increased beyond one, and probabilistic or stochastic considerations are added to this nonprobabilistic or deterministic model. Portfolio analysis might be especially applicable to a personal injury plaintiff or defense lawyer trying to decide

how to allocate his scarce resources among a set of cases, each one of which has a probability of victory and each of which has an estimated monetary value if the case is won.

48. See section I-C.

4 Equilibrium Models Applied to the Defendant and the Prosecutor

I. Results of Clashes between Different Bargainers

Since a high percentage of, but not all, negotiations between defendants and prosecutors result in out-of-court settlements, a useful model should be capable of indicating when a settlement is likely to occur and why a settlement occurs in such a high percentage of criminal cases. The model also should be able to indicate at what amount settlement is likely to occur and what other alternatives are likely to be selected if a settlement does not occur. In showing how the model presented in chapter 3 is capable of answering these types of questions, chapters 4 and 5 will present the general situation and also other situations involving special conditions concerning the defendant's strategies toward the alternatives and both parties' degree of knowledge of the contingent probabilities.[1]

A. General Equilibrium

1. When Convergence Is Likely to Occur. Geometrically speaking, convergence to an equilibrium solution is likely to occur if in a figure like figure 3-1 the defendant's limit at his perceived probability of conviction (PC) is greater than the prosecutor's limit at his perceived PC. Thus, in figure 3-1 if the defendant's $PC = .5$, his maximum limit is 5 years. If the prosecutor's $PC = .4$, his maximum limit is 3.2 years. With those facts one can see in figure 3-1 that the circle corresponding to the defendant's limit is higher than the circle corresponding to the prosecutor's limit. Convergence is likely to occur in that situation because the defendant-buyer is willing to accept a greater sentence than the prosecutor-seller has as his minimum, or the prosecutor-seller is willing to accept a lesser sentence than the defendant-buyer has as his maximum. By using a market analogy, convergence is likely to occur in that situation, because the prosecutor-seller is willing to sell for less than the price at which the defendant-buyer is willing to buy.

On the other hand, if the defendant perceives his PC to be .2, his maximum limit would be 2 years. A circle corresponding to the defendant's limit then would be below the prosecutor's limit of 3.2. In that situation, convergence would be unlikely because the prosecutor would be willing to accept a solution no lower than 3.2 years, and the defendant would accept no sentence higher than 2 years. This assumes, of course, that sentence maximization and minimization are the goals of the respective parties.

Convergence may fail to occur not only because the defendant perceives his conviction probability as being substantially lower than the prosecutor's perception of *PC*, but also because the defendant perceives his payoff cells in table 3-1 to be substantially less than those payoffs perceived by the prosecutor. Thus, even if both the defendant and the prosecutor perceive *PC* to be .4, there will be no convergence if the defendant perceives that his maximum sentence on being convicted at trial (cell *d*) would be 5 years. At *PC* = .4, the defendant perceives that his likely sentence would be only 2 years since $LS_1 = 0 + 5(.4) = 2$ years. Thus, the defendant's 2-year maximum would be below the prosecutor's 3.2-year minimum.

Plea bargaining is in a sense a non-zero-sum game since both parties are likely to come out ahead of their fall-back limits. In other words, when a plea bargain is struck, the defendant is getting more satisfaction out of the waiver which the prosecutor gives him of both trial and unbargained judicial pleading than the years he is giving up, since without that waiver he anticipates he would give up even more years. Similarly, the prosecutor is getting more satisfaction from the years the defendant gives him than the waiver or sentence recommendation since he anticipates he would get even less years if the case were resolved at trial or before a judge by a nonnegotiated plea bargain. Plea bargaining may be less fruitfully viewed as a zero-sum game, in which whatever the defendant gives up the prosecutor gains. The years paid by the defendant are years received by the prosecutor in the same way a price is paid and received for merchandise in our buyer-seller analogy. Perhaps, though, plea bargaining should be analyzed as being neither a non-zero-sum game nor a zero-sum game, but rather a game against nature in which both parties are trying to outguess the contingent probabilities and cell payoffs rather than outguess each other. Nevertheless, they probably do try to confuse each other by bluffing. From a methodological perspective, one nice thing about the plea bargaining situation is that it enables one to draw simultaneously upon concepts and methods from the theory of games, decisions, bargains, static equilibrium, and dynamic equilibrium.[2]

Therefore, if *LD*[3] is greater than *LP*,[4] a settlement is likely to be reached, whereas if *LD* is less than *LP*, settlement is unlikely to be reached, unless the adjustments for nonsentence goals cause *ALD* to be greater than *ALP*.[5] Similarly, if *LD* − *LP* in a second situation is positive and greater than *LD* − *LP* in a first example, then the likelihood of a settlement is greater in the second situation. The model, however, does not provide a way of assigning probabilities to the likelihood of settlement, because the degree of probability of a settlement when *LD* is greater than *LP* depends on the

Equilibrium Models Defendant/Prosecutor

bluffing activities of the parties which, unlike *LD* and *LP*, are not predictable from the basic payoff and *PC* perceptions of the parties. More will be said about the dynamics of bluffing after further discussion of the likely equilibrium (in general and under special conditions) without considering bluffing elements.

2. Results of Convergence and Nonconvergence. When convergence does occur (meaning *LD* is likely to be higher than *LP*), the settlement point, in general will, be near the midpoint between *LD* and *LP* in the absence of any additional information concerning the bargaining methods of the parties. In a specific case, one side may have the ability to bargain or bluff the other side closer to the other side's limit.[6] In a large number of cases, however, with approximately equal bargainers, the midpoint should be reasonably accurate. If S^* is the likely sentence at the point of equilibrium, then generally $S^* = .5(LD + LP)$, provided that *LD* is greater than *LP*.

What happens, though, if *LD* is not greater than *LP* in the solution $S^* = .5(LD + LP)$? The answer can be best understood by looking at figure 3-1. In the example where the defendant had $PC = .2$ and thus a 2-year limit, and the prosecutor had $PC = .4$ and thus a 3.2-year limit, the negotiations would break off unless the parties changed their *PC* perceptions or their payoff perceptions. Upon breaking off the negotiations, the defendant would proceed to go to trial since going to trial at his *PC* of .2 is his best alternative decision.[7]

If, however, the defendant had a *PC* of .6, in effect he would perceive his likely sentence as being 5.8 years since $LS_2 = 4 + (7 - 4)(.6) = 5.8$ years.[8] His payoff matrix from table 3-1, as graphed in figure 3-1, indicates that he perceives he could, on average, obtain a sentence of 5.8 years by pleading guilty before a judge in a nonnegotiated plea. At $PC = .6$, the defendant would not want to go to trial, because trial would produce on average a 6-year sentence $[LS_1 = 0 + 10(.6) = 6$ years].[9] In fact, given the defendant's payoff perceptions, he would prefer to plead guilty before a judge rather than go to trial whenever his *PC* is greater than .57.[10] Suppose further that the prosecutor perceives $PC = 1.0$; then his minimum limit (*LP*) would be 6 years, the likely or average sentence he perceives the defendant would get from a guilty plea before a judge at $PC = 1.0$. Thus, in this hypothetical situation, there would be no convergence because *LP* is greater than *LD*. Unlike the previous hypothetical situation, however, the defendant would plead guilty before the judge rather than go to trial when negotiations break off with the prosecutor. This alternative, which presumes that the defendant perceives he can receive a different sentence by pleading guilty before a judge than by plea-bargaining with the prosecutor, may not be the case in all jurisdictions or in all cases in the same jurisdiction.

The overall algebraic or symbolic solution to the location of the S^* equilibrium point is thus summarized in the following three convergence rules:

1. If LD is greater than or equal to LP, then $S^* = .5(LD + LP)$.
2. If LD is less than LP (meaning convergence unlikely) and the defendant's LS_1 (likely sentence upon going to trial) is greater than his LS_2 (likely sentence from a nonnegotiated plea), then the defendant will plead guilty before a judge in a nonnegotiated plea.
3. If LD is less than LP and the defendant's LS_1 is less than his LS_2, then the defendant will go to trial.

Note that S^* represents the likely sentence or settlement which arises from plea bargaining when there is a convergence. The likely sentence from trial or from a guilty plea before a judge is unknown with the given data.[11] This is so because the basic data, as given in table 3-1, merely show what the defendant and the prosecutor perceive to be the payoffs, not what the payoffs in fact are, as known only to an omniscient being. Even if the perceived PC's of the parties were averaged in order to derive a better prediction of the probability of conviction, the true probability of conviction would still not be known. In other words, this plea bargaining model is not a judicial decision-making model, although one might try to predict payoff cells[12] and conviction probabilities.[13]

3. Why Convergence Occurs so Frequently. How does the model explain why such a high percentage of criminal cases are settled through plea bargaining? The explanation probably is not caused by defendants perceiving the payoff cells or conviction probabilities as being higher than do prosecutors. There are good reasons for thinking defendants might perceive the situation as being more severe than the prosecutor does (such as awareness of his own guilt and of aggravating circumstances).[14] Similarly, the defendant might also perceive the situation as being less severe (such as wishful thinking based on having more at stake than the prosecutor does). These reasons tend to neutralize each other. Indeed, an empirical survey might reveal that the limit lines of defense counsel and prosecutors as well as their PC's tend to be approximately the same in a given case or set of hypothetical facts, assuming only sentence minimization and maximization are involved.

What propels the defendant and the prosecutor toward equilibrium convergence is the fact that sentence minimization and maximization are not the only goals in plea bargaining. The defendant may have other goals which will tend to raise his unadjusted LD.[15] For example, a defendant will increase his limit for his litigation costs, including (1) the cost of imprisonment pending trial if the defendant cannot afford bail, (2) the cost of hiring an attorney if the defendant is not poor enough to receive a court-appointed attorney but is still unable to easily absorb expensive attorney fees, and (3) the cost to one's reputation where one is more sensitive to adverse publicity. Likewise, the prosecutor's other goals tend to reduce his unadjusted *LD*. His litigation costs include (1) his limited budget, which prohibits taking all cases to trial, (2) the pressures to reduce court congestion, and (3) the pressures to build a record with a high percentage of convictions.

In other words, the defendant is willing to add a bonus on his *LD* maximum limit, and the prosecutor is willing to deduct a discount from his *LP* minimum limit. Thus, even if *LD* = *LP* in a given case, those adjustments are likely to make *ALD* substantially higher than *ALP*. The three convergence rules previously given should therefore be adjusted so that *ALD* (or limit of the defendant adjusted for nonsentence goals) is substituted for *LD*.[16] Similarly, wherever those rules say *LP, ALP* (or limit of the prosecutor adjusted for nonsentence goals) should be used. Most of the cases are likely to follow convergence rule 1 rather than nonconvergence rules 2 and 3, since *ALD* is likely to be greater than *ALP* a high percentage of the time.[17] As a result, most criminal cases are settled through the plea bargaining process.

The exceptional case is where the bargaining settlement costs are greater than the litigation costs. This may be true from the point of view of the defendant in traffic violations and many minor misdemeanor cases like city ordinance violations. In those cases, the defendant may consider it more expensive to plea-bargain with a prosecutor than to simply plead guilty before a judge. The settlement costs may outweigh the litigation costs from the point of view of the prosecutor at the other end of the seriousness continuum where, for example, a heinous child murder is involved. In that kind of a case, the prosecutor may feel he has more to lose politically by settling for a reduced charge or sentence than by expending the time and money in trial.[18]

B. Equilibrium under Special Conditions

In order to further clarify the kind of equilibrium, convergence, or settlement point, if any, that is likely to be produced by plea bargaining, the nature of the equilibrium should be discussed, since the parties may have difference strategies toward the alternatives and different degrees of knowledge of the conviction probabilities.

1. The Limits Matrix. Table 4-1 shows the bargaining limits for various kinds of defendants and prosecutors, depending on how they are positioned

Table 4-1
The Bargaining Limits of Certain Types of Defendants and Prosecutors (The Limits Matrix)

	Conditions of Knowledge Concerning the Probability of Conviction								
	Certainty of Acquittal or Conviction (PC Perceived at 0 or 1.0)		Ignorance of PC (PC Perceived between 0 and 1.0)				Condition of Risk (PC Perceived as Risk Point between 0 and 1.0)		
Strategy toward Alternatives	D's Upper Limit (LD)	P's Lower Limit (LP)	D's Upper Limit (LD)		P's Lower Limit (LP)		D's Upper Limit (LD)	P's Lower Limit (LP)
	$PC = 0$ $PC = 1.0$	$PC = 0$ $PC = 1.0$	O	M	P	O	M	P	Assuming $PC = .5$	Assuming $PC = .4$
Maximax or D sees only trial line (Limit = trial line)	c d	c d	c	$\frac{c+d}{2}$	d	d	$\frac{d+c}{2}$	c	$a + (b-a)(PC)$, or $(1-PC)(c) + (PC)(d)$ 5 years (i.e., LS_1)	$c + (d-c)(PC)$, or $(1-PC)(c) + (PC)(d)$ 3.2 years (i.e., LS_1)
	0 10	0 8	0	5	10	8	4	0		
Minimax or D sees only plead line (Limit = plead line)	a b	a b	a	$\frac{a+b}{2}$	b	b	$\frac{b+a}{2}$	a	$a + (b-a)(PC)$, or $(1-PC)(a) + (PC)(b)$ 5.5 years (i.e., LS_2)	$a + (b-a)(PC)$, or $(1-PC)(a) + (PC)(b)$ 4.2 years (i.e., LS_2)
	4 7	3 6	4	5.5	7	6	4.5	3		
Mixed strategy or D sees both lines (Limit = thick line)	c b	c b	c	5	b	b	4	c	LS_1 or LS_2, whichever lower 5 years.	LS_1 or LS_2, whichever lower. 3.2 years
	0 7	0 6	0	5	7	6	4	0		

O = optimistic PC, M = middling PC or .5, P = pessimistic PC.

The defendant of a given type will accept any offer below the bargaining limit shown in the cell of that type.
The prosecutor of a given type will accept any offer above the bargaining limit shown in the cell of that type.
The limits of D should have a bonus added for nonsentence benefits received by D.
The limits of P should have a discount deducted for nonsentence benefits received by P.

on two dimensions. The first dimension relates to strategies toward the alternative decisions. It includes (1) defendants who see only their trial line, possibly because they are maximax strategists, (2) defendants who see only their plead line, possibly because they are minimax strategists, and (3) defendants who are mixed strategists and thus see both lines in their strategies graph and both rows in their payoff matrix.[19]

The second dimension relates to conditions of knowledge toward PC. It includes defendants or prosecutors (1) who are certain of either acquittal or conviction, (2) who are totally ignorant of what PC might be, and (3) who think PC is at some fairly precise risk point between $PC = 0$ and $PC = 1.0$. This third category includes those parties who think of PC in terms of a range but who tend to round off to lower PC boundary, the midpoint, or the upper PC boundary, depending on whether they are optimistic, neutral, or pessimistic.

The numbers in the cells of table 4-1 indicate the upper limit for the defendant and the lower limit for the prosecutor, depending on how each party is positioned on those two dimensions. For example, in the cell in the upper left-hand corner, the limit of the defendant who is certain that he will be acquitted, viewing trial as the only meaningful alternative to plea bargaining is shown. Such a defendant will not accept an offer from the prosecutor unless the offer is at or below the defendant's limit of 0 years in jail, assuming he wants only to minimize his sentence. In other words, the cells do not show what bonus should be added to indicate the nonsentence benefits received by the defendant.

As an example at the opposite end of the table, in the cell in the lower right-hand corner, the limit of the prosecutor who perceives the probability of conviction at .4 and who perceives the defendant as working with the two alternatives to plea bargaining, namely going to trial or pleading guilty before a judge, is shown. Such a prosecutor will not accept an offer from the defendant unless the offer is at or above 3.2 years. The 3.2 years is the expected sentence from a trial at $PC = .4$ given the cell payoffs as perceived by the prosecutor. The prosecutor perceives the defendant as being more likely to plead guilty before a judge when $PC = .4$ because pleading guilty before a judge at $PC = .4$ is perceived as producing an expected sentence of 4.2 years.

At the left side of the table are shown the LD's and LP's for defendants and prosecutors certain of acquittal ($PC = 0$) or conviction ($PC = 1.0$). In the middle of the table, when the reasonable range of PC is the total range between 0 and 1.0, the LD's and LP's are also shown. In the latter situation, the LD depends on whether the defendant is optimistic ($PC = 0$), middling ($PC = .5$), or pessimistic ($PC = 1.0$). On the other hand, the LP depends on whether the prosecutor is optimistic ($PC = 1.0$), middling ($PC = .5$), or pessimistic ($PC = 0$). On the right side of the table, the LD's of a defendant who perceives $PC = .5$ and the LP's of a prosecutor who perceives $PC = .4$ are shown. A separate LD and LP are shown in all three parts of the table depending on whether the defendant sees only the trial line, only the plead line, or both lines.[20]

In table 4-1, there are many types of defendants and many types of prosecutors. There are, in fact, three types of defendants who operate under a condition of risk, namely, a maximax risk defendant, a minimax risk defendant, and a mixed-strategy risk defendant. In addition, there are nine types of defendants who operate under conditions of ignorance since there are three strategies corresponding to each of the three optimism-pessimism points. Moreover, there are six types of defendants operating under conditions of certainty since there are two conditions of certainty and three strategies toward the alternatives. This makes eighteen types for the defendant and eighteen types for the prosecutor.

Even though there are eighteen possible types of defendants and prosecutors shown in table 4-1, this does not necessarily mean that all types correspond to defendants and prosecutors who frequently exist, and especially not in equal numbers. For example, at least two defendant types probably represent null classes. One is the defendant who sees only the plead line even though he is certain of acquittal. Any defendant who is certain of acquittal is unlikely to consider pleading guilty, unless a minor traffic or parking violation is involved. This "unless" limitation is not true for the hypothetical felony for which the defendant could conceivably receive at least 10 years' maximum penalty. The other null class is the defendant who sees only the trial line even though he is certain of conviction. Any defendant who is certain of conviction in unlikely to go to trial where his sentence is likely to be higher than pleading guilty before a judge.[21] The most common situations in table 4-1 are probably conditions of risk (that is, the right side) with defendants pursuing a mixed strategy that involves considering both the trial line and the plead line (that is, the bottom row possibilities).

2. The Results Matrix. Table 4-2 shows the results of clashes between certain types of defendants and prosecutors. If each of the 18 types of defendants was pitted against the 18 types of prosecutors shown in table 4-1, then 324 scenarios would be generated, which is a rather large number of clashes to show in one results table. To make the table more manageable, table 4-2 just deals with 8 types of defendants and 8 types of prosecutors (and thus 64 scenarios) by dealing with only the middling optimism-pessimism type of party under conditions of ignorance and only the mixed strategist type of party under conditions of certainty. The reader can stage any of the remaining scenarios if he wishes to do so.

To read table 4-2, find the cell corresponding to any particular clash between a hypothetical defendant and prosecutor. Take, for instance, the cell in the lower right-hand corner where each party is operating under conditions of risk and each one is considering both the trial alternative and the plead alternative. In that scenario, the hypothetical defendant has an upper limit (*LD*) of 5 years, and our hypothetical prosecutor has a lower limit of

Equilibrium Models Defendant/Prosecutor

Table 4-2
Results of Clashes between Certain Types of Defendants and Prosecutors (The Results Matrix)

Type of Defendant		Certainty (Just Both Lines) $PC = 0$	Certainty (Just Both Lines) $PC = 1$	Ignorance (Only Middling O-P) Trial Line	Ignorance (Only Middling O-P) Plead Line	Ignorance (Only Middling O-P) Both Lines	Risk (Only $PC = .4$) Trial Line	Risk (Only $PC = .4$) Plead Line	Risk (Only $PC = .4$) Both Lines
Certainty (Just both lines)	$PC = 0$	0 / 0 / 0	0 / T / 6	0 / T / 4	0 / T / 4.5	0 / T / 4	0 / T / 3.2	0 / T / 4.2	0 / T / 3.2
	$PC = 1$	7 / 3.5 / 0	7 / 6.5 / 6	7 / 5.5 / 4	7 / 5.75 / 4.5	7 / 5.5 / 4	7 / 5.1 / 3.2	7 / 5.6 / 4.2	7 / 5.1 / 3.2
Ignorance (Only middling O-P)	Trial Line	5 / 2.5 / 0	5 / T / 6	5 / 4.5 / 4	5 / 4.75 / 4.5	5 / 4.5 / 4	5 / 4.1 / 3.2	5 / 4.6 / 4.2	5 / 4.1 / 3.2
	Plead Line	5.5 / 2.75 / 0	5.5 / T / 6	5.5 / 4.75 / 4	5.5 / 5 / 4.5	5.5 / 4.75 / 4	5.5 / 4.35 / 3.2	5.5 / 4.85 / 4.2	5.5 / 4.35 / 3.2
	Both Lines	5 / 2.5 / 0	5 / T / 6	5 / 4.5 / 4	5 / 4.75 / 4.5	5 / 4.5 / 4	5 / 4.1 / 3.2	5 / 4.6 / 4.2	5 / 4.1 / 3.2
Risk (Only $PC = .5$)	Trial line	5 / 2.5 / 0	5 / T / 6	5 / 4.5 / 4	5 / 4.75 / 4.5	5 / 4.5 / 4	5 / 4.1 / 3.2	5 / 4.6 / 4.2	5 / 4.1 / 3.2
	Plead Line	5.5 / 2.75 / 0	5.5 / T / 6	5.5 / 4.75 / 4	5.5 / 5 / 4.5	5.5 / 4.75 / 4	5.5 / 4.35 / 3.2	5.5 / 4.85 / 4.2	5.5 / 4.35 / 3.2
	Both lines	5 / 2.5 / 0	5 / T / 6	5 / 4.5 / 4	5 / 4.75 / 4.5	5 / 4.5 / 4	5 / 4.35 / 3.2	5 / 4.6 / 4.2	5 / 4.1 / 3.2

Key:

```
| LD |
| R  |
| LP |
```

R = Result which can be S^*, T, J, or F

Conditions of convergence: Convergence if $LD \geq LP$; nonconvergence if $LD < LP$.
Results of Convergence: $S^* = .5(LD + LP)$
Results of Nonconvergence:
T = Sentence determined by D going to trial. $LD < 5.71$.
J = Sentence determined by D going to judge and pleading guilty. $LD > 5.71$.
F = Coin flip or related random method will determine whether D goes to trial or pleads before judge. $LD = 5.71$

3.2 years. Since the defendant's upper limit is greater than the prosecutor's lower limit, there is likely to be convergence, and the likely convergence point (S^*) should be near the midpoint between LD and LP (that is, 4.1).

Some of the scenarios, on the other hand, involve an LD that is lower than the LP for that scenario. For example, if the defendant, given his perceived cell payoffs and his perceived PC of .5, considers both the trial and plead lines or alternatives, then he will have $LD = 5$. If, however, the prosecutor is certain the defendant will be convicted and the prosecutor also considers both lines, then the prosecutor will have $LD = 6$ as shown in column 2 of the bottom row. Therefore, convergence will not occur, and the defendant will resort to either trial or pleading guilty before a judge. Which alternative he chooses will depend on whether LD is greater or less than LS^*, which is the likely sentence at the point where $LS_1 = LS_2$. In this specific hypothetical situation, since $LD = 5$ and $LS^* = 5.71$, the defendant will go to trial as his alternative to a settlement through plea bargaining.

There are no cells in table 4-2 where nonconvergence was resolved by the defendant electing to plead guilty before a judge. A hypothetical situation could be created, though, where such a resolution would have occurred in our results matrix. A defendant with the same payoffs as in table 3-1 but who perceives his probability of conviction as being greater than .57 (rather than just .5) would elect to plead guilty before a judge. In that situation, if LD is less than LP, the hypothetical defendant will elect a guilty plea in order to minimize his sentence.[22] That defendants tend to think their conviction probabilities are low partly explains why they may be more likely to resort to trial as an alternative to plea bargaining. Part of the explanation also may relate to the fact that in many jurisdictions judges ask for the prosecutor's sentencing recommendation if the defendant pleads guilty, and thus the judge may not serve as a sufficiently independent alternative to the prosecutor.[23]

Both the defendant and the prosecutor would like to know the other side's payoff cells, PC perceptions, and thus bargaining limits so that each side could strike a bargain that will maximize his side's gain and minimize the other side's gain, but still obtain convergence. They both, however, try to make their own payoff and PC perceptions (and thus their limits) reflect reality as accurately as possible rather than reflect the other side's possible misperceptions, especially where they have encouraged pessimistic misperceptions by the other side. That kind of bluffing encouragement comes out more clearly in discussing the dynamic equilibrium model.

II. The Dynamics of Converging toward Equilibrium

A. The Time Path Graph

In tables 4-1 and 4-2 were calculated the equilibrium points likely to be determined by different types of defendants with different payoff and PC

perceptions.[24] The discussion highlighted the given data and the results. However, the process whereby one moves from the givens to the results was not discussed. Thus, the equilibrium discussion so far has been a static rather than a dynamic or process equilibrium. More specifically, it has been a comparative static equilibrium because the equilibrium points produced by different types of situations have been compared. Now it seems appropriate to extend the model to explain in simple arithmetic terms the process of moving from the givens to the results.

Figure 4-1 introduces a time dimension on the horizontal axis as contrasted to the probability dimension on the horizontal axis of figure 3-1.

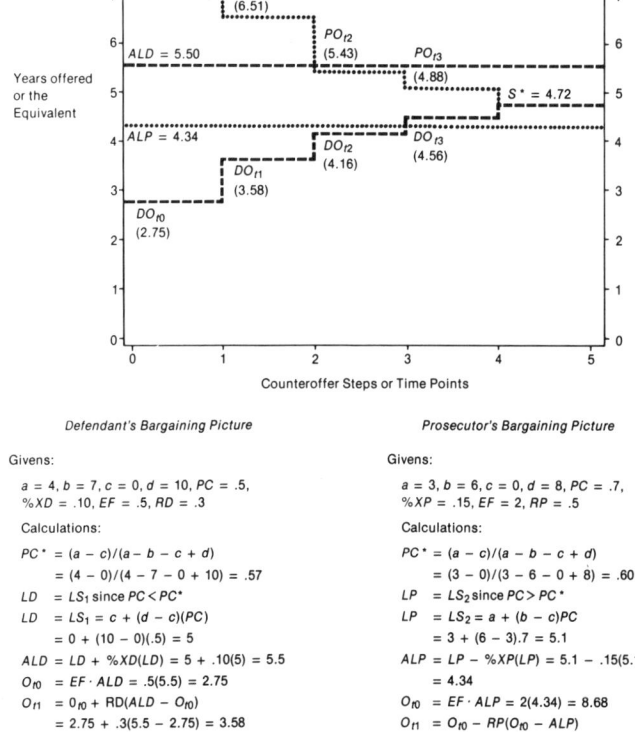

Defendant's Bargaining Picture

Givens:

$a = 4, b = 7, c = 0, d = 10, PC = .5,$
$\%XD = .10, EF = .5, RD = .3$

Calculations:

$PC^* = (a - c)/(a - b - c + d)$
$ = (4 - 0)/(4 - 7 - 0 + 10) = .57$
$LD = LS_1 \text{ since } PC < PC^*$
$LD = LS_1 = c + (d - c)(PC)$
$ = 0 + (10 - 0)(.5) = 5$
$ALD = LD + \%XD(LD) = 5 + .10(5) = 5.5$
$O_{r0} = EF \cdot ALD = .5(5.5) = 2.75$
$O_{r1} = O_{r0} + RD(ALD - O_{r0})$
$\phantom{O_{r1}} = 2.75 + .3(5.5 - 2.75) = 3.58$

Prosecutor's Bargaining Picture

Givens:

$a = 3, b = 6, c = 0, d = 8, PC = .7,$
$\%XP = .15, EF = 2, RP = .5$

Calculations:

$PC^* = (a - c)/(a - b - c + d)$
$ = (3 - 0)/(3 - 6 - 0 + 8) = .60$
$LP = LS_2 \text{ since } PC > PC^*$
$LP = LS_2 = a + (b - c)PC$
$ = 3 + (6 - 3).7 = 5.1$
$ALP = LP - \%XP(LP) = 5.1 - .15(5.1)$
$ = 4.34$
$O_{r0} = EF \cdot ALP = 2(4.34) = 8.68$
$O_{r1} = O_{r0} - RP(O_{r0} - ALP)$
$\phantom{O_{r1}} = 8.68 - .5(8.68 - 4.34) = 6.51$

Figure 4-1. Dynamic Plea Bargaining from Initial Offers to Counteroffers to Equilibrium (Time Path Graph).

The vertical axes on both figures represent sentence severity or charge severity where there is bargaining over the charge instead of, or in addition to, bargaining over the sentence. In figure 3-1, however, the vertical axis represents years likely to be received at different conviction probabilities, whereas in figure 4-1 the vertical axis represents years offered by the defendant or the prosecutor at different stages in the negotiation process. Figure 4-1 is referred to as a time path graph because it shows how converging or diverging variables change over time. The variables in this situation are the defendant's offers and the prosecutor's offers.

Most of the data used in figure 4-1 comes from the payoff matrices of table 3-1, the bargaining limits of figure 3-1 and table 4-1, and the previous discussion of the defendant's bonus factor and the prosecutor's discount factor.[25] The only change from the previous examples is to set the prosecutor's perceived probability of conviction at .7 rather than .4. This makes the prosecutor and the defendant initially farther apart, so that the convergence process will occur more slowly for observation. As indicated at the bottom of figure 4-1, the defendant's upper limit is 5 years when only considering sentence minimization and 5½ years when adjusted by a 10 percent bonus to consider other goals. Similarly, the prosecutor's lower limit is 5.1 years when only considering sentence maximization and 4.34 years when adjusted by a 15 percent discount to consider other goals. Over the time points in the dynamic bargaining process, either *ALD* or *ALP* can change as a result of new information or new values. For the sake of simplicity, however, figure 4-1 shows *ALD* and *ALP* as being constant across the graph.

B. Initial Offers and Bluffing

In order to better understand figure 4-1, it is necessary to introduce two new concepts which intervene between the givens of table 4-1 and the results of table 4-2. The concepts are initial offer and counteroffer. These concepts are easier to understand if we recall the comparison of the defendant (or prosecutor) to a buyer (or seller) who is seeking the lowest (or highest) price possible in a bargaining bazaar without fixed prices. Under those circumstances, the initial offer of the defendant logically would be lower than the limit he is finally willing to accept. Similarly, the initial offer of the prosecutor would be higher logically than the limit he is willing to accept. A better understanding of the nature of initial offers in plea bargaining is quite helpful in understanding the dynamics of going from the inputs to the outputs of the bargaining process, especially with regard to bluffing or exaggerating one's statements about outer limits, the likely sentence, or the probability of conviction.

1. Calculating Initial Offers. Thus, the defendant's initial offer should be calculated by multiplying his limit by a decimal (or percentage) less than 1.

That decimal can be called the *defendant's exaggeration factor*, since it represents a coefficient of the degree to which he exaggerates the lowness of the limit. Multiplication of the defendant's limit by such a decimal, in effect, reduces the defendant's upper limit to indicate his low initial position. For the want of better information,[26] assume the hypothetical defendant has an exaggeration factor of .5, meaning his initial offer is one-half of his bargaining limit.

The size of the defendant's exaggeration factor (*EF*) depends partly on the psychology of his bluffing strategy. If he sets his exaggeration factor at .1 or an extremely low point, he may cause the prosecutor to consider the defendant unreasonable. The prosecutor may then break off negotiations even though the defendant really may have been willing to settle at a mutually good bargain. On the other hand, if he sets his exaggeration factor at .9 or an extremely high point, he may yield too much just to obtain an agreement. Where in this range the defendant sets his exaggeration factor depends partly on what he perceives the prosecutor's likely reaction to be, although the defendant may have an opportunity to remedy an unduly high or unduly low exaggeration factor by compensating on his first counteroffer. The defendant's credibility, however, will be disrupted if his first counteroffer is a lot higher than his initial offer in order to compensate for an unduly low initial offer. Similarly, the defendant's reasonableness or good faith will be put in doubt if his first counteroffer involves a backward move or trivial difference upward from his initial offer in order to compensate for an unduly high initial offer. The *credibility* of an offer refers to telling the truth when stating one' limits. The *reasonableness*, or *good faith*, of an offer refers to being willing to make concessions.[27]

The point at which the defendant sets his exaggeration factor and thus his initial offer also depends on his willingness to go to trial.[28] The more willing he is to go to trial, the more he will exaggerate the lowness of his bargaining limit, since he is not so concerned with making an offer the prosecutor will eventually accept. In these cases, the defendant is more likely to have an exaggeration factor of .1 rather than .9. Thus, if his adjusted limit is 5 years, then the defendant more willing to go to trial is likely to have an initial offer of 6 months rather than 4½ years.

To calculate the prosecutor's initial offer, multiply his limit by an integer greater than 1 or an improper fraction like ³⁄₂. Multiplying the prosecutor's limit by such a number increases the prosecutor's lower limit to indicate his high initial position. For the want of better information,[29] the hypothetical prosecutor may be assumed to have an exaggeration factor of 2, meaning he tends to double his initial offer. Like the defendant, the exact position of the prosecutor's exaggeration factor depends partly on the psychology of his bluffing strategy in dealing with the defendant and on the prosecutor's willingness to go to trial.[30]

The higher the defendant's limit, the higher is his initial offer if his exaggeration is held constant, since his initial offer is the product of his exaggeration factor times his limit. The same is true of the prosecutor. If the defendant's limit is high, however, the defendant also is likely to exaggerate more how low his limit is by using a smaller decimal for an exaggeration factor. This may be true because defendants may be more willing to go to trial (particularly to benefit from the safeguards for the innocent) when (1) the crime is more severe, (2) thus the likely sentence is greater, and (3) the defendant-buyer's bargaining limit or maximum price is therefore higher. As previously mentioned, the more willing the defendant is to go to trial, the more he may exaggerate in a downward direction his bargaining limit by setting a low initial offer because he cares less about the negotiations breaking down. If the exaggeration factor is partly determined by *ALD* (the defendant's limit), then the exaggeration factor is at least partly an endogenous variable (determined by one of the variables which can be calculated) rather than a given or exogenous variable. Nevertheless, for both the defendant and the prosecutor, probably the exaggeration factor is mainly determined by the psychology of bluffing strategies.[31]

Bluffing involves communicating information that the communicator thinks is false to the other party with regard to the communicator's limits or with regard to facts relevant to the sentence payoffs or the conviction probability. Bluffing is not likely to have any effect on whether there will be convergence if bluffing merely understates the defendant's *ALD* or overstates the prosecutor's *ALP* at the initial offer stage or a counteroffer stage. Whether convergence will occur is mainly dependent on whether *ALD* is greater than *ALP*. The exception to this rule is where the bluffing is strong enough and persisted in long enough to cause the other side to break off negotiations prematurely. Bluffing as to *ALD* and *ALP*, however, can influence the point of convergence, since convergence tends to be at the midpoint between the bluffed or claimed *ALD* and the bluffed or claimed *ALP*. Bluffing can affect the convergence point especially if it causes the defendant to think the payoff sentences and conviction probability are higher than they really are, or if the bluffing causes the prosecutor to think the payoffs and *PC* are lower than they really are.

If each side refrained from engaging in any bluffing or exaggeration, but instead immediately informed the other side what his limits are, then approximately the same agreement or nonagreement could be reached much more quickly, assuming the bluffing on both sides is evenly balanced in degree of exaggeration and credibility. It is, however, unrealistic to expect competitive sides with valuable stakes to be that cooperative and trusting. Likewise, agreement could be reached more quickly (and with results that come closer to the true sentence which would be arrived at through a trial) if the parties would share information concerning the probability of conviction and the sentence payoffs, rather than try to bluff each other into thinking *PC* and the payoff cells are lower or higher than they really are. Discovery can force a more honest sharing of information.[32]

By applying the defendant's exaggeration factor of .5 to his adjusted limit of 5½ years, his initial offer should be 2.75 years. That initial offer is symbolized DO_{t0} for defendant's offer at time 0. Applying the prosecutor's exaggeration factor of 2 to his adjusted limit of 4.34 years, his initial offer, or PO_{t0} is 8.68 years. One might ask how a prosecutor with any credibility or ethical reasonableness could ask initially for 8.68 years when the defendant "knows," according to figure 4-1, that the worst that is likely to happen is he will get 5 years by going to trial or 5.5 years by pleading guilty before a judge. The answer is that the defendant really is not absolutely certain that his estimate is correct, since he may be too low in his perception that .5 is his conviction probability and he may be too low in his perception of the cell payoffs for trial and pleading. Indeed, the prosecutor will try to convince the defendant that his perceptions are too low.[33] Similarly, the defendant will try to convince the prosecutor that the prosecutor's perceptions are too high, giving the defendant's initial offer more credibility and reasonableness.

2. Ordering Initial Offers. Once the considerations involved in calculating the initial offers have been determined, then the next question is, Who shall make the first initial offer? Who makes the first offer is irrelevant to whether and at what point an equilibrium will be attained, but it is relevant to describing the dynamics of plea bargaining negotiation. Like the exaggeration factor, the order of the initial offers is determined largely by the psychology and personalities of the bargainers[34] rather than through the deductive, axiomatic reasoning used to arrive at the defendant's limit, the prosecutor's limit, and their equilibrium point.

Nevertheless, perhaps one can say that if the prosecutor perceives *PC* as being low, he is more likely to make an initial offer to avoid trial than if he perceives *PC* as being high. Similarly, if the defendant perceives *PC* as being high, he is more likely to make an initial offer to avoid trial than if he perceives *PC* to be low. A high *PC* in this context can be defined as one above *PC**, and a low *PC* as one below *PC**. Normally, both the prosecutor and the defendant would perceive *PC* as being about equally high or equally low. If, however, the prosecutor perceives *PC* as being high and the defendant perceives *PC* as being low, both will want to avoid trial. In that case, the initial offer would probably be made by the side whose perceived *PC* is closest to his maximum pessimistic position. In other words, if the *PC* of the prosecutor minus 0.0 is smaller than 1.0 minus the *PC* of the defendant, then the prosecutor will tend to make the initial offer. Otherwise, the defendant will. More empirically valid procedures could be established for determining which party should make the first offer,[35] but for the purposes of this model this formula should be satisfactory.

In applying this analysis to the data shown at the bottom of figure 4-1, the defendant perceives *PC* as being low, since his perceived *PC* of .5 is below his *PC** of .57. Therefore, the defendant has a preference for trial as compared to pleading guilty before a judge without a bargain. In addition, the prosecutor perceives *PC* as being high, since his perceived *PC* of .7 is above his *PC** of .60. The prosecutor also is not so anxious to avoid trial since he perceives trial as likely to produce a longer sentence than that produced by pleading guilty before a judge. The defendant, however, is likely to be less enthusiastic about going to trial than the prosecutor since .5 is only .07 less than .57, whereas .7 is .10 more than .60. Thus, the defendant is more likely to make the initial offer. The same conclusion could be reached by observing that the distance between .5 and 1.0, the worst *PC* the defendant could have, is less than the distance between .7 and 0.0, the worst *PC* the prosecutor could have. In other words, since the defendant perceives his trial alternative as less attractive than the prosecutor views his own trial alternative, the defendant is more likely to make the first move toward settlement.

3. Relation to Convergence. It should be noted that one cannot tell whether there will be convergence by simply observing the relative rank or closeness of the initial offers. Convergence occurs if the adjusted limit of the defendant is greater than or equal to the adjusted limit of the prosecutor. Convergence fails and negotiations break down if the adjusted limit of the defendant is less than the adjusted limit of the prosecutor. In either situation, however, the initial offer of the prosecutor will be greater than the initial offer of the defendant. Likewise, even though the initial offers of the prosecutor and the defendant may be very far apart, they will still reach convergence if *ALD* is greater than *ALP*. The corollary is that if the initial offers of the prosecutor and the defendant are very close together, they may still not reach convergence if *ALD* is smaller than *ALP*.

The reason the initial offer of the prosecutor is almost always likely to be greater than the initial offer of the defendant is that neither the prosecutor nor the defendant is ever likely to cross over the other in making either his initial offer or his counteroffers. In other words, if the prosecutor initially offers 7 years, the defendant's first offer is not going to be greater than 7 years if he is seeking to minimize his sentence. Likewise, if the defendant's initial offer is 3 years, the prosecutor's first offer is not going to be less than 3 years if he is seeking to maximize the sentence. This is true at any stage in the negotiation process.

As a result, given the data in figure 4-1, the defendant is likely to make the first offer, which should be 2¾ years. The prosecutor is then likely to initially offer about 8⅔ years. In a dynamic scenario the defendant is now ready to make his first counteroffer.

C. Calculating Counteroffers

A *counteroffer* is any offer by a party after his initial offer. It seems reasonable to expect each counteroffer of the defendant to be higher than his low initial offer. In other words, the defendant's offer reasonably should be expected to ascend in staircase fashion (although not necessarily in equal jumps) from his initial offer to his bargaining limit. Likewise, it seems reasonable to expect the prosecutor's offers to descend in staircase fashion from his high initial offer to his bargaining limit. In bargaining, one normally makes bigger concessions or bigger jumps in the beginning and then smaller concessions as one gets closer to one's limit or a settlement point. There may be some situations, of course, where either the prosecutor or the defendant backtracks either because he feels he has gone too far in light of his new perceptions of *PC* or the payoffs or because the other side seems especially willing to concede. Nevertheless, the general trend of the defendant's counteroffers is upward, and that of the prosecutor's counteroffers is downward, as shown in the time path graph of figure 4-1.

1. First Counteroffer. In light of the previous discussion, the first counteroffer of the defendant equals his initial offer plus an increment. Likewise, the first counteroffer of the prosecutor equals his initial offer minus a decrement. The increment for the defendant equals a portion of the distance between his last offer and his bargaining limit. The decrement for the prosecutor equals a portion of the distance between his last offer and his bargaining limit.[36] The portion of that distance for either the defendant or the prosecutor is a decimal less than 1 assuming the defendant or the prosecutor does not jump to his bargaining limit. That decimal or "splitting rate" can be symbolized *RD* for the defendant and *RP* for the prosecutor.

Thus, the first counteroffer for the defendant can be defined as

$$DO_{t1} = O_{t0} + RD(ALD - O_{t0})$$

and the first counteroffer for the prosecutor as

$$PO_{t1} = O_{t0} - RP(O_{t0} - ALP).$$

The product of the splitting rate and the distance to be covered is preceded by a plus sign for the defendant since it is a positive increment. A minus sign is used for the prosecutor, because his is a negative decrement. DO_{t0} is subtracted from ALD in determining the distance left to be covered by the defendant, because ALD is always larger than DO_{t0}; but ALP is subtracted from PO_{t0} in determining the distance to be covered by the prosecutor, because PO_{t0} is always larger than ALP.[37]

The splitting rates for the defendant and the prosecutor are determined by the same kind of considerations with regard to the psychology of bluffing strategy and one's willingness to go to trial that determined the exaggeration factors.[38] For lack of any better information, assume the defendant has a splitting rate of .3 and the prosecutor has a splitting rate of .5. Perhaps they should have had closer splitting rates since their exaggeration factors are reciprocals of each other. On the other hand, since the hypothetical defendant is more anxious to avoid trial, perhaps he should have a higher splitting rate than the prosecutor. However, given the greater financial pressures on the prosecutor, perhaps he should have a higher splitting rate, since empirical reality may indicate that prosecutors generally are more willing to settle out of court than are defendants. Since good arguments can thus be made for different relative rankings of the RD and RP splitting rates, $RD = .3$ and $RP = .5$ should be reasonable. Over the time points in the dynamic bargaining process, either RD or RP can vary as a result of changes in one's willingness to go to trial or one's bluffing psychology or the reactions of the opponent. For the sake of simplicity, however, figure 4-1 shows RD and RP as being constant across the graph.

In applying the formulas for calculating the first counteroffers of the defendant and the prosecutor to the data provided in figure 4-1, the defendant's first counteroffer is predicted to be 3.58 years, or about 3½ years. Likewise, the prosecutor's first counteroffer is determined to be 6.51 years, or about 6½ years. The calculations are shown at the bottom of figure 4-1. Thus, at stage 1 the bargainers have not yet converged on a common settlement sentence. In fact, neither side has yet crossed the limit of the other side. Before we proceed to the next stage, it seems appropriate to briefly develop some formulas that have greater generality and insight value in calculating counteroffers.

2. Incremental Counteroffer. From the above definitional equations of the first counteroffers, a general incremental equation determining the counteroffer at any stage can be derived. That general equation is

$$O_{ti} = O_{ti-1} + R(L - O_{ti-1}).$$

In this equation, O_{ti} is the counteroffer at time i; O_{ti-1} is the counteroffer of the previous stage or time i minus 1 time unit; R is the splitting rate for either the defendant or the prosecutor; and L is the bargaining limit for either party. Since L for the defendant is greater than any of his counteroffers, $L - O_{ti-1}$ will be positive, and R times that distance will be a positive increment for the defendant. Since L for the prosecutor is less than any of his counteroffers, $L - O_{ti-1}$ will be negative, and R times that distance will be a negative decrement for the prosecutor.

With the general counteroffer equation we can derive a number of other useful equations. The absolute difference between L and O_{ti-1} is the distance left to be covered after stage $O_{ti-1} \cdot R(L - O_{ti-1})$ is the positive or negative increment to be added to O_{ti-1} to get O_{ti}. The sum of all the increments from the initial offer to O_{ti} can be added to O_{t0} to get O_{ti}. If O_{ti} is the infinite stage, then the sum of all the increments added to O_{t0} will equal the bargaining limit toward which the offers are moving. Since each increment represents only a portion of the remaining distance, there is never an increment that completes the remaining distance to the bargaining limit unless the bargainer changes his splitting rate or his increment. At any point in the process, a bargainer can change his splitting rate or his bargaining limit if he acquires new perceptions of *PC,* the payoff cells, or how far he can push the other side.

Applying this general formula for determining counteroffers, we find that the second counteroffer for the defendant equals $O_{t2-1} + RD(ALD - O_{2-1})$, or 4.16, that is, $3.58 + .3(5.5 - 3.58)$. Likewise, the second counteroffer for the prosecutor equals $O_{2-1} - RP(ALP - O_{2-1})$, or 5.43, that is, $6.51 - .5(6.51 - 4.34)$. The defendant's second counteroffer of 4.16 years still has not crossed above the prosecutor's lower limit of 4.34 years, even though the prosecutor's second counteroffer of 5.43 years has crossed under the defendant's upper limit of 5.50 years. This means the prosecutor may be getting a little frustrated, not because he has crossed the defendant's upper limit, which he is not likely to know, but rather because the defendant has still not crossed the prosecutor's lower limit. The defendant, on the other hand, may be gloating because he is succeeding in getting a good bargain, but like a good poker player he will push for an even bigger pot if he can get it.

3. General Solution Counteroffer. One problem with the general equation for determining the counteroffer at any given stage is that it requires knowing the counteroffer at the previous stage, which requires knowing the counteroffer at the stage before that, and back to the initial offer. That was no problem when the first counteroffer was calculated. At later counteroffers, though, a more useful equation should state the value of O_{ti} (or the counteroffer at any stage or time i) in terms of the initial offer, the limit, and the splitting rate without requiring knowledge of the previous counteroffers. This involves solving for O_{ti} in terms of O_{t0}, L, and R with no O_{ti-1} on the right side of the equation. The general definitional or incremental equation cannot be solved for O_{ti} by simple high school algebra. Instead, the methods developed in slightly more advanced algebra for solving difference equations must be used. A *difference equation* is an equation that involves an expression (like O_{ti}) which is a function of itself at an earlier or later integer point in time (like O_{ti-1}) plus or minus an increment, as in the equation

$$O_{ti} = O_{ti-1} + R(L - O_{ti-1}) \qquad \text{(definition)}$$

The solution of this equation involves using a combination of the rules of difference equations, high school algebra, and geometric progressions,[39] and it is

$$O_{ti} = L + (1 - R)^{ti} (O_{t0} - L) \qquad \text{(solution)}$$

The meaning of the solution equation is fairly simple given the equations previously explained. To find O_{ti} in the definitional equation, add an increment for the defendant or subtract a decrement for the prosecutor from their previous counteroffers. To find O_{ti} in the solution equation, subtract from the defendant's bargaining limit or add to the prosecutor's bargaining limit. In the solution equation, $O_{t0} - L$ is the distance to be covered from the initial offer to the bargaining limit. It is a negative number for the defendant and a positive number for the prosecutor. The $1 - R$ raised to the exponent *ti* indicates that a smaller portion of that total distance to be covered is added as a positive or negative increment to L at each successive stage *ti*. The $1 - R$ will always be a decimal smaller than 1; and when a decimal smaller than 1 (unlike an integer) is raised to the exponent 3 (the third time stage), the resulting decimal is smaller than when the decimal is raised to the exponent 2 (the second time stage). For example, $(.7)^2 = .49$, but $(.7)^3 = .34$. The reason the expression $1 - R$ is used rather than just R is that we are going backward from the bargaining limit to O_{ti} rather than going forward from O_{ti-1} to O_{ti}.

By applying the new solution equation to stage 3, the third counteroffer of the defendant equals $ALD + (1 - RD)^{ti} (O_{t0} - ALD)$, or 4.56, that is, $5.50 + (1 - .3)^3(2.75 - 5.50)$. That is exactly the same result determined by the definitional equation, calculating each successive counteroffer until the counteroffer for stage 3 is found. Similarly, the third counteroffer for the prosecutor equals $ALP + (1 - RP)^{ti} (O_{t0} - ALP)$, or 4.88, that is, $4.34 + (1 - .5)^3(8.68 - 4.34)$. Note that the solution equation not only saves time but also avoids clerical and rounding errors which can occur from successive calculations with the incremental or definitional equation.[40]

D. Convergence: Its Occurrence, Meaning, and Likelihood

At stage 3, the prosecutor *and* the defendant are now within each other's bargaining limits. This means there will be convergence. The parties would be likely to converge from the very beginning, since the defendant's limit is higher than the prosecutor's limit; but coming within each other's bargaining limits makes convergence more nearly certain. However, just because both parties are within each other's bargaining limits does not mean the counteroffers are completed. If counteroffers at the next stage do not cross over each other, then another set of counteroffers will be made. In figure 4-1, however, at stage 4 the defendant's counteroffer would be 4.84, or about 5 years, and the prosecutor's counteroffer would be 4.61, or about 4½ years. It is impossible or at least very unlikely for the prosecutor to ask the defendant to go to jail for 4½ years when the defendant wants to go to jail for 5 years, or for the defendant to want to go to jail for 5 years when the prosecutor is asking for only 4½ years. Therefore, stage 4 is an unrealistic occurrence, and convergence is likely to be at the midpoint, or 4.72, between the two stage 3 counteroffers of 4.88 and 4.56.[41]

In using the static equilibrium approach, the settlement point was the midpoint between the bargaining limits of the defendant (5.50) and of the prosecutor (4.34), namely, 4.92. Which convergence point makes more sense, 4.72 or 4.92? The 4.72 arrived at through the dynamic equilibrium, difference-equation approach makes more sense because it uses more information, assuming, of course, that this information has some degree of accuracy and is not mere random numbers. To arrive at a settlement sentence, the dynamic equilibrium approach uses the bargaining limits (the only information used in the static equilibrium approach) plus EF, R, and the difference equations.

In discussing convergence under the static equilibrium model[42] and with regard to initial offers,[43] the discussion emphasized that when ALD is greater than ALP, the defendant and the prosecutor should be able to agree somewhere between those two limits, since then they will both be coming out ahead of their fall-back positions. However, evey if ALD is greater than ALP, strong and persistent bluffing could lead to a break-off in negotiations in which both sides sacrifice the opportunity for a mutually beneficial agreement.[44] This is more likely to happen if the negotiations involve considerable emotion and name calling, where a potential agreement collapses because the parties feel that agreement under such emotional circumstances involves losing face. This fear provides further justification for encouraging the adoption of discovery procedures, which will enable both sides to have a greater awareness of what the conviction probabilities and sentencing payoffs are likely to be, and to thereby decrease the distrust and short-sighted emotion which may otherwise preclude effective negotiations.

Who won the plea bargaining contest? In a sense, both sides won. The defendant won, since he was willing to go to jail for as long as 5.50 years but plea-bargained a sentencc of only 4.72 years. The prosecutor also won, since he was willing to let the defendant off with only 4.34 years but instead obtained a longer sentence of 4.72 years.[45] In a way, the defendant won more, since the difference between 5.50 and 4.72 (that is, .78) is larger than the .38 difference between 4.72 and 4.34. On the other hand, the extent to which the defendant or prosecutor won probably should be judged by what limits the defendant and prosecutor both should have had if they were omniscient beings accurately perceiving *PC* and the payoff cells. Judged by that standard, the defendant may have been cheated because he set his limit too high, or he may have had a surprise windfall if he set his limit too low. This is also true for the prosecutor. In another sense, the prosecutor could be said to have won more than the defendant since he did obtain a conviction. In that sense, the prosecutor won 4.72 years, and the defendant lost 4.72 years, although that interpretation fails to recognize possible opportunity costs to both parties with regard to what they could have had. Thus who won depends on whether one talks in terms of a victory over what could have been or simply in all-or-nothing terms of conviction or acquittal. The problem is largely semantic and psychological and is really not that relevant to analyzing the process of plea bargaining.[46]

Rather than try to analyze who won or will win in a plea bargaining situation, it is more meaningful to analyze or predict whether a plea bargaining settlement will be reached. The circumstances that lead to static equilibrium or disequilibrium already have been discussed in terms of the static model variables of payoff perceptions, probability conviction perceptions, and special types of defendants and prosecutors.[47] The subsequent dynamic equilibrium model increases the understanding of when convergence will be reached by emphasizing the role of bluffing strategies, partly manifested in exaggeration factors, and the role of gullibility or psychological willingness to make big jumps in one's counteroffers. As in poker playing, these kinds of factors can cause a defendant or a prosecutor to break off negotiations much as a poker player drops out of a hand, even though convergence could have been reached given the respective bargaining limits of the parties.

The dynamic equilibrium material is also valuable for analyzing the speed at which convergence will be reached since the speed of the process is largely dependent on the exaggeration factors and splitting rates of the parties. Convergence speed is also partly dependent on how close the limits of the parties are, which, in turn, is influenced by their perceptions of *PC* and the cell payoffs, not to mention their bonus and discount factors. Nevertheless, if the limit of the defendant is only slightly higher than that of the prosecutor, then the parties will still not converge quickly if one or both are prone to exaggerate or are very parsimonious about splitting the difference between the last offer and the limit. This is especially true if the parties lack accurate information about the payoffs, the conviction probabilities, and each other's likely limits. With more accurate information, then, gross exaggeration and unreasonable parsimony are less likely to be pursued and less likely to waste the time of the bargainers and the criminal justice system.

Notes

1. Section I-A, on general equilibrium, is based on chapter 3, section II-B-1 (regarding general bargaining limits) and section II-C-1 (regarding general *PC* calculations). Similarly, section I-B on special equilibrium is based on chapter 3, section II-B-2 (regarding special bargaining limits) and sections II-C-2 to II-C-4 (regarding special *PC* calculations).

2. For an example of a model that views plea bargaining in game theory terms, see the forthcoming dissertation of Ivan Orton in the political science department at the University of Texas. He views the prosecutor as a threat maker analogous to a blackmailer who can accept the defendant's payment or punish him. He also views the defendant as the victim of a blackmailer who can either comply with the blackmailer's demands or resist them. These dichotomous positions for each side yield a four-cell payoff matrix. Orton also views the defendant as analogous to a blackmailer and the prosecutor as the victim of a blackmailer, yielding another four-cell payoff matrix. These two matrices are manipulated to provide some insights into the plea bargaining relations between prosecutor and defendants, although on a verbal rather than a quantitative level. His basic idea comes from Ellsberg, "The Theory and Practice of Blackmail" (unpublished paper written at Harvard University, 1961).

3. LD is defined to be the bargaining limit of the defendant. See chapter 3, section II-A.

4. LP is defined to be the bargaining limit of the prosecutor. See chapter 3, section II-A.

5. ALD and ALP are the adjusted bargaining limits of the defendant and prosecutor, respectively. See chapter 3, section II-D-2.

6. At the midpoint between LD and LP, the gain of the defendant under LD is equal to the gain of the prosecutor over LP. In other words, where S^* is the settlement sentence, $LD - S^* = S^* - LP$. If both parties have equal bluffing power, their gains from S^* should be equal. See A. Rappaport, *Two-Person Game Theory: The Essential Ideas* 94-122, esp. 109 and 120 (University of Michigan Press, 1966).

7. Chapter 3, section I-A.

8. LS_2 is defined to be the likely sentence from pleading guilty before the judge in a nonnegotiated plea. See chapter 3, section II-A.

9. LS_1 is the likely sentence from going to trial. See chapter 3, section II-A.

10. Chapter 3, section II-B-3.

11. The true sentence if the defendant goes to trial (known before trial only to an omniscient being) can be symbolized S' (S prime). If the legal system is a just legal system, the S' should also bear a close relation to the sen-

tence that would be given by an omnibenevolent being. The extent to which plea bargaining tends to arrive at such a sentence is discussed in section II-B-2 of chapter 5 dealing with the policy implications of the plea bargaining model.

12. See chapter 3, section I-B.
13. See chapter 3, section II-C.
14. See chapter 3, section I-A.
15. See chapter 3, section II-D.
16. See notes 10 and 11 and accompanying text.
17. See chapter 3, section II-D.
18. An alternative perspective to figure 3-1 for analyzing the general equilibrium situation is the Edgeworth box diagram which is like that shown here:

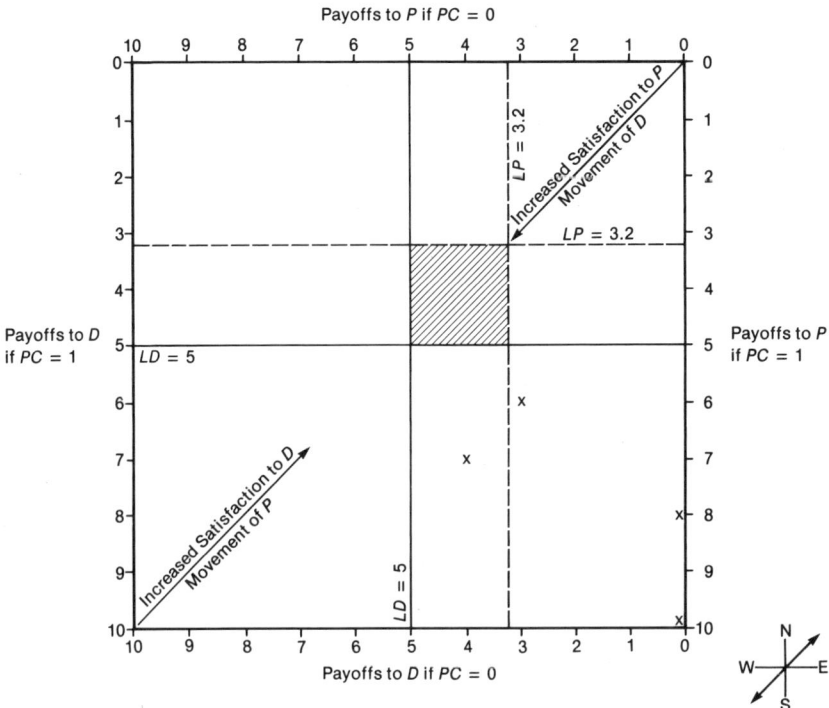

The continuous lines show that the defendant's bargaining limit is 5 years, and the dashed lines show that the prosecutor's bargaining limit is 3.2 years. The defendant obtains increased satisfaction by moving across indifference curves or lines not shown toward the northeast, wheras the prosecutor obtains increased satisfaction by moving across indifference or equal-satisfaction lines toward the southwest. In their bargaining, the defendant moves from near the northeast corner toward the southwest, and the prosecutor moves from near the southwest corner toward the northeast. If they both get into the shaded area which is the feasible region, an agreement will be reached.

This perspective, however, provides less information than figure 3-1 because this perspective provides only one limit point for the defendant and one for the prosecutor, since it does not show probabilities of conviction on any axis. It also provides less information than figure 4-1, since it does not show time stages on any axis. The main value of the Edgeworth box is that it can show degrees of risk preference or risk avoidance as nonsentence goals by the shape of the indifference curves which pass through the defendant's payoff points at (0, 10) for going to trial and (4, 7) for pleading before a judge, or which pass through the prosecutor's payoff points at (0, 8) for going to trial and (3, 6) for pleading before a judge. If the defendant's trial point is on a higher, lower, or the same indifference curve as his pleading point, then he is a risk preferrer, risk avoider, or risk-neutral, respectively. For further detail on this perspective, see W. Baumol, *Economic Theory and Operations Analysis* (Prentice-Hall, 1965); J. Cross, *Economics of Bargaining* (Basic Books, 1969).

The Edgeworth box would be more useful if the two goods being exchanged were both intervally measured and shown on each axis. The defendant, however, is paying years in jail to the prosecutor (which can be intervally measured) in return for a waiver of litigation (which is a yes-no dichotomy).

19. A defendant also may see only his trial line not because he is a maximax strategist, but because it is the only line to see in some places or cases where pleading guilty before the judge is not a meaingful alternative to going to trial or to plea bargaining with the prosecutor. Also a defendant may see only his plead line not because he is a minimax strategist, but because for reasons of time, money, or stigma he just cannot possibly consider going to trial. The first dimension also includes prosecutors who perceive a given defendant to be a maximax strategist, a minimax strategist, or a mixed strategist.

20. In addition to stating the number of years that corresponds to each type of defendant and prosecutor, the table also gives the formula that was used to calculate the *LD* or *LP* years. The formulas are stated in terms of the defendant's or the prosecutor's *a, b, c,* and *d* perceived cell payoffs. All the formulas in the first and second thirds of the table on the left side are simplified versions of the formulas in the last third of the table on the right side. For example, the optimistic prosecutor who lacks any knowledge of *PC* and who operates in a jurisdiction where going to trial is the only alternative to plea bargaining has an *LP* of 8 years based on cell *d*. That 8 could also be calculated from the formula $LS_1 = 0 + (8 - 0)(1.0)$, or from the formula $LS_1 = (1 - 1.0)(0) + (1.0)(8)$, both of which are given in the last

third of the table. To review what is involved in calculating an *LD* or an *LP*, the reader can check the calculations for all or any of the cells in table 4-1 by using the raw data from table 3-1 and the graphical approach of figure 3-1.

21. The defendant will not plead guilty if he knows the judge will give him a more severe sentence than the jury will in those unusual places where juries can determine sentence. See chapter 3, section I-A.

22. We could have also had some *J*'s in table 4-2 by changing the defendant's payoff cells so that with a *PC* of .5 or even lower, his *LD* would be greater than his *LS**. Doing so would involve decreasing cells *a* and *d* and/or increasing cells *c* and *d*. Table 4-2 would also have some *J*'s in it if we had included the pessimistic defendant operating under conditions of ignorance rather than just the middle defendant, since the pessimistic defendant perceives *PC* to be 1.0.

There seem to be no empirical data available indicating what percentage of the time the defendant turns to the judge with a nonbargained guilty plea rather than go to trial when plea bargaining negotiations break down. Donald Newman's data indicates that in the Wisconsin county he studied, 6 percent of all the felony cases went to trial, 56 percent were settled by plea bargaining [that is, 60(.94)], and 38 percent were settled by nonbargained guilty pleas [that is, .40(.94)]. See chapter 3. However, the data do not indicate (1) what proportion of the 38 percent involving guilty pleas never involved plea bargaining or (2) what proportion did involve plea bargaining that broke down. Similarly, the data do not show (3) what proportion of the 6 percent who went to trial never involved plea bargaining or (4) what proportion did involve plea bargaining that broke down. To determine the most common alternative occurrence when plea bargaining breaks down, one must compare proportions 2(.38) with 4(.06). Writers on plea bargaining often assume that if plea bargaining were made more difficult, the quantity of trials would increase greatly, causing the criminal justice system to collapse. Such writers tend to think that the only alternative to plea bargaining is to go to trial rather than to plead guilty before a judge who is likely to give a lower sentence after a guilty plea than after a trial conviction. *Brady* v. *United States,* 397 U.S. 742 (1970); President's Commission on Law Enforcement and Administration of Justice, *Task Force Report: The Courts* 10 (Government Printing Office, 1967); and Hoffman, "Plea Bargaining and the Role of the Judge." 53 *F.R.D.* 499 (1971). Pleading guilty before a judge without plea bargaining consumes some judicial resources, but not nearly as much as a trial.

23. Because we sought to simplify the arithmetic in the example by using a defendant with a *PC* of .5, we introduced some repetition into table 4-2 and table 4-1 whereby the defendant's limit, if he were ignorant of *PC* and middling on the optimism-pessimism scale, was the same as if he knew

that $PC = .5$ in his case. It is not artificial repetition, however, that on any given row in table 4-2 the *LD* of the defendant remains the same. That is so because neither the payoff cells nor the *LD* of the defendant is changed by the type of prosecutor he is dealing with, except in the sense that the more competent the prosecutor is, the higher the defendant should perceive *PC* to be; and also the more severe and influential the prosecutor is, the higher the defendant should perceive the payoffs to be. Likewise on any given column the *LP* of the prosecutor remains the same because the *LP* is not changed by the type of defendant or defense counsel he is dealing with, except in the sense that the more sympathy-arousing or competent the other side is, the lower the prosecutor should perceive *PC* and the payoff cells to be.

24. See section I.

25. See chapter 3, section II-D-2.

26. Perhaps a questionnaire survey will reveal more precisely how much the average defendant or defense counsel tends to underoffer in stating his initial bargaining position.

27. For further discussion of the psychology of bluffing and other negotiation techniques, see J. Ilich, *The Art and Skill of Successful Negotiation* (Prentice-Hall, 1973); C. Karrass, *The Negotiating Game* (World, 1970); R. Walton and R. McKensie, *A Behavioral Theory of Labor Negotiation* (McGraw-Hill, 1965).

28. His willingness to go to trial is governed by his position on the maximax-minimax dimension regarding his perception of the trial-pleading alternatives, the optimism-pessimism dimension regarding his narrowing of the *PC* or cell payoff ranges, and the risk preferrer-risk avoidance dimension regarding his attitude toward risk as a nonsentence goal. His willingness to go to trial also varies with the severity of the crime in the sense that the more severe the crime, the less likely it is that the defendant will plead guilty. Likewise, the defendant is more willing to go to trial if his litigation costs are lowered and his settlement costs are raised.

29. See note 26.

30. In our hypothetical example, the defendant's exaggeration factor is the reciprocal of the prosecutor's exaggeration factor, and vice versa. This is coincidental since they are determined separately, although a prosecutor may tend to exaggerate his lower limit more if he perceives that the defendant is highly exaggerating his upper limit, and vice versa.

31. The splitting rate discussed in section II-C is also a function of bluffing psychology. On the mathematics of bluffing, see Cross, *Economics of Bargaining*, pp. 166-180. As Cross emphasizes and as both our static and dynamic models tend to show, where the parties start in their bargaining generally has little effect on the point of agreement (S^*) which is largely determined by the defendant's limit (*ALD*) and the prosecutor's limit (*ALP*). In the model, as is clarified in section II-B-3, the initial offers have

no bearing on whether convergence will be reached since that is determined by whether *ALD* is greater than *ALP*. The initial offers along with the splitting rates, however, do determine the last counteroffers before the parties cross over, and the midpoint between those last counteroffers is the likely settlement point. See Section II-D.

32. See section II-B-1.

33. The prosecutor's initial offer can still be meaningful even if it is greater than either the defendant's or the prosecutor's perception of cell *d*, which shows the likely sentence if the defendant is convicted after a trial. The prosecutor's initial offer cannot be meaningful or ethical, though, if it is greater than the statutory maximum allowed for the crime involved.

34. See notes 26 to 33 and accompanying text.

35. This matter of who initiates plea bargaining may, however, be determined more by institutionalized procedures for different crime categories than by the evidence in specific cases. Thus we have in the ordering of initial offers another side aspect of our model which can be empirically tested through a questionnaire and interviewing survey.

36. The increment for the defendant would never be so great as to make the defendant's next offer equal a sentence greater than the prosecutor's last offer. Likewise, the decrement for the prosecutor would never be so great as to make the prosecutor's next offer equal a sentence less than the defendant's last offer. This is true at any stage in the negotiation process, as discussed in sections II-B-3 and II-D.

37. By changing the first sign and reversing the order of the limit and the initial offer, an alternative way to write the prosecutor's first counteroffer would be

$$O_{t1} = O_{t0} + RP(ALP - O_{t0})$$

which would achieve the same effect although in a less obvious manner. The defendant's first counteroffer could be similarly rewritten.

38. See notes 26 to 34 and accompanying text.

39. The solution is as follows:

1. $O_{ti} = O_{ti-1} + R(L - O_{ti-1})$ (Definitional equation)

2. $O_{ti+1} = O_{ti} + R(L - O_{ti})$ (Eq. 1 applied to stage $ti + 1$)

3. $O_{ti+1} = O_{ti} + RL - RO_{ti}$ (multiplying by R to remove parentheses)

4. $O_{ti+1} = O_{ti}(1 - R) + RL$ (Factoring out O so it appears only once on the right side)

Equilibrium Models Defendant/Prosecutor

5. $O_{t1} = O_{t0}(1 - R) + RL$ Eq. 4 applied to stage $t1$)

6. $O_{t2} = [O_{t0}(1 - R) + RL]$
   $(1 - R) + RL$ (Combination of Eqs. 4 and 5 applied to stage $t2$)

7. $O_{ti} = O_{t0}(1 - R)^{ti} + RL(1 - R)^{ti-1}$
   $+ \cdots + RL(1 - R)^{ti-ti}$ Simplifying and removing brackets from Eq. 6)

8. $O_{ti} = O_{t0}(1 - R)^{ti} + L - L(1 - R)^{ti}$ (Inserting and simplifying the sum of a geometric progression for the "$+ \ldots +$" expression in Eq. 7)

9. $O_{ti} = L + (1 - R)^{ti}(O_{t0} - L)$ (Simplifying Eq. 8)

Note the sum of the geometric progression (for example, .2 + .4 + .8 + .16 + .32) in Eq. 7 is $[RL - (RL)(1 - R)^{ti}] / [1 - (1 - R)]$.

For further detail on solving difference equations, see M. Brennan, *Preface to Econometrics* 71-74, 238-240 (Southwestern, 1973); Dinwiddy, *Elementary Mathematics for Economists* 199-216 (Oxford, 1967). For further detail on finding the sum of a geometric progression, see Moore, *Algebra* 138-44 (Barnes and Noble, 1952).

40. A possibly easier, although normally less accurate and less informative, way of arriving at a general solution counteroffer equation is to use the incremental or definitional equation to calculate two counteroffers along with the initial offer. The values of A and B are calculated in the regression equation

$$O_{ti} = A(T + 1)^B$$

where O_{ti} is the counteroffer at stage i and T is the stage number. For example, to fit such a power function to the defendant's ascending staircase in figure 4-1, the logarithms of 2.75, 3.58, and 4.16 as the dependent-variable scores and the logarithms of 1, 2, and 3 as the independent-variable scores are fed into the linear regression analysis. The computer output then informs us that the power function which best fits the defendant's ascending staircase is

$$O_{ti} = 2.75(T + 1)^{.38}$$

This equation tells us that when $T = 0$, the initial offer will be 2.75; when $T = 1$, the first counteroffer will be 3.58; when $T = 2$, the second counteroffer will be 4.17; and when $T = 3$, the third counteroffer will be 4.66. This third counteroffer is slightly higher than the 4.56 calculated by the more accurate way. Applying the same method to the prosecutor's descending staircase, we get the equation

$$O_{ti} = 8.70(T + 1)^{-.43}$$

This approach to solving a difference equation is especially helpful if one wants to know what the counteroffer is at some time between the integer time stages, as might be the case in some other substantive problem. In effect we are approximating a solution for a differential equation which is generally even more difficult to solve than a difference equation where T must always take integer values.

41. See chapter 3 for the discussion of the logic behind finding convergence at the midpoint between the last two counteroffers before the parties criss-cross.

42. See section I-A.

43. See section II-B-3.

44. See section II-B-1.

45. If the defendant and the prosecutor are both considered to have won something, then a Pareto optimum solution is obtained, since both sides won relative to their limits, or more narrowly defined, no one lost relative to his limits and at least one party won relative to his limits. If plea bargaining tends to produce such Pareto optimum solutions, it can be considered a Pareto optimizing process.

46. The discussion focuses on who won or lost when a plea bargaining settlement is reached. The interesting question of who is likely to win and by how much if the case goes to trial and sentencing is not discussed. See chapter 3, section II-C (on determining the conviction probabilities of who is likely to win) and section I-B (on determining the payoff sentences).

47. See section I-A.

5 Civil Analogies and Implications for Policy and Research

I. Out-of-Court Civil Settlements

One useful way to review the mathematical model just presented for handling the plea bargaining process is to apply it to the simpler situation of out-of-court settlements in civil cases. Analyzing civil settlements and the related literature also may help generate insights regarding policy variables, which by analogy could influence the likelihood of settlement in criminal cases. Civil settlements are easier to analyze mainly for two reasons. First, virtually all the goals of both the defendant and the plaintiff can be measured in terms of dollars. Dollars represent a common unit that can be added and subtracted even for different kinds of costs and benefits. Working with dollars provides a more precise scale on which to position the costs and benefits as well as an easier method for obtaining meaningful data.

A second major reason why civil settlements are easier to analyze is there are only two sellers whom the defendant-buyer can buy from or deal with in a civil case. The defendant can either negotiate with the plaintiff or go to trial. Pleading guilty before a judge is not a meaningful alternative for the defendant in a civil case. If a civil defendant pleads guilty before a judge, then the judge in a civil case can only find the defendant liable and assess the damages for which the plaintiff asks. Only through a bench or jury trial or an out-of-court settlement can a damage figure be reached other than the figure stated in the plaintiff's complaint.[1]

A. From the Payoff Matrices to the Dynamic Equilibrium

In light of these two simplifying considerations, both sides are, in effect, working with payoff matrices that have only a bottom or trial row (that is, that have only cells c and d present). In cell c is the dollar amount that the plaintiff is likely to receive if he goes to trial and does not win a judgment in his favor (that is, when $PL = 0$ where PL is the probability of liability being established). Thus, cell c is 0 dollars. In cell d is the dollar amount that the plaintiff is likely to receive if he goes to trial and wins a judgment in his favor (that is, when $PL = 1.0$). Cell d can be determined by methods similar to those used in calculating cell d in the plea bargaining situation.[2] Thus, the payoff matrices in the civil situation reduce to one row, because there is only one alternative to negotiation. Indeed, the matrices reduce to just one cell, because one of the two cells in that one row will always be zero.

Given those simplified payoff matrices or simply the payoff amount perceived by the defendant and the payoff amount perceived by the plaintiff, a strategies graph like figure 3-1 can be constructed easily. It consists of only two lines. Both are trial lines starting at the zero origin. The defendant's trial line slopes upward toward his perception of the payoff amount, and the plaintiff's trial line slopes upward toward his perception of the payoff amount. The horizontal axis of the figure shows the perceived probability that liability will be established (that is, PL). Thus, the defendant's unadjusted maximum bargaining limit is the point on his trial line at which he perceives PL, and the plaintiff's unadjusted minimum bargaining limit is the point on his trial line at which he perceives PL. Good estimates of PL can be determined by using methods like those discussed for determining PC.[3] Regardless of what PL is determined, the unadjusted limit of a party is calculated by multiplying his perceived PL by his perception of the payoff amount.[4]

To adjust the defendant's limit (LD), add a bonus factor. The bonus factor consists of litigation costs (analogous to the criminal defendant's nonsentence goals which tend to turn him away from *litigating*) minus settlement costs (analogous to the criminal defendant's nonsentence goals which tend to turn him away from *settling* through plea bargaining). Thus, as in the criminal situation, ALD, the adjusted limit of the defendant, is $ALD = LD + XD$, but here $XD = \$L - \$S$, where $\$L$ is litigation cost and $\$S$ is settlement cost. To adjust the plaintiff's limit (LP), subtract a discount factor. As with the defendant, the discount factor (XP) consists of litigation costs (analogous to the prosecutor's nonsentence goals which tend to turn him away from litigating) minus settlement costs (analogous to the prosecutor's nonsentence goals which tend to turn him away from settling through plea bargaining). Thus, the adjusted limit of the plaintiff is $ALP = LP - XP$, where $XP = \$L - \$S$ of the plaintiff.

As in the criminal situation, convergence is likely to be reached if and only if ALD is greater than or equal to ALP. If, on the other hand, ALD is less than ALP, then they will go to trial as the only alternative available, unless at least one of the parties changes his adjusted limits.

The special equilibrium conditions shown in table 4-1 with regard to certain types of criminal defendants and prosecutors do not apply in the civil case. This is so because there is only one alternative to negotiation (namely going to trial). Thus, civil defendants and plaintiffs cannot be divided into those who see alternative 1, alternative 2, or both alternatives. However, the civil defendants and plaintiffs can be divided on the basis of their degree of knowledge for determining the probability of liability being established under the categories for certainty, ignorance, and risk. That categorization, though, merely indicates that the party to which it applies sees *PL* as being 0.0 or 1.0 if he is operating under certainty, as being .5 if he is operating under ignorance with middling optimism-pessimism, or as being something between 0.0 and 1.0 if he is operating under risk.[5]

The dynamic equilibrium model is virtually the same for criminal or civil cases. As in criminal cases, the initial offer of the defendant represents his adjusted limit minus an exaggeration factor. Similarly, the initial offer of the plaintiff represents his adjusted limit plus an exaggeration factor. From his low initial offer, the defendant proceeds upward by splitting the difference between his last offer and his relatively high adjusted limit. Likewise, from his high initial offer, the plaintiff proceeds downward by splitting the difference between his last offer and his relatively low adjusted limit. Once each side comes within the adjusted limits of the other side, convergence is virtually assured.

B. Time Discounting

The only complicating aspect of the civil model is the fact that generally the monetary payoff amounts are substantially into the future. Therefore, they need to be discounted for the passage of time. In other words, assume the average civil personal injury case in a big city like Chicago takes five years to go to trial and to judgment. If the plaintiff is offered $2,500 now, should he accept it? If he perceives *PL* to be .80 and the judgment to be $5,000, then the $5,000 has an expected monetary value (analogous to a likely or expected sentence in criminal cases) of $4,000 [or, .80($5,000)]. If the defendant's litigation costs are 40 percent of the expected judgment of $4,000 and his settlement costs are 25 percent of the judgment,[6] then $L - $S = $1,600 - $1,000. This means the adjusted expected monetary value is $3,400, that is, $4,000 - $600. In other words, the plaintiff's lower bargaining limit is $3,400. Without regard to time discounting, he would thus reject the defendant's offer of $2,500.

The time discounting question asks, in essence, whether the $2,500 offer is worth more or less than $3,400 expected value five years hence. It would be helpful to know how much principal would have to be set aside at the current annual rate of interest in order to have in today's money $3,400 five years from now. Assuming the current interest rate is 6 percent and the inflation rate is 4 percent, then the amount of principal is equal to $3,080, that is, $3,400/[1 + (.06 - .04)]^5, or algrbraically $P = A/[1 + (r - i)]^t$, where A is the future value or amount of the investment, r is the interest rate, i is the inflation rate, and t for time is the number of years). In other words, the plaintiff would have to be offered $3,080 now to be receiving the equal of $3,400 five years from now. Since he is only being offered $2,500, he should reject the offer.

Time discounting is important to the defendant also. For example, if the defendant is made a final settlement offer by the plaintiff of $3,080, the defendant must decide whether paying the plaintiff $3,080 now will be cheaper than paying the plaintiff $3,900 five years from now, assuming $3,900 is the adjusted upper limit of the defendant.[7] To determine which is the better deal for the defendant, he must decide what is the value five years hence of $3,080 paid out now. Assuming the 6 percent interest rate and the 4 percent inflation rate, the future value for an investment of $3,080 in principal is equal to $3,400, that is, $3,080(1 + .02)^5$, or algebraically $A = P(1 + r)^t$. In other words, the plaintiff's request for $3,080 now is the equivalent to paying the plaintiff $3,400 five years from now. Since the defendant has an adjusted upper limit of $3,900, the $3,400 figure is a good bargain for the defendant.[8]

The notion of time discounting does not apply to criminal cases in the same way that it does to civil cases, because there is a much shorter passage of time between the settlement negotiations and the subsequent trial (if there is a trial) in a criminal than in a civil case. Civil cases also deal with money damages (or injunctions against business practices, which can be translated into dollars) rather than jail sentences, and the future value of money compared to the present value can be more meaningfully measured than the future and present value of jail sentences. The criminal defendant's lowered bonus factor[9] does take into consideration that a defendant might be pushed toward going to trial and possibly appeal because he would rather serve 5 years starting three years from now than 4 years starting today. Similarly, the prosecutor may offer a bigger discount factor because he would rather put the defendant in jail now, even if it is only a 4-year sentence, than put him in jail three years from now after a trial and possible appeal even if the trial yields a 5-year sentence. Thus, even in the matter of time discounting, the criminal plea bargaining situation involves more considerations which are difficult to measure and more complexities than the civil negotiation situation does. Nevertheless, worthwhile insights can be acquired by applying elementary mathematical modeling to both situations.

C. The Decision to Sue and Other Analogies

Before getting to the plea bargaining stage, the prosecutor must decide that he is going to bring a formal charge against the defendant. In a civil case, that decision is analogous to the plaintiff's lawyer deciding that he is going to file a formal complaint. It might be interesting to analyze briefly the general considerations involved in deciding to initiate a civil lawsuit as a grounds for better understanding both the analogous considerations involved in deciding to initiate a criminal lawsuit and the subsequent plea bargaining process.

In the simplest terms, a plaintiff should initiate a lawsuit if the expected benefits of doing so will exceed the expected costs. The expected benefits to the plaintiff equal the predicted damage award ($$D$) times the probability of establishing liability (PL) minus one-third of $$D$ times PL to cover the lawyer's usual contingency fee, or $D(PL) - \frac{1}{3}(D)(PL)$. The expected benefits to the plaintiff's lawyer equal one-third of $$D$ times PL. The expected costs to the plaintiff or the plaintiff's lawyer equal the amount of hours each one is likely to have to spend pursuing the case multiplied by how much their time is worth per hour, plus the out-of-pocket costs or other nonmonetary expenses involved in pursuing the case. The expected costs also include the cost of the missed opportunities to do other more profitable things with one's time where these things cannot be done simultaneously.[10] Predicting damages that will be awarded is analogous to predicting the trial sentence in criminal cases.[11] Determining the probability of liability is analogous to determining the probability of conviction in criminal cases.[12]

Applying these concepts to the prosecutor, one could say that a prosecutor should likewise initiate a lawsuit if the expected benefits of doing so will exceed the expected costs. His expected benefits equal his predicted sentence multiplied by the probability of obtaining that sentence through trial, a guilty plea without a bargain, or a guilty plea with a bargain. A prosecutor generally prefers longer sentences to shorter sentences, since a longer sentence tends to indicate that he has caught a more dangerous criminal and since the public seems to prefer longer sentences. Like the plaintiff's lawyer in personal injury cases, the prosecutor includes his time, expenses, and other competing cases (that cannot be diverted) into his expected costs. Unlike the plaintiff's lawyer, however, the prosecutor may be operating under other constraints. For political and legal reasons, often he must prosecute or formally charge many cases that are not profitable in a benefit-cost sense, although he need not try the case since he still has considerable bargaining discretion. Private defense counsel is more like a private personal injury lawyer in being able to choose his clients. The public defender is more like an insurance company defense counsel since he is required to take all legally eligible cases, although with discretion in out-of-court bargaining.[13]

Many other aspects of the decision-making activities of lawyers in civil cases are applicable by analogy to the decision-making activities of lawyers in criminal cases besides the settlement process, time discounting, and the decision to sue. Just as one can gain insights into plea bargaining from civil settlements, one can also gain insights into the civil settlement process from analyzing plea bargaining. Thus, much of the earlier discussion on plea bargaining is applicable by analogy to civil cases, although generally in a more simplified form. In addition, the model is also applicable to civil cases by deducing the effects of various judicial process changes on the likelihood and level of settlements being reached.[14] Similarly, suggestions for empirical research on testing hypotheses and methodological tools concerning plea bargaining could also be applied to research on out-of-court civil settlements.[15]

II. Practitioner and Policy Implications

A. Scholars, Lawyers, and Society

The main purpose of these chapters is to present a mathematical model that captures the essence of the plea bargaining process in criminal cases. The model should have value to legal scholars interested in why the legal process operates as it does. As such, the model can generate hypotheses which can be empirically tested with data obtainable from questionnaires, interviews, and court records. The model can also serve to integrate related findings that have already been developed concerning the nature of the legal process.

Although the main purpose is the development of conceptual, methodological, and causal theory, the model is also meant to be useful to practicing lawyers and legal policy makers. Practicing lawyers like states' attorneys, public defenders, and private defense counsel may find insights in the model that will be useful to them in their plea bargaining activities. In personal injury civil practice, there now exist looseleaf services and mathematical how-to-do-it articles designed to aid plaintiffs, lawyers, and insurance counsel in their negotiation activities.[16] Perhaps similar tools will become available in criminal case work.

These looseleaf services may be expensive for some attorneys. Therefore it might be useful to determine how much they improve the accuracy of the average practitioner in predicting the percentage of plaintiff victories in onehundred cases and in predicting the mean amount of damages awarded. If such a determination were made, then one could better decide whether the extra accuracy is worth the extra cost. To determine how much the defendant or prosecutor would benefit from the improved knowledge gained from such a looseleaf service, one could calculate the absolute value of $S - S'$, where S is the predicted settlement sentence without the use of those services and S' is the predicted settlement sentence with the improved knowledge. $S = (ALD + ALP)/2$, where ALD is greater than ALP. $S' = (ALD' + ALP')/2$, where ALD' is greater than ALP' and where ALD' and ALP' are the defendant's and prosecutor's limits based on improved knowledge of the payoffs and of PC. These same calculations can be used to help determine the extent to which the improved knowledge increases the likelihood of settlement, as well as the accuracy of individual practitioners.[17]

If practicing lawyers in criminal cases can improve their bargaining techniques partly through a better understanding of decision theory and equilibrium models, then society will receive at least four kinds of benefits. First, improving the effectiveness of the prosecutor is socially beneficial, since he represents society in the judicial enforcement of social norms. Second, improving the effectiveness of public defenders and defense counsel is socially beneficial to the extent that effective representation improves the respect for the law of people accused of crimes. Many inmates object to how their plea bargaining was handled more than to any other aspect of the criminal justice process.[18] Third, improving the plea bargaining of both the prosecutor and the defendant reduces the occurrence of undersentencing and oversentencing. Both kinds of sentencing are socially undesirable since undersentencing may decrease the deterrent effect of the law and oversentencing may generate unnecessary antisocial bitterness. Both undersentencing and oversentencing can thus lead to an increase in crime and crime costs. Fourth, saving time is important in the criminal justice process, and improved plea bargaining may enable the prosecutor and defense counsel to arrive at agreements more quickly.

B. *The Role of Discovery, Defense, Bail, and Delay*

In addition to the direct practitioner and indirect social benefits, an empirically valid plea bargaining model can also be useful for generating ideas among policy makers with regard to how to facilitate fair out-of-court settlements in criminal cases and also the effects of other policies and changes on the settlement process. If a legislature wants to encourage plea bargaining in order to reduce court congestion, save money, and resolve cases more quickly, then the most meaningful policy reform that could be adopted is probably the improvement of the criminal discovery process. The model does indicate that if the defendant and the prosecutor are both knowledgeable as to the true payoff cells and the true conviction probability, then they are quite likely to converge at a settlement point, because (1) their unadjusted bargaining limits will then be equal, (2) the adjusted bargaining limit of the defendant will increase in order to avoid the defendant's litigation costs, and (3) the adjusted bargaining limit of the prosecutor will decrease in order to avoid the prosecutor's litigation costs. Through discovery techniques analogous to those used in civil cases, the defendant and the prosecutor can become more knowledgeable about the available evidence, which is valuable in accurately determining the true conviction probability and the sentencing payoffs.[19]

The model can aid the policy maker not only in stimulating ways of facilitating settlements, but also in clarifying the impact on the settlement process of policy and nonpolicy changes in the criminal justice system. Two of the most important criminal justice policy changes in recent years have been the increased availability of provided counsel to the indigent and the increased release of arrested persons pending trial. Both reforms have reduced litigation costs for defendants. The bonus factor will then be reduced which, in turn, decreases the likelihood of settlement. Free counsel clearly reduces litigation costs to the defendant although there are two offsetting considerations. First, free counsel tends to consist of a public defender who is pressed to settle because of his heavy caseload and lack of financial and personal resources. Second, increasingly expensive attorneys' fees for those who are not eligible for free counsel may be increasing the settlement rate among nonindigent defendants.

Bail reform also reduces litigation costs because one of the defendant's trial costs is that of having to remain in jail until trial. That can be a high cost in terms of lost income and discomfort which pushes jailed defendants toward settlement (that is, offering a larger bonus factor). That bonus element is no longer important when more defendants are being released pending trial. Pointing out these effects of providing free counsel and more liberal pretrial release is not meant to attack those reforms. On the contrary, the purpose is to indicate first that the due process benefits which the changes provide are partly offset by their settlement reduction costs and second that possibly there is a need for other policies (like improved discovery techniques) to counteract that settlement reduction. It also should be pointed out that although providing effective counsel and pretrial release may decrease the likelihood of reaching a settlement, they may cause the resulting settlement to be closer to the true sentence which would have been given at trial since the defendant's artificially high bonus factor is reduced.[20]

An example of a nonpolicy change in recent years that has probably affected the likelihood of plea bargaining convergence is the increased delay in processing criminal cases.[21] This delay is due to increases in population, crime rates, and urbanization, although it is partly offset by new court management techniques and new legal rules requiring speedier trials. If there is long delay from arrest to trial, this increases the willingness of a defendant to settle if he is held in jail pending trial. On the other hand, it decreases the willingness of a released defendant to settle since a distant trial penalty is less of an incentive to settle than one closer in time. Long delay, however, may increase the prosecutor's willingness to settle since he has a difficult burden of proof, which generally becomes harder to meet as witnesses become more forgetful or disappear. In anticipation of that happening, the prosecutor tends to be willing to offer a bigger discount factor. Given these conflicting effects of delay, it is hard to say how increased delay affects cases in general. Specific cases categorized in terms of whether the defendant is in or out of jail and whether the prosecutor is relying on evidence that has a high or low time-decay rate may be better explained.[22]

C. Changes in Conviction Probabilities and Sentencing Payoffs

What does the model indicate about the effect of increasing or decreasing *PC* or the cell payoffs on settlement likelihood? Clearly, if the defendant is made to think *PC* or the cell payoffs are higher than they really are, he will be more willing to settle. Likewise, if the prosecutor is made to think *PC* or the cell payoffs are lower than they really are, he also will be more willing to settle. As previously mentioned, however, they will both be quite willing to settle if they simply perceive *PC* and the cell payoffs accurately (rather than falsely upward for the defendant and downward for the prosecutor) since the defendant's bonus factor and the prosecutor's discount factor will then put the defendant's bargaining limit above that of the prosecutor.

What if the true *PC* increases or decreases from improved or worsened investigative and presentation abilities by the prosecutor relative to defense counsel, or from changes in the rules of evidence? Figure 3-1 helps answer that question. It reveals that if both parties accurately perceive the same true *PC*, then the defendant's upper limit will be higher than the prosecutor's lower limit without regard to that jointly perceived, true *PC*. The gap between the defendant's upper limit and the prosecutor's lower limit, however, is wider when $PC = 1.0$ than when $PC = 0.0$. That is partly due to the relative payoffs of the defendant and prosecutor shown in table 3-1. If they both had the same payoffs, then they would have the same limit lines and they would be willing to set the same price at any jointly perceived low or high *PC*. If, however, the defendant is willing to give a smaller bonus at a lower *PC*, then he will be less willing to settle at a lower *PC*. This, however, may be offset by the fact that the prosecutor is willing to give a higher discount and more willing to settle at a lower *PC*. Thus, improving or worsening the probability of conviction does not generally affect the likelihood of a settlement being reached except in those situations where the defendant perceives the payoffs as being higher than the prosecutor does [and thus settlement will be more likely at higher *PC*'s, or where the defendant increases his bonus more for a higher *PC* than the prosecutor decreases his discount (and settlement will thus also be more likely at higher *PC*'s)].

What if the true payoffs increase or decrease from more harsh or lenient sentencing? Figure 3-1 is also helpful in elucidating the effect of that kind of policy change. If sentencing became more harsh, the limit lines of both the defendant and the prosecutor would still start at the zero origin on the left vertical axis since the defendant would receive no sentence if he goes to trial when his probability of conviction is zero. The limit lines of both parties would, however, be higher on the right vertical axis. For example, those intercept points are now 7 and 6 for the defendant and prosecutor, respectively; but with 20 percent harsher sentences they might become about 8½ and 7, respectively. Nevertheless, the parties still would be as likely to reach a settlement, unless the defendant perceived the increase as being substantially greater than the prosecutor (which would increase the likelihood of settlement) or the defendant perceived the increase as substantially less than the prosecutor (which would decrease the likelihood of settlement). If figure 3-1 were redrawn so that both parties initially perceived the payoff cells alike and thus had the same limit lines, then an upward or downward change in sentencing practices would simply cause their common limit line to shift up or down without affecting the likelihood of settlement, assuming they both accurately perceive the sentencing shift. The same results are true if changes in sentencing practices affect only pleading before a judge, going to trial, or one of the four cells.[23] This, however, assumes that the increase or decrease in sentencing practices does not affect the relative size of the defendant's bonus and the prosecutor's discount. The more severe a case is, the less willing the defendant might be to offer a large bonus for a plea bargaining settlement and, in effect, plead for a long jail sentence; but this is offset by the possible fact that the more severe a case is, the more willing the prosecutor might be to offer a large discount to avoid an expensive trial.[24]

This discussion of the noneffects of increasing *PC* or increasing the likely sentences on settlement likelihood seems to run contrary to the commonsense notion that if *PC* and the likely sentences are increased, then the defendant should be more willing to settle and avoid a likely conviction carrying a stiff sentence. However, this commonsense notion assumes, perhaps falsely, that the plea bargaining process on the part of the prosecutor and the defendant fails to consider the upward shift in *PC* or in the likely sentences. In other words, to the extent that the prosecutor and the defendant correctly perceive those upward shifts and rationally incorporate them into their bargaining limits, then the results of the plea bargaining will still be convergence, although at a higher sentence than would otherwise be the case. This means the defendant would be no more likely than before to reach a plea bargaining settlement, since such a settlement will now mean a higher sentence. At the same time, however, he will be no less likely to reach a settlement since the alternative sellers from whom the defendant-buyer can buy now also have raised their prices. The most important meaning of this analysis, though, is that rational plea bargaining can just as capably produce meaningful sentences where the parties accurately perceive *PC* and the sentencing payoffs as can the trial process, although plea bargaining does so with less expenditure of social resources.

The same kind of conclusion could have been reached by noting that commonsensically one might think that if *PC* and the likely sentences decrease, then the defendant will be less willing to settle because the prosecutor cannot so effectively threaten him. This kind of common sense, however, also fails to consider that the *PC* reduction and sentence reduction tend to get incorporated into the plea bargaining on both sides, so that the parties are now logically bargaining between lower limits. This means that the defendant will be no less willing than before to reach a settlement, since such a settlement will now imply a lower sentence. At the same time, he will be no more likely to reach a settlement, since all the alternative sellers from whom the defendant-buyer can buy have now also lowered their prices.

As a result, plea bargaining thus tends to result in sentences that reflect the true probabilities of conviction and the true likely sentences[25] *provided that:*

1. The parties are as capable as possible of accurately perceiving *PC* and the sentence payoffs, which can be facilitated by better discovery procedures and more objective sentencing.
2. The defendant is not forced to offer an excessive bonus (or any bonus), which he otherwise might be if he were being held in jail pending a distant trial, if he could not afford an expensive lawyer and was not eligible for a free one, or if he had a public defender who did not have the time or resources to take cases to trial where a trial would bring a lower likely sentence than plea bargaining would.
3. The prosecutor is not forced to offer an excessive discount (or any discount), which would otherwise be true if he did not have the time or resources to take cases to trial where a trial would bring a higher likely sentence than plea bargaining would.[26]

Figure 5-1 summarizes the effect of judicial system changes on the likelihood of a plea bargaining settlement being reached and at what level. One can say the following in light of the model presented, as summarized in that figure:

1. A change that decreases the defendant's bonus factor (such as increased free counsel or pretrial release) will lower the defendant's adjusted bargaining limit without affecting the prosecutor's limit. This will narrow the room for settlement and lower the level of the new settlement, assuming that a settlement can still be reached and that it will still be roughly at the midpoint between the defendant and the prosecutor's limits. The opposite occurs from a change that increases the defendant's bonus factor. A prosecutor who is aware that a change has occurred which decreases the defendant's bonus factor can offset the decreased settlements by offering better offers. He might especially want to do that if the decreased settlements add to his court congestion and thereby increase his desire to raise his discount factor.

Defense Counsel Strategy:

1. Accept offer if less than:
   (Perceived probability of conviction)
   times (Sentence if convicted)
   plus (% Bonus to avoid litigation)
2. Otherwise go to trial

Prosecutor's Strategy:

1. Accept offer if greater than:
   (Perceived probability of conviction)
   times (Sentence if convicted)
   minus (% Discount to avoid litigation)
2. Otherwise go to trial.

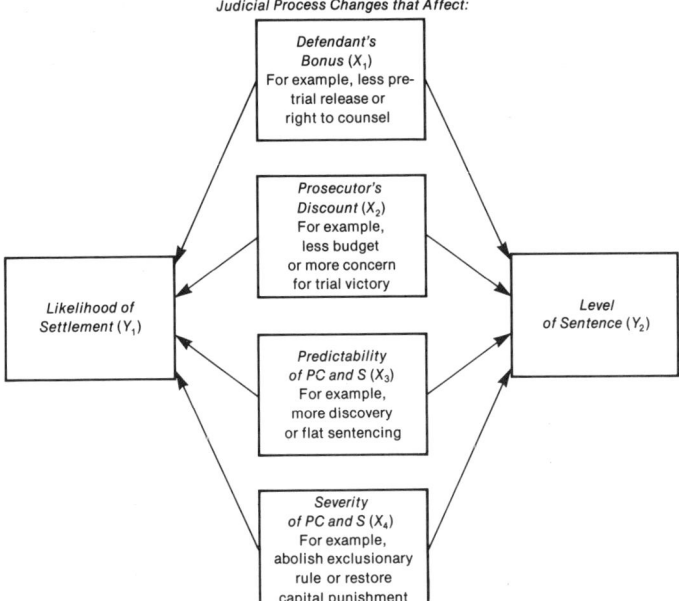

+ means an increase in X causes an increase in Y, or a decrease in X causes a decrease in Y.
− means an increase in X causes a decrease in Y, or a decrease in X causes an increase in Y.
0 means X is not related to Y. All three types of relations assume other variables are held constant.

Figure 5-1. The Impact of Judicial Process Changes on Plea Bargaining Settlements.

2. A change that decreases the prosecutor's discount factor (such as more resources to the prosecutor, thereby lowering the cost of litigation) will raise the prosecutor's adjusted bargaining limit without directly affecting the defendant's limit (although more resources to the prosecutor may affect the probability of conviction also). This will narrow the room for settlement and increase the level of the new settlement if one can still be reached. The opposite occurs from a change that increases the prosecutor's discount factor.

Civil Analogies for Policy and Research 153

3. A change that improves the ability of one or both sides to predict more accurately the probability of conviction or the sentence upon conviction such as pretrial discovery proceedings or flat sentencing)[27] will increase the likelihood of settlements by decreasing misperceptions of their bargaining limits by the respective parties. In the normal case, if both parties accurately perceive the probability of conviction and the sentences and thus have the same nonadjusted limits, then a settlement should be reached when the bonus factor raises the defendant's limit and the discount factor lowers the prosecutor's.
4. A change that increases the probability of conviction (such as more lenient admissibility of police-obtained evidence) or that increases sentencing payoffs in any of the decision matrix cells (such as new mandatory minimum sentences) will raise both the defendant's adjusted limit and the prosecutor's adjusted limit (if they both accurately perceive the effects of those judicial system changes on *PC* and on sentencing) since their respective limits at least partly reflect the product of the perceived *PC* (or 1 − *PC*) times the sentence associated with each decision-making possibility. The new limits will then still allow as much room for settlement as before, but they will both be higher, thereby resulting in settlement at a higher level.[28] A change that decreases the probability of conviction or the sentencing payoffs will have the opposite effect.[29]

III. Future Research

This chapter could conceivably lead to two kinds of future research. One kind would relate to the plea bargaining model. The other kind would involve applying the decision theory and equilibrium modeling concepts and methods to other legal process and related problems.

A. Plea Bargaining Research

Future plea bargaining research can serve at least three useful purposes with regard to the model presented. One is to test the meaningfulness of the measuring instruments suggested in this chapter. The measuring instruments include the methods for (1) deriving the payoff matrices through questioning knowledgeable persons or analyzing case data;[30] (2) converting the payoff cells into relative or ordinal utility measures;[31] (3) determining conviction probabilities for specific cases or types of cases;[32] (4) obtaining an optimism-pessimism coefficient and applying it to narrowing to a point the estimation range on *PC* or a payoff cell;[33] and (5) seeing if and how nonsentence goals can be meaningfully reduced to a percentage against which the defendant's upper sentence bargaining limit or the prosecutor's lower sentence bargaining limit can be multiplied in order to determine the bonus or discount factor.[34]

A second purpose to the testing is to determine the extent to which various hypotheses directly generated by the model are true. These hypotheses relate to the internal workings of the plea bargaining process. They can be tested through depth interviewing or possibly through mailed questionnaires that are carefully structured and directed toward prosecutors, defense attorneys, judges, or defendants in various places.[35]

A third purpose for future plea bargaining research relevant to the model is to determine the extent to which various hypotheses indirectly generated by the model are true. These hypotheses relate to the effect of external policies, events, or changes on the plea bargaining process. They require studying plea bargaining in different communities, in the same communities over time, or in different cases using large random or matched samples.[36]

A purpose that cannot be served by empirical research like that just listed is the testing of the basic assumptions of the model. This is so because those assumptions are almost definitional tautologies. The basic assumption is that both defendants and prosecutors want to maximize their satisfaction. This is almost a tautology, since one can define satisfaction as what one receives when he chooses one alternative action over another, given his values and the information he has available at the time he makes the choice. Thus, even masochistic and martyr-prone defendants seek to maximize their satisfaction, although they have an unusual value system. Similarly, defendants who represent themselves when they could have court-provided counsel are also seeking to maximize their satisfaction, although they may have a faulty information system about the functions performed by defense counsel. At a less basic level, the model assumes that the satisfaction of defendants will increase if their sentences decrease, and the satisfaction of prosecutors will increase if the sentences they obtain also increase, unless some offsetting nonsentence goals are being achieved by the defendant or prosecutor. This assumption is also practically a tautology, since the concept of nonsentence goals is broad enough to include any unusual reason why a defendant would not receive satisfaction from a lower sentence, or why a prosecutor would not receive satisfaction from a higher sentence.[37]

If defendants and prosecutors are assumed to want to maximize their respective satisfactions, then this is like saying they both are rational (or not irrational) if *rational* simply means choosing the alternative action that gives the most satisfaction given one's values and the information he has available at the time he makes the choice. In this context being rational does not necessarily mean being consistent in one's values, informed of relevant information, intelligent in IQ, or even capable of functioning with psychiatric sanity. Laymen, however, often use the term *rational* in these narrower senses, which makes the term not as meaningful in decision theory as the phrase *wanting to maximize one's satisfaction*.[38] In spite of the simplicity of our basic assumptions, they are the only goal assumptions on which the essence of the plea bargaining model is based.[39] The calculation of limits like *LD, LP, ALD,* and *ALP* and the calculation of convergence points like S^* are deduced from these axioms or assumptions.

B. Other Decision and Game Theory Applications

Perhaps the most important value of the presentation of this plea bargaining model is to stimulate the application of decision theory and equilibrium modeling to legal and political problems other than plea bargaining. Decision theory and equilibrium models are not easy to find in the literature on legal policies and the legal process. That may, however, reflect only the newness of these approaches rather than reflect adversely on their applicability.

Probabilistic decision theory (or decision theory under uncertainty) seems to be especially applicable to many of the fundamental decision problems in the legal process. These include analyzing the behavior of judges in the context of (1) deciding whether to release an arrested person pending trial or confine him to jail by setting a bail figure higher than he can meet, or (2) deciding whether to imprison a convicted defendant or allow him freedom on a suspended sentence or probation. In the bail context, there are two alternative decisions comprising the rows of the four-cell payoff matrix, namely, release the defendant or hold him in jail pending trial. The key probabilistic event is the probability of the defendant failing to show up for trial.[40] If the probability is 0 that the defendant will fail to show up (meaning that it is virtually certain he will appear in court), then we receive our worst payoff if we hold the defendant and our best payoff if we release him. If the probability is 1.0 that the defendant will fail to show up, then we receive our next to the best payoff if we hold him and our next to the worst payoff if we release him.[41] The order of those payoffs might be changed by one who has less concern for freeing the nonwrongdoer (that is, for freeing someone who will not violate his promise to show up in court).[42]

Probabilities of skipping out could be obtained for individual defendants or types of defendants.[43] Payoff values also could be calculated through a survey of relevant persons. The payoff values produced by the survey could be expressed as index numbers or relative distances rather than as absolute units like prison sentences or dollars. The decision theory methodology could be used to determine for any given case or type of case whether the defendant should be released or held in jail.[44] The decision would depend on whether the expected value of release is greater or less than the expected value of holding the prisoner, by calculating for each case or case type $a(1 - P) + b(P)$ versus $c(1 - P) + d(P)$, where P is the probability of skipping out and a, b, c, and d are the cell payoffs analogous to those in table 3-1.

If case data are available that closely approximates the data in a given city, an average city, or a type of city, the above decision theory analysis may well result in an extremely low percentage of cases in which defendants should be held in light of the probabilities of skipping out and in light of the cell payoffs perceived by the respondents. If so, this might indicate that more arrested persons should be released or that more arrested persons should be held if the optimum release percentage shown by the decision theory analysis is substantially higher than the actual release percentage. Such a decision theory analysis may also provide insights into the value structures and probability perceptions of arraigning magistrates, regardless whether the decision theory model is close or far from the actual release percentage. A similar analysis could be made of the incarceration-probation decision, except that the key probabilistic event would be the likelihood of the defendant repeating his crime.

Probably the most useful application of the bargaining aspects of decision theory (besides criminal and civil settlement negotiations) is in obtaining a better understanding of certain aspects of contract law. The traditional common law of contract tended to operate on the assumption that (1) the buyer sought to maximize the gap between his upper bargaining price and the settlement price with no conflicting goals, (2) the seller sought to maximize the gap between the settlement price and his lower bargaining price, and (3) both parties had perfect information. The courts refused to interfere with contractual arrangements, arguing implicitly or explicitly that both buyers and sellers under such assumptions would benefit from the equilibrium agreements that would be freely determined. Clarifying those assumptions through geometric and algebraic bargaining theory should help clarify defects in the assumptions and the adverse effects they can produce. Such recognition has led to increased government regulation of contracts dealing with employment, landlord-tenant relations, consumer purchases, and other matters on behalf of the party who is likely to have less information and who is more likely to be influenced by noneconomic goals. Even when the assumptions are accurate, the analysis has helped illustrate the need for increased governmental intervention to prevent the parties from contracting to the detriment of the community through such matters as the building of a glue factory in a residential neighborhood or the nonreconstruction of a strip mine. The analysis should also illustrate the method for restoring in a meaningful way the parties to the position where they would have been in a freely negotiated, fully informed agreement which one side has breached.[45]

Closely related to the two-person bargaining in contract law is the multiple-person bargaining associated with coalition formation within collegial courts. This is one area of decision game theory that has been well developed in the political science literature. Some political scientists have analyzed how the nine judges on the Supreme Court come together in majority and minority coalitions. For example, Glendon Schubert hypothesizes certain goals that each judge or group of judges might have in coalition formation. He then observes their behavior to see if it fits the hypothesized goals. If the behavior does fit the goals, he considers that as providing support for the accuracy of the hypothesized goals, although the behavior could be directed toward other goals or the goals could be achieved by other behavior. If the behavior does not fit the goals, Schubert considers that as a rejection of the hypothesized goals. Although the judges may really have those goals, they may be unable to behave accordingly, because they may misperceive factual means-ends relations or because they may have other conflicting goals.[46]

Walter Murphy, on the other hand, has been among those seeking to explain the dynamic bargaining process on the Supreme Court, although he uses a verbal approach rather than a quantitative one.[47] David Rohde has shown particular concern for testing hypotheses that relate to the size of the winning coalition in the sense that anything more than $5/9$, or 56 percent, represents possible waste with regard to what judicial principles could have been established, unless an image of unanimity was being sought.[48] Sidney Ulmer has developed a number of formulas for analyzing the relations between coalition size and the likelihood of error, which have important policy implications for the issue of what minimum-size coalition should be allowed for jury convictions.[49]

C. Other Equilibrium Modeling Applications

Mathematically speaking, equilibrium models involve two or more simultaneous equations or inequalities that intersect when graphed in such a way that the points of intersection represent the points toward which the behavior of an individual or individuals tends to move. In that sense, probabilistic decision theory is a type of equilibrium model since the intersection or intersections of the highest or lowest payoff lines are points where one's strategy should change from one alternative decision to another. Two-person bargaining and multiple-person coalition models are thus also equilibrium models since often they hypothesize a point toward which the bargainers gravitate or a point that represents a kind of natural coalition like the minimum winning coalition. The most common equilibrium models in elementary economics are the supply and demand model, the consumer model, and the firm model. All three have numerous potential applications to legal policy problems.[50]

The supply and demand, or market, model says that two simultaneous equations determine the equilibrium price and equilibrium quantity in a competitive market. One equation shows quantity demanded as a function of price, and the other shows quantity supplied as a function of price. Where those two equations intersect is where the prevailing price and quantity bought and sold will tend to be. This is so because at any higher price, suppliers will supply a larger quantity than buyers will buy, and thus suppliers will lower their selling price to sell the surplus. At any lower price, buyers will demand a larger quantity than suppliers will supply, and therefore buyers will raise their buying price to encourage more production. This model can be used to get a better partial understanding of how the salaries of legal process personnel like judges, prosecutors, and public defenders are determined. Those salaries, in turn, may have a substantial influence on the quality of legal process personnel. This model also can be used to get a better partial understanding of the market price for prostitution, gambling activities, stolen goods, hired killers, and other criminal services. Indeed, a whole school of criminology may be in the process of developing which emphasizes that the way to decrease crime is to increase the costs of committing crimes, including the missed opportunity costs (that is, shift the supply curve to the left so that at a given price less will be supplied because of higher costs), and decrease the benefits which cause people to demand or seek criminal activities (that is, shift the demand curve to the left so that at a given price less will be demanded because of lower benefits from the product).[51]

The consumer model says that the consumer is in optimal equilibrium when the marginal benefit-cost ratios of all products that he buys are equal. The *marginal ratio* of a product or good is the ratio of the benefit to be received from buying one additional unit to the cost to be paid for that one additional unit. If not all the marginal benefit-cost ratios are equal, then the consumer should buy more of those products which have higher marginal or incremental ratios and less of those products which have lower ratios. This model applies to many legal policy problems where one is seeking to get an optimum mix among a variety of goods.[52] All these optimum mix situations involve somewhat difficult problems in measuring benefits or satisfaction and measuring costs or effort. The measurement methods, however, may be less difficult than those involved in measuring the plea bargaining cell payoffs, the conviction probabilities, and especially the nonsentence goals.

The model of the firm says that a one-product firm is in optimal equilibrium if its total profits are maximized when its marginal revenue equals its marginal cost. *Marginal revenue,* or *benefit,* is the additional unit of income which comes from producing one additional unit of the firm's product. *Marginal cost* is the additional unit of cost which comes from producing one additional unit of the firm's product. If marginal or incremental revenue were greater than marginal cost, then the firm should keep producing more units of its product, because more income than cost has been produced from each additional unit. If marginal revenue were less than marginal cost, then the firm should cut back on the number of units it produces because at least the last few units have been costing more to produce than the revenue they generate. This equilibrium model may have more applicability to legal policy problems than any of the previous equilibrium models. It could help provide a better understanding of what is involved in finding the optimum level of due process to produce in criminal and civil cases. The optimum level would be the point where the marginal cost of convicting the innocent (which can be considered a negative benefit or negative marginal revenue) equals the marginal cost of acquitting the guilty. This same firm model could also help provide a better understanding of what is involved in finding the optimum level of severity for economic regulation laws, divorce laws, and other substantive laws. The optimum level would be the point where the marginal cost of being undersevere (which is like negative marginal revenue) equals the marginal cost of being oversevere.[5]

As with the plea bargaining model, one may have to resort to nonprecision forms of measurement in order to apply to model of the firm, the consumer, and the market to legal policy problems. Even then, however, these models can be insight-provoking. They provide insights for comparing optimum or equilibrium behavior with empirical behavior so that one can make policy recommendations to bring the empirical closer to the optimum, or so that one can revise the values he attributes to the policy makers in order to bring the optimum closer to the empirical. They provide insights for understanding the effects on other variables of changing legal policies and decisions, as well as the effects on legal policies and decisions of changing other variables. They help to clarify assumptions, goals, alternative means, payoffs from alternative means, contingent probabilities, and other elements essential to understanding more fully the basic simplicities and subtle complexities of law and the legal process.

Notes

1. For further discussion of the application of mathematical modeling to out-of-court civil settlements, see Friedman, "An Analysis of Settlement," 22 *Stan. L. Rev.* 67 (1969); Johnston and Tersine, "The Mathematical Evaluation of Trial versus Settlement," *Case & Comment* 3-10 (January 1973); and Posner, "An Economic Approach to Legal Procedure and

Judicial Administration," 2 *J. Legal Studies* 399-458 (1973). For a good, nonmethematical approach to civil negotiation, see Ross, *Settled out of Court* (Aldine, 1970).

2. See chapter 3, section I-B.

3. See chapter 3, section II-C-1.

4. A strategies graph would look like the following for the unadjusted plaintiff's limits and the unadjusted defendant's limits, using the hypothetical data mentioned in section I-A-2.

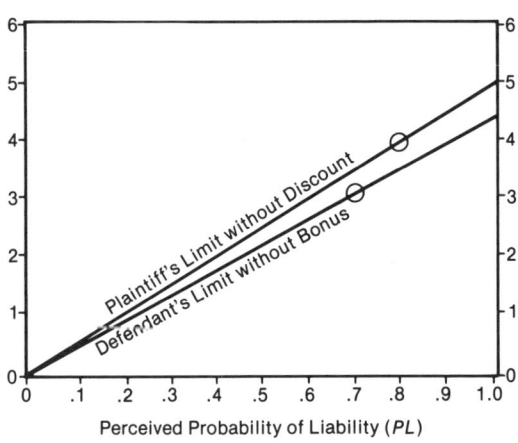

5. See chapter 3.

6. The main settlement cost is the one-third contingency fee that usually has to be paid to one's attorney. It represents 33 percent of the settlement. If the expected judgment is higher than the settlement, then 25 percent of the expected judgment might be about equal to 33 percent of the settlement. One often settles for a settlement less than the expected judgment in order to save litigation costs which include (1) the cost of having one's money tied up for a substantial period of time and (2) the higher contingency fee percentage which personal injury lawyers often charge for going to trial rather than negotiating an out-of-court settlement.

7. The $3,900 *ALD* was arrived at by assuming that the hypothetical defendant perceives the payoff amount to be $4,500 if the case goes to trial. He also perceives *PL* to be .70, and thus the unadjusted limit is $3,150. We further assume that his litigation costs will be $1,200 if the case goes to trial and his settlement costs will be $450 if the case is settled out of court. Thus, his bonus factor is $750, and his adjusted limit is $3,900.

8. For further detail on time discounting, see Dinwiddy, *Elementary Mathematics for Economists* 199-216 (Oxford, 1967); C. Bell and L.J. Adams, *Mathematics of Finance* 247-68 (Holt, 1949). The plaintiff and defendant need not operate under the same discount rate since they may be

able to obtain interest on their respective investments at different rates, and they may perceive the inflation rate differently. Similarly, they need not perceive the interest rate or inflation rate as holding constant in each future year. If X changes from year to year (where $X = r - i$), then the formula for calculating P is

$$P = a/(1 + X_1)(1 + X_2) \cdots (1 + X_n)$$

and the formula for calculating A is

$$A = P(1 + X_1)(1 + X_2) \cdots (1 + X_n)$$

where the subscripts indicate the first year, the second year, and so on. If the defendant were to offer the plaintiff a certain or varying amount of income each year rather than a lump sum, the discounted present value would be calculated by summing the quotient of each year's income divided by $[1 + (r - i)]^{t-1}$, where t is 1 for the first year, 2 for the second year, and so on. Such an offer is unlikely to be made by the average defendant, but it is a common situation in benefit-cost analysis in deciding between two or more social-income-producing government investments. See E. Mishan, *Economics for Social Decisions* 112-40 (Praeger, 1972).

9. See chapter 3, section II-D.

10. For analyzing the decision to sue in civil cases, see R. Hunting and G. Neuwirth, *Who Sues in New York City? A Study of Automobile Accident Claims* (Columbia University Press, 1962); F.B. MacKinnon, *Contingent Fees for Legal Services* (Aldine, 1964); Nagel, "Statistical Prediction of Verdicts and Awards," in *Modern Uses of Logic in Law* 135 (1963); Schwartz and Mitchell, "An Economic Analysis of the Contingent Fee in Personal Injury Litigation," 22 *Stan. L. Rev.* 1125 (1970).

11. See chapter 3, section I-B.

12. See chapter 3, section II-C.

13. For analyzing the decision to formally charge in criminal cases, see F. Miller, *Prosecution: The Decision to Charge a Suspect with a Crime* (Little, Brown, 1969); Abrams, "Prosecutional Charge Decision Systems," 23 *UCLA L. Rev.* 1 (1975); and McIntyre and Lippman, "Prosecutors and Early Disposition of Felony Cases," 56 *A.B.A.J.* 1154 (1970). The discretionary decision of private criminal defense counsel to accept a client is discussed in A. Wood, *Criminal Lawyer* 96-101 (College and University Press, 1967).

14. See section II.

15. See section III.

16. Hermann, "Predicting Verdicts in Personal Injury Cases," 9 *Prac. Law.* 83 (1963); H. Liebenson and L. Miller, *Medical and Legal Evaluation of Disability in Personal Injury Cases: A Practical Guide for Doctors and*

Lawyers (Callaghan, 1962); Reeder, "Formulae for Evaluation of Damages," *ABA Law Notes* (January 1967); Johnston and Tersine, "The Mathematical Evaluation of Trial versus Settlement." The *Verdict Expectancies* looseleaf service of the Jury Verdict Research Company provides probabilities of liability for a large variety of factual situations. The *Valuation Handbooks* of the Jury Research Company and the *Current Money Awards* of the Lawyers Co-operative Publishing Company provide expected damage award payoffs also for a large variety of situations.

17. See S. Richmond, *Operations Research for Management Decisions* 540-556 (Ronald, 1968), for a discussion of some of the mathematical considerations involved in determining the incremental value of additional information.

18. Casper, *American Criminal Justice: The Defendant's Perspective* 100-125 (Harper & Row, 1972); Blumberg, "The Practice of Law as Confidence Game: Organizational Cooptation of a Profession," 1 *Law & Society Rev.* 15 (1967); and Stover and Eckart, "The Indigent's Right to Counsel: How Much Does it Help?" (Mimeographed paper presented at the Midwest Political Science Association convention, 1973).

19. These discovery techniques include requiring both sides to provide lists of witnesses in advance, transcripts of confessions, itemized lists of materials obtained through search warrants or other searches, and requiring both sides to answer questionnaire interrogatories subject to the privilege against self-incrimination. Related techniques that have been used in civil cases to make both sides more knowledgeable and thereby facilitate settlements include pretrial conferences and examinations by impartial medical experts and other experts.

On discovery in criminal proceedings, see Symposium, "Pre-trial Discovery in Criminal Proceedings," 27 *Brooklyn L. Rev.* 318 (1961); Louisell, "Criminal Discovery: Dilemma Real or Apparent?" 49 *Cal. L. Rev.* 56 (1961); R. Nimmer, *The Omnibus Hearing: An Experiment in Relieving Inefficiency, Unfairness and Judicial Delay* (ABA, 1971). Providing more discovery to both sides does not necessarily mean requiring pretrial conferences or omnibus hearings. It would be wasteful to require discovery conferences in all criminal cases because many would result in a nonnegotiated guilty plea without necessitating such a conference, and many might be unlikely to result in a negotiated guilty plea even with such a conference. The only types of cases, if any, for which such conferences should be required are those that have characteristics (possibly revealed at the preliminary hearing stage) that are likely to benefit from such a conference. Relevant characteristics might include the severity of the initial charge and the initial offers, if any, by the prosecutor and the defendant. If the severity is very low, the conference can be optional since guilty pleas are still likely to be high. If the parties are very close on their initial offers, they will probably reach convergence without a compulsory conference; and if they are very far apart on their initial offers, a compulsory conference will not be so likely to bring convergence.

20. See section II-B-2. Providing more counsel to the indigent and more pretrial release decreases *ALD*, not only by decreasing the defendant's litigation costs, but also possibly by decreasing the defendant's perception of his conviction probability and his sentencing payoffs. Defendants are less likely to be severely convicted when they have a lawyer and when they have been released prior to trial so that they can better prepare their cases. The prosecutor's perception of the conviction probability and the sentencing payoffs may also thereby be decreased. This can result in a new midpoint between *ALD* and *ALP* that comes closer to the "correct" sentence if by correct sentence one means that it is not influenced by the discriminatory absence of defense counsel and pretrial release.

21. Instead of noting the effect of delay on the likelihood of plea bargaining settlement, one might note that plea bargaining may be one of the causes of delay if continuances are often required to allow plea bargaining to occur and a large percentage of plea bargaining negotiations break down. See Levin, "Delay and Related Policy Topics in Five Criminal Courts" (Mimeographed paper presented at the American Political Science Association convention, 1973). That relation possibly further emphasizes the need to facilitate convergence in plea bargaining by making both sides more knowledgeable through discovery procedures.

Abolishing or restricting plea bargaining normally would increase delay in the criminal justice system by increasing the number of trials. The amount of delay depends on the number of trials, the number of persons available to try cases, and the average length of a trial. One could thus offset the increased delay by increasing the number of persons available to try cases or decreasing the average length of trial. The prosecutor could also offset the increased delay by dismissing more cases. There may, however, be no increased trials or delays if the decrease in plea bargains is offset by an increase in guilty pleas without a bargain out of fear that the likely sentence on trial would be greater than the sentence following a nonnegotiated plea. That is what seems to have happened when plea bargaining was abolished in certain types of cases in Phoenix, Arizona. Berger, "The Case against Plea Bargaining," 62 *A.B.A.J.* 621 (1976).

22. For futher discussion on the role of discovery, defense, bail, and delay in determining settlements, see Landes, "An Economic Analysis of the Courts," 14 *J. L. & Econ.* See also H. Kalven, Jr. and B. Buchholz, *Delay in the Court* 111 (1959); M. Rosenberg, *The Pretrial Conference and Effective Justice* (1964); Posner, "An Economic Approach to Legal Procedure, and Judicial Administration," 2 *J. Legal Studies* 399-458 (1973).

23. Landes, in "An Economic Analysis of the Courts, pp. 69-71, however, states that the more severe a case is, the more resources the defendant devotes to fighting the case, which decreases his *PC* and thereby increases

his willingness to go to trial and his unwillingness to agree to a plea bargain settlement. That analysis, however, may fail to recognize that the more severe a case is, the more resources the prosecutor devotes to fighting the case, which may restore the decreased *PC* to where it was. Even if the prosecutor does not devote additional resources to the more severe case, if he is a perceptive prosecutor, he will perceive that *PC* has gone down as a result of the defendant's increased resources. The prosecutor's new lower *PC* will then result in a lowered bargaining limit point for the prosecutor, which will still enable a settlement to be reached. This is so since *LP* will be equal to *LD* when both sides perceive *PC* and the payoff cells alike, and *ALP* will be lower than *ALD* when the litigation costs are greater than the settlement costs.

24. See chapter 3, section II-D. In Posner, "An Economic Approach to Legal Procedure, and Judicial Administration," 2 *J. Legal Studies* 399-458 (1973), at 421, however, the writer says that if the stakes become higher in civil cases, then the parties are less likely to settle. The only example he gives is the addition of an interest rate percentage onto the damage award rather than a fixed addition or subtraction. This, if in Posner's example, $LD = \$100$ and $LP = \$120$, then the initial gap is $-\$20$. If 6 percent interest is added to each limit, then $LD = \$106$, $LP = \$127$, and the new gap is a larger $-\$21$. If, however, a \$6 penalty had been added to the damage award for delay rather than 6 percent interest, then $LD = \$106$, $LP = \$126$, and the gap is still $-\$20$.

More important, Posner assumes the perceptions (and thus the limits of the parties) are unequal with *LD* begining unrealistically lower than *LP*. If an *LD* of \$100 were equal to an *LP* of \$100, as in the perfect discovery situation, then after adding 6 percent interest, $LD = \$106$, $LP = \$106$, and the gap remains the same. If more realistically *ALD* were to be \$120 after the bonus factor and *ALP* were to be \$100 after the discount factor, then the 6 percent interest would make $ALD = \$127$ and $ALP = \$106$, for a gap of \$21 which is more likely to induce a settlement since it allows more room for convergence than a gap of \$20 when *ALD* is greater than *ALP*. In other words, the bigger the gap, the less likely the settlement when *ALD* is smaller than *ALP*; but the bigger the gap, the more likely the settlement when *ALD* is larger than *ALP*.

Posner also assumes that the likelihood of settlement is dependent only on the size of the gap between the limits of the parties, and not on the gap ratio. Clearly, the size of the gap is more important than the gap ratio in that the parties would be more likely to settle in case 1 than in case 2: in case 1, $LD = \$10$, $LP = \$11$, the gap $= -\$1$, and the gap ratio $= .91$ (or \$10/\$11); in case 2, $LD = \$1$ million, $LP = \$1,100,000$, the gap $= -\$100,000$, and the same gap ratio $= .91$. Nevertheless, if the gap is held roughly constant, the case with the larger gap ratio is more likely to be settled such that case 2 is more likely to involve a settlement than case 3 where in case 3, $LD = \$1$, $LP = \$100,001$, the same gap $= -\$100,000$, but the gap ratio $= .00001$. In other words, in case 2 the defendant-buyer can come up to 91 percent of the plaintiff-seller's asking price, whereas in case 3 the defendant-buyer can only come up to 1/1,000 of 1 percent of the plaintiff's asking price even though in both cases they are $100,000 apart. This problem of the relative importance of the gap and the gap ratio is related to the fundamental benefit-cost decision problem of the importance of maximizing benefits minus cost $(B - C)$ versus maximizing benefits divided by costs (B/C), assuming both benefits and costs can be measured in the same units. Analogous to the gap and gap ratio comparison, $B - C$ is the preferable criterion; but if two investments are equal on $B - C$, then one should prefer the investment with the higher B/C ratio. The above examples could illustrate that principle by changing LP to B and LD to C. See McKean, *Efficiency in Government through Systems Analysis* 25-49 (Wiley, 1958); F. Mishan, *Economics for Social Decisions* 134-135 (Praeger, 1972).

25. One might argue that even if plea bargaining could be made to arrive at sentences that on the average equal those that would be arrived at through trials, the plea bargaining system would still be defective for at least two reasons. First, plea bargaining does not give the appearance of due process that a trial does, and therefore defendants who are convicted by way of plea bargaining might be more likely to feel antisocial resentment. This is currently likely where defendants feel they are coerced into pleading guilty for lack of resources to take cases to trial. If, however, public defenders did have overly adequate resources, defendants might feel they were getting such a break under the system that the system might lose some of its deterrent power. Second, even if the plea bargaining averages equal the trial averages, it would not be any consolation to tell an individual who receives an above-average sentence in a plea bargain that someone else got an offsetting below-average sentence. What is needed is to strive to have a system whereby every plea bargain, not just the average plea bargain, equals the trial sentence. This means not only adequate resources for the defense and prosecution, but also possibly pretrial discovery and flat sentencing, whereby both sides can come close to predicting with certainty whether the defendant will be convicted and with what sentence.

26. For further discussion on the accuracy and fairness of plea bargaining, see American Bar Association Project on Minimum Standards for Criminal Justice, *Standards Relating to Pleas of Guilty* (ABA, 1967); National Advisory Commission on Criminal Justice Standards and Goals, *Courts* 42-65 (Government Printing Office, 1973); Gallagher, "Judicial Participation in Plea Bargaining: A Search for New Standards," 9 *Harv. Civ. Rights-Civ. Lib. L. Rev.* 29 (1974); Kuh, "Balancing the Scales of Justice: How to Make Plea Bargaining Work," *The New Leader* 10-14 (Janu-

ary 7, 1974); D. Newman, *Conviction: The Determination of Guilt or Innocence without Trial* 7-52, 231-243 (Little, Brown, 1966).

The most practical sentence to arrive at in plea bargaining is for S^* (the settlement sentence) to equal $PC'(d')$ where PC' is the true value of PC, which would be 0.0 or 1.0, and where d' is the true value of cell d. The values of PC' and d' cannot be known with certainty before trial except by an omniscient being, but both values can be known after trial. The S^* will equal $PC'd'$ if (1) the defendant, the prosecutor, and the pleading judge perceive PC as PC'; (2) they perceive d as d'; (3) $a = b = d$, which means the same sentence is given on plea as on trial; and (4) the defendant's bonus factor to be added to LD equals the prosecutor's discount factor to be subtracted from LP. With these four conditions,

$$LS_1 = c + (d - c)(PC) = 0 + (d' - 0)PC' = PC'd'$$

and

$$LS_2 = a + (b - a)(PC) = d' + (d' - d')(PC') = d'$$

Thus both LD and LP equal d' if $PC' = 1$, and both LD and LP equal 0 if $PC' = 0$. Therefore, given those four conditions,

$$S^* = ALD + ALP/2 = PC'd'$$

The most ideal sentence to arrive at in plea bargaining is $PG(d'')$, where PG is the true probability of actually being guilty rather than just being convicted and d'' ("d double prime") is the sentence which is deserved in light of the crime and the defendant's characteristics (according to an omnibenevolent being, a survey of public opinion, or whatever source one regards as ultimate). The value of $PC'd'$ can be objectively determined even before trial with some statistical accuracy (see chapter 3, sections I-B and II-C-1) but not the value of PGd''.

This symbolism is useful for obtaining a better understanding of the four roles which Albert Alschuler perceives the prosecutor as having. Alschuler, "The Prosecutor's Role in Plea Bargaining," 36 *U. Chi. L. Rev.* 50 (1968). The four roles include those of (1) the administrator who will settle for anything greater than ALP, where ALP equals LP minus a large discount, or $\%XP$, to avoid trial; (2) the advocate who will try for a bargain as much greater than LP as possible, where LP equals LS_1 or LS_2, whichever is lower with no discount to promote administrative convenience; (3) the judgelike prosecutor who strives for a settlement at what he perceives d to be, or the true empirical value of cell d; and (4) the legislatorlike prosecutor who strives for a settlement at what he perceives d'' to be, or the righteous normative value of cell d.

27. Flat sentencing, whereby the legislature removes judicial discretion to sentence after conviction, increases the predictability of all the cells in the decision theory matrix. Thus, if the statute specifies a 10-year sentence for a given crime, then cells a, b, and d will all have 10's in them, and cell c will continue to have a 0. Predictability may, however, be decreased in some nontypical cases if the statute allows the judge to award probation as an alternative to flat sentence, or if the judge or jury frequently refuses to convict in a trial because they consider the flat sentence out of line with the nature of the circumstances.

An important effect of flat sentencing on plea bargaining would be a shift from bargaining over sentencing recommendations to bargaining over the charge. Prosecutors may not be so willing to reduce the charge if a reduced charge means a defininte sentence reduction, as it does under flat sentencing but as it often does not under indeterminate sentencing. Another effect would be that going to trial would always be a more favorable alternative than a nonnegotiated plea of guilty, given the possibility of an acquittal. This might mean more cases going to trial when plea bargaining breaks down than at present, although the extent to which nonnegotiated pleas provide an alternative to plea bargaining must be empirically determined. The effect of practically abolishing nonnegotiated pleas might cause the prosecutor to be more willing to make concessions on the charge in order to avoid trials, cover the nontypical case, and relieve himself of the increased burden stemming from more cases being through into lengthy plea bargaining because the defendant no longer has the option of a nonnegotiated plea followed by a light sentence.

The prosecutor's bargaining position mainly would be strengthened and the defendant's weakened if the new flat sentencing results in higher likely sentences than the old, more indeterminate sentencing, or if the likely sentences are perceived as being higher by defendants who formerly may have wishfully misperceived likely sentences as being lower than they actually turned out to be. If the nonnegotiated plea formerly provided a more attractive alternative to the defendant (as it probably would if PC were high), then abolishing it would strengthen and thereby raise the prosecutor's limit and weaken or lower the defendant's limit. Thus, the effects of flat sentencing are more complicated than merely improving the predictability of sentences by decreasing their variation. This is so in view of the fact that the flat-sentence level could conceivably be higher, lower, or the same as the former sentence generally was or was perceived to be, and in view of the influence of the level of *PC* on the impact of the sentence change on plea bargaining. In general, flat sentencing provides sentences substantially above the former average sentences, but the flat sentences are subject to being reduced close to the average by reductions of one day for each day of good time served in prison.

28. Although the model enables one to determine the probable direction of the effects of judicial process changes on the likelihood and level of plea bargaining settlements, one cannot determine the exact magnitude of such effects in an individual case because doing so depends on the individual prosecutor, defendant, defense counsel, and case facts. However, the magnitude of the effects on the average prosecutor of a given type, the average defendant of a given type, or the average case of a given type can be discussed, at least after compiling further empirical data (see section III-C-1). One can also talk about certain judicial procedures as being more or less conducive to increasing settlements than other judicial procedures, such as statements that there will be more settlements if pretrial detention averages 6 months than if it averages 3 months and other things are held constant.

29. Oaks and Lehman argue that "when the overall rate of conviction at trial goes down, so would the proportion of guilty pleas." Oaks and Lehman, *Criminal Justice and the Indigent* 57-58 (University of Chicago Press, 1968). Such reasoning seems to assume that a drop in *PC* affects only the behavior of the defendant, who now demands a lower sentence to reflect his lowered bargaining limit. In light of the model and the data presented by Oaks and Lehman, which they consider contrary to their common sense, it seems reasonable to expect that the prosecutor now offers a lower sentence to reflect his also lowered bargaining limit. As a result, the percentage of cases settled through plea bargaining should remain about the same unless one side perceives the drop as being greater than the other side, although the new average sentences should now be lower. It is an empirical question as to which side (if either) has a greater tendency to perceive a *PC* drop or a sentencing drop as being bigger, although perhaps there is more of a knowledge lag on the part of less knowledgeable defense counsel than there is on the part of prosecutors, who tend to be involved in criminal work more full-time than the average defense attorney. This differential would explain why when *PC* went down in the Illinois data, prosecutors made better offers resulting in a higher percentage of bargained guilty pleas. In other words, given the small one-year time lag that Oaks and Lehman looked at, there was insufficient time for the original percentage of settlements to restore itself as a result of defense counsel demanding better offsetting settlements.

30. See chapter 3, section I-B.
31. See chapter 3, section I-C.
32. Methods to be tested for determining conviction probabilities for specific cases or types of cases might include the averaging of knowledge-

able persons and the use of the three-point estimate system. See chapter 3, section II-C-1.

33. See chapter 3, section II-C-3.

34. See chapter 3, section II-D-2.

35. They include such statements as these: (1) Pleading guilty before a judge produces a lower sentence than being convicted at trial for the same crime. (2) Pleading guilty before a judge is used as an alternative to plea bargaining with the prosecutor. (3) Defendants and prosecutors have fairly clear notions of what the likely sentences are for going to trial and pleading when the evidence is extremely weak or extremely strong. (4) Defendants and prosecutors have fairly clear notions of what the probability of conviction is under various circumstances. (5) Defendants perceive the likely sentences and conviction probabilities to be higher or maybe lower than prosecutors do. (6) Defendants and prosecutors have a number of other goals besides sentence minimization and maximization, respectively. (7) The nonsentence goals pushing toward settlement are stronger than the nonsentence goals pushing toward litigation. (8) The nonsentence goals vary with the severity of the case, the time discounting, and the risk-oriented personalities of the parties. (9) Plea bargaining settlements occur in a high percentage of felony cases. (10) Defendants and prosecutors exaggerate their initial offers. (11) Defendants and prosecutors try to make the other side think the conviction probabilities and the sentencing payoffs are lower or higher, respectively, than they perceive them to be. (12) Who makes the initial offer depends more on local custom than on which side has the greater need to avoid trial. (13) Counteroffers of the defendant tend to move upward with bigger jumps at first rather than later. (14) Counteroffers by the prosecutor tend to move downward with bigger jumps at first rather than later. (15) Both the defendant and the prosecutor feel they have gained something from a plea bargaining settlement over what they expected to get by going to litigation in terms of sentence or nonsentence goals.

For examples of such survey research to determine average and deviant practices, see Vetri, "Guilty Plea Bargaining: Compromises by Prosecutors to Secure Guilty Pleas," 112 *U. Pa. L. Rev.* 865 (1964); Note, "The Influence of the Defendant's Plea on Judicial Determination of Sentence," 66 *Yale L. J.* 204 (1956). In hypothesis 15, as elsewhere in this chapter, the concept of "litigation" as an alternative to plea bargaining refers to going to trial, pleading before a judge, or both, depending on what litigation alternatives are perceived as available to the defendant.

36. These hypotheses include statements like the following: (1) The presence of criminal discovery laws facilitates plea bargaining settlements. (2) The increased availability of court-provided counsel and pretrial release has decreased settlements. (3) Increased delay in prosecuting criminal cases increases settlements where evidence likely to decay is involved, but

decreases settlements where defendants are not in jail pending trial. (4) Changes in the conviction probabilities or sentencing payoffs do not affect settlement rates.

For examples of such cross-sectional or over-time studies to determine relations between practices and varying policies or environments, see Alschuler, "The Prosecutor's Role in Plea Bargaining," 36 *U. Chi. L. Rev.* 50 (1968); Landes, "An Economic Analysis of the Courts," 14 *J. L. & Econ.* In addition, see a symposium on the comparative study of prosecutors in 5 *The Prosecutor* 237 (1969).

Thomas Church and William Morris are developing an intensive study of the before and aftereffects of the discontinuance of charge-reduction plea bargaining in Oakland County, Michigan, in which the sale of narcotics is first charged. Church and Morris, "Charge Reduction Plea Bargaining and the Courts: A Model Based on Quasi-Experimental Data" (Unpublished paper prepared at Oakland University, 1975). They plan on working with a probabilistic decision theory model although as with most plea bargaining models, they do not consider the option of pleading guilty before a judge without a negotiated bargain, the determination of the bargaining limits of the parties, the dynamics of convergence, the occurrence of bluffing and other psychological elements, and the difficulties in measuring subjective benefits rather than more objective sentences. Their model, like most models, however, will aid in generating hypotheses to test and in synthesizing the data which are compiled. Such an approach can be contrasted with a massive compilation of raw data that has little theoretical direction for hypothesizing or integrating, such as Miller, Dash, and McDonald, "Plea Bargaining in the United States" (Funded LEAA application prepared at Georgetown Law School, 1975).

37. The model does not assume that it is possible for the defendant and the prosecutor to bargain with each other since the model allows in section II-B-2 for the possibility that the defendant's only alternatives are trial or judicial pleading. On axiomatic theory or the deduction of conclusions from empirical premises, see E. Meehan, *Contemporary Political Thought: A Critical Study* 287-349 (Dorsey, 1967); Bailey, "Evaluating Axiomatic Theories," in *Sociological Methodology* ed. E. Borgatta (1970); Land, "Formal Theory," in *Sociological Methodology* ed. H. Costner (1971).

38. On rationality, see Friedland, *Introduction to the Concept of Rationality in Political Science* (General Learning Press, 1974).

39. In addition to the above assumptions about the goals of the parties, certain data givens can be assumed (which are shown at the bottom of figure 3-2) in order to provide a more concrete illustration of the model. Those data givens, however, can be changed to any numbers, and the conclusions of the model will still hold, especially with regard to the basic conclusion

Civil Analogies for Policy and Research 171

that generally there will be convergence when and only when ALD is greater than or equal to ALP.

40. Pretrial release statutes specify that the main criterion for release is the probability of appearance. See, for example, *Illinois Criminal Code,* ch. 38, art. 110-2; Rule 46-c of the *Federal Rules of Criminal Procedure.* The model, however, can also consider the probability that the defendant will commit a crime while released, as is discussed in note 42.

41. For a discussion of how to work with payoff matrices that involve ranking or ordinal data (like the above-mentioned pretrial release matrix) rather than interval data (like our plea bargaining, likely-sentences matrix), see J.D. Williams, *The Compleat Strategyst: Being a Primer on the Theory of Games of Strategy* 198-206 (McGraw-Hill, 1954). If, as mentioned before in discussing the pretrial release matrix, cell c is worst, a is best, d is good, and b is bad, then those cells can be given rank-order payoff scores of $c = 1$, $a = 4$, $d = 3$, and $b = 2$. The two-alternative payoff matrix can be graphed where line 1 or $LP_1 = a + (b - a)(PS) = 4 - 2(PS)$, and line 2 or $LP_2 = c + (d - c)(PS) = 1 + 2(PS)$. The LP_1 is the likely payoff from holding the defendant; the LP_2 is the likely payoff from releasing the defendant; and PS (or just P) is the probability of skipping out. Such a strategies graph like figure 3-1 would involve intersecting pairs of lines. The point of intersection, or PS^*, is (as in figure 3-1) the point where $LP_1 = LP_2$, or $4 - 2(PS) = 1 + 2(PS)$. Solving for PS in this equation gives $PS^* = .75$. This means that given those cell payoffs, one should release anyone whose PS is below .75 and hold anyone whose PS is above .75. This decision theory analysis would reflect community values even more so if the payoffs were based on a survey and if the respondents were allowed to indicate relative or interval differences between the cell payoffs rather than just rank orders. Additional data gathering can indicate what percentage of the defendants in a given city fall below PS^* or above PS^*, as well as what percentage of the defendants are actually released or actually held. The important matter to note, however, is that one does not need to work with absolute units like sentence years or dollars in constructing payoff matrices, but instead can work adequately with relative units or index numbers.

42. As a supplement to the payoff matrix with the probability of skipping out as the key contingent event, one could also have a payoff matrix with the probability of committing a crime (while released) as a second contingent event. This would mean that for a defendant to be released, his probability of skipping out would have to be below PS^* (that is, the intersecting probability of skipping out discussed in note 40) and PW^* (that is, the intersecting probability of criminal wrongdoing where PW^* is calculated in a manner similar to PS^*).

43. See chapter 3, section II-C-1.
44. Ibid.

45. See Birmingham, "Damage Measures and Economic Rationality: The Geometry of Contract Law," 1969 *Duke L. J.* 49-71 (1969). See also Birmingham, "Legal and Moral Duty in Game Theory: Common Law Contract and Chinese Analogies," 18 *Buffalo L. Rev.* 99 (1969); Birmingham, "A Second Look at the Suez Canal Cases: Excuse for Nonperformance of Contractual Obligations in the Light of Economic Theory," 20 *Hastings L. J.* 1393 (1969).

46. See G. Schubert, *Quantitative Analysis of Judicial Behavior* 173-269 (Free Press, 1959); Schubert, "The Study of Judicial Decision-Making as an Aspect of Political Behavior," 52 *Am. Pol. Sci. Rev.* 1022 (1958); Schubert, "Policy without Law: An Extension of the Certiorari Game," 14 *Stan. L. Rev.* 284 (1962).

47. See Murphy, *Elements of Judicial Strategy* (University of Chicago Press, 1964); Danelski, "The Influence of the Chief Justice in the Decisional Process of the Supreme Court," in Murphy and Pritchett, *Courts, Judges, and Politics* 525 (1974); Murphy, "Marshaling the Court: Leadership, Bargaining, and the Judicial Process," 29 *U. Chi. L. Rev.* 640 (1962).

48. See Rohde, "Policy Goals and Opinion Coalitions in the Supreme Court," 16 *Midwest J. Pol. Sci.* 208 (1972); Rohde, "A Theory of the Formation of Opinion Coalitions in the U.S. Supreme Court," in *Probability Models of Collective Decision-Making* eds. R. Niemi and H. Weisberg (Merrill, 1972). Rohde draws heavily upon W. Riker and P. Ordeshook, *Positive Political Theory* (Prentice-Hall, 1973) and Riker, *The Theory of Political Coalitions* (Yale University Press, 1962).

49. See Ulmer, *Courts as Small and Not so Small Groups* (General Learning Press, 1971); Ulmer, "Quantitative Analysis of Judicial Processes: Some Practical and Theoretical Applications," 28 *Law & Contemp. Prob.* 176 (1963); Zeisel, "... And Then There Were None: The Diminution of the Federal Jury," 38 *U. Chi. L. Rev.* 710 (1971). Political scientists have also studied such matters as the measurement of cohesion in judicial coalitions, the extent to which judges with similar background characteristics tend to be in the same coalitions, and the measurement of the pivotal power or other power indices of coalitions. Much of this literature is reviewed in the first Ulmer article above. Most of it, however, does not contain a bargaining element or a deductive mathematical model like that associated with decision game theory.

50. For materials which deal with multiple applications of economic modeling to law, see the *Journal of Legal Studies,* the *Journal of Law and Economics,* the *Journal of Criminal Justice;* R. Posner, *Economic Analysis of Law* (Little, Brown, 1972); and G. Tullock, *The Logic of the Law* (Basic Books, 1971). For those who think they need an introduction to or review of basic enonomic models of the market, the consumer, or the firm, see any elementary economics textbook such as P. Samuelson, *Economics: An Introductory Analysis* (McGraw-Hill, 1972).

51. See R. Andreas and J. Siegfried, *The Economics of Crime: An Anthology of Recent Works* (forthcoming); L. Kaplan, *An Economic Analysis of Crime* (Charles C. Thomas, 1976); A.J. Rogers, *The Economics of Crime* (Dryden, 1974); G. Tullock, *The Economics of Crime* (Basic Books, forthcoming); S. Rottenberg, ed., *The Economics of Crime and Punishment* (1973); and Becker, "Crime and Punishment: An Economic Approach," 76 *J. Pol. Economy* 169 (1968).

52. Examples include finding an optimum mix between (1) law reform and case handling in the OEO Legal Services Program; (2) free press and fair trial in prejudicial pretrial press reporting; and (3) voting, schools, criminal justice, housing, public accommodations, and employment civil rights activities in promoting equality improvement. See S. Nagel, *Minimizing Costs and Maximizing Benefits in Providing Legal Services to the Poor* (Sage, 1973); S. Nagel and M. Neef, *The Application of Mixed Strategies: Civil Rights and Other Multi-Policy Activities* (Sage, 1976); Nagel, Reinbolt, and Eimermann, "A Linear Programming Approach to Problems of Conflicting Legal Values like Free Press versus Fair Trial," 4 *Rutgers J. of Computers & Law* 420 (1975).

53. S. Nagel, P. Wice, and M. Neef, *The Policy Problem of Doing Too Much or Too Little: Pretrial Release as a Case in Point* (Sage, 1976); R. Ridker, *Economic Costs of Air Pollution* (Praeger, 1967); and Posner, "An Economic Approach to Legal Procedure and Judicial Administration," 2 *J. Legal Studies* 399-458 (1973).

Appendix 5A.
Glossary of Symbols

Symbol	Represents	First Appearing
Parties:		
D	The defendant or defense counsel	I-A, Ch. 3
P	The prosecutor	I-A, Ch. 3
Defendant's Alternatives:		
Alternative 1, or T	Defendant goes to trial	I-A, Ch. 3
Alternative 2, or J	Defendant pleads guilty before a judge without a bargain	I-A, Ch. 3
Alternative 3	Defendant settles with the prosecutor	I-A, Ch. 3
F	Coin flip or other random method to determine whether defendant goes to trial or pleads before a judge	I-B-2, Ch. 4
MR	Method of nonbargain resolution (trial or non-negotiated plea)	I-B, Ch. 3
Payoff Cells:		
a	Cell showing perceived sentence if defendant pleads guilty when probability of conviction is low	I-A, Ch. 3
b	Cell showing perceived sentence if defendant pleads guilty when probability of conviction is high	I-A, Ch. 3
c	Cell showing perceived sentence if defendant goes to trial and is acquitted	I-A, Ch. 3
d	Cell showing perceived sentence if defendant goes to trial and is convicted	I-A, Ch. 3
d'	True value of cell d known only to an omniscient being	II-C, Ch. 5
d''	Sentence which is deserved by the defendant in light of his characteristics and in light of the crime	II-C, Ch. 5
Utility Units:		
DIS	Dissatisfaction or negative satisfaction units in a payoff cell, not just sentence years	I-C, Ch. 3
SAT	Satisfaction units in a payoff cell, not just sentence years	I-C, Ch. 3
Probabilities:		
PC	Perceived probability of defendant being convicted	I-A, Ch. 3
PC'	True probability of conviction as known by an omniscient being	II-C-1, Ch. 3

Symbol	Represents	First Appearing
PCD	Probability of conviction as perceived by the defendant	II–C-1, Ch. 3
PCP	Probability of conviction as perceived by the prosecutor	II–C-1, Ch. 3
PG	Probability of whether the defendant is actually guilty	II–C-1, Ch. 3
PL	Perceived probability of liability being established in a civil suit	I–A-1, Ch. 5

Threshold Probabilities:

Symbol	Represents	First Appearing
PC^*	Probability of conviction on trial that makes going to trial or pleading guilty without a bargain seem like equally desirable alternatives	II–B-3, Ch. 3
PS^*	Probability of a released defendant showing in court that makes holding or releasing him prior to trial seem like equally attractive alternatives	III–B, Ch. 5
PW^*	Probability of a released defendant committing a wrong or a crime that makes holding or releasing him prior to trial seem like equally attractive alternatives	III–B, Ch. 5

Sentences and Settlements:

Symbol	Represents	First Appearing
LS	Likely sentence in years or expected sentence value from either trial or nonnegotiated plea	I–A, Ch. 3
LS_1	Likely sentence from going to trial	II–A, Ch. 3
LS_2	Likely sentence from nonnegotiated plea	II–A, Ch. 3
LS^*	Likely sentence at point where going to trial or pleading without a negotiated bargain are equally attractive alternatives	II–B-3, Ch. 3
R	Result of clash between defendant and prosecutor	I–B-2, Ch. 4
S^*	Likely settlement at point of equilibrium or convergence point between the adjusted limits of defendant and prosecutor, where defendant's limit is higher than the prosecutor's	I–A-2, Ch. 4
S'	True settlement as known to an omniscient being	II–B-1, Ch. 5

Bonus Factors, Defendant:

Symbol	Represents	First Appearing
XD	Defendant's bonus factor in bargaining to be added to the defendant's unadjusted bargaining limit to obtain ALD	II–D-2, Ch. 3
$\%XD$	Defendant's percentage bonus factor to be multiplied by the defendant's unadjusted bargaining limit to obtain XD	II–D-2, Ch. 3

Discount Factors, Prosecutor:

Symbol	Represents	First Appearing
XP	Prosecutor's discount factor in bargaining, to be subtracted from the prosecutor's unadjusted bargaining limit to obtain ALP	II–D-2, Ch. 3
$\%XP$	Prosecutor's percentage discount factor, to be multiplied by a prosecutor's unadjusted bargaining limit to obtain XP	II–D-2, Ch. 3

Appendix

Bargaining Limits:

ALD	Adjusted bargaining limit of defendant	II-D-2, Ch. 3
ALP	Adjusted bargaining limit of prosecutor	II-D-2, Ch. 3
L	Bargaining limit for defendant or prosecutor	II-B-3, Ch. 4
LD	Defendant's unadjusted bargaining limit	II-A, Ch. 3
LP	Prosecutor's unadjusted bargaining limit	II-A, Ch. 3

Attitudes of Bargainers:

M	Middling attitude on optimism–pessimism scale	I-B-1, Ch. 4
O	Optimistic attitude	II-B-1, Ch. 4
O–P coefficient	Optimism–pessimism coefficient on a 0–1.00 scale	II-C-3, Ch. 3
P	Pessimistic attitude	I-B-1, Ch. 4

Exaggeration Factors:

EFD	Fraction less than 1 by which defendant multiplies his adjusted limit in order to arrive at initial offer	II-A, Ch. 4
EFP	Number more than 1 by which prosecutor multiplies his adjusted limit in order to arrive at initial offer	II-A, Ch. 4

Offer (Symbol can be preceded by a *D* or *P*)

O_{t0}	Initial offer, or offer at time 0	II-A, Ch. 4
O_{t1}	First counteroffer	II-A, Ch. 4
$O_{t2}\cdots O_{tn}$	Subsequent bargaining offers	II-A, Ch. 4
O_{ti}	Counteroffer at any time *i* or at any stage	II-C-2, Ch. 4
O_{ti-1}	Counteroffer of any previous stage, or time *i* minus one time unit	II-C-2, Ch. 4

Splitting Rates:

R	Splitting rate for defendant or prosecutor	II-C-2, Ch. 4
RD	Splitting rate in defendant's bargaining, or fraction of distance between his last offer and his bargaining limit	II-A, Ch. 4
RP	Splitting rate in prosecutor's bargaining, or fraction of distance between his last offer and his bargaining limit	II-A, Ch. 4

Time Designation:

t	Time (used as subscript like **i** and **n**)	II-A, Ch. 4
i	Time point *i* or stage *i* corresponding to any stage	II-C-3, Ch. 4
n	The last time point	
T	Stage number from 1 to *N* (used as variable)	II-C-3, Ch. 4

Benefits and Costs:

B	Benefits	II-C, Ch. 5
B/C ratio	Benefit/Cost ratio	III-C-3, Ch. 5
C	Cost	II-C, Ch. 5

Symbols	Represents	First Appearing
$L	Litigation costs in civil suit	I-A-1, Ch. 5
$S	Settlement costs in civil suit	I-A-1, Ch. 5

Discounting Future Value of Settlements:

A	Amount or future value of future payoff	I-A-2, Ch. 5
P	Principal or present value of future payoff	I-A-2, Ch. 5
r	Interest rate of an investment minus the inflation rate	I-A-2, Ch. 5

Variables, Types of:

X	Independent variable used to predict from	II-A, Ch. 3
Y	Dependent variable to be predicted to	II-A, Ch. 3

Regression Coefficients:

A or a	Value of variable being predicted to when variables being predicted from have zero values in a linear or log-linear relation	I-B, Ch. 3
B or b	Ratio between change in variable being predicted to and 1-unit change in the variable being predicted from, holding other variables constant	I-B, Ch. 3

Appendix 5B.
Basic Formulas Used

1. Expected values (or likely sentences associated with each choice):

$LS_2 = (1 - PC)(a) + (PC)(b)$ $LS_2 = a + (b - a)(PC)$

$LS_1 = (1 - PC)(c) + (PC)(d)$ $LS_1 = c + (d - c)(PC)$

2. Nonadjusted bargaining limits:

$$LD \text{ or } LP = LS_1 \text{ or } LS_2, \quad \text{whichever is lower}$$

3. Adjusted bargaining limits:

$ALD = LD + XD$ $XD = (\%XD)(LD)$

$ALP = LP - XP$ $XP = (\%XP)(LP)$

4. Likely settlement:

$$S^* = .5(ALD + ALP)$$

5. Threshold PC and LS (where either going to trial or pleading guilty without a bargain is equally attractive):

$$PC^* = \frac{a - c}{a - b - c + d}$$

$$LS^* = \frac{ad - bc}{a - b - c + d}$$

6. Offers:
   a. Initial offer:

   $$DO_{t0} = EFD(ALD) \quad PO_{t0} = EFP(ALP)$$

   b. First Counteroffer:

   $O_{t1} = O_{t0} + RD(ALD - O_{t0})$ $O_{t1} = O_{t0} - RP(O_{t1} - ALP)$

c. General counteroffer in terms of prior counteroffer:

$$O_{ti} = O_{ti} + R(L - O_{ti-1})$$

d. General counteroffer in terms of initial offer:
$$O_{ti} = L + (1 - R)^{ti} (O_{t0} - L)$$

7. Present value in time discounting:

$$P = \frac{A}{(1 + R)^t}$$

Note: See appendix 5A for the definitions of the symbols.

Part III.
Other Applications of Decision Theory to the the Legal Process

Introduction to Part III

Part I dealt with the one-person decision situation. Part II dealt with the two-person bargaining situation. This third part deals with other applications of decision theory to the legal process. An important other application involves group decision making as reflected in the work of juries and multiple-judge courts. Most of the research on juries has not involved a decision theory perspective, whereby jurors are viewed as seeking to maximize perceived benefits minus costs, discounted by the probabilities of the benefits and the costs occurring. Instead, much jury research has emphasized statistically explaining the variance between judges and jurors, among jurors, or among cases in actual or simulated jury trials. Other jury research has emphasized attitudes toward juries, delay reduction, juror characteristics, and jury deliberation.[1] A decision theory perspective is particularly useful in analyzing juror decision making because it enables one to establish in a meaningful way the threshold probability for individual jurors, as described in chapter 6. One can then test hypotheses concerning the effect of instructions and other variables on those threshold probabilities which, in turn, influence juror decisions. Such testing is substantially easier than trying to determine directly the effect of instructions and other variables on actual or experimental juror decisions. Such testing may be quite useful for increasing the objectivity, legal conformity, and accuracy of juror decision making.

Another important application of decision theory to group decision making in the legal process involves the decision of jurors or judges on multiple-judge courts to join with one coalition or another. That kind of decision making has not been studied with regard to jurors from a decision theory perspective as contrasted to a statistical perspective, but it has with regard to multiple-judge courts, especially the U.S. Supreme Court. For example, Glendon Schubert hypothesizes certain goals that each judge or group of judges might have in coalition formation. He then observes their behavior to see if it fits the hypothesized goals. If the behavior does fit the goals, he considers that as providing support for the accuracy of the hypothesized goals, although the behavior could be directed toward other goals or the goals could be achieved by other behavior. If the behavior does not fit the goals, Schubert considers that as a rejection of the hypothesized goals. The judges, however, may really have those goals, but may be unable to behave accordingly, because they may misperceive factual means-ends relations or because they may have other conflicting goals.[2] Walter Murphy, on the other hand, has been among those seeking to explain the dynamic bargaining process present on the Supreme Court, although he uses a verbal approach rather than a quantitative one.[3] David Rohde has shown particular concern for testing hypotheses that relate to the size of the winning coalition in the sense that anything more than 5/9, or 56 percent, represents possible waste with regard to what judicial principles could have been established, unless an image of unanimity was being sought.[4] Sidney Ulmer has developed a number of formulas for analyzing the relations between coalition size and the likelihood of error, which has important policy implications for the issue of what minimum-size coalition should be allowed for jury convictions.[5]

Chapter 7 links the decision theory perspective with the perspective of finding an optimum level or mix which is emphasized in the companion volume of Nagel and Neef, *Legal Policy Analysis: Finding an Optimum Level or Mix* (D.C. Heath, Lexington Books, 1977). That chapter on "Allocating Resources among Court Cases by Legal Counsel" belongs with decision theory since it involves making decisions in light of the contingent probabilities of obtaining a conviction in criminal cases or of establishing liability in personal injury cases. The decision, however, is not simply one of accepting rather than rejecting a client, or going to trial rather than settling out of court. Instead, it involves finding an optimum level of time to allocate to each case or an optimum mix of one's total time among a set of cases. As such, it is like the optimizing decisions that relate to finding an optimum percentage of defendants to release prior to trial, an optimum jury size, an optimum allocation of resources to various civil rights activities, or an optimum allocation of anticrime dollars to various cities and states. Decision makers and researchers who combine decision theory and optimization techniques in their methodological tool kits are better equipped to cope with diverse situations in the legal and political process. Such a tool kit will help them to deduce more accurately the effects of policy changes before the changes are adopted, as well as to determine an optimum decision strategy for maximizing given goals under varying conditions.

Chapter 8 deals with the important decision theory application of using decision theory to influence decision makers to make more socially desired decisions, especially in the context of would-be criminal law violators, pollution violators, or noncomplying public officials. This use can be contrasted with using decision theory (1) to arrive at optimum decisions from given values and facts, (2) to deduce a decision maker's factual perceptions from his values and decisions, (3) to deduce his values from his factual perceptions and decisions, or (4) to deduce what his decisions would be from changing his factual perceptions or value judgments. Attempting to influence his decisions as a fifth purpose is closely related to the fourth purpose of deducing or predicting changes in his decisions from relevant system changes. That fourth purpose, however, is not explicitly concerned with trying to engineer system changes that will produce socially desirable (or desired) decision changes.

Examples of the other four purposes have been given in the previous six chapters. Chapters 1 and 2 discussed optimizing behavior in making pretrial release decisions, and chapters 3, 4, and 5 discussed optimizing behavior in arriving at out-of-court settlements. Chapter 6 mentioned the problems of deducing a juror's perception of the probability of a defendant's guilt from knowing a juror's normative threshold probability and his decision to convict or acquit. It also mentioned deducing the high value judges place on obtaining convictions from knowing that judges do not instruct jurors in quantitative terms concerning the meaning of *beyond a reasonable doubt* and from reasonably assuming that judges are aware such instructions would reduce convictions. Chapter 5 was particularly concerned with the fourth purpose in the context of predicting changes in the likelihood and level of plea bargaining settlements from other changes in the judicial process. The fifth purpose of encouraging socially desired decisions has already been partly illustrated by the concern in chapter 1 for getting arraignment judges to show relatively more sensitivity to holding errors rather than convicting errors and in chapter 6 for getting jurors to have higher and more uniform threshold probabilities for voting to convict. Chapter 8 provides a fitting ending to this book by integrating many of the prior chapters into a context which emphasizes their relevance for encouraging socially desired behavior and which brings out how decision theory can suggest prescriptive proposals, generate predictive hypotheses, organize ideas, help test proposals, explain findings, and suggest data to gather in legal process research.

Notes

1. See references cited in note 2 of chapter 6.

2. See G. Schubert, *Quantitative Analysis of Judicial Behavior* 173-269 (1959); Schubert, "The Study of Judicial Decision-Making as an Aspect of Political Behavior," 52 *Am. Pol. Sci. Rev.* 1007, 1022 (1958); and Schubert, "Policy without Law: An Extension of the Certiorari Game," 14 *Stan. L. Rev.* 285 (1962).

3. See Murphy, *Elements of Judicial Strategy* (1964); Danelski, "The Influence of the Chief Justice in the Decisional Process of the Supreme Court," in Murphy and Pritchett, *Courts, Judges, and Politics* 525 (1974); and Murphy, "Marshaling the Court: Leadership, Bargaining, and the Judicial Process," 29 *U. Chi. L. Rev.* 640 (1962).

4. See Rohde, "Policy Goals and Opinion Coalitions in the Supreme Court," 16 *Midwest J. Pol. Sci.* 208 (1972); and Rohde, "A Theory of the Formation of Opinion Coalitions in the U.S. Supreme Court," in *Probability Models of Collective Decision-Making*, eds. R. Niemi and H. Weisberg (1972). Rohde draws heavily upon W. Riker and P. Ordeshook, *Positive*

Political Theory (1973) and W. Riker, *The Theory of Political Coalitions* (1962).

5. See Ulmer, *Courts as Small and Not so Small Groups* (1971); Ulmer, "Quantitative Analysis of Judicial Processes: Some Practical and Theoretical Applications," 28 *Law & Contemp. Prob.* 164, 176 (1963); and Zeisel, "And Then There Were None: The Diminution of the Federal Jury," 38 *U. Chi. L. Rev.* 710 (1971). Political scientists have also studied such matters as the measurement of cohesion in judicial coalitions, the extent to which judges with similar background characteristics tend to be in the same coalitions, and the measurement of the pivotal power or other power indices of coalitions. Much of this literature is reviewed in the first Ulmer item above. Most of it, however, does not contain a bargaining element or a deductive mathematical model like that associated with decision game theory.

6 Decision Theory and Juror Decision-Making

The purpose of this chapter is to describe how a decision theory perspective can be helpful in obtaining a better understanding of how jurors make decisions to convict or acquit and how those decisions are influenced by the characteristics of the jurors and the cases. Such an understanding, in turn, can be helpful in developing more meaningful instructions designed to increase the objectivity, legal conformity, and the accuracy of juror decision-making.[1]

The emphasis in this chapter is on individual juror propensities, rather than on the interaction among jurors or collective decision making. Individual juror propensities are the building blocks which combine to make the interaction patterns and the collective decisions. Both the individual and the interacting perspective may need more study, particularly from the viewpoint of individual decision theory, collective choice, and other deductive models that can help generate empirically testable hypotheses and synthesize empirical findings.[2]

I. The Basic Decision Theory Model

Decision theory refers to a perspective for analyzing decision which emphasizes that decision makers choose the alternative decision which they implicitly perceive as providing the greatest expected benefits minus costs of the other available decisions. In this context expected benefits mean the benefits which are perceived as following a given decision, discounted by the probability of the occurrence of some contingent event on which those benefits depend. Likewise, in this context expected costs mean the costs perceived as following a given decision, discounted by the probability of an event on which those costs depend.[3]

In the juror decision-making context, the alternative decisions are basically to vote to convict or to acquit. Sometimes the alternative decisions may include a question as to what the charge or crime should be, such as whether to convict or acquit of murder or manslaughter. In some states, jurors still participate in the sentencing decision, and the conviction alternative would thus have many subalternatives with regard to the sentence to recommend. In personal injury cases, the basic decisions are to vote to find the defendant liable or not liable, and if liable, how much damages to award. This chapter will emphasize the conviction-acquittal decision, but will also refer to other types of juror decisions.[4]

The amount of benefits (or satisfaction) and costs (or dissatisfaction) that a juror receives from voting to convict or acquit depends partly on whether the defendant is guilty or innocent. Those relations can be seen more clearly in figure 6-1, which provides a four-cell payoff matrix showing symbolically the amount of satisfaction and dissatisfaction for each of the four possible outcomes. Those outcomes include (1) voting to convict when the defendant is guilty, yielding a $+B$ quantity of satisfaction; (2) voting to convict when the defendant is innocent, yielding a $-A$ quantity of dissatisfaction; (3) voting to acquit when the defendant is guilty, yielding a $-B$ quantity of dissatisfaction; and (4) voting to acquit when the defendant is innocent, yielding a $+A$ quantity of satisfaction.[5]

To make the payoff matrix more meaningful, numbers are inserted to indicate what scores might be inserted by William Blackstone on a scale going from -100 (indicating maximum dissatisfaction) to $+100$ (indicating maximum satisfaction). The numbers reflect the fact that Blackstone stated that it is better for ten guilty persons to go free rather than convict one innocent person. Thus if convicting an innocent person yields a -100 level of dissatisfaction, then for Blackstone acquitting a guilty person would yield a -10 level of dissatisfaction, or would be one-tenth as bad. Likewise, for Blackstone, acquitting an innocent person would be ten times as satisfying as convicting a guilty person, yielding the numbers $+100$ and $+10$ for the two satisfaction-producing cells in the matrix.

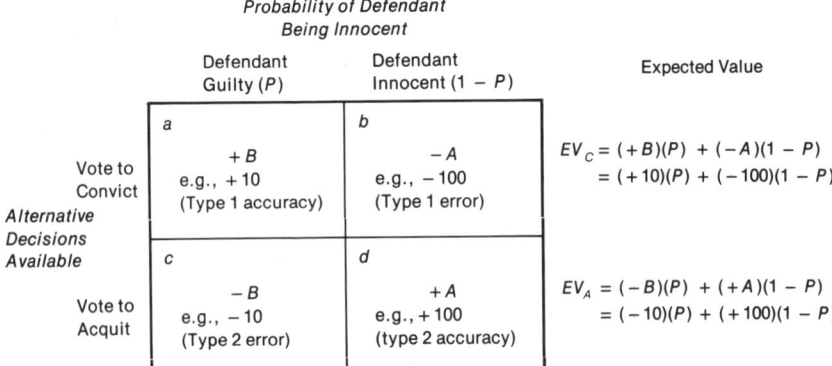

General Presumption: Defendant is innocent. Type 1 error rejects presumption when true. Type 2 error accepts presumption when false.

The values in this table are those for William Blackstone, who said ten guilty persons should go free rather than convict one innocent person.

Threshold probability: $P^* = A/(A + B) = 100(100 + 10) = .91$, meaning Blackstone would require greater than .91 probability of guilt before he would convict.

Figure 6-1. The Basic Decision Theory Model of Juror Decision Making.

The expected value of convicting is logically equal to the benefits of convicting minus the costs. The benefits are symbolically, $+B$, or numerically $+10$ in the Blackstone example, and the costs are symbolically $-A$, or numerically -100. We cannot, however, simply determine the difference between $+10$ and -100 in order to calculate the expected value of convicting, since (1) the $+10$ satisfaction is achieved only if the defendant is guilty, which we can symbolically say has a probability of P, and (2) the -100 satisfaction is achieved only if the defendant is innocent, which we can symbolically say has a complementary probability of $1 - P$. Thus, the expected benefits are $+B$ discounted or multiplied by P; the expected costs are $-A$ discounted by $1 - P$; and the expected net benefits thus represent the benefits $(+B)(P)$ plus the costs $(-A)(1 - P)$, as indicated to the right of the first row of the payoff matrix. The same kind of analysis can be done to determine the expected value of acquitting. It is equal to the expected benefits of acquitting $(-B)(P)$ plus the expected costs of acquitting $(+A)(1 - P)$, as indicated to the right of the second row of the payoff matrix.

Given those expected net benefits of convicting and of acquitting, the next logical thing to calculate might be the value of P (that is, the perceived probability of guilty) when those two expected values are exactly equal. To calculate that equilibrium or threshold P, we simply solve for P as one unknown in the one equation

$$(+B)(P) + (-A)(1 - P) = (-B)(P) + (+A)(1 - P)$$

Doing so reveals that the threshold P (symbolized P^*) equals $A/(A + B)$. For Blackstone, his threshold P would thus be $100/(100 + 10)$, or .91. This means that for Blackstone the perceived probability of guilt would have to be greater than .91 for Blackstone to vote to convict, and would have to be less than .91 for him to vote to acquit if he wanted to always vote for the alternative that would give the highest expected value or benefits minus costs.[6] As a general statement, P^* so calculated means the perceived probability of guilt above which a juror would vote to convict and below which a juror would vote to acquit. If $P = P^*$, then voting neither to convict nor to acquit would give a greater expected value, and a decision could be reached by flipping a coin, although it is probably extremely rare that a given juror in a given case perceives P to be exactly at P^*.[7]

The basic formula of $P^* = A/(A + B)$ can be made both more complicated and more simple. One complication is to drop the assumption that the amount of satisfaction received from acquitting an innocent defendant is equal but opposite in sign to the amount of dissatisfaction received from convicting an innocent defendant. Likewise, one can drop the simplifying assumption that the amount of satisfaction from convicting a guilty defendant is equal but opposite in sign to the amount of dissatisfaction received from acquitting a guilty defendant. If one drops those assumptions, then instead of labeling the four cells $+B$, $-A$, $-B$, and $+A$, one can label them a, b, c, and d to represent the amount of satisfaction or dissatisfaction received from each possibility. Doing so makes the expected value of convicting equal to $(a)(P) + (b)(1 - P)$ and the expected value of acquitting equal to $(c)(P) + (d)(1 - P)$. If one sets those two expressions equal to each other and solves for P, then P^* becomes $(d - b)/(a - b - c + d)$. Under that approach, one can still numerically anchor the most satisfying alternative at $+100$ and the most dissatisfying alternative at -100.

A simplifying approach is to think not in terms of determining four values to arrive at P^*, namely a, b, c, and d, or even two values, namely $-A$ and $-B$. Rather, one can calculate P^* for any given juror in any given type of case by determining what the juror's trade-off ratio is between $-A$ and $-B$, which is the same thing as asking how many times worse does he or she consider it to convict an innocent defendant as contrasted to acquitting a guilty defendant. That trade-off ratio can be symbolized X, and then P^* can be calculated by the formula $P^* = X/(X + 1)$, which is algebraically equal to $P^* = A/(A + B)$ and also algebraically equal (if one makes the converse assumptions about the relations between cells 1 and 3 and cells 2 and 4) to $P^* = (d - b)/(a - b - c + d)$.

The approach of calculating $P^* = X/(X + 1)$ is especially useful where one is trying to determine one's own threshold probability and there is no concern with the honesty of the answers received. It is also useful if many threshold probabilities are to be calculated for different cases since the other approaches might involve an excessive number of like questions that may bore or irritate the respondents. The approach of calculating P^* from information on all four cells is especially useful where respondents do not indicate that cells b and c are dissatisfying and that cell b is the more dissatisfying. No matter how unusual the respondent's preferences or values are, a meaningful P^* can still be calculated by using the four-cell approach. For example, a respondent may indicate that all four cells are equally satisfying or dissatisfying. Inserting a $+100$ for a, b, c, and d (or a -100) yields $P^* = .50$, meaning such a respondent should logically vote to convict whenever the perceived probability of guilt is greater than $.50$. Likewise, by using the four cell formula, a respondent who indicates receiving more dissatisfaction from acquitting the guilty than convicting the innocent (and more satisfaction from convicting the guilty than acquitting the innocent) will receive a P^* of less than $.50$. A respondent who considers it more satisfying to acquit than convict a defendant regardless whether the defendant is guilty or innocent will receive a P^* greater than 1.00, meaning no perceived probability of guilt exists which will enable such a respondent to vote to convict. Likewise, the respondent who considers it more satisfying to convict rather than acquit an innocent or guilty defendant in a given case will receive a P^* less

Decision Theory and Juror Decision-Making 191

than 0, meaning no P exists which will enable such a respondent to vote to acquit; that is, no perceived probability can exist below 0.[8]

To summarize the basic decision theory model, we can say that it conceives juror decision making (D) as a function of a juror's perception of the probability that the defendant is guilty (P) and the juror's threshold probability above which he will vote to convict and below which he will vote to acquit (P^*). The model further conceives of P^* as a function of the juror's relative cost evaluation of a type 1 error of convicting an innocent defendant (A) and a type 2 error of acquitting a guilty defendant (B). Those relations logically follow from the basic assumption that people, when confronted with a choice, will choose the alternative that they perceive as providing them with the greater benefits minus costs in light of their own benefit-cost values.[9] The interesting methodological questions relate to, How can we measure the key variables in the model, namely D, P, A, and B? The interesting empirical or causal questions are, What causes variations in those variables across people and across cases? The interesting normative or policy questions are, What rules can be established in light of the model and the possible empirical findings so as to (1) minimize variations across people and across cases, (2) bring P^* up to a range that the law seems to require, and (3) increase the accuracy of the perceived probability of guilt? Those are the questions discussed in the subsequent sections of this chapter.

II. Measuring the Variables

Figure 6-2 provides the key parts of a questionnaire with which the authors have been working to ascertain the relative values of a type 1 error versus a type 2 error of psychology students and other potential jurors. This questionnaire approach, in effect, asks for only two values from the payoff matrix rather than the more complicated four-values approach. It avoids the simpler approach of just asking for a trade-off ratio, though, because it is felt that some subtlety is needed in order to keep students from responding by simply giving what they consider to be a socially desirable or legally accepted answer rather than their true personal feelings.

Obtaining true values in a simple way is the main advantage of this measurement approach over alternatives that might be used. For example, asking respondents directly what their threshold probability of guilt is above which they would vote to convict and below which they would vote to acquit has the dual disadvantage of (1) being harder to understand and more likely to produce nonsense responses, and (2) if understood, being likely to produce fudged responses in the .90 to .99 range, which people seem to think is what the law requires. This is a problem with any kind of attitudinal questioning where one must be subtle enough to get at the

General Statement: Two things can happen if you *convict* someone. One is that he is guilty (possibility *a*), and the other is that he is innocent (possibility *b*). Likewise, two things could happen if you *acquit* someone. One is that he is guilty (possibility *c*), and the other is that he is innocent (possibility *d*).

Question (Using the two-cell approach)   *Response*

1. Which one or more of these four possibilities, if they were to occur, would make you feel more displeased than pleased?

    _____
    (*a, b, c,* or *d*)

2. Of those dissatisfying occurrences, which is the most dissatisfying? Let's score this −100 to have a lower anchor point.

    _____
    (*a, b, c,* or *d*)

3. If the most dissatisfying alternative is scored −100 on a 0 to −100 scale, then where would you score the next to the most dissatisfying alternative? Zero means neither dissatisfying or satisfying, and −100 means most dissatisfying.

    _____
    (0 to −100)

Note to the researcher: To determine the respondent's threshold probability from the above information, calculate $100/(100 + c)$ where c is the unsigned response to question 3 assuming the response to question 1 is *b* and *c* and the response to question 2 is *b*. If those assumptions do not apply, then use the four-cell approach to obtain a threshold probability.

Question (Using the four-cell approach)   *Response*

1. Which one or more of these four possibilities, if they were to occur, would make you feel more displeased than pleased?

    _____
    (*a, b, c,* or *d*)

2. Of those dissatisfying occurrences, which is the most dissatisfying? Let's score this −100 to have a lower anchor point.

    _____
    (*a, b, c,* or *d*)

3. If the most dissatisfying alternative is scored −100 on a 0 to −100 scale, then where would you score the next to the most dissatisfying alternative? Zero means neither dissatisfying or satisfying, and −100 means most dissatisfying.

    _____
    (0 to −100)

4. Which one or more of these four possibilities, if they were to occur, would make you feel more pleased than displeased?

    _____
    (*a, b, c,* or *d*)

5. Of those satisfying occurrences, which is the most satisfying? Let's score this +100 to have an upper anchor point.

    _____
    (*a, b, c,* or *d*)

6. If the most satisfying alternative is scored +100 on a 0 to +100 scale, then where would you score the next to the most satisfying alternative?

    _____
    (0 to +100)

The following questions are optional:

7. Are you sure you want your next to the best choice to be that close or that far away from the best choice, and that close or that far away from the neutral position? If not, please revise your answer accordingly.

    _____
    (possible revised number for question 3)

8. Are you also sure you want your next to the worst choice to be as close or as far away from your worst choice as you initially put it? If not, please revise that evaluation accordingly.

    _____
    (possible revised number for question 6)

Note to the researcher: To determine the respondent's threshold probability from the above information, calculate $(d - b)/(a - b - c + d)$ where those letters correspond to the signed values of each of the four cells.

Figure 6-2. Some Questions for Obtaining a Person's Values regarding a Conviction-Acquittal Decision.

respondent's true feelings, but not so subtle as to lose meaningful communication.

This approach to obtaining the relative values of a type 1 error versus a type 2 error can be applied to a variety of different case types like rape, robbery, or consumer fraud. In doing so, one need not specify detailed facts as one would in setting up a hypothetical case situation. In fact, we would not want much detail because we are trying to determine an individual's threshold of probability with regard to broad case types rather than specific cases. We also have found that the more cases an individual is presented with in this context, the more the individual's threshold probabilities tend to be alike. In other words, after a few cases, a respondent tends to give answers similar to his or her previous answers, possibly out of a feeling that doing otherwise would be inconsistent or out of a lessening interest to think out different responses. Therefore, the order in which the case types are presented has to be varied so the threshold probabilities will not be influenced by the order.

In the context of measuring the variables, the most important variables to measure that might account for variance on the key dependent variable of P^* are (1) variables that relate to the respondent's characteristics like sex, liberalism, and occupation or occupational aspirations, which can be measured the way they traditionally are; (2) variables that relate to the case characteristics which, as mentioned before, can be measured by simply specifying before each set of six questions like those in figure 6-2 what type of case is involved; and (3) variables that relate to instructions that might be given by a judge to a jury. These instructions can be inserted at the beginning of the questionnaire schedule. However, only one set of instructions should be used; the instructions change during the questionnaire, the earlier instructions tend to influence the later decisions. For example, one set of respondents could be instructed that to convict in criminal cases requires the probability of guilt to be established beyond a reasonable doubt. Another set of respondents could be instructed that to convict in criminal cases requires the probability of guilt to be established beyond a 9 out of 10 probability, and third set of respondents could receive no instruction concerning a conviction standard.

Other variables appropriate to measure as part of the testing of the causal and policy implications of the basic model might include the respondent's perception of the probability of guilt. This can be determined by simply asking each respondent what percentage of the time he or she thinks defendants in general or defendants in specific types of cases are truly guilty. Asking those questions may be quite useful for determining the reciprocal relations between the perceived probability of guilt and the threshold probability for voting to convict or acquit. However, asking those questions in so general a manner would not be useful for determining whether the voting of a respondent or juror is a function of both the respondent's perceived probability of guilt and his threshold probability, as stated in the model. Making that determination would require providing the respondent with at least one very specific hypothetical case and then asking him or her what he perceives the defendant's probability of guilt to be in that case (P) and whether he would vote to convict or acquit (D). Doing so would provide a useful check on both the model and the measuring system because if respondents do not consistently vote to convict when their perceived P is greater than their P^* and consistently vote to acquit when their perceived P is less than their P^*, then something must be wrong with either the model or the measurement. There is more likely, though, to be something wrong with the precision of the measurement, since the model seems so logically simple.[10]

One desirable aspect of the model and the measurement is that the respondent is unable to force a consistency between his decision, his perceived P, and his threshold P^*. This is so because if the respondent says he perceives the probability of guilt as being .70, he does not know whether that .70 is above or below his P^* figure because he is unlikely to know how to translate his responses concerning the relative value of type 1 and type 2 errors into a threshold probability. He may, however, have a notion that the threshold probability is supposed to be about .90, even though his values yield a threshold probability of .65. He may therefore vote to acquit because his perceived P is below his notion of what P^* is supposed to be, even though his actual P^* is .65; therefore, if he is being logical, he should vote to convict. This illustrates the need for adding one or more questions to the analysis to ask the respondent what he thinks the threshold probability for conviction should be in probability terms. Doing so, however, is likely to force a consistency among his decision, his perceived P, and his normative P^*, as contrasted to his actual P^*. The confounding influence of what we have just referred to as a respondent's normative P^* would have to be statistically controlled for in order to test the empirical validity of the model's basic idea that juror voting is a function of P and actual P^*, assuming other variables are held constant.

This discussion raises the fundamental question of which of those two measures is a more valid reflection of a respondent's true standard for convicting, namely, his P^*, which is obtained by directly asking him, or his P^*, which is obtained by asking him about his relative values of a type 1 and type 2 error and then inputting that information into a decision theory calculation discussed in figure 6-1. The advantage of the direct approach is that it is probably easier for the respondent to handle, and thus one need not worry that his responses reflect a misunderstanding of the question. The advantage of the indirect approach, which probably makes it more valid, is that it is not so easy for the respondent to understand what is happening and thus not so easy for him to give a response which reflects what he thinks ought to be the threshold probability or what he thinks the law requires, while at the same time the indirect approach is not so subtle as to necessarily lead to misunderstanding and miscommunication.[11]

Although an indirect approach may be desirable for obtaining P^* through A and B, an indirect approach for obtaining P^* through P and D, or for obtaining P through P^* and D, does not make sense. For example, knowing that an individual perceives the probability of guilt as being .70 and votes to convict merely tells us that his P^* must be less than .70; but we cannot know how much less unless we have a series of cases to observe exactly when his lowered P results in a vote to acquit rather than convict. Likewise, if he had voted to acquit with a P of .70, we would only know that his P^* was greater than .70, but not how much greater. Also, if we know an individual has a P^* of .80 and votes to convict, this merely tells us that he must have perceived the probability of guilt as being greater than .80, but we cannot know how much greater. Likewise, if he had voted to acquit, that would merely tell us that his P must be below .80, but not how much below.

Another variable to be measured is the threshold probability which the law requires in criminal cases. By that P^* we do not mean the threshold probability of a given individual measured directly or indirectly for criminal cases in general for specific types of criminal cases. We also do not mean what the respondents think the law requires. Rather, we are referring to an analysis of the court cases to try to translate the language used there into a probability figure. Such an analysis, however, seldom yields quantitative information. Instead, judges either use the phrase *beyond a reasonable doubt* without defining it, or they define it in terms of other words, like *a very high standard of conviction*. They may also define it by saying what it is not, as when a judge says "beyond a reasonable doubt does not mean beyond any doubt at all, and it does not mean by a mere preponderance of the evidence."[12]

Perhaps the best quantitative statement for what the constitutional framers meant in referring to due process in the Constitution was the Blackstone conviction standard that it is better to let ten guilty go free than to convict one innocent person, which, as we have seen, logically translates into a .91 probability threshold. Further evidence that a figure in the .90 range is what the law implicitly, although not explicitly, requires is given by the survey which Rita Simon made of judges asking them what *beyond a reasonable doubt* meant to them in probability terms.[13] The responses did tend to be over .90. That is a useful figure to compare with the threshold probabilities calculated for the potential jurors in an empirical survey, and it is particularly useful as a goal to seek to push jurors toward through appropriate judicial instructions, that is, appropriate in the sense of being effective in changing their threshold probabilities to be about .90.[14]

The discussion concerning the measurement of the variables within the model and the variables that might explain variance on P^*, P, and D has proceeded from the perspective of conducting a questionnaire survey of potential jurors rather than actual jurors. Everything said, though, could be applied to actual jurors after they have heard and decided a criminal case. They could be asked their relative type 1 and type 2 error values, their perception of the probability of the defendant's guilt, how they voted, their notion of what *beyond a reasonable doubt* means or ought to mean in probability terms, and other attitudinal and background questions. Before doing so, however, the model and measurement should be tested further and applied in the context of nonjurors who could become jurors. The testing that has been done so far has been quite preliminary and has involved mainly psychology and political science students at the University of Illinois. The findings are too preliminary to be reported in a quantitative manner. They are, however, quite suggestive of some interesting hypotheses, which are reported in the subsequent sections of this chapter and which will be more meaningfully tested by the authors and possibly by others.

III. Characteristics of the Jurors and Cases that Influence the Model Inputs and Outputs

The preliminary analysis that has been done involved applying questions like those in figure 6-2 to determining the threshold probabilities of various types of respondents in rape, robbery, and consumer fraud cases. Often the samples were quite small, and all we can report here are some general tendencies with reasons why they might make sense. The variables that explain variance in the threshold probabilities are also the same variables that explain variance in the perceived probability of guilt and in the voting decisions. Therefore, it usually seems appropriate to discuss what accounts for variance in the threshold probabilities.

In general, the threshold probabilities tend to be quite low compared to the .90 figure that the law seems to require and the close-to-.90 figure that most of the respondents said they thought the law requires or ought to require. The actual threshold probabilities tended to average about .55 and thus were no different from what one might expect to find if the respondents were operating under the civil case standard of *by a preponderance or a majority of the evidence,* rather than the criminal case standard of *beyond a reasonable doubt.*[15] Some of the respondents who considered themselves to be staunch civil libertarians were quite surprised to see their threshold probabilities calculated so far below .90. After the calculation was made, some of them sought to revise the values they had assigned to the cells in the payoff matrix in order to raise their P^* calculation. This was especially the case where they had been asked to assign values to all four cells rather than just the two error cells and were thus less able to fudge their answers to make P^* approximately .90. As an interesting experiment, the reader might try applying the questions of figure 6-2 to one of his or her civil libertarian friends to see if similar reactions are received.

Although the indirectly calculated threshold probabilities tend to be substantially lower than the threshold probabilities that respondents think they should have for both liberal and conservative respondents, liberal respondents do have somewhat higher threshold probabilities than conservative respondents. This is more so, as one would expect, where liberalism is measured by attitudinal items that specifically deal with sensitivity to the safeguards for the innocent in criminal proceedings, rather than general civil libertarian liberalism or liberalism that includes economic matters. On demographic variables like sex and career aspirations, the differences are too small to be worth mentioning, especially when the measuring instrument deals with the respondent's general threshold probability rather than his threshold probability in specific types of cases. Likewise, the differences across types of cases tend to be small if the demographic groups are equally represented. For example, the threshold probability in rape cases is about the same as that in robbery cases if there are an equal number of males and females responding to both types of cases.[16]

On the other hand, the differences between demographic groups and types of cases become quite substantial if one makes comparisons that take into consideration the interactions between those two dimensions. For example, the threshold probabilities of males in rape cases are quite higher than females in rape cases, meaning males are relatively more concerned about convicting an innocent defendant in rape cases and females are relatively more concerned about acquitting a guilty defendant. Likewise, the threshold probability in robbery cases is higher than the threshold probability in rape cases if one compares only those two types of cases with female respondents, meaning females are relatively more concerned about convicting an innocent defendant in robbery cases than they are in rape cases. Liberal females seem to be even less sensitive to convicting an innocent defendant in rape cases than conservative females, although liberal females and males are generally more sensitive to convicting innocent defendants than conservative females and males.

In the consumer fraud cases, business students indicated higher threshold probabilities than liberal arts students. Likewise, conservative students also indicated higher threshold probabilities, given the positive correlation between being a business student and being more conservative on both economic and civil libertarian liberalism. That conservatism manifested itself in a lower threshold and lower sensitivity to convicting the innocent in robbery cases which balanced their higher threshold and higher sensitivity to convicting the innocent in consumer fraud cases. Open-ended interviewing tended to reveal that the concept of defendant or innocent defendant was not as applicable to businessmen defendants by liberal students as to robbery defendants, and the concept of defendant or guilty defendant was not as applicable to businessmen defendants by business students as to robbery defendants.

In addition to accounting for variations on P^* (and also on P and D) by looking to the characteristics of the cases and the respondents, one can also account for variations on P^* by looking to variations on P and D, and vice versa. Those relationships are not just spurious correlations in the sense that P^*, P, and D are all three determined by case and juror characteristics. Rather, the preliminary analysis tends to show that P^* is partly determined by P and D, and P is partly determined by P^* and D, although the basic model indicates only that D is determined by P^* and P, which are independent of each other. More specifically, one finding stemming from the preliminary analysis, for example, is that if a respondent through judicial instructions is forced to raise his P^* value from .60 to .90, then doing so tends to have the effect of causing his P values in the same cases to go up from something like .65 to .95 so that he can continue to convict. Likewise, if we force a lowering of P^* from .90 to .60 for respondents who formerly perceived P as being .85, they might now perceive P as being .55 so they can continue to acquit.[17]

Given the possibly reciprocal causation nature of P and P^*, further experimentation might also reveal that if we change the case facts so that P goes down from .82 to .62, then individuals who were formerly convicting with a P^* of .80 might change their P^* to .60 so they could still convict. Likewise, if we change the case facts so that P goes up from .62 to .82, then individuals who were formerly acquitting with a P^* of .65 might change their P^* to .85 so they could still acquit. In other words, what may often be happening is a kind of knee-jerk decision (D) based on general notions of liberalism and conservatism with the assessments of P and P^* being at least partly rationalizations for the decision rather than implicit preliminary calculations leading to the decision.

The extent to which P and P^* are implicit preliminary calculations leading to a decision probably depends on the cost of gathering and processing information relevant to P and P^*. That cost (C) is additional to the cost of making an error of convicting an innocent defendant (A) and the cost of acquitting a guilty defendant (B). The value of C, in turn, probably depends on how intensely the individual feels about his or her general conservatism-liberalism or his conservatism-liberalism specific to the type of case involved. C also probably depends on the amount of education and intelligence the individual has, since thinking rationally (rather than out of knee-jerk habit) is probably easier and thus costs less for better educated, more intelligent people, although the emotional intensity variable may be more important than the intelligence-education variable.[18]

Bayesian probability theory provides a method whereby the perceived probability of guilt, given the evidence, is calculated from (1) the probability of guilt regardless of the evidence and (2) the capability or likelihood of the evidence indicating guilt. More specifically, the theory states that jurors implicitly follow, or rationally should follow, a four-step process. First, determine the odds[19] of the defendant being guilty regardless of the evidence, which equals $P(G)/P(-G)$. Second, determine the likelihood ratio, which equals $P(E|G)/P(E|-G)$. This is the probability of the evidence given that the defendant is guilty divided by the probability of the evidence given that the defendant is not guilty. Third, multiply those two ratios to determine the odds of the defendant being guilty, given the evidence, which is symbolized $P(G|E)/[1 - P(G|E)]$. Fourth, convert those odds into a probability of guilt, given the evidence, which is symbolized $P(G|E)$, or simply P. To make that conversion use the formula $P = \text{odds}/(\text{odds} + 1)$ which follows algebraically from the formula $\text{odds} = P/(1 - P)$. Nothing in our decision theory model conflicts with the notion that the perceived probability of guilt is based on the above kind of reasoning. However, this kind of four-step, decomposed reasoning does seem sufficiently complicated that it is questionable whether jurors do it implicitly, let alone explicitly, as contrasted to arriving at P via a more holistic or Gestalt approach. Arriving at D by thinking in terms of P and P^* seems more feasible, although both D and P may be arrived at via a holistic approach or both via a decomposed approach that involves combining separate elements.[20]

One type of variable that might explain variations in threshold probabilities across different places would be the characteristics of those places. For example, one would expect a higher threshold probability (that is, a higher than 10-to-1 trade-off ratio) in those places where there is more liberalism, less fear of crime, higher prison holding costs, and more property owners where one is dealing with crimes against property. In the preliminary analysis, there was no breakdown of the student respondents by urban versus rural community, by North versus South, or by demographic type of state or city. There is, however, probably more variance across individuals than across places, and many of the characteristics of places are just aggregate characteristics of individuals.

In summary, our preliminary causal findings tend to indicate the following. (1) In general, the threshold probabilities tend to be substantially lower than the .90 level implied by Blackstone and explicitly stated by judges in direct questioning, regardless of the type of jurors or cases which we surveyed. (2) In specific types of cases, the threshold probabilities tend to differ substantially from one group of potential jurors to another. (3) Jurors often may decide first on whether to convict or acquit and then an appropriate probability of guilt and a conviction standard. Those findings raise the questions of (1) how can jurors be better instructed to apply higher threshold probabilities, (2) how jurors can be better instructed in order to decrease the differences across different background and attitudinal groups, and (3) how jurors can be better instructed so as to increase the likelihood that they will consciously think about the defendant's probability of guilt and the conviction standard before, not after, deciding how to vote.

IV. Judicial Instructions to Increase Objectivity, Conformity with the Law, and Accurate Decision Making

Our preliminary findings indicate that the conviction threshold probabilities of males are substantially higher than females in rape cases. The male threshold probability, however, is likely to go down and the female threshold probability is likely to go up if they are instructed in the following manner:

> Social science research tends to show that males are more reluctant to convict rape defendants than females. When you go into the jury room if you are a male and you feel reluctant to convict, ask yourself whether your reluctance is based on the facts of the case or on your identifying with the defendant. If you are a female and you feel relatively willing to convict, ask yourself whether your willingness is based on the facts of the case or on your identifying with the victim.

One could develop a similar instruction for other types of cases in which different types of jurors tend to differ substantially in their threshold probabilities in order to reduce those differences. One, however, might raise the question of whether such instructions are eliminating bias or introducing an opposite bias. *Group bias* in this context as contrasted to individual bias can be defined as being present when one demographic group decides certain cases substantially different from the opposite demographic group, whether the groups be males versus females, young versus old, or business-oriented versus consumer-oriented jurors. There is no need to say that one group in those pairs is biased or more biased as compared to the other group, only that certain cases bring out a divergence or difference between the groups. Perhaps the word *divergence* is a better, more neutral word than *bias* or *lack of objectivity*. In light of that definition of bias, an instruction which reduces the divergence is reducing bias and not introducing an opposite bias unless it causes a divergence in the opposite direction such that females now have a substantially higher threshold probability in rape cases than males.

Although the above equalizing type of instruction does seem to reduce divergence, as indicated by our rough pilot study, that type of instruction does not substantially increase conformity with the legal notion that the threshold probability should be about .90. More specifically, what seems to be happening is that males in rape cases who are uninstructed start out with an average threshold probability of about .70, and females who are uninstructed start out with an average threshold probability of about .50. If one then takes another random group of males and gives them the equalizing instruction, their threshold probability tends to drop to about .60; and if one takes another random group of females and gives them the equalizing instruction, their threshold probability tends to rise to about .60. Both groups, however, are substantially below the .90 figure.

As part of a crude experiment to raise the threshold probability of potential jurors, we randomly divided small samples of students into (1) those who received no instructions, (2) those who were instructed by being told that to convict requires evidence that the defendant is guilty beyond a reasonable doubt, (3) those who were instructed that to convict requires evidence that the defendant is guilty beyond a .90 probability of guilt, or a 9-out-of-10 probability, and (4) those who were instructed that leading constitutional authorities have been quoted as saying that it is ten times as bad to convict one innocent person as it is to acquit one guilty person.

The sample sizes of males and females in each of those four groups were too small for the results to be statistically significant, but the pattern which may be found in further testing might run roughly as follows:

	Males	*Females*
No instruction	.65	.45
Beyond reasonable doubt	.75	.60
.90 probability	.85	.75
10-to-1 trade-off	.90	.90

That pattern is an oversimplification, but it illustrates the idea that threshold-raising instructions can have the simultaneous effect of raising the probability of threshold and equalizing divergent probability thresholds. This pattern also points up that one is likely to find that merely using words like *beyond a reasonable doubt* does not sufficiently raise the threshold probability, whereas more quantitative instructions do, at least as measured by our payoff matrix approach, especially quantitative instructions that emphasize Blackstone's 10-to-1 trade-off.

Few jurisdictions provide for instructing jurors as to the meaning of *beyond a reasonable doubt*. The justifications offered for not providing such instructions tend to emphasize that attempting to define a conviction standard will merely confuse or bias jurors.[21] The real justification might be that legislators and state supreme court judges who promulgate judicial instructions may be aware that giving more explicit precision to the notion of "beyond a reasonable doubt" will tend to increase the probability of threshold and make convictions more difficult.[22] It might be interesting to ask judges whether they perceive more precise instructions on conviction standards as likely to decrease convictions and whether they think conviction rates are too low, in order to determine the extent to which those two attitudes go together. It might be even more interesting to determine the extent to which the increased probabilty threshold stemming from more precise instructions would actually increase convictions. As was pointed out in the previous section, merely raising P^* does not necessarily change D if raising P^* causes P to go up proportionately or if P was already higher than the new P^*.

One variation on the instructions which seems to affect the threshold probabilities of jurors is to talk about a given crime, sometimes mentioning the penalty and sometimes not mentioning it. As one might hypothesize, when the severity of the penalty is mentioned, the threshold probability for conviction tends to go up, and the likelihood of conviction may thus tend to go down. Along related lines, one might note that asking potential jurors about benefits and costs of convicting and acquitting guilty and innocent persons may, in general, lead to lower threshold probabilities and an increased likelihood of conviction than jurors actually have. This may be so because the potential jurors are not hearing actual cases in which a defendant's freedom is at stake. Under those more realistic circumstances, actual jurors may have higher threshold probabilties and a decreased likelihood of conviction. That occurrence, however, should not substantially affect the findings that relate to the extent to which different types of jurors, cases, and instructions correspond to relatively higher or lower threshold probabilities.[23]

One type of instruction that we did not try even in our crude pilot study is an instruction to use the rational model approach to jury decision making. In other words, the basic decision theory model around which this chapter has been built can be used not just to describe juror decision making, which it may not do so well because of what we have referred to as knee-jerk or habituated decisions. In addition to that use, the basic model can also serve a prescriptive purpose by instructing jurors roughly as follows:

> Before voting to convict or acquit, you should decide for yourself what is the probability that the defendant is guilty. By *probability* in that context, we mean that if the circumstances and evidence in this type of case were to come up about 100 times, how many times out of those 100 do you think the defendant would be truly guilty? Before voting to convict or acquit, you should also bear in mind that our legal system requires a high probability of guilt before we will allow someone to be convicted. By *high probability* in that context, we mean the evidence should indicate the defendant is so guilty that 90 out of 100 people with this evidence would be truly guilty; or, to put the matter differently, our legal system considers it about 10 times as bad to convict an innocent person as it is to acquit a guilty person.

With an instruction like that, it seem plausible that the tendency would decrease for P, (or the perceived probability of guilt) to go up or down depending on one's P^* value. Likewise, it seems plausible that the tendency would decrease for P^*, (or the threshold probability) to go up or down depending on one's perceived P in a given case. In other words, that kind of instruction may be shown to be capable of reducing the rationalization approach of partly deciding first and then justifying one's decision in terms of an appropriate P and P^*. Doing so should result in more accurate decisions in the sense of decisions that reflect the facts, rather than facts made to fit the decisions.[24]

Instructions like the above should also result in decisions that are more in conformity with the law as clarified by Blackstone's commentary and surveys of judges concerning the high threshold probability which the law requires. In addition, instructions like the above should result in decisions that involve a minimum of divergence between different demographic groups.[25] It will be interesting to see what future experimentation yields with this kind of decision theory model, and what impact such future experimentation might have on improving judicial instructions.[26]

Notes

1. The authors are grateful to Martin Kaplan of the Psychology Department at Northern Illinois University, Judge David Strawn of the Florida Eighteenth Judicial Circuit, Michael Fried of the State's Attorneys Office in Detroit, and James Davis of the Psychology Department at the University of Illinois for their helpful comments and stimuli concerning this chapter.

2. For surveys of jury research see Rita James Simon, ed., *The Jury System in America: A Critical Overview* (Sage, 1975); Elizabeth Prescott, *Facets of the Jury System: A Survey* (National Center for State Courts, 1976); Howard Erlanger, "Jury Verdict Research in America: Its Past and Future," 4 *L. & Soc. Rev.* 345-370 (1970); James Davis, Robert Bray, and Robert Holt, "The Empirical Study of Social Decision Processes in Juries," in *Law, Justice and the Individual in Society,* eds. June Tapp and Felice Levine (Holt, Rinehart and Winston, 1977); Amiram Elwork and Bruce Dennis Sales, "Psycholegal Research on the Jury and Trial Processes" in *Modern Legal Medicine and Forensic Science,* eds. C. Petty, W. Curran, and L. McGarry (F.A. Davis, 1978); and Rita James Simon and Prentice Marshall, "The Jury System," in *The Rights of the Accused: In Law and Action,* ed. S. Nagel (Sage, 1972). For other deductive models applied to the legal process besides a decision theory perspective, see S. Nagel, ed., *Modeling the Criminal Justice System* (Sage, 1977); and S. Nagel and M. Neef, *The Legal Process: Modeling the System* (Sage, 1977).

3. On decision theory in general, see Robert Behn and James Vaupel,

Analytical Thinking for Busy Decision Makers (Basic Books, 1978); Rex Brown, Andrew Kahr, and Cameron Peterson, *Decision Analysis for the Manager* (Holt, Rinehart, and Winston, 1974); Ruth Mack, *Planning on Uncertainty: Decision Making in Business and Government Administration* (Wiley-Interscience, 1971); and Howard Raiffa, *Decision Analysis: Introductory Lectures on Choices under Uncertainty* (Addison-Wesley, 1968). On decision theory applied to the legal process see Gordon Tullock, *The Logic of the Law* (Basic Books, 1971); Gail Monkman, *Readings in Correctional Economics* (ABA Center for Correctional Economics, 1974); and S. Nagel and M. Neef, *Decision Theory and the Legal Process* (D.C. Heath, Lexington Books, 1978).

4. For applications of decision theory specifically to juror decisions, see Michael Fried, Kalman Kaplan, and Katherine Klein, "Juror Selection: An Analysis of Voir Dire" in *The Jury System in America: A Critical Overview,* ed. Rita Simon (Sage, 1975); John Kaplan, "Decision Theory and the Factfinding Process," 20 *Stan. L. Rev.* 1065-1092 (1968); Catherine Marshall and James Wise, "Juror Decisions and the Determination of Guilt in Capital Punishment Cases: A Bayesian Perspective," in *Utility, Probability, and Human Decision Making,* eds. Dirk Wendt and Charles Vlek (Reidel, 1975); Ewart Thomas and Anthony Hogue, "Apparent Weight of Evidence, Decision Criteria, and Confidence Ratings in Juror Decision Making," 83 *Psych. Rev.* 442-465 (1976); Karen Peterson, "The Juror's Decision: The Effect of Sentencing on Type I and Type II Errors" (M.A. thesis, Stanford University, 1975); Alan Cullison, "The Model of Rules and the Logic of Decision," in *Modeling the Criminal Justice System,* ed. S. Nagel (Sage, 1971); and Lawrence Tribe, "An Ounce of Detention: Preventative Justice in the World of John Mitchell," 56 *V. L. Rev.* 371, 385-390 (1970).

5. See appendix 6A for a summary of the meaning of the symbols used in this chapter and appendix 6B for a summary of the basic formulas used. Those appendixes also help bring out the relations among the symbols and formulas, and they help one see the basic concepts and methods on a more general level.

6. The P^* (or threshold probability) for a given individual is not affected algebraically by using a 0 to 100 scale or a $-1,000$ to $+1,000$, rather than a -100 to $+100$ scale. However, a 0 to 100 scale does not get at the notion of some payoffs being negative or costs, and some payoffs being positive or benefits. A $-1,000$ to $+1,000$ scale may involve numbers that are too big for most respondents to handle. As a result, those alternative anchoring points may create confusion or lessened understanding such that the results are less valid than those obtained from a -100 to $+100$ anchoring scale.

7. An algebraically equal formula is developed in R.A. Howard, "The Science of Decision Making," in *Readings in Decision Analysis* (Stanford

Research Institute, 1977). However, he works with absolute dollar amounts for the cell values rather than with the relative index number approach used in figure 6-1. For cell *a,* he assesses the cost of convicting a guilty person as being $2,000 per year prison incarceration cost. For cell *b,* he assesses the cost of convicting an innocent person at the $2,000 incarceration cost plus $100,000 cost for the injustice. For cell *c,* the cost of letting a guilty person go free is assessed at a $7,000 annual gain to the national income from the income the defendant will be able to earn minus $10,000 in damages he is expected to incur as a result of crimes he may commit during that one-year period. For cell *d,* the payoff from acquitting an innocent defendant is the positive $7,000 income gain. Although those figures are questionable and unnecessary, his manipulation of them results in the same P^* value of .99, which would be arrived at by translating those figures into numbers on a -100 to $+100$ scale.

8. An alternative decision theory perspective for analyzing juror decision making and arriving at a threshold probability is through the use of a regret matrix. Such a matrix is a four-cell table labeled exactly like figure 6-1. The difference is that in each cell one does not show a number representing the relative costs or benefits of the outcome corresponding to the cell, as is done in figure 6-1. Instead one shows in each cell the relative amount of regret one is likely to feel as a result of the outcome corresponding to each cell. Thus cell *a* would generally have a 0 in it, since one would not normally have any regret about voting to convict a guilty defendant (except regret that the crime was committed in the first place). Likewise cell *d* would generally have a 0 in it, since one would not normally have any regret about voting to acquit an innocent defendant (except regret that the defendant was arrested in the first place). Cells *c* and *b* would both have numbers other than 0 in them, since they both involve errors that an aware juror would normally regret. Between those two cells a regret value of 1 gets assigned to the less regretted outcome, and a regret value equal to 1 or greater gets assigned to the more regretted outcome, showing how much relatively more regretted that outcome is. Thus William Blackstone generally would have a regret matrix with cell entries of 0, 10, 1, and 0 for cells *a, b, c,* and *d,* rather than $+10$, -100, -10, and $+100$. The regret matrix is then manipulated in the same way as the payoff matrix in figure 6-1 to give a threshold probability, which in the case of William Blackstone would be .91. The regret matrix approach, though, is probably more difficult for respondents to handle. It is used to analyze juror decision making in Richard Lempert, 75 *Mich. L. Rev.* 1021-1057 (1977).

9. The research on which this chapter is based did not significantly attempt to deal with juror decisions on sentencing, as contrasted to juror decisions on whether the defendant should be convicted. A rational sentencing decision would be one in which the decision maker seeks to minimize the

sum of the holding costs plus the releasing costs when deciding upon a sentence. The holding costs mainly consist of jail maintenance and loss of gross national product while a defendant is held in prison. The releasing costs mainly consist of the damage done by releasing defendants who commit further crimes which they would not have committed if they had been held in prison. Arriving at optimum sentences involves cost calculations for which jurors do not have adequate information, or adequate training to process the information if it were available. Therefore, sentencing should be mainly a legislative function, especially if sentences are to be (1) largely nondiscretionary, in order to provide objectivity, and (2) based on data showing the relation between various sentences and both holding costs and recidivism costs. See S. Nagel, M. Neef, and T. Weiman, "A Rational Method for Determining Prison Sentences," 61 *Judicature* 371-375 (1978).

10. On how probabilities of guilt can be calculated as contrasted to how they are actually determined, see Paul Slovic and Sarah Lichtenstein, "Comparison of Bayesian and Regression Approaches to the Study of Information Processing in Judgment," 6 *Org. Behavior & Human Performance* 649-744 (1971); and S. Nagel, "Judicial Prediction and Analysis from Empirical Probability Tables," 41 *Ind. L. J.* 403-419 (1966). On how one can use a questionnaire survey to elicit probability perceptions from respondents, see Philip Kotler, *Marketing Decision Making: A Model Building Approach* 583-595 (Holt, 1971); and Huber, "Methods for Quantifying Subjective Probabilities and Multi-Attribute Utilities," 5 *Decision Sci.* 430 (1974). On the problems of working with perceived probabilities that represent a range between 1.00 and 0 rather than a specific probability, see Nagel and Neef, "Plea Bargaining, Decision Theory, and Equilibrium Models," 51 and 52 *Ind. L. J.* 1010-1018. The reasoning there also applies where the payoff cell entries represent ranges rather than specific quantities. Under those circumstances, one could hypothesize that the juror operates at the midpoint of those ranges, or that he operates toward the higher or lower end depending on his degree of propensity to convict or acquit. An alternative approach would be to work with both the high and low points of the probability and payoff cell ranges and thus wind up with a P^* or threshold probability that is also a range like .60 to .80. Under those circumstances such a juror would not vote to convict unless the range of the perceived probability was completely above the range of the threshold probability, unless the juror could compress those ranges into a specific P and P^*.

11. In order to simultaneously obtain the benefits of various ways of measuring P^*, one could average the results from the alternative methods. For example, a more accurate, indirect method could average the P^* arrived at through the two-cell indirect method and the four-cell indirect method.

Likewise, a more accurate, direct method could average the P^* arrived at by asking respondents what probability of guilt they personally think should be required before a conviction vote is merited and what probability of guilt they think the law requires. One could then average those two averages for the indirect method and the two averages for the direct method to obtain a P^* estimate that may predict more accurately decisions given a respondent's perceived probability of guilt (P) than any of the separate P^*-estimating methods.

12. To illustrate the nonquantitative language that tends to dominate how *beyond a reasonable doubt* is defined, one might quote *U.S.* v. *McGuire* (300 *Fed. Rept.* 98, 102 (1924), where the court metaphorically says, "Beyond a reasonable doubt may be linked to the summit of a high mountain, and probable cause to a halfway station on the mountain side. Few may reach the summit, but many may reach the halfway station." Other verbal definitions tend to emphasize providing other negative definitions or synonyms like *moral certainty, Fidelity Mutual Loan Association* v. *Mettler,* 185 U.S. 308 (1902); *entirely convinced, State* v. *Harris,* 223 N. Car. 697 (1943); or *beyond question,* In re Meckley, 137 *Fed. Rept.* 2d 310 (1943). In the case of In re Winship, 90 Sup. Ct. 1068 (1970), the U.S. Supreme Court indicated how important the standard is by requiring that it be applied to juvenile cases as well as adult cases, although the court does not attempt to define the standard or indicate how juries are to be instructed as to its meaning. The court indicates that there should be a difference between the reasonable-doubt standard and the civil standard of a mere preponderance of the evidence, but the court cites no evidence that jurors or even judges decide differently when given those two different standards.

13. Rita James Simon, "Beyond a Reasonable Doubt: An Experimental Attempt at Quantification," 6 *J. Applied Behavioral Sci.* 203-209 (1970).

14. It makes sense to talk about an optimum threshold probability of about 10 to 1 in view of the Blackstone analysis and the judicial survey, although other legal scholars have recommended other trade-off ratios. For example, Hale though the ratio of wrongful acquittals that a society should be willing to tolerate in order to avoid one wrongful conviction should only be 5 to 1. Matthew Hale, *Pleas of the Crown* (Professional Books Limited, 1972 reprint of 1678 edition). Fortescue thought the ratio should be 20 to 1. John Fortescue, *A Learned Commendation of the Laws of England* (W.J. Johnson, 1969 reprint of 1567 edition). It does not, however, make sense to talk about an optimum level or number of convictions. This is so because each defendant's guilt or innocence should be judged in terms of his own case, not in terms of what has happened in previous cases, the way students are graded on a curve. One could argue either way, though, on the question

of whether the trade-off ratio on which P^* is based should be the same for all types of criminal cases or whether there should be a higher P^* required where the penalty is more severe and thus the type 1 error costs of convicting an innocent person are higher. Where the penalty is more severe, however, the crime is also more severe; and thus the type 2 error costs of releasing a guilty person may be higher, offsetting the higher type 1 error costs, thereby holding P^* constant.

15. Threshold probabilities are low, even when jurors are questioned about conviction standards using the direct approach by asking them to translate the phrase *beyond a reasonable doubt* into a statement of probability. Rita Simon, for example, found the probability answers of jurors were almost indistinguishable from the "preponderance of the evidence" standard in civil cases, unlike the judges in her survey. Rita James Simon and Linda Mahan, "Quantifying Burdens of Proofs: A View from the Bench, the Jury, and the Classroom," 5 *L. & Soc. Rev.* 319-330 (1971). Contrary to the Rita Simon findings, Kalven and Zeisel hypothesize that juries have a higher conviction threshold than judges as a partial explanation for why juries are less prone to convict. Harry Kalven, Jr., and Hans Zeisel, *The American Jury* (Little, Brown, 1966), 182-190. The two viewpoints can be reconciled by noting Rita Simon is, in effect, asking judges and jurors what they think the law requires, whereas Kalven and Zeisel are talking about what threshold probability judges and jurors actually tend to apply. Jurors may tend to apply higher threshold probabilities and to perceive lower probabilities of guilt because of a greater empathizing with the defendant, who is more likely to share economic class values with jurors than with judges.

16. Peterson, "The Juror's Decision," finds that the threshold probability rises when she presents a murder trial to her respondents in which the possible penalty is capital punishment rather than life imprisonment. In the Nagel-Lamm pilot studies, the type of cases were varied between rape, robbery, and consumer fraud, but no explicit variations were made with regard to the degree of punishment. It does, however, seem reasonable that jurors would demand a higher probability of guilt where the stakes of making a type 1 error of convicting the innocent are greater, although in more severe crimes there may be a greater desire to obtain a conviction.

17. Experimental evidence that one's empirical perceptions can influence one's values is given in Thomas Ostrom, "Perspective as a Determinant of Attitude Change," 6 *J. Exp. Psych.* 280-292 (1970). One could establish that perceptions can influence values in the juror decision-making context by determining the values (that is, the threshold probabilities) of a group of subjects before and after they perceive some relevant situations. If

their values change in accordance with their differing perceptions, this could be interpreted as evidence that those perceptions caused the value changes. Likewise, one could establish that values influence perceptions in juror decision making by determining the guilt perceptions (that is, the empirical probabilities) of a group of subjects before and after they evaluate some relevant situations. If their perceptions change in accordance with their differing values, this could be interpreted as evidence that those evaluations caused the perception changes.

18. The concept of a cost C is designed to bring out that a juror reaching a decision is faced with costs other than type 1 error costs (A) and type 2 error costs (B), namely information gathering and processing costs. To avoid those costs, the juror may tend to vote at least partly on the basis of his or her generalized notion of the probability (P) of a defendant's being guilty, rather than the probability of this specific defendant being guilty. More important are the thinking costs involved in arriving at a threshold probability (P^*). The juror who wants to save those mental costs may tend to operate under a notion that the cost of making a mistake of convicting an innocent person (regardles of the specific case) is generally much greater than the cost of acquitting a guilty person such that some jurors are quite reluctant to ever vote to convict or, in the opposite situation, to acquit.

19. *Odds* can be defined as the ratio between the probability of a certain outcome occurring and the probability of the certain outcome not occurring; that is, odds = $P/(1 - P)$. *Probability* can, in turn, be defined as the proportion or fraction of times that a certain outcome is likely to occur over a large number of opportunities. By .43 odds (where $P = .30$, and $P/(1 - P) = .30/.70$, or $.43/1.00$), we mean that if one wants to bet the defendant will be found guilty, then for every $1.00 he puts into the betting pot, the other side should put in $.43. If the defendant is found guilty, our bettor collects the pot: otherwise, the other side gets the pot. If odds equal .43, then $P = .30$ since $P = $ odds/(odds + 1.00), or $.43/1.43$, or .30.

20. That jurors reason implicitly in a Bayesian way is hypothesized in John Kaplan, "Decision Theory and the Factfinding Process," but empirical data tend to indicate otherwise, as presented in Catherine Marshall and James Wise, "Juror Decisions and the Determination of Guilt." On the Bayesian and other approaches to handling information to arrive at posterior odds from both prior odds and a likelihood ratio, see Richard Lempert, "Modeling Relevance," 75 *Mich. L. Rev.* 1021-1057 (1977); Peter Lindsey and Donald Norman, *Human Information Processing* (Academic Press, 1972), 549-556; Martin Kaplan and Gwen Kemmerick, "Juror Judgment as Information Integration: Combining Evidential and Nonevidential Information," 30 *J. Personality & Social Psych.* 493-499 (1974);

and David Schum, "Contrast Effects in Inference: On the Conditioning of Current Evidence by Prior Evidence," 18 *Organ. Behavior & Human Performance,* 217-253 (1977).

To illustrate the Bayesian approach to calculating a probability of guilt, assume 100 hypothetical cases distributed as follows:

	Not Guilty ($-B$)	(Guilty (G)	
Have Evidence (E) (for example, eyewitness)	2	38	40
Not Have Evidence ($-E$)	8	52	60
	10	90	100

Those data yield the following probabilities, where $P(A|B)$ reads "probability of A given B":

$P(G)$	= 90/100 = .90		$P(E)$	= 40/100	= .10
$P(-G)$	= 10/100 = .10		$P(-E)$	= 60/100	= .60
$P(G\|E)$	= 38/40 = .95		$P(G\|-E)$	= 52/60	= .87
$P(-G\|E)$	= 2/40 = .05		$P(-G\|-E)$ =	8/60	= .13
$P(E\|G)$	= 38/90 = .42		$P(E\|-G)$	= 2/10	= .20
$P(-E\|G)$	= 52/90 = .58		$P(-E\|-G)$ =	8/10	= .80

With those probabilities, one can calculate the odds of the defendant being guilty regardless of the evidence. This equals .90/.10, or 9/1, or 9.00. One can also calculate the likelihood ratio of the evidence indicating guilt. This equals .42/.20, or 2.10. By multiplying those two figures, one obtains the odds of the defendant being guilty given the evidence. This, in turn, equals 18.90. One can then translate those odds into a probability or P, which equals 18.90/19.90, or .95. That .95 could have been arrived at more simply by merely observing that $P(G|E) = .95$.

21. A simple instruction that the jury should acquit if they have a reasonable doubt as to the defendant's guilt of the crime charged in the indictment is ordinarily sufficient. Charles McCormick, *Handbook of the Law of Evidence* (West, 1954); and *People* v. *Russell,* 94 Pac. 2d 400, 403 (1939). McCormick justifies not defining *beyond a reasonable doubt* on the grounds that it needs a skillful definer to make it plainer by multiplication

of words, and the explanations themselves often need more explanation than the terms explained, citing *Hoffman* v. *State,* 97 Wis. 576 (1897) and *State* v. *Sauer,* 38 Minn. 438 (1888). In the latter case, Judge Mitchell states: "It may be doubted whether any attempt to define it (that is, beyond a reasonable doubt) will not be more likely to confuse than to enlighten a jury." In *Illinois Pattern Jury Instructions: Criminal* (Burdette-Smith Co., 1968), the drafting committee recommended that no instructions be given defining reasonable doubt, favorably citing *People* v. *Malmenato,* 14 Ill. 2d 52, 61, 150 N.E. 2d 806, 811 (1958) in which the Illinois Supreme Court stated "Reasonable doubt is a term which needs no elaboration and we have so frequently discussed the futility of attempting to define it that we might expect the practice to be discontinued." On the art and science of instructing juries, see Bruce Sales, Amiram Elwork, and James Alfini, "Improving Comprehension for Jury Instructions" in *Perspectives in Law and Psychology,* ed. Bruce Sales (Plenum, 1978) and Amiram Elwork, Bruce Sales, and James Alfini, "Juridic Decisions: In Ignorance of the Law or in Light of It?" 1 *Law & Human Behavior* 163-189 (1977).

22. In her research, Rita Simon found that instructing jurors to consciously determine the probability that the defendant is guilty does result in reducing conviction votes. Simon and Mahan, "Quantifying Burdens of Proof."

23. If P and P^* are derived from a questionnaire or a simulated jury experiment rather than a real jury situation, the decision to convict or acquit should still be a function of P and P^*. In real jury trials, however, the perceived probability of guilt (P) from a given set of facts may be lower than in simulations, and likewise the threshold probability of guilt (P^*) may be higher given the greater reluctance of real jurors to convict a real defendant.

24. There are other ways of increasing the accuracy, legality, and objectivity of juror decisions besides changing the nature of the instructions which they are given. For example, more factually accurate decisions can be encouraged by making sure both the prosecution and the public defender are represented by attorneys who have adequate resources for investigation and presentation. More legalistic decision making can be encouraged by requiring potential jurors to have certain educational qualifications that indicate a better ability to understand what is meant by *beyond a reasonable doubt,* although such selection standards might conflict with the representativeness of juries. More objectivity or sameness across demographic groups in jury decision making could be facilitated by encouraging more deliberation and oral balloting, since it has been found that twelve people deciding collectively tend to have a smaller spread in their decisions than twelve people deciding separately.

25. As an alternative to the above instruction, Rita Simon suggests that jurors should not decide the guilt or innocence of defendants, but rather should merely decide the probability of guilt, presumably by averaging their twelve probability perceptions. The judge would then decide whether that jury-perceived P is above or below the P^* of about .90 which the law seems to require. The same procedure can be used in civil cases, although working there with a P^* of .51. Simon and Mahan, "Quantifying Burdens of Proof." That procedure assumes the role of juries is only that of a fact finder rather than a normative evaluator.

26. A decision theory perspective on juror decision making not only is useful for purposes of measurement, causation, and improvement of the legal process, but also can be of value to the practicing lawyer. Fried, Kaplan, and Klein, "Juror Selection," emphasize that kind of orientation in analyzing the juror selection process. They, in effect, recommend that prosecutors should seek jurors whose threshold probabilities are likely to be below their perceived probabilities, and prosecutors should seek to shape the P^* values and P perceptions of jurors so that P will be greater than P^*. They likewise recommend that defense attorneys seek jurors whose threshold probabilities are likely to be above their perceived probabilities, and defense attorneys should seek to shape the P^* values and P perceptions of jurors so that P will be less than P^*.

Appendix 6A. Glossary of Symbols and Terms

Symbol	Represents	Section First Appearing
Payoff Values:		
$+B$ (cell a)	Satisfaction gained from voting to convict when defendant is guilty	I
$-A$ (cell b)	Dissatisfaction gained from voting to convict when defendant is innocent (type 1 error cost)	I
$-B$ (cell c)	Dissatisfaction gained from voting to acquit when defendant is guilty (type 2 error cost)	I
$+A$ (cell d)	Satisfaction from voting to acquit when defendant is innocent	I
X	Trade-off ratio, or how many times worse one considers it to convict an innocent defendant ($-A$) as contrasted to acquitting a guilty defendant ($-B$)	I
P^*	Threshold or normative probability such that a juror votes to convict if the observed probability is greater than this figure, and votes to acquit if the observed probability is less than this figure (a function of X which is a function of $-A$ and $-B$).	I
Probability Perceptions:		
P	Observed probability of defendant being guilty	I
$(1-P)$	Observed probability of defendant being innocent	I
Odds	The ratio between favorable outcomes and unfavorable outcomes	I
New odds	The perceived odds a defendant is guilty after evidence is heard	I
Old odds	The perceived odds a defendant is guilty before evidence is heard	I
Expected Values (Combined values and perceptions):		
EV_C	Expected value of voting to convict a defendant	I
EV_A	Expected value of voting to acquit a defendant	I
Decisions:		
D	Decision of a juror to convict (scored 1) or acquit (scored 0)	I
C	The cost of gathering and processing information relevant to P and P^*	I

See the list of formulas in appendix 6B for how various concepts are calculated and the context in which they are used.

Appendix 6B.
Basic Formulas Used

Symbol	Represents	Section First Appearing
Payoff Values:		
$P^* = A/(A + B)$ $= X/(X + 1)$	Threshold probability of guilt required before voting to convict	I
$P^* = (ad - bc)/(a - b - c + d)$	In terms of payoff cells	I
$P^* = A/(A + B)$	In terms of error costs	I
$P^* = X/(X + 1)$	In terms of trade-off ratio	I
Probability Perceptions:		
Prior or initial probability of guilt = Number of convictions/Number of trials		III
Prior or initial odds = Number of convictions/Number of acquittals		III
Likelihood ratio = Probability of evidence being present given convicted defendants/ Probability of evidence being present given acquitted defendants		III
Posterior or subsequent odds = Prior odds x Likelihood ratio		III
Posterior or subsequent probability = Posterior odds/Posterior odds + 1)		III
Expected Values:		
$EV_C = (+B)(P) + (-A)(1 - P)$	Expected value of voting to convict a defendant	I
$EV_A = (-B)(P) + (+A)(1 - P)$	Expected value of voting to acquit a defendant	I
Decisions: Expressed as a function of P and P^*:		
$D = \begin{cases} 1 & \text{if } P > P^* \\ 0 & \text{if } P < P^* \end{cases}$		I
Expressed as a function of EV_C and EV_A: $D = \begin{cases} 1 & \text{if } EV_C > EV_A \\ 0 & \text{if } EV_C < EV_A \end{cases}$		

See appendix 6A for definitions of the symbols.

7. Allocating Resources Among Court Cases by Legal Counsel

Statistical analysis has been applied to predicting the verdict (or who will win) in various types of personal injury, criminal, and other cases.[1] Such analysis has also been applied to predicting what damages will be awarded if a personal injury plaintiff wins, what sentence will be handed down if a prosecutor wins, and to other types of judgments.[2] A related problem that has not been analyzed is how legal counsel can use that kind of information in order to allocate his or her resources among pending court cases. The purpose of this chapter is to discuss some of the methodological problems involved in optimally allocating scarce time resources among court cases by legal counsel.[3]

The methodology described is somewhat analogous to an investment company trying to decide how to allocate its scarce resources among various stock purchases. Both court cases and stocks involve payoffs that depend on risks or probabilities. Taking those payoffs and probabilities into consideration in order to develop an optimum mix with one's scarce resources is sometimes referred to as portfolio analysis. Such an analysis can sometimes be quite complicated, although it is ultimately based on simple common sense. In this chapter, simplicity will be emphasized not only to make the methodological discussion more understandable, but also because allocation of court cases is inherently a much simpler or at least clearer problem than the stock market investment problem.[4] The court cases allocation problem becomes even simpler as it is further developed in subsequent sections of this chapter, to cover variations on the basic model, more cases, more types of cases, related decisions, and implementation problems.[5]

I. A Basic Example

A. Defective Strategies

For the sake of simplicity, suppose a lawyer, law firm, or government agency has only two cases. (Later the problem can be expanded to include any number of cases.) Suppose also that the cases are two plaintiff's personal injury cases where the judgement is likely to be expressed in terms of dollars, although later the problem can be expanded to include judgments expressed in terms of years in jail, severity of an injunction, or other units of measurement. Suppose further that it has been estimated that case 1 has a

.80 probability of being won and case 2 has a .40 probability of being won. How should our hypothetical law firm allocate its resources? At first glance one might say: (1) allocate all one's resources to the better case; (2) allocate 80/120, or .67, of one's resources to the better case and 40/120, or .33, of one's resourcses to the case less likely to succeed; (3) allocate as much resources as are needed in order to win both cases; (4) allocate as little resources to the case less likely to succeed as one might be ethically obligated to do so and the remainder of one's resources to the better case; (5) allocate the same amount of resources to case 1 as has been allocated in the past to the average case of the case 1 type, and do likewise with case 2; or (6) use some other alternative allocation.

All those possibilities lack common sense. Allocating all our resources to the better case (as in alternative 1) might be wasteful because we might have 100 hours of time to allocate but need only 50 in order to obtain a victory; and if we allocate all our resources to case 1, we will miss the possibility of receiving any judgment from case 2, which might mean suffering a substantial opportunity cost and be unethical as well if we have already agreed to take case 2. Allocating our resources proportionately (as in alternative 2) would mean giving 67 hours to case 1 and 33 hours to case 2 (if we had 100 hours available) which might be wasteful since maybe case 1 needs less than 67 hours to cross the threshold between being a loser and a winner; and maybe case 2 needs more than 33 hours, although not necessarily a lot more. Allocating as much resources as are needed to win both cases (as in alternative 3) may be meaningless if by *to win* we mean with 1.00 certainty since even an infinite number of hours devoted to each case may not be capable of achieving that, or if by *to win* we mean with more than a .50 probability since achieving that for case 2 may require more than the 100 hours we have available. The fourth alternative of allocating a minimum to the worse case and the rest to the better case will not exceed our hours available (unlike alternative 3) or violate our ethical oblications (unlike alternative 1), but it may represent an excessive allocation to case 1 and an opportunity cost for case 2 (just like alternatives 1 and 2). The fifth alternative of allocating in terms of past averages has the defect that it assumes what we have been doing on the average in the past has been optimal or rational in allocating our scarce resources.[6]

The answer to our simple hypothetical problem, as the reader may have already figured out, is that we need more information. What may not be so obvious, though, is what additional information we need and what we should do with it. For a starter, it might help to know if case 1 results in a victory, what the damage award is likely to be, and likewise for case 2. If the damage award in case 1 upon a plaintiff victory is $10,000, then that case can be said to have an expected value of $8,000 (or .80 times $10,000). If, however, the damage award in case 2 upon a plaintiff victory is $30,000, then that case has an expected value of $12,000 (or .40 times $30,000). Now it looks like case 2 is the better case. If, however, we apply our five alternative strategies with this new information, we will still come up with the same answers that all five lack common sense for the same reasons, and we still need more information.

B. Equalizing Marginal Rates of Return

The additional information that we especially need besides victory probabilities (P's) and likely damage awards (D's) is how those figures are affected by putting in additional hours (H's). For example, suppose a looseleaf service shows that in cases like case 1 there is a relation between P and H of the form $P = a(H)^b$. The *lowercase a* and *b* are numbers that can be arrived at through a computerized regression analysis on a large number of personal injury cases in which the looseleaf service has access to (1) whether the plaintiff won or lost the case and (2) how many hours the plaintiff's attorney put into the case.[7] The b is likely to be a decimal between 0 and 1 showing that as additional hours are allocated, the probability of victory increases, but at a diminishing rather than at a constant rate. Suppose further that the looseleaf service or other research source shows that in cases like case 1 there is a relation between D and H of the form $D = A(H)^B$. The A and B are two other numbers which can also be arrived at through an analysis of cases won by the plaintiff, where one knows for each case the damages awarded and the hours of the plaintiff's attorney. The looseleaf service or researcher can also obtain a similar pair of equations for cases like case 2. Now we may have all the information we need, but what do we do with it?

The answer may not be obvious common sense, but it is fairly simple, at least as a matter of hindsight. Logically if we have 100 hours available, we want to allocate them to the two cases so as to obtain from both an equal *marginal rate of return* (MRR). By that, we mean we want to be in a position of equilibrium such that there is nothing to be gained by shifting an hour of our time from one case to the other. In this simple situation, arriving at that position merely involves solving on a desk calculator the value of H_1 (the hours to be devoted to case 1) and H_2 (the hours to be devoted to case 2) in the following pair of equations:

$$H_1 + H_2 = 100 \qquad (7.1)$$

$$[(b + B)(aA)(H)^{b+B-1}]_1 = [(b + B)(aA)(H)^{b+B-1}]_2 \qquad (7.2)$$

The first equation says we want the sum of the hours allocated to be 100 because we have no more than that available (or some other figure) and because we feel we would suffer missed opportunities if we worked less. The second equation says the marginal rate of return for case 1 should be equal to the marginal rate of return for case 2. The *a, b, A,* and *B* in the first set of brackets correspond to the numerical coefficients of the probability equation and the damage equation for cases of type 1, and the symbols in the second set of brackets correspond to cases of type 2.

At this point, one is likely to be asking where that second equation came from, or at least where the left side came from, since knowing that would enable one to know where the right side came from. All we are doing, first of all, is calculating the expected value for each type of case. This is no more complicated than the probability of victory (P) times the damage that would be awarded (D) if victory occurs, or, put differently, the damages discounted by the probability of receiving them. Since we know $P = a(H)^b$ and $D = A(H)^B$, we can substitute $a(H)^b A(H)^B$ for $P(D)$. The expression $a(H)^b A(H)^B$ can be simplified to read $(aA)(H)^{b+B}$ by multiplying the two multipliers and by remembering that one sums the exponents when multiplying expressions with the same base but different exponents. That new expression, however, does not look like the left side of the second equation, although it does look like we are getting closer to explaining it.

If we were to set that new expression, $(aA)(H)^{b+B}$, for cases of type 1 equal to the analogous expression for cases of type 2, we would be equalizing the expected values between the two cases. It is, however, the marginal rates of return between the two cases that we want to equalize. In high school algebra, one learns that if one has the equation of the form $Y = a + bX$, then the slope, or marginal rate of return, on Y of a one-unit increase in X is equal to b. On a slightly more advanced level, if one has an equation of the form $Y = aX^b$, then the slope, or marginal rate of return, on Y of an increase in X is equal to baX^{b-1}. Thus, the marginal rate of return for the expression $(aA)(H)^{b+B}$ is logically $(b + B)(aA)(H)^{b-1}$, where the exponent also becomes a multiplier, and 1 is subtracted from the exponent. This is what appears on the left side of equation 7.2.

Solving these two equations simultaneously merely involves four steps. (1) Substitute the numbers for the eight coefficients (that is, four for each case), and perform the arithmetic involved. (2) Note from equation 7.1 that if $H_1 + H_2 = 100$, then $H_2 = 100 - H_1$, and substitute that expression, $100 - H_1$, for H_2 in the right side of equation 7.2. (3) Try different guessed values for H_1 in this new version of equation 7.2 until the guesses converge so as to make both sides equal. (4) Subtract that equalizing or optimum value of H_1 from 100 to arrive at the optimum value for H_2.

A closely related allocation approach that is substantially easier to handle, although less accurate, involves recognizing that the amount of hours optimally allocated to case 1 depends on the values of a, b, A, and B for case 1; likewise, the amount of hours allocated to case 2 depends on the values of a, b, A, and B for case 2. Thus, one could simply allocate the 100 hours to case 1 by giving case 1 a proportion of the 100 hours equal to the product $(abAB)_1$ divided by the sum of the product for case 1 and the product for case 2. In other words, allocate to case i in accordance with the formula

$$G[(abAB)_i / \Sigma\, abAB]$$

where G is the grand total of hours available. This method has the big advantage of not requiring any solving of simultaneous equations, and that cost- and time-saving advantage will generally be enough to offset the somewhat lessened accuracy.[8]

II. Simplifying and Varying the Basic Model

A. Constant, Linear, and Nonlinear Relations

Although the basic allocation model involves only solving a pair of simultaneous equations, that model can be simplified further. For example, if the probability of victory is not affected by the number of hours spent on a case, then the expected value becomes $P \cdot A(H)^B$, and the left side of equation 7.2 becomes $BPA(H)^{B-1}$, with a similar change to the right side. Likewise, if the amount of damages is not affected by the number of hours spent on a case but the probability of victory is, then the expected value becomes $a(H)^b \cdot D$, and the left side of equation 7.2 becomes $bDa(H)^{b-1}$, with a similar change to the right side. If neither the probability of victory nor the amount of damages is affected by the number of hours spent on a case, in effect that means that both b and B equal zero on both sides of equation 7.2, which makes equation 7.2 disappear, leaving one unsolvable equation and two unknowns. In more commonsense terms, if P and D are not affected by H, then one may as well spend no time at all on either case and the result will be the same as if one were to spend an infinite amount on both cases. That statement emphasizes that it is nonsense to think P and D are totally unaffected by attorney hours, although within a given range of hours there may be little change in P or D.[9]

Another related simplification, which may also be an oversimplification, involves saying that maybe the relation between probability, damages, or fees, on the one hand, and hours, on the other hand, is a linear relation of the form $Y = a + bX$, rather than a nonlinear relation of the form $Y = aX^b$. For example, if an attorney were being paid a flat fee of $30 an hour rather than a fee contingent on victory, then his fee (F) could be calculated by the equation $F = 0 + 30(H)$. By $30 an hour in that context, we do not mean the billing rate which may be $60 an hour, but rather the actual rate which takes into consideration that our hypothetical lawyer has to put in about 2 hours' clock time in order to develop 1 hour of chargeable or billing time. In such an equation or relation, the marginal rate of return is 30 since one additional hour of work will yield an additional $30. If attorney 1 has two types of cases, one of which pays a constant $30 an hour and the other of which pays a constant $40 an hour, then the best strategy would be to devote all 100 hours to the cases that pay $40 an hour if one can get 100 hour's worth of them. If attorney 2 has two types of cases, of which one pays $30 an hour (meaning a $30 an hour marginal rate of return) and the other has a nonlinear marginal rate of return like that of case 2 in equation 7.2, then the optimum allocation would involve solving for H_1 and H_2 in the pair of equations:

$$H_1 + H_2 = 100 \quad \text{and} \quad 30 = (b + B)(aA)(H_2)^{b+B-1}$$

Those two attorney examples involved either a pair of flat-fee cases or one flat fee and one contingency fee. The linear-type relationship also can occur with regard to determining the probability or the damages when two contingency-fee cases are involved. For example, if P bears a linear relation to H of the form $P = a + b(H)$, then the expected value of those cases will be

$$[a + b(H)]A(H)^B$$

or

$$a \cdot A(H)^B + b(H) \cdot A(H)^B \quad \text{by mutiplying}$$

or

$$(aA)(H)^B + (Ab)(H)^{b+1} \quad \text{by simplifying further}$$

The marginal rate of return of that expression is then $BaA(H)^{B-1} + (B + 1)(Ab)(H)^B$. Likewise, if D bears a linear relation to H of the form $D = A + B(H)$ but P bears a nonlinear relation, then the expected value of those cases will be

$$a(H)^b[A + B(H)]$$

or

$$(aA)(H)^b + (aB)(H)^{b+1} \quad \text{by multiplying and simplifying}$$

The marginal rate of return for that expression is

$$baA(H)^{b-1} + (b + 1)(aB)(H)^b$$

Allocating Resources Among Court Cases

If both P and D bear a linear relationship to H, then the expected value is

$$[a + b(H)][A + B(H)]$$

or

$$aA + aB(H) + Ab(H) + bB(H)^2 \quad \text{by multiplying}$$

and the marginal rate of return is

$$aB + Ab + 2bB(H)$$

Saying that P and D bear a linear or constant relation to H is more realistic than saying P and D bear no relation to H. It seems more realistic, however, to think that when only a few total hours are involved, an extra hour makes more difference than when many total hours are involved, which means that a nonlinear, diminishing relation is present. In doing the regression analysis designed to get the numerical parameters for either $Y = a + bX$ or $Y = aX^b$, the computerized regression analysis reads out a correlation coefficient for each equation which informs us which approach better fits the data.[10]

B. Other Ways of Conceiving the Basic Equations

One might react to equations 7.1 and 7.2 by saying several things. (1) They fail to take into consideration the one-third contingency-fee arrangement. (2) The equations consider only income, not expenses. (3) It may be impossible to equalize the MRRs within 100 hours. (4) Some attorneys may prefer to minimize their hours subject to a desired income rather than maximize their income subject to a given number of hours. (5) Hours are unlimited because there are always more hours in the future or more people can be hired. (6) The equations do not consider other variable that determine victory probabilities and damages, besides hours. (7) The equations could be simplified by looking to only the fee received, not the victory probabilities or the judgments.

If case 1 involves a one-third contingency fee, then its expected value is $.33a(H)^b A(H)^B$, or $.33(aA)(H)^{b+B}$ by multiplying and simplifying. The marginal rate of return for such an expression is then $(b + B)(.33aA)(H)^{b+B-1}$. If both case 1 and case 2 involve a one-third contingency fee, then the .33 on each side of the second equation can be canceled out by dividing both sides of the equation by .33. Thus, the one-third contingency fee has no bearing on the optimum values of H_1 and H_2 if both cases involve the same contingency fraction. If, however, case 1 involves a higher, lower, or no contingency fraction as compared to case 2, then that does make a difference in the optimum values of H_1 and H_2, since then the contingency fractions will not cancel out in the equation.

On the matter of expenses, case 1 may involve, for example, $50 in out-of-pocket expenses like a filing fee. Thus, the expected value of case 1 should be $a(H)^b A(H)^B - \$50$, or $(aA)(H)^{b+B} - 50$ by multiplying and simplifying. In other words, its expected net value is its expected income minus its known expenses. The marginal rate of return of income to hours for that expression, however, is still $(b + B)(aA)(H)^{b+B-1}$, as it was without subtracting the $50. This is so because the $50 is a constant not affected by the quantity of hours devoted to the case. If, however, expenses like income do increase as more hours are put in, then considering expenses would affect the MRR of net income to hours. That would be the situation where we are figuring hours as an expense at $30 per actual hour rather than per billing hour. Then the expected net value would be $a(H)^b A(H)^B - \$30(H)$, or $(aA)(H)^{b+B} - 30(H)$ by multiplying and simplifying. The marginal rate of return for that expression is $(b + B)(aA)(H)^{b+B-1} - 30$. This type of MRR is more appropriate to use in equation 7.2 since it does take into consideration the relation between hours and both income (that is, P time D) and expenses, not just income.

It is possible that cases of type 1 have a very high MRR, which in our context means that an extra hour continues to produce a high quantity of extra income after 50, 75, and even 100 hours. It is also possible that cases of type 2 have a very low MRR. In our context this means that an extra hour even in the beginning with only a total of 10 hours, 5 hours, or 1 hour still does not produce a high enough extra income that the MRR from case 2 at its less productive hours can equal the MRR from case 1 at its more productive hours. Under those unusual circumstances, there would be no numerical values to H_1 and H_2 that would satisfy both our basic equations. In other words, we would then put all our extra time into case 1 up to our 100 hours since diminishing returns in case 1 would not be great enough to justify moving 1 hour from case 1 to case 2.[11]

With a slight adjustment the basic equations can take into consideration the attorney who prefers to minimize his hours subject to a desired income, rather than maximize his income subject to a given number of hours. Suppose our hypothetical attorney wants to make only $2,000 a month from his law practice and wants to work the minimum number of hours necessary to earn that salary. Such an attorney still would want to equalize the MRR across his cases and thus would still use equation 7.2 if he were working with just our two cases or types of cases. For equation 7.1, however, he would logically substitute an equation of the form $[a(H)^b A(H)^B]_1 + [a(H)^b A(H)^B]_2 = \$2,000$. That equation, in effect, says the expected value of case 1 (that is, P_1 times D_1) plus the expected value of case 2 should equal $2,000. Solving that pair of simultaneous equations will inform our hypothetical attorney of the minimum number of hours he needs to work at each type of case in order to earn $2,000. That minimum number of hours may be more than 100 hours, and it may be more business than our hypothetical attorney is capable of generating. Therefore he may have to lower his $2,000 goal per month or generate more hours of work.

It is not meaningful to consider the total quantity of hours as being unlimited because (1) cases have to be resolved within a finite, although flexible, time; (2) hiring extra people cost money that we would prefer to allocate more efficiently within our present staff or man-hours available; and (3) treating time as infinitely available results in the unreasonable conclusion to allow an infinite amount of time to each case. That is like saying there is no relation between victory probabilities or damages and working hours and then unreasonably concluding that the quantity of hours devoted to a case makes no difference in terms of one's goals. Likewise, one cannot arrive at optimum allocations by defining H not as hours but as a percentage of the whole time budget, which is quantified as 1.00, or 100 percent. That would lead to meaningless results since the percentage of time to allocate to one of two cases might be quite different if we have a total time budget of 10 hours rather than 100 hours. With only 10 hours, it might be optimal to allocate 0 percent to case 1 and 100 percent to case 2; but with 100 hours, it might be optimal to allocate 30 percent to case 1 and 70 percent to case 2. Within the time period under consideration, it might be meaningful to allocate 0 hour to a given case because it is set for trial beyond that time period. It is, of course, meaningless to allocate less than 0 hour to a case regardless how low or even negative its MRR might be.[12]

Other variables which determine victory probabilities and damages besides hours can be taken into consideration. The main variable that determines those probabilities and damages is the type of case. Thus, the probability of plaintiff victory is much higher where the plaintiff suffered a rear-end automobile collision than when the plaintiff was a child pedestrian hit while running into the street. Likewise, damages are much greater where the plaintiff has lost a leg or arm than where the plaintiff has suffered a dog bite. As of now, the Jury Verdict Research Corporation of Cleveland, Ohio, does publish a looseleaf service giving probabilities and damages for many categories of case types. With a little extra effort, they could send questionnaires to the plaintiff and defense attorneys in each case which they use in their analysis asking how many hours the attorneys' records show were devoted to the case. With that information, the looseleaf service could publish *by type of case* an average probability, an average damages figure, the a and b parameters for the equation $P = a(H)^b$, and the A and B parameters for the equation $D = A(H)^B$. Doing so, in effect, holds constant the most important nonhours variables or elements determining the probabilities and damages.

A substantially different way of conceiving the basic equations would involve ignoring the victory probabilities and the judgments and just looking to the fee received in each previous case in the data base. One would then relate those fees to the actual working hours by way of the computerized regression analysis to obtain linear equations of the form $F = a + b(H)$, or diminishing-returns equations of the form $F = a(H)^b$. Those linear equations, however, would not make sense since they imply that for every additional hour a plaintiff's attorney devotes to a personal injury case, his fee goes up at a constant rate. This is not true if his fee is the usual contingency fee rather than an unusual hourly fee and if additional hours make little difference after a while. Those nonlinear equations fail to take into consideration that the probability of victory may bear a different relation to working hours than the amount of damages does. Working with the fee received as the dependent variable on the left side of the equation is also the equivalent of assuming that the probability of victory is always .33 when one works with $P(D)$ as the dependent variable, which is contrary to reality. Further empirical analysis is needed to determine how fees received, victory probabilities, and damages awarded relate to hours devoted to different types of cases. The $P(D)$ (or expected value) model has many interesting characteristics which the more gross fee-received model lacks; but one should be flexible in being able to switch to alternative models, perspectives, or conceptualizations if empirical data show the alternatives better fit reality and are more practical to work with.[13]

III. More Cases and More Types of Law Practice

A. From a Personal Injury Plaintiff's Perspective

As indicated in discussing the looseleaf service of the Jury Verdict Research Corporation, the basic model can be applied to a law firm that has hundreds of cases, not just two cases. The important thing is to think in terms of types of cases, not individual cases, and the quantity of basic types of cases is manageable. Those basic types can be combined, if necessary, in a variety of ways. For example, one basic type might be a rear-end collision case. Another basic type might be the urban area case. That combination could be handled by giving separate numerical parameters for rear-end collisions in urban areas and separate numerical parameters for rear-end collisions in rural areas. As an alternative to partitioning the cases into so many subsets, the publisher or researcher could generate from the data base a series of equations in which either the probability of victory or the damages awarded are a function of both hours worked and whether the cases came from an urban or a rural area. Such equations would have the form

$$P = a(H)^{b_1}(U)^{b_2} \quad \text{and} \quad D = A(H)^{B_1}(U)^{B_2}$$

In those equations U stands for urbanism and could be coded 1 for urban and 0 for rural, or coded to show the exact city size. The parameters for those equations are obtained by inputting into the computerized regression analysis for many cases (1) whether the plaintiff won (or what the damages were if the plaintiff did win), (2) the hours worked by the plaintiff's attorney, and (3) the size of the city in which the case occurred. Separate equations could be generated for rear-end collisions versus other kinds of personal injury cases, or a third variable could be added to the equations which could be coded 1 for rear-end collision involved and 0 for no rear-end collision involved.[14]

Suppose we have the numerical parameters for the general types of cases that interest us. If our hypothetical firm has 20 cases of type 1 and 40 cases of type 2, how should it allocate its 1,000 attorney hours among those cases? At first glance, one might think answering that question merely involves substituting 1,000 for 100 in the first of our two basic equations. Doing so might indicate we should spend 700 hours on type 1 cases and 300 hours on type 2 cases. We then might say the 700 hours should be allocated among the 20 type 1 cases by giving each of them 700/20 hours, or 35 hours, apiece, and the 300 hours should be allocated to the 40 type 2 cases by giving each of them 300/40 hours, or 7½ hours, apiece. The fallacy in this reasoning is that it does not take into consideration how many cases of each type we have. The same 700 to 300 distribution of our 1,000 hours would occur if we had only 1 case of type 1 and 50 of type 2, or 50 of type 1 and 1 of type 2.

To make the matter simpler, suppose our firm has only 3 cases instead of 60, and suppose 1 is a type 1 case and 2 are type 2 cases. Determining how to optimally allocate our 1,000 hours among those 3 cases would involve solving the following three equations simultaneously:

$$H_1 + H_2 + H_3 = 1,000$$

$$[(b + B)(aA)(H)^{b+B-1}]_1 = [(b + B)(aA)(H)^{b+B-1}]_2$$

$$[(b + B)(aA)(H)^{b+B-1}]_2 = [(b + B)(aA)(H)^{b+B-1}]_3$$

The first equation says that we want the sum of the hours we spend on each case to total the 1,000 hours available. The second and third equations say we want the marginal rates of return to be equal for all three cases. If we follow the above reasoning, then for 60 cases we would need 60 equations of the following form:

$$H_1 + H_2 + \cdots + H_{60} = 1{,}000$$

$$\text{MRR}_1 = \text{MRR}_2$$

$$\text{MRR}_{59} = \text{MRR}_{60}$$

Fortunately, there is an easier way to solve for the optimum value of each H that does not involve any equations. That method is referred to as nonlinear programming. To apply it requires a packaged computer program such as the P-CON routine or other similar routines available at university computing centers and other computing facilities.[15] In using this approach, the only input statements needed in order to obtain the optimum H values are statements like the following:

Maximize: $\quad 20[a(H)^b A(H)^B]_1 + 40[a(H)^b A(H)^B]_2$

Subject to: $\quad$ DO 5 I = 1, 60

$\quad\quad\quad\quad\quad$ 5 SUMH = SUMH + H(I)
$\quad\quad\quad\quad\quad$ G(1) = SUMH − 1,000

The first statement tells the computer to maximize income, which consists of the expected income from 20 cases of type 1 and from 40 cases of type 2. In writing that statement for the computer, numerical values would be substituted for the a, b, A, and B in case 1 and for the a, b, A, and B in case 2. The brackets and subscripts would then be eliminated, and multiplication and exponentiation signs would be added. X's would be substituted wherever H's appear since X is the more general symbol for unknowns to be solved. The remaining three statements inform the computer that we have a maximum sum of 1,000 hours to work with. The "G(1) =" means "less than or equal to 0." Thus, the last of those three statements, in effect, says the sum of the hours minus 1,000 should be less than or equal to 0. If the sum of the hours is greater than 1,000, then that inequality constraint will be violated. The two preceding statements involve a DO loop which says the subscript of H should be incremented from 1 through 60 in order to calculate the sum of the H's.

The P-CON nonlinear programming routine and other such routines can also be used if one wants to inform the computer that each type 1 case should be allocated a certain minimum number of hours and likewise for each type 2 case. That is done by adding the following statements to the basic statements given before:

Allocating Resources Among Court Cases

Subject to: $DO\ 6\ I = 1, 20$

$6\ G(I) = 2 - H(I)$

$DO\ 7\ I = 21, 60$

$7\ G(I) = 3 - H(I)$

The first pair of statements informs the computer that for the first 20 cases which are all type 1, the amount of time allocated to each case should be greater than 2 hours. In other words, 2 hours should be less than H_i (that is, the hours allocated to case i), which means the same as $2 - H_i$ should be less than 0 (that is, $2 - H(I)$ should be negative). The second pair of statements informs the computer that the next 40 cases which are all type 2 cases should be allocated a minimum of 3 hours apiece. Those minimums roughly conform to the ethical obligations a lawyer has in representing a client, or else the lawyer could be involved in a malpractice action. Those minimums also keep all types of cases from being allocated zero time regardless how long or negative their MRRs might be.

For the law firm that wants to minimize its hours worked subject to a desired income of $2,000, the nonlinear programming statements would be as follows:

Minimize: SUMH

Subject to: $G(1) = 2,000 - 20[a(H)^b A(H)^B]_1$
$+ 40[a(H)^b A(H)^B]_2$

Before saying to minimize SUMH (that is, the sum of the hours across all the cases), one would insert the previously mentioned two-statement DO loop that defines SUMH. The second statement indicates that $2,000 minus the sum of the expected values of the cases should equal zero or a negative number, meaning the expected income should be greater than $2,000. One can also insert the four statements that indicate the minimum hours per type of case as constraints in the optimizing problem.

B. From Other Law Practice Perspectives

To further illustrate the meaningfulness of the model, it seems appropriate to indicate how it can be applied by a personal injury defense counsel, a criminal prosecutor, and a criminal defense attorney. Those are the main types of attorneys who are involved in court cases. In personal injury cases, the plaintiff's lawyer wants to allocate his time so as to maximize the expected value of his cases (that is, so as to maximize the sum of the *PD* or $a(H)^b A(H)^B$ values of his cases). Defense counsel, on the other hand, wants to minimize the expected value of the same cases. In other words, the plaintiff wants the probability of a plaintiff victory (*P*) and the size of the damages awarded (*D*) to be as high as possible, whereas the defendant wants both *P* and *D* to be as low as possible.

Given that general orientation, it follows logically that if defense counsel were engaged in the same two cases as our hypothetical plaintiff's attorney, then the defense side would also solve the same pair of equations as equations 7.1 and 7.2 in order to determine how to optimally allocate his time if he had only 100 hours available. The difference in the defense perspective is that the *a, b, A,* and *B* for case 1 would be different for the defense side since those parameters would be arrived at by inputting into a computer for type 1 personal injury cases (1) whether the plaintiff or defendant won, (2) how much the damages were, and (3) how many hours the defense side put into each case, rather than how many hours did the plaintiff side put into each case. Obtaining those parameters would require a little extra effort by whatever looseleaf research service might be doing the same work for personal injury plaintiff attorneys, or the work could be done by a group of insurance companies interested in improving the efficiency of their personal injury lawyers. The same pair of equations with different parameters makes sense for either the defense or the plaintiff side because both sides would like to rationally equalize the MRRs of their cases so that nothing can be gained by shifting time from one case to another, although graphing both perspectives should produce substantially different graphs. For the plaintiff, the relation is positive (like the left side of a hill) between the probability of plaintiff victory (or of damages awarded) and the working hours of the plaintiff's attorney. For the defendant, the relation is negative (like the left side of a valley or a children's slide) between the probability of plaintiff victory (or damages awarded) and the working hours of the defense attorney.

The alternative nonlinear programming perspective for the defense side would involve computer statements like the following:

Minimize: $[a(H)^b A(H)^B]_1 + [a(H)^b A(H)^B]_2$

Subject to: $G(1) = 2 - H(1)$

$G(2) = 3 - H(2)$

$G(3) = H(1) + H(2) - 100$

The first statement indicates defense counsel wants to minimize the expected values of the two cases rather than maximize them as the plaintiff does. The second statement says 2 hours minus the hours allocated to case 1 should be less than or equal to 0, meaning case 1 should receive a minimum of 2 hours. The third statement says case 2 should receive a minimum of 3 hours. The fourth says the sum of the hours allocated to case 1 and case 2 minus 100 hours should be less than or equal to 0, meaning $H_1 + H_2$ should be less than or equal to 100.[16]

In criminal cases, we have a situation analogous to personal injury cases, although dollar awards are not involved. More specifically, a good prosecutor, like a personal injury plaintiff lawyer, is interested in going after the cases in which he has a good chance of winning and that involve important matters. In other words, a prosecutor wants to allocate his time so as to maximize the sum of the expected values across his cases. In determining the expected value for each case, one needs to consider the probability of a prosecutor victory (P). One also needs to consider the severity of the case or the likely sentence if the case is won (S). That S (or sentence value) is analogous to the D (or damages value) in personal injury cases. Thus, each criminal case in which a complaint has been filed (or in which the complainant is seeking to have the prosecutor file a complaint) has a $P(S)$, or expected value.

A state's attorney in a large county, or a group or association of state's attorneys, could compile information on many criminal cases with regard to (1) who won, (2) what sentence was handed down, and (3) how many hours were devoted by the state's attorneys to the case. That information could then be processed for different types of cases through a computerized log-linear regression analysis in order to obtain the parameter values expressing the relation (1) between probability of victory and hours put in [that is, $P = a(H)^b$], and (2) between the sentence received in those case where the defendant was convicted and the prosecutor's hours [that is, $S = A(H)^B$]. The expected value of a given criminal case or type of case is then $a(H)^b A(H)^B$ as it is in personal injury cases, although the parameters differ since they are based on criminal cases and prosecutors' hours. Thus, for two cases, the prosecutor could allocate a given number of hours by solving for simultaneous equations 7.1 and 7.2. For a larger number of cases, he could use the nonlinear programming approach discussed in section III-A.

The defense side in criminal cases is analogous to the defense side in personal injury cases. They are both interested in minimizing, rather than maximizing, the expected values of their cases. For example, a public defender who has many criminal cases would seek to concentrate on those in which he has the best probability of winning and of substantially reducing the defendant's sentence by putting in some extra hours. A public defender with many cases, or a group or association of public defenders, might find it worthwhile to obtain the a, b, A, and B parameters for various types of criminal cases with the H input being defense counsel hours. The same log-linear regression approach mentioned before can be used to obtain those parameters. Perhaps a commercial looseleaf service might find providing that information to be financially profitable for both personal injury lawyers and criminal lawyers. With those parameters a public defender's staff of attorneys could allocate their time more efficiently as attorneys for personal injury insurance companies could do, as discussed before. Private defense counsel in criminal cases, however, would not have as much incentive for using those methods since private defense counsel tends to be paid a flat fee of so many dollars per hour per case, whereas an increased caseload in a public defender's office does not necessarily mean an increase in salary or staff and thus time has to be allocated more in accordance with victory probabilities, likely sentences, and their relations to hours spent.

One could easily talk in terms of the probability of victory for cases other than personal injury or criminal cases. Likewise, one could develop outcome measures analogous to damages or sentences for probate cases, divorce cases, or other types of cases. Many types of cases, however, involve an hourly fee arrangement where the expected value of the case is not contingent on the outcome of the case. In other words, the probability of victory is not relevant to the fee received just as it is irrelevant in most doctor-patient relations. In those flat-fee cases, the expected value equals $R(H)$, where R is the hourly rate. The optimum allocation of a lawyer's time under those circumstances is to simply concentrate as much as he can on those accepted cases that have the highest hourly income rate. If those cases do not fill out his available time, then he should logically take on the next most profitable cases until he satisfies either his maximum time constraint or his desired income, assuming money and time are his only considerations as contrasted to the nonmonetary benefits that might come from taking on unprofitable public interest cases.

IV. Related Problems

A. The Decisions to Accept a Client and to Go to Trial

The analysis thus far has assumed that our hypothetical attorneys have agreed to take certain cases, and the question simply has been how they should allocate their time among those cases in order to maximize their income, subject to time and ethical constraints, or minimize their hours, subject to desired-income and ethical constraints. Making that allocation decision is separate from the decisions of whether to take on a prospective client and whether to go to trial.

The decision to accept a *plaintiff* client in a personal injury case, as with any rational decision, should be based on the benefits minus costs of accepting the potential client versus the benefits minus costs of rejecting the client.

Allocating Resources Among Court Cases

If we think just in terms of monetary benefits and not psychological benefits, one could say a personal injury plaintiff should accept a prospective client when one-third the expected value of the case (PD) is greater than the product of the hours to be allocated to the case (H) times how much the lawyer considers 1 hour of his time to be worth (R). The H, or hours to be allocated, can be explicitly or implicitly determined by the methods discussed in the previous sections of this chapter. In terms of symbols, one could say a plaintiff should be (1) accepted as a client if $.33(P)(D)$ as benefits is greater than $(R)(H)$ as costs and (2) rejected if it is less than $(R)(H)$ unless the plaintiff is willing to pay a flat hourly fee greater than R or an overall flat fee greater than $(R)(H)$. [If the contingency-fee rate is other than .33, that other rate should be substituted in the expression $.33(P)(D)$.] To give a dollar value to that expression, the attorney can consult the references and looseleaf services mentioned at the beginning of this chapter dealing with predicting victory probabilities (P) and damages (D). The *defense* side of personal injury cases is generally a salaried insurance company lawyer who has no choice as to which clients he will represent. He must defend all policy holders of the company who are involved in automobile or other accidents.[17]

The decision by a *prosecutor* to take on a client is somewhat analogous to the personal injury plaintiff. The prosecutor should prefer accepting complaints where there is a good probability (P) of getting a conviction and where the sentence (S) is likely to be relatively substantial, given the prosecutor's scarce time resources. However, we cannot say the prosecutor should accept cases when $(P)(S)$ is greater than $(R)(H)$ because $(P)(S)$ is measured in time units like months or years and $(R)(H)$ is measured in dollars.[18] To resolve that kind of measurement problem, each prosecutor could ask himself a series of questions that have been developed by psychologists whereby one can convert into a common unit (like dollars or satisfaction) something of value (that is, a benefit), like a prosecutor obtaining a 20-year conviction, and something of disvalue (that is, a cost), like a prosecutor putting in 50 hours of work on a case.[19] A simpler approach more in line with this chapter would be for the prosecutor to accept all complaints that satisfy a minimum probable-cause threshold of about a .30 probability of getting a conviction. Then, the cases with a low $(P)(S)$ value probably would wind up being allocated a very small number of hours under our rational allocation procedures, or they would wind up being settled for a plea of guilty to a rather minor charge under a rational set of plea bargaining procedures.

The public *defender* in criminal cases is like defense counsel for an insurance company in that he is obligated to represent all defendants found to be indigent, and he thus has no discretion as to whom he will take for a client as contrasted to whom he will take to trial. Private defense counsel, on the other hand, might rationally only represent those clients who are willing to pay (1) a flat hourly fee greater than what he considers 1 hour of his time to be worth or (2) an overall fee greater than his personal hourly rate times what quantity of hours he perceives the case will generally consume, or better yet, the quantity of hours to be allocated to the case if it were accepted.[20]

A *plaintiff's* attorney should decide to go to trial rather than accept an out-of-court settlement if $.33(P)(D) - (R)(H)$ is greater than what the defense side is offering. To be more exact, $(P)(D)$, or the expected value from going to trial, should be discounted or decreased in value for the fact that those dollars will not be received for a number of months or time periods (t), whereas defense counsel presumably will make a settlement payment immediately. The discounted formula is $(P)(D)/(1 + r)^t$, where r is the prevailing interest rate at which the money being offered by the defendant could be invested for t time periods.

A *defendant's* attorney should decide to go to trial rather than make a greater out-of-court offer if his offer becomes greater than what he perceives $(P)(D)$ to be. To be more exact, the defense attorney should be willing to add on a bonus to cover his litigation costs that he would be avoiding by an out-of-court settlement. Thus, he should be willing to raise his offer until it equals $(P)(D)$ plus his $(R)(H)$, just as the plaintiff's attorney subtracts $(R)(H)$ from $(P)(D)$. To be still more exact, defense counsel should take into consideration that he would be better off paying the plaintiff anything less than $1,060 a year from now than paying $1,000, because the $1,000 that would be paid now could be put into a savings account at 6 percent interest and be worth $1,060 a year from now. Thus, defense counsel should be willing to raise his offer until it equals $(P)(D)(1 + r)^t + (R)(H)$ in order to simultaneously consider the expected value of the case, the bonus for saving litigation costs, and the interest-gaining advantage of paying later.[21]

A *prosecutor* in a criminal case should be willing to go to trial rather than offer to accept a guilty plea to a lesser charge so long as the sentence associated with the lesser charge involves a number of years or months less than $(P)(S)$. The prosecutor, however, should be willing to deduct something from that $(P)(S)$ for the litigation time that he would save by an out-of-court settlement. Therefore, he should be willing to go to trial only if the pretrial sentence agreed to is less than $(P)(S)$, minus the litigation hours (H) he would have to put in or allocate, multiplied by what 1 hour is worth to him (R). If the hourly rate is expressed in terms of dollars, then $(R)(H)$ dollars cannot be subtracted from $(P)(S)$ years or months, and it may be too difficult to express R by saying 1 hour of the prosecutor's time is worth to him something like one extra month of jail time imposed on the defendant. It may, however, not be so difficult for the prosecutor to say in a given case

Allocating Resources Among Court Cases 235

that he would be willing to subtract a 10 percent discount (or other percent) off the $(P)(S)$ to avoid litigation. Thus, the prosecutor should be willing to go to trial only if the defendant is unwilling to agree to a sentence as high as $(P)(S) - \%(P)(S)$, where "%" is the discount percentage the prosecutor will offer to avoid litigation.

Likewise, the *defendant* should be willing to go to trial rather than accept the prosecutor's offer if the prosecutor is unwilling to come down to what the defendant perceives the expected value, or $(P)(S)$, of the case to be. Just as the prosecutor should be willing to offer a discount to avoid litigation, however, so also the defendant or defense counsel should be willing to add a bonus to avoid litigation. Thus, defense counsel should be willing to go to trial only if the prosecutor is unwilling to agree to a sentence as low as $(P)(S) + \%(P)(S)$, where "%" in this context is the bonus percentage defense counsel will offer to avoid litigation.[22]

By clarifying what is basically involved in the decision to accept a client and the decision to go to trial in both personal injury cases and criminal cases, we can see more clearly how those decisions relate to and differ from the decisions of how to allocate one's hours among one's cases. The decision to accept a client depends, as has been mentioned, on how much time will be allocated to the case. The decision to allocate, however, will not be implemented unless the case is accepted. Thus, the allocation decision is a prerequisite to the decision to accept, and the decision to accept is a prerequisite to carrying out the allocation decision. Once a case is accepted, hours should be tentatively allocated to it as if it might go to trial for many reasons: (1) That attitude is likely to lead to a better negotiated settlement. (2) It is difficult to predict which cases will be satisfactorily settled. (3) It would be contrary to the minimum ethical constraint to close out the possibility of going to trial when doing so might be in the best interest of the client. (4) Existing looseleaf service data are available for trial cases only. (5) Anticipated trial results affect negotiations. (6) One has less to lose by tentatively allocating too much time to a case than too little time. (7) If a case does not go to trial and thus does not use up its allocation, that allocation can be returned to the total hours available for reallocation to other cases. Thus, the decision to go to trial is irrelevant to the hours-allocation decision if one operates on the tentative assumption that all cases will go to trial.[23]

B. Implementing the Model

Throughout the chapter we have been mentioning various aspects of the work involved in implementing the model presented for allocating resources among court cases by legal counsel. It seem appropriate, however, to bring those ideas and related ones together at this point by way of summary and further clarification.

A key implementation problem relates to the argument that every case is unique and that one cannot allocate hours to a given case simply by knowing what type of case it is. In other words, no two rear-end collision cases are alike. One may require 30 hours and the other 10 hours. One answer to that point is the model never says any given type of case should be assigned a given number of hours. It says the number of hours assigned to a given case depends partly on the other cases one has accepted, their MRRs, and how many total hours are available. The quantitative allocations should also be treated as rough guidelines and not as straitjackets. Just as in flat sentencing judges are allowed to deviate from the determinate sentences by plus or minus a given percentage in view of aggravating and mitigating circumstances, likewise it might make sense for an attorney to deviate to some extent from the quantitative allocations in view of complicating circumstances that justify taking more time on a given case or mitigating circumstances that justify taking less time. An example of a complicating circumstance might be doing an especially good job on a low-return divorce case for a corporate officer in anticipation of receiving corporate law business. An example of a mitigating circumstance might be doing a below-allocation job (although above the minimum ethical level) on a criminal defense matter where the client is personally obnoxious, but for some reason had to be accepted and a withdrawal is not possible.

Another key implementation problem is how to make available to lawyers the parameters for the equations relating working hours (H) to victory probabilities (P), damages (D), and sentences (S) in various types of cases. By *parameters* we mean the numerical value of the a's and b's in the equations of the form $P = a(H)^b$ and the A's and B's in the equations of the form $D = A(H)^B$ or $S = A(H)^B$. To obtain those parameters for personal injury cases involves (1) obtaining a large, relevant sample of personal injury cases; (2) determining for each case whether the plaintiff won, what the damages were, and approximately how many working hours were spent by the attorneys for the plaintiff and the defendant; (3) inputting those data into a computerized, log-linear regression analysis with the data divided by different types of cases; and (4) recording those outputted parameters in a looseleaf service or other medium than can be updated periodically. To obtain the analogous parameters for criminal cases involves the same procedures although by substituting prosecutor for plaintiff, criminal defendant for civil defendant, and sentence in months or years for damages.[24]

The work of obtaining and processing those data and making available the results can be done by (1) a commercial firm like the Jury Verdict Research Corporation; (2) an association of personal injury lawyers or criminal lawyers; (3) an insurance company or group of insurance companies; (4) a government agency like the Justice Department, a state attorney general, or a group of states' attorneys or public defenders; or (5) a large law firm or group of law firms. Once the results are made available, however, they can be used by law firms or lawyers of any size in more rationally allocating their time among court cases.

The best way for a lawyer to use those parameters would be to have access to a terminal that connects to a computer system. The system would continuously store the parameters and their periodically updated versions, the amount of time the lawyer has available for one year or time period ahead of the present time, and data on what cases the lawyer has accepted as part of his pending cases and their deadlines. Whenever a potential new client comes in, the lawyer can decide whether to accept the client on an impressionistic basis or by doing a more quantitative analysis. Such an analysis might involve typing into the terminal some information that would enable the computer system to instantly feed back an hours allocation figure for the case so the lawyer could decide whether the probable fee (for example, $.33PD$) merits the hours involved or how to price the case to the client (for example, the total fee in an hourly rate case).

For determining the probable fee, the same computer system could supply the attorney with information concerning the probability of victory and the likely damages if the plaintiff does win. That information could also be useful in making decisions on whether to settle or go to trial. If the case is rejected or completed, it is removed from the computer storage. The computer would be programmed to do the nonlinear programming analysis discussed in section III in order to optimize the allocation of the attorney's scarce time in light of the case parameters. The continuous-storage terminal can periodically print out the updated allocations of all previous pending cases in light of what cases are completed and what new cases are added. It can also print out for each case how much time has been consumed on what activities, deadlines to watch for, and what activities are left. Other options also could be provided such as informing the attorney who wants to achieve only a certain income how many hours he would have to work over a given set of cases or how many cases he would have to add to his pending-cases agenda. The increased availability of computer terminals at low prices that are connected to time-sharing computer systems makes this scheme quite technologically feasible, especially if enough attorneys are interested in subscribing to the service.

For attorneys who cannot afford that kind of computer terminal arrangement of for the time being until such computer terminal arrangements are developed, attorneys can work directly with the information that could be provided by a looseleaf service, supplemented by a desk calculator. In its simplest form, the looseleaf service would mainly indicate the average quantity of hours spent by a sample of attorneys in various types of cases.

Those figures could then become the allocation figures or be helpful in supplementing a lawyer's knowledge of his own average time for various types of cases. In a somewhat more sophisticated form, the looseleaf service could provide the parameters relating fees received (F) in personal injury cases (or other cases not involving flat fees) to working hours (H) but only by using linear relations of the form $F = a + b(H)$.[25] That information could be used as part of the following optimizing model:

1. Initially allocate to each case the minimum hours necessary to satisfy ethical constraints.
2. Allocate the remaining hours equally among cases of the type that has the highest marginal rate of return (that is, the highest b parameter in the set of $P = a + bH$ equations), up to the maximum point where the looseleaf service indicates no substantial gains are made by adding additional hours.
3. Allocate the still-remaining hours equally to cases of the type that has the next highest MRR up to their maximum, and so on to cases having the third, fourth, and nth marginal rate of return until there are no remaining hours left to be allocated.

On a still more sophisticated level, the looseleaf service could provide the parameters for diminishing-returns relations of the form $F = a(H)^b$, $P = a(H)^b$, and $D = A(H)^B$. Using that information to optimally allocate one's hours involves solving either simultaneous equations (as discussed in sections I-B and III-A) or a nonlinear programming problem (as discussed in sections III-A and III-B). If a large number of cases were involved, however, either type of solutions would require punching the data on IBM cards or tape and then processing the cards or tape at a local computing center where an equation-solving program or a nonlinear programming routine is likely to be available. Doing that might be relatively easy for an insurance company or a government agency which has easy access to computer equipment and personnel, but not so easy for a small law firm or a lawyer. However, many insurance companies, government agencies, large law firms, and others could benefit from even this most sophisticated allocation model without having to wait for the next step of continuous-storage terminal operation.

Both the simultaneous-equation approach and the nonlinear programming approach require access to computers and relevant computer routines. One can, however, work with diminishing-returns relations by allocating to the cases in proportion to their *abAB* products, as discussed at the end of section I-B. Doing so requires only pencil and paper or a desk calculator, plus a looseleaf service or other means of circulating the parameters which relate fees received, victory probabilities, damages, and sentences to hours spent.

C. Other Applications of Portfolio Analysis to the Legal Process

As mentioned at the beginning of this chapter, the methodology we have been using is a variation on the more general methodology sometimes referred to as portfolio analysis. Its distinctive characteristic is that it involves allocating scarce resources in order to maximize one's goals in light of the fact that the relations between outputs and inputs depend on the probabilities of uncertain events (say, whether a case will be won or lost or whether a stock will pay a high or low dividend).[26]

As applied to the stock market, portfolio analysis involves first determining for each stock its average yield rate over the last few years. By *yield rate* in this context is meant the ratio of (1) the stock's incremental value at the end of each year, including both dividends and growth, to (2) the stock's initial value at the beginning of each year. Those ratios can be averaged over the last five or so years to obtain an average yield rate. For each stock, one then obtains a measure of spread around that average. The average deviation or the standard deviation can be used for such a measure.[27] If all other things are held constant, we would prefer the stocks which have the smallest spread or variance around their average yield rate, just as we perfer cases that are close to certainty of victory or at least not so unstable in their predictability.

The second step in generalized portfolio analysis is to input into the computer the yield rate for each stock for each year over the last five or so years. The computer is then instructed to determine the correlation between the yield rate of each stock and the yield rate of each other stock. The larger the correlation, the more risk is involved in purchasing those two highly correlated stocks since they are likely to fall or rise together. If all other things are held constant, we would prefer pairs of stocks or sets of stocks which have a small average correlation among them so as to avoid "having all the eggs in one basket." This is analogous to a law firm seeking to diversify its law practice by not being dependent exclusively on one type of case since the market for that type of case could fall out, leaving no alternative cushion.

The third step in a common version of portfolio analysis is to input into a nonlinear programming routine the average yield rate for each stock, the spread score for each stock, and the correlation between each pair of stocks. Along with that information goes an indication of how much capital is to be invested, what minimum yield rate we want on that quantity of capital, and a request to determine the optimum allocation of that capital among the stocks with no stock receiving less than zero dollars. By *optimum allocation* is meant one that minimizes a combination of average spread per stock bought and the average correlation among the stocks bought, while not exceeding our total budget or going below our requested average yield. It is possible that no allocation of the total budget will meet the requested average yield, especially if we also demand that the average spread and average correlation be below a given maximum. If that possibility occurs, then we might have to bring forth more capital or be satisfied with a lower average yield, just as an attorney allocating his hours to a set of cases might have to put in more hours or be satisfied with a lower income.

Having this more general picture of what portfolio analysis involves may stimulate thinking about its other applications to the legal process besides the allocation of time or other resources to the court cases of a personal injury or criminal lawyer. One interesting example proposed by Peter Aranson of the University of Miami Law and Economics Program conceptualizes sentencing as a portfolio analysis problem.[28] There are just so many years of penitentiary space available to be allocated among convicts. The problem is how to allocate those scarce units among convicted defendants in light of the facts that each defendant, given the nature of his crime, has a probability (P) of repeating his crime or another crime and each crime has a degree of societal damages (D). Deterrence theory assumes that the probability (P) of recommitting one's crime is partly a function of the length of one's sentence (S). If we could obtain recidivism data for many convicted defendants and data on how long they were imprisoned, then we could determine the parameters for the relationship $P = a(S)^b$, using the same kind of analysis previously discussed for determining the relationship between victory probabilities and working hours, or $P = a(H)^b$. The expected value for a given sentence would thus be D discounted by P, or $Da(S)^b$. Then the problem becomes one of allocating our total sentencing capacity so as to minimize the sum of those expected values across types of cases, just as we would allocate our total time capacity to maximize the sum of the expected values if we were a personal injury plaintiff's lawyer.

In Aranson's proposal, he is concerned more with the decision to jail or not jail certain types of convicts than with the length of sentence that should be imposed. That decision is more analogous to the decision whether to accept a client, or the decision whether to buy a stock, rather than the more difficult decision of how much time to allocate to a client or how many dollars to allocate to a stock. Also Aranson is impliedly concerned with the optimum mix of burglars, robbers, rapists, and others in the penitentiary population in view of the limited penitentiary space, the probabilities of recidivism, and the damage done if various crimes are repeated. As another insight, Aranson sees the problem as one of seeking the smallest amount of damages for a given level of risk or the smallest amount of risk for a given level of damages, much like the investment banker who seeks the highest expected return at a maximum allowable risk or the lowest risk at a minimum expected return. This example of sentencing allocation illustrates the many new insights that a portfolio analysis perspective can stimulate. Stimulating such new insights in the legal process or other processes is the main function of a good deductive model, of which portfolio analysis is a good example.[29]

V. Some Conclusions

The essence of the allocation model presented is simply to try to have balance across one's cases so that the time one is allocating to different cases is done in such a way that nothing is to be gained by transferring time from one case or type of case to another. The model also emphasizes the need to think in terms of how much extra income will be received as a result of putting in extra time. In other words, it emphasizes the marginal rate of return on an investment of time, rather than the more traditional and less optimal approach of thinking in terms of the benefit-cost ratio between income and hours in a given case, which is the equivalent of the average rather than the marginal rate of return.

That basic model has been discussed in the context of simplifications with regard to constant, linear, and nonlinear relations between hours worked and either victory probabilities or judgments. The basic model can be varied to consider (1) contingent fees, (2) expenses, (3) the need to increase one's available hours, (4) the alternative goal of minimizing hours subject to a desired income, (5) the flexibility of one's hours, (6) other variables besides hours worked which determine victory probabilities and judgments, and (7) thinking in terms of fees received rather than victory probabilities and judgments.

The basic model can be expanded to include large quantities of cases or types of cases which can be processed so as to arrive at optimum allocations through the use of newly developed nonlinear programming routines. The basic model also can be expanded to include the allocation perspective of both the plaintiff and the defense side in personal injury cases, both the prosecution and the defense in criminal cases, and also other types of cases. The model fits well with other models that deal with the decisions to accept a client and to go to trial. At this stage, what the model especially needs are some applications by looseleaf services, associations of lawyers, insurance companies, government agencies, or large law firms. Those applications will help to further refine the basic model and render it even more useful.

Even if the model is not implemented soon by way of the continuous-storage terminal approach or the looseleaf services approach, just thinking in terms of the types of concepts involved can improve the allocative efficiency of legal counsel by emphasizing balance across one's cases and marginal analysis. The model provokes questions that may lead to further analysis and research concerning (1) how attorneys actually allocate their hours among their cases, (2) what attorneys consider to be the ethical minimums required by various types of cases, (3) how attorneys determine their maximum hours available within a given time period, (4) what attorneys consider to be a desired income beyond which it may not be worth working additional hours, and (5) to what extent attorneys could handle a more quantitative approach for allocating hours, deciding what cases to accept, and deciding whether to settle or go to trial. The portfolio analysis model also has potential for providing insights into the allocation of other scarce resources in the legal process besides the time of attorneys, where the optimum allocation depends on the payoffs from the activities or places to which resources are allocated, with the payoffs being contingent on the probability of the occurrence of intervening events. In general, this kind of optimizing perspective may have good potential for better understanding and improving various aspects of the legal process. It is hoped this chapter will help stimulate the development of that potential.

Notes

1. [Since 1962] *Jury Verdict Expentancies Service* (Statewide Jury Verdicts Publishing Co.); J. Grossman and J. Tanenhaus, eds., *Frontiers of Judicial Research* 307-372 (Wiley, 1969); G. Schubert, ed., *Judicial Decision-Making* 111-200 (Free Press, 1963); Baade, "Jurimetrics," 28 *Law & Contemp. Prob.* 1 (symposium issue 1963); and S. Nagel, *The Legal Process from a Behavioral Perspective* 125-172 (Dorsey, 1969).

2. [Since 1962] *Valuation Handbook Service* (Statewide Jury Verdicts Publishing Co.); [since 1963] *Current Money Awards* (Lawyers Co-operative Publishing Co.); R. Hand and R. Singer, *Sentencing Computation Laws and Practice: A Preliminary Survey* (ABA, 1974); Reeder, "Formulae for Evaluation of Damages," *Law Notes* (January 1967); Nagel, "Statistical Prediction of Verdicts and Awards," *Modern Uses of Logic in Law* 135 (1963); and J. Hogarth, *Sentencing as a Human Process* (Toronto University Press, 1971).

3. Other studies dealing with the allocation of resources among court cases by legal counsel include Forst and Brosi, "A Theoretical and Empirical Analysis of the Prosecutors," 6 *J. Legal Stud.* 177 (1977); Landes, "An Economic Analysis of the Courts," 14 *J. Law & Econ.* 61 (1971); J. Lachman, "An Economic Model of Plea Bargaining in the Criminal Court System" (Unpublished Ph.D. dissertation in the Michigan State University Department of Economics, 1975); and Schwartz and Mitchell, "An Economic Analysis of the Contingent Fee in Personal Injury Litigation," 22 *Stan. L. Rev.* 1125 (1970). In those criminal justice studies, however, the allocation decision generally is only a part of a broader economic model of the behavior of prosecutors or the criminal justice system. In the personal injury study by Schwartz and Mitchell, the emphasis is on the optimum number of hours to allocate to a single case taken out of the context of other cases that are competing for one's scarce time. Both the prior criminal and civil studies are relatively more concerned with describing and explaining attorney decision making by using an economic model, than with trying to improve the efficiency of attorney decision making by using an implement-

able management science or operations research model. A more recent and relevant paper is Noam, "Case Quotas in the Court: An Analysis of Judicial Resource Allocation" (Unpublished paper available from the author at Columbia University, May 1978). Noam's paper, however, is oriented more toward a mathematical and statistical analysis of what percentage of the trial court cases should be devoted to robbery, burglary, larceny, automobile theft, and assault in light of various criteria, rather than how legal counsel should allocate time to cases.

4. At first glance, the symbolism and formulas in this chapter may not seem so simple. Appendixes 7A and 7B help clarify the meanings of and the relations among the symbols and the formulas, respectively. Relatively technical matters are left to the notes, as are references where further detail can be provided. Variations on the basic methodology are simple enough to be applied by a nonquantitative lawyer with pencil and paper or a desk calculator, as will be described presently, provided that certain input parameters are supplied to lawyers by commercial research firms, associations of lawyers, insurance companies, government agencies, or in-house researchers working within larger law firms.

5. For further detail on the methodology for finding an optimum mix in general, see S. Richmond, *Operations Research for Management Decisions* 277-404 (Ronald, 1968); W. Baumol, *Economic Theory and Operations Analysis* 167-294 (Prentice-Hall, 1965); M. Brennan, *Preface to Econometrics: An Introduction to Quantitative Methods in Economics* (Southwestern, 1973); and S. Nagel and M. Neef, *Legal Policy Analysis: Finding an Optimum Level or Mix* (Lexington Books, 1977). For further detail on the portfolio analysis perspective for finding an optimum mix under conditions of uncertainty, see C. McMillan, *Mathematical Programming: An Introduction to the Design and Application of Optimal Decision Machines* 177-180 (Wiley, 1970); W. Baumol, *Portfolio Theory: The Selection of Asset Combinations* (General Learning Press, 1970); S. Kassouf, *Normative Decision Making* 55-64 (Prentice-Hall, 1970); and J. Dickinson, *Portfolio Analysis: A Book of Readings* (Lexington Books, 1974).

6. This strategy is analogous to developing a flat sentencing law by merely codifying the average sentences for each type of crime. Doing so may increase sentencing objectivity by eliminating disparties in the sentences of defendants convicted of the same crime. Doing so, however, will not necessarily generate sentences that are optimum in the sense of minimizing the sum of the recidivism costs and the jail maintenance costs, or optimum in terms of achieving some other purpose besides sameness in sentences. It would, however, be helpful for attorneys to know on the average how much time is spent by plaintiff's or defendant's counsel in different types of personal injury cases so they can know how they are doing in comparison to their fellow lawyers, just as it is helpful for judges to know on the

average what damages are granted in different types of personal injury cases or sentences in criminal cases. If no better information is available or easily acquired, emulating the previous average behavior may make the most sense, assuming that human decision makers on the average do tend to implicitly maximize their benefits minus costs even if they do not explicitly use quantitative optimization methods.

7. For further detail on using computerized regression analysis to relate a variable being predicted (like P) to a variable being predicted from (like H), see section IV-B which deals with implementing the model.

8. For further accuracy while still avoiding the solving of simultaneous equations, one can allocate to each case in accordance with the product of the multiplier or scale coefficient of its marginal rate of return, that is, $(b + B)(aA)$, and the exponent or elasticity coefficient, that is, $b + B - 1$), rather than just the $abAB$ product. As described later, computerized regression analysis can provide the numerical values for the a, b, A, and B parameters. In allocating proportionately, one would give only the minimum number of hours required to a case having a negative $abAB$ product, or else the case would not be taken in the first place. Thus, in allocating proportionately, the only $abAB$ products summed into the denominator would be positive ones, that is, cases where additional hours produce increased expected income.

9. Under a workmen's compensation system, the amount of damages is predetermined by statute or administrative rule once liability has been established. Working extra hours, though, can influence the damages awarded by establishing liability for a more severe injury. Likewise, under a flat sentencing system, the sentence is predetermined by a statute once guilt has been established, but working extra hours can result in establishing guilt to a more severe charge. In the Forst and Brosi model, however, only the probability of guilt is influenced by the prosecutor's expenditure of resources, not the length of the sentence even under traditional discretionary sentencing. Forst and Brosi, "A Theoretical and Empirical Analysis of the Prosecutor."

10. There are other nonlinear ways of relating victory probabilities or damages awarded to hours spent besides $P = a(H)^b$ or $D = A(H)^B$. For example, a better fit to the data might be a cubic relation of the form $P = a + b_1H + b_2H^2 + b_3H^3$. That type of relation implies that additional hours at a low or high level of hours results in no substantial increase in the probability of victory, but that in the middle range additional hours can substantially increase the probability of victory. Working with nonlinear equations of that form, however, would make the analysis substantially more complicated probably without sufficiently offsetting benefits in terms of increased accuracy.

11. It may be impossible to equalize the marginal rates of return, not only because of the limited total hours available but also because the regres-

sion analysis may show a negative slope between hours and expected values for a given type of case. Under those circumstances, cases of that type should be given whatever minimum amount of time is necessary to satisfy the ethical constraints. A case with a negative slope does not mean it is unprofitable. It merely means that putting additional hours into such a case relates to a decrease in the probability of victory or damages received rather than an increase. Such a relation is unlikely to be a causal relation but may reflect either an unduly small sample of cases on which the slope is based or the fact that additional hours tend to occur coincidentally with some variable that relates to reduced victory or reduced damages.

12. Allocation models dealing with how would-be criminals might allocate their time between legal and illegal activities also operate with a concept of a finite amount of time. See Becker, "Crime and Punishment: An Economic Approach," 76 *J. Pl. Economy* 169 (1968), and Correa, "A Mathematical Model of Rational Choice between Criminal and Non-Criminal Activities," *Modeling Simulation* 516 (1976).

13. Another variation on this fee-received variation would involve combining types of cases into a single equation. In other words, the fee-received model involves having one equation of the form $F = a(H)^b$ for each case or type of case and then attempting to equalize the MRRs across the cases by solving for a set of equations of the form $[ba(H)^{b-1}]_1 = [ba(H)^{b-1}]_2$, and $H_1 + H_2 = G$, where G is the grand total of hours available. The variation on that model involves having one equation of the form $F = a(H_1)^{b1}(H_2)^{b2}$ which includes all cases simultaneously. One could then optimally allocate G to each case that has a positive exponent or elasticity coefficient by simply allocating in proportion to those exponents; that is, case i would get a proportion of G equal to b_i divided by the sum of the positive b's. That is algebraically the equivalent of equalizing the marginal rates of return in light of this new combination equation, while spending the grand total of hours available. One defect in that approach, however, is that it is meaningful with only the fee-received model rather than the model that decomposes expected fees into victory probabilities and damages awarded, since only fees or damages can be meaningfully combined, but not probabilities of two cases in this context. The approach also has the defect of combining cases in one equation such that their elasticity coefficients become less meaningful as a result of being too dependent on what other cases happen to be in the equation and the intercorrelations among the cases.

14. For further detail on multivariate regression analysis see E. Tufte, *Data Analysis for Politics and Policy* 135-163 (Prentice-Hall, 1974); and J. Guilford and B. Fruchter, *Fundamental Statistics in Psychology and Education* 326-395 (McGraw-Hill, 1973). Probabilities for hours spent and urbanism can be combined by using Bayesian probability formulas. F. Mosteller, *Probability with Statistical Applications* 143-150 (Addison-Wesley,

1961). Here, however, we are interested in deriving new parameters from the data base, not in combining old parameters or probabilities to create new ones.

15. The P-CON nonlinear programming routine was developed at Livermore Laboratories in Livermore, California. It is based on an algorithm developed by M.J.D. Powell. A copy of the program deck is available on request from the authors at the University of Illinois. For further detail on this program and nonlinear programming in general, see Powell, "An Efficient Method for Finding the Minimum of a Function without Calculating Derivatives," 7 *Computer J.* 155 (1964); D. Himmelblau, *Applied Nonlinear Programming* (McGraw-Hill, 1972); and McMillan, *Mathematical Programming.*

16. A more sophisticated but unnecessarily complicated approach would involve determining the relation between the probability of a plaintiff victory (P) or damages awarded (D) and both the hours of the plaintiff attorney (H_p) and the hours of the defense attorney (H_d) in equations of the form

$$P = a(H_p)^{b_1}(H_d)^{b_2} \quad \text{and} \quad D = A(H_p)^{b_1}(H_d)^{b_2}$$

To use those parameters, the plaintiff's attorney would plug in the average number of hours for the defense side, and he or she then would use the equation-solving or nonlinear programming approach to find the optimum number of hours for his side. The defense attorney would do likewise with those kind of parameters.

17. The decision to accept a client in a personal injury case is discussed in Schwartz and Mitchell, "An Economic Analysis of the Contingent Fee"; Jury Verdict Research, Inc., *How to Use the Personal Injury Valuation Handbooks to Predict Personal Injury Verdicts* (Jury Verdict Research, Inc., 1967); and F. MacKinnon, *Contingent Fees for Legal Services: A Study of Professional Economics and Responsibilities* (Aldine: 1964).

18. At first glance, one might say we do have a common unit of measurement already, namely time. That, however, is not true. Only the benefits are measured in time or years in jail, that is, $(P)(S)$. The costs are measured in dollars or a monetary value of time, that is, $(R)(H)$. If we drop the R, then both benefits and costs would be measured in time. That would not make sense, though, since the cost is not just hours but how much they are worth. More important, one hour of a prosecutor's time spent on a case clearly does not produce the same dissatisfaction or cost as an hour taken off a defendant's sentence.

19. R. Keeney and H. Raiffa, *Decisions with Multiple Objectives: Preferences and Value Tradeoffs* (Wiley, 1976); J. Cochrane and M. Zeleny, eds., *Multiple Criteria Decision Making* (University of South Carolina

Press, 1973); and A. Easton, *Complex Managerial Decisions Involving Multiple Objectives* (Wiley, 1973).

20. The decision to accept a client in criminal cases is discussed in J. Jacoby, *Pretrial Screening in Perspective* (LEAA, 1976); J. Jacoby, *The Prosecutor's Charging Decision: A Policy Perspective* (LEAA, 1977); Abrams, "Prosecutorial Charge Decision System," 23 *UCLA L. Rev.* 1 (1975); F. Miller, *Prosecution: The Decision to Charge a Suspect with a Crime* (Little, Brown, 1969); and A. Wood, *Criminal Lawyer* 96-102 (College and University Press, 1967).

21. The decision to settle or go to trial in a personal injury case is discussed in Friedman, "An Analysis of Settlement," 22 *Stan. L. Rev.* 67 (1969); Johnson and Tersine, "The Mathematical Evaluation of Trial versus Settlement," 78 *Case & Comment* 3 (1973); and Posner, "An Economic Approach to Legal Procedure and Judicial Administration," 2 *J. Legal Stud.* 399 (1973).

22. The decision to settle or go to trial in a criminal case is discussed in Nagel and Neef, "Plea Bargaining, Decision Theory, and Equilibrium Models," 51 *Ind. L. J.* 987 (1976), 52 *Ind. L. J.* 1 (1976); Landes, "An Economic Analysis of the Courts"; Lachman, "An Economic Model of Plea Bargaining"; and G. Tullock, *The Logic of the Law* 174-186 (Basic Books, 1971).

23. Another related interesting decision that attorneys often face is the order in which cases should be handled. If one is seeking to minimize the average amount of time spent on cases from the date the case is opened until it is closed, then the optimum strategy generally is to take the shortest cases first while making sure the longest cases are handled before their deadlines expire, rather than handle cases on a first come, first served basis. J. Byrd, *Operations Research Models for Public Administration* 152-156 (Lexington Books, 1975); R. Conway, W. Maxwell, and L. Miller, *Theory of Scheduling* (Addison-Wesley, 1967); and Nagel and Neef, "Time-Oriented Models and the Legal Process: Reducing Delay and Forecasting the Future" (Unpublished paper presented at the annual meeting of the American Society for Public Administration, 1978).

24. For further detail on computerized regression analysis whereby one uses many cases to determine a diminishing-returns relation between a variable to be predicted and a variable to be predicted from, see N. Nie, C. Hull, J. Jenkins, K. Steinbrenner, and D. Bent, *Statistical Package for the Social Sciences* 320-373 (McGraw-Hill, 1975); Tufte, *Data Analysis for Politics and Policy,* pp. 1-134; and H. Blalock, *Social Statistics* 361-413 (McGraw-Hill, 1972).

25. To determine the parameters for that equation involves inputting into a computerized regression analysis for many cases the fee received in each case and the hours worked in each case. The fees are sometimes zero in

personal injury cases where the plaintiff's attorney loses the contingency fee by not winning the case. If by *fee* we mean the net fee (that is, income minus expenses), then the fees are sometimes negative where money has been spent for filing, investigation, or other costs and no income is received.

26. For references to portfolio analysis, see note 5.

27. The average deviation is determined by summing for each year the difference between the actual yield and the average yield and then dividing by the number of years, ignoring whether the difference is positive or negative. The standard deviation is determined by summing the squares of those differences, dividing by the number of years, and then taking the square root of that quotient.

28. P. Aranson, "Post-Conviction Decisions in Criminal Justice" (Unpublished paper, presented as a research proposal to the Law Enforcement Assistance Administration, 1975).

29. Alvin Klevorick finds the concepts of portfolio analysis to be helpful in discussing optimum jury composition. Klevorick, "Jury Composition: An Economic Approach," in *The Interaction of Economics and the Law,* B. Siegan, (Lexington Books, 1977). The analogy does not apply to the prosecutor who would like to have all prosecution-oriented jurors, or to defense counsel who would like to have all defense-oriented jurors, rather than a mixed portfolio. The Supreme Court would like to see a representative mix on juries in order to satisfy the Equal Protection clause. Portfolio analysis supports that notion by virtue of its concern for not having all one's eggs in one basket, which is analogous to not having all jurors of one type. Perhaps, however, an optimal jury is not necessarily a representative one, but rather one that has people all of one type, namely the type of people who are unlikely to convict an innocent person or to acquit a guilty person. Representativeness, though, may be a more important equal protection consideration than quality of outcomes, since representativeness may be more important for legitimacy of governmental action in a democracy. The reasoning in the above note also applies to civil cases.

Appendix 7A.
Glossary of Symbols

Symbol	Represents	Section First Appearing
Basic Variables:		
1. Specific		
P	Probability of victory in a given case. The actual probability for a single case that has already been decided is either 0 or 1.00. The predicted probability derived from a regression analysis can range from 0 to 1.00.	I-B
D	Damages awarded in a given case, either actual damages or predicted damages	I-B
F	Fee received in a given case, either actual or predicted	I-B
S	Sentence received in a given case, either actual or predicted	III-B
H, H^*	Hours spent in a given case, either actual (H) or optimum (H^*)	I-B
2. General		
Y	A defendent variable to be maximized or minimized such as P, D, S, or F	I-B
X	An independent variable which influences Y and whose quantity needs to be determined, such as H	I-B
Basic Parameters:		
1. In relations of the nonlinear form $Y = aX^b$ or $Y = AX^B$		
a	Victory probability or fee received if $H = 1$. Also referred to as the *scale coefficient* or *multiplier* in the relation	I-B
b	Percentage of increase in P or F when H goes up 1 percent. Also referred to as the *elasticity coefficient* or *exponent* in the relation	I-B
A	Quantity of damages or length of sentence if $H = 1$	I-B
B	Percentage of increase in D or S when H goes up 1 percent	I-B
2. In relations of the linear from $Y = a + bX$ or $Y = A + BX$:		
a	Probability of victory if $H = 0$	II-A
b	Increase in P when H goes up 1 unit	II-A
A	Quantity of damages or length of sentence if $H = 0$	II-A
B	Increase in D or S when H goes up 1 unit	II-A

Symbol	Represents	Section First Appearing
Accepting a Client and Settling out of Court:		
R	Amount a lawyer considers one of his hours to be worth	IV-A
r	Prevailing interest rate at which money being offered by a personal injury defendant could be invested	IV-A
t	Time periods between when a settlement offer might be accepted and when a trial judgment might be received	IV-A
%	Discount percentage the prosecutor is willing to offer to avoid litigation, or the bonus percentage defense counsel is willing to offer to avoid litigation	IV-A
Miscellaneous Symbols:		
MRR	Marginal rate of return, or increase in P, D, F, or S when H goes up a small unit in either a nonlinear or linear relation	III-A
SUMH, G	The sum (Σ) or grand total of the hours available, or the goal to be minimized when one is seeking to minimize work while providing a given income	III-A
i	ith case, or any case	III-A
U	Urbanism or city size as an independent variable which influences P, D, F, and S in addition to the influence of H	III-A
$G(i)$	Zero is greater than or equal to what follows. The i indicates the number of constraint.	III-A

See the list of formulas in appendix 7B for how various concepts are calculated.

Appendix 7B.
Basic Formulas Used

Symbol	Represents	Section First Appearing
Basic Relations:		
1. General:		
$Y = aX^b$	A nonlinear relation in which changes in X do not produce constant changes in Y, but rather diminishing or increasing returns	I-B
$Y = a + b(X)$	A linear relation in which a 1-unit change in X constantly produces the same b change in Y	I-B
2. Specific:		
$P = A(H)^b$ and $P = a + b(H)$	Relating victory probabilities to hours spent in either a linear or nonlinear relation	I-A
$D = A(H)^B$ and $D = A + B(H)$	Relating damages awarded to hours spent	I-B
$S = A(H)^B$ and $S = A + B(H)$	Relating sentences received to hours spent	III-B
$F = a(H)^b$ and $F = a + b(H)$	Relating fees received to hours spent, for example $F = 0 + 30(H)$, where an attorney is paid a fee of $30 an hour rather than a fee contingent on victory; or for example, $F = 500 + O(H)$ where an attorney is paid a flat fee of $500 regardless of hours or victory	II-B
$P = a(H)^{b_1}(U)^{b_2}$	Relating victory probabilities to both hours spent and the urbanism or city size of the cases	III-A
D or $S = A(H)^{B1}(U)^{B2}$	Relating damages or sentences to both hours spent and urbanism or city size of the cases	III-A
Expected Values (EV's):		
1. General:		
$P(D)$ or $P(S)$	The predicted damages discounted by the probability of victory for plaintiff, or the predicted sentence discounted by the probability of victory for the prosecutor	I-B
2. Nonlinear, Linear, and Constant Relations:		
$a(H)^b A(H)^B$ or $(aA)(H)^{b+B}$	Expected value of case where P, D, and S bear a nonlinear relation to H	I-B
$(a + bH)(A + BH)$	Expected value of case where P, D, and S bear a linear relation to H	II-A

Symbol	Represents	Section First Appearing
$P \cdot A(H)^B$	Expected value of case where D and S bear a nonlinear relation to H, but P bears no relation	II-A
$a(H)^b\, D$ and $a(H)^b\, S$	Expected value of case where P bears a nonlinear relation to H, but D and S bear no relation	II-A

3. Considering Contingency Fees and Expenses:

$.33a(H)^b A(H)^B$	Expected value of personal injury case to a plaintiff's attorney considering a one-third contingency fee (C), assuming nonlinear relations between P, D, and H	II-B
$a(H)^b A(H)^B - E$	Expected value of case considering the nonhours expenses (E) that need to be subtracted from expected income	
$a(H)^b A(H)^B - R(H)$	Expected value of case considering the deduction from expected income for hours spent times rate per hour (R) which lawyer considers his time to be worth	II-B

Note: Additional expected values can be created depending on how one combines different types of the above expected-value relations and whether one includes C, E, and RH.

Marginal Rates of Return:

1. General:

b	When $Y = a + bX$	II-A
baX^{b-1}	When $Y = aX^b$	I-B

2. Specific:

$(b+B)(aA)(H)^{b+B-1}$	When $EV = a(H)^b A(H)^B = (aA)(H)^{b+B}$	I-B
$aB + 2bB(H)$	When $EV = (a + bH)(A + BH)$	II-A
$BPA(H)^{B-1}$	When $EV = P \cdot A(H)^B$	II-A
$bDa(H)^{b-1}$	When $EV = a(H)^b D$	II-A
$(b+B)(C)(aA)(H)^{b+B-1}$	When $EV = Ca(H)^b A(H)^B$	II-B
$(b+B)(aA)(H)^{b+B-1}$	When $EV = (aA)(H)^{b+B} - E$	II-B
$(b+B)(aA)(H)^{b+B-1} - R$	When $EV = a(H)^b A(H)^B - R(H)$	II-B

Optimum Hours to Spend:

1. General:

$H_1 + \cdots + H = G$ $MRR_1 = \cdots = MRR$	The equations that need to be satisfied simultaneously in order to optimally allocate hours across cases, assuming at least some nonlinear relations and assuming one wants to maximize income or net income subject to limited hours	I-B

Appendix 253

2. Variations:

$H_1^* = G[(abAB)_i / \sum(abAB)]$	Equation for allocating to each case that has a positive $abAB$ product in proportion to those products	II-B
$EV_1 + \cdots + EV = \min Y$ $MRR_1 = \cdots = MRR_n$	Equations that need to be satisfied simultaneously in order to optimally allocate hours across cases, assuming one wants to minimize hours subject to a minimum income	II-B
Maximize: $EV_1 + \cdots + EV_n$ Subject to: $H_1 + \cdots + H_n \leq G$	Objective function and key constraint in a nonlinear programming way of expressing the problem of allocating hours to maximize income subject to a maximum time available	III-A
Minimize: $H_1 + \cdots + H_n$ Subject to: $EV_1 + \cdots + EV_n \geq \min Y$	Objective functions and key constraint in a nonlinear programming way of expressing the problem of allocating hours to minimize time subject to a minimum income	III-A

Note: Any of the above ways of expressing the optimum hours to spend could involve grouping the cases into types and could include minimum time constraints for specific cases or types of cases.

Accepting a Client and Settling out of Court:

1. Some Acceptance Criteria:

$(C)(P)(D) \lessgtr (R)(H)$	For plaintiff's lawyer in personal injury case: Accept client if CPD greater than RH; otherwise, reject	IV-A
$F \lessgtr R(H)$ or $R(H^*)$	For private defense counsel in criminal case: Accept client if F greater than RH; otherwise, reject	IV-A

2. Some Settlement Criteria:

$(C_2)(P)(D)/(1+r)^t - (R)(H)$ $\lessgtr (C_1)D$'s offer	For plaintiff's lawyer in personal injury case: Accept D's offer if first expression is less than second expression; otherwise reject. C is contingent-fee rate if case goes to trial, and C is contingent-fee rate if case is settled. H in this context represents trial and trial preparation hours.	IV-A
$(P)(D)(1+r)^t + (R)(H)$ $\lessgtr P$'s offer	For defense lawyer in personal injury case: Accept P's offer if first expression is greater than P's offer; otherwise, reject	IV-A
$(P)(S) - \%(P)(S)$ $\lessgtr D$'s offer	For prosecutor in criminal case: Accept D's offer if first expression is less than D's offer; otherwise, reject	IV-A
$(P)(S) + \%(P)(S)$ $\lessgtr P$'s offer	For defense lawyer in criminal case: Accept P's offer if first expression is greater than P's offer; otherwise, reject	IV-A

See the glossary in appendix 7A for definitions of the symbols.

8

Using Decision Deterrence Theory to Encourage Socially Desired Behavior

Much has been written in recent years designed to test the extent to which increasing the probability of being caught or increasing the severity of punishments has a substantial impact on decreasing criminal behavior.[1] Most of that research involves at least two limitations. First, the research tends to be highly statistical with an emphasis on having a large amount of quantitative data, but it generally lacks a causal theoretical orientation. Second, the research tends to be confined almost exclusively to street crimes, as contrasted to business and governmental wrongdoing. One purpose of this chapter is to discuss the applicability of decision theory and deterrence theory to generating ideas for encouraging socially desired behavior even in the absence of quantitative data. A second purpose is to attempt to apply deterrence ideas across diverse would-be wrongdoers who might engage in traditional criminality, economic regulation violations, or noncomplying governmental behavior.

By *decision theory* we mean the study of which available decision should be reached in order to maximize benefits minus costs in light of the probable occurrence of uncertain events. In the context of encouraging socially desired behavior, the decision theory problem basically involves how to increase the perceived expected benefits minus costs of doing the socially desired act relative to the socially undesired act. The key uncertain events are the probability of being (1) detected, (2) determined to be a wrongdoer, and (3) negatively sanctioned.[2]

By *deterrence theory* we mean a perspective or body of knowledge that emphasizes wrongdoing behavior as being due to implicit benefit-cost considerations by the wrongdoer, rather than as being due to having a deviant or diseased personality that is in need of therapy. The deterrence perspective thus tends to view wrongdoers as being more analogous to entrepreneurs seeking profitable activities than to tuberculosis patients in need of an antibiotic. "Decision deterrence theory" thus involves a combination of the deductive modeling that is associated with decision theory and the criminological substance that is associated with deterrence theory.[3]

I. Criminal Law Applications

Figure 8-1 attempts to apply decision deterrence theory to the problem of how to deter store robberies, or, stated more positively, how to encourage

256   Decision Theory and the Legal Process

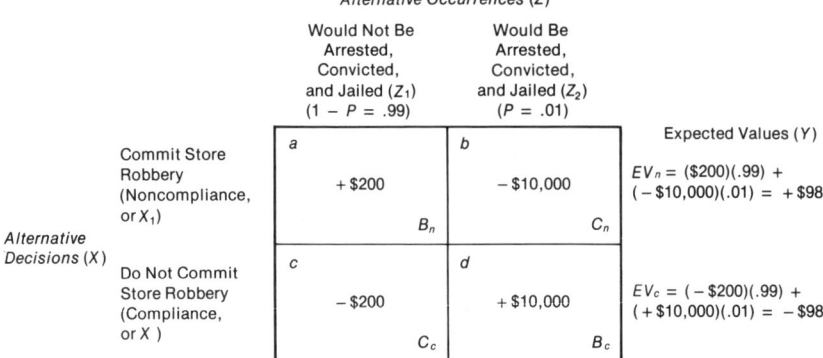

To make EV of compliance greater than EV of noncompliance:

I. Increase perceived probability of being arrested, convicted, and jailed (that is increase P).
   A. Relatively conservative approach: Lessen due process
   B. Relatively liberal approach: More professionalism in police and prosecution
   C. Threshold P or $P^* = c/(c + b) = \$200/\$10,200 = .02$
II. Decrease perceived benefits of noncompliance and costs of compliance (that is, decrease Z_1).
   A. Conservative: Harden the targets by, for example, having less accessible cash.
   B. Liberal: Rechannel peer group approval.
   C. Threshold Z_1 or $Z_1^* = Pd/(1 - P) = \$100/.99 = \$101$
III. Increase perceived costs of noncompliance and benefits of compliance (that is, increase Z_2)
   A. Conservative: More suffering in prison
   B. Liberal: More alternative opportunity costs
   C. Threshold Z_2 or $Z_2^* = (1 - P)(a)/P = \$198/.01 = \$19,800$.

Abbreviations: B = benefits, C = costs, n = noncompliance, c = compliance; a, b, c, d = cell entries or outcome payoffs; EV = expected value, or $B - C$.

General Rule: Comply if EV of compliance is greater than EV of noncompliance.

Figure 8-1. Increasing Compliance in the Criminal Law Context.

would-be store robbers to decide against committing a store robbery. The figure involves a payoff matrix in which the alternative decisions are listed to the left of the rows. Those decisions consist of either committing the store robbery (the noncomplying or socially undesired decision) or not committing the store robbery (the complying or socially desired decision). The alternative possibilities relevant to the uncertain event are listed on the columns. There are two possibilities: the decision maker would not be arrested, convicted, and imprisoned, or the decision maker would be arrested, convicted, and imprisoned. We could increase the number of decisions available by specifying alternatives to or ways of committing the store robbery, but starting with the choice between two decisions will help to clarify the model. Likewise, we could later increase the number of alternative outcome possibilities by, for example, thinking in terms of (1) not being arrested and thus not being convicted or imprisoned, (2) being arrested by not being convicted and thus not imprisoned, (3) being arrested and convicted but not imprisoned, and (4) being arrested, convicted, and imprisoned.

A. Clarifying the Payoff Matrix

The four cells in the payoff matrix indicate the benefits or costs associated with each combination of decision alternative on the rows and outcome possibility on the columns. Thus, cell *a* indicates the benefits of not complying (B_n) when one would get away with noncomplying behavior. Cell *b* indicates the costs of not complying (C_n) when one would not get away. Cell *c* indicates the costs of complying (C_c) when one would be able to successfully not comply, that is, successfully commit the store robbery. Cell *d* indicates the benefits of complying (B_c) when one otherwise would be arrested, convicted, and imprisoned.

To clarify further this simple decision theory model, we can try inserting some dollar values into the cells, although the decision theory often works well by merely inserting relative values into the cells with the worst cost anchored at ÷100 and the best benefit anchored at +100. The dollar values should reflect the subjective perceptions of our would-be average store robber. Those values could be determined by interviewing a sample of convicted store robbers or possibly using street-wise insiders to interview unconvicted store robbers. Perhaps such interviewing might reveal that the average respondent interviewed or a specific interviewee perceives the average store robbery of a given type of store to be good for $200, as indicated in cell *a*. For the sake of simplicity, we can assume there are no costs involved in a successful store robbery such as time or other expenses, or we can assume the $200 represents a net gain after subtracting such expenses. Also, for the sake of simplicity and logical consistency, it is reasonable to say that if committing a successful store robbery nets $200, then deciding not to commit the store robbery when one could have done so successfully means an opportunity cost of a lost $200. That $200 could have also been determined by calculating the average take from store robberies, although such a calculation would reflect the actual benefits and costs of the first column rather than the more important perceived benefits and costs.

Determining the benefits and costs in the second column is a more difficult undertaking because the cost of being arrested, convicted, and imprisoned is so inherently subjective. A researcher, however, could interview convicted or unconvicted store robbers, asking them how many dollars would they be willing to pay (if they had the money) to avoid being arrested, convicted, and imprisoned for what they perceive to be the average prison sentence for an unsuccessful store robbery. With our data, we have indicated that our hypothetical store robber would be willing to pay $10,000 to avoid such imprisonment. Thus, if our would-be store robber chooses not to commit the store robbery when he would have been arrested, convicted, and imprisoned, then he has, in effect, saved himself $10,000 worth of cost or suffering. The $10,000 in cell d does not mean he gets paid $10,000 for not committing a store robbery. Rather, it is an opportunity benefit just as the $-\$200$ in cell c is an opportunity cost, that is, a benefit or a cost from not taking advantage of the opportunity to rob the store in question.

The next logical step in the analysis is to determine what the benefits minus costs are for each alternative decision. However, it would not make sense to calculate the benefits minus costs of committing a store robbery by simply combining the $200 positive benefit and the $10,000 negative cost and thereby arrive at a figure of $-\$9,800$. Instead, those benefits and costs need to be discounted by the probability of their occurring before they can be combined. The probability of suffering the $10,000 cost is equal to the perceived probability of being arrested, convicted, and imprisoned (symbolized P). One could arrive at an actual probability by determining what proportion of the store robberies in a given city resulted in somebody being arrested, convicted, and imprisoned. Again, though, the more important probability is the one perceived by our would-be store robber. In this hypothetical example, he perceives his odds of getting away as being about 100 to 1, or in probability terms 100 out of 101, or .99 (symbolized $1 - P$), which means only a .01 probability of being arrested, convicted, and imprisoned.

Thus, the expected benefits minus costs of committing a store robbery equal (1) the $200 benefit discounted or multiplied by the .99 probability of occurrence and (2) the $10,000 cost discounted by the .01 probability of occurrence. That combination of expected benefits and expected costs equals $198 minus $100 for an expected net benefit figure of $98. Likewise, the expected benefits minus costs of not committing the store robbery equal (1) the $10,000 benefit discounted by the .01 probability of occurrence and (2) the $200 cost discounted by the .99 probability of occurrence, or $100 minus $198 for an expected net benefit figure of $-\$98$. In other words, in this example, our would-be store robber would perceive a higher expected value from committing the store robbery, rather than from refraining from doing so. If our would-be store robber is motivated by only these monetarized considerations, then logically he or she would choose to commit the store robbery.[4]

B. Determining the Threshold Values

One useful purpose of this type of mathematical model is to inform criminal justice policy makers what the threshold values of P, B_n (or C_c), and B_c (or

C_n) are, such that our average store robber would switch from deciding to rob the store to not robbing it, assuming everything else is held constant. To calculate the threshold value of P, we set $(\$200)(1 - P) + (-\$10,000)(P)$ equal to $(-\$200)(1 - P) + (+\$10,000)(P)$, and then solve for P. Doing so reveals a threshold P of .02. One could algebraically show that .02 can be arrived at more simply by just dividing $200 by $10,200, or $c/(c + b)$. The .02 means that if the would-be robber perceived his probability of being imprisoned as being greater than .02, then he would be better off not robbing the store, given the $200 and $10,000 payoff values. Likewise, he would rob the store if he perceived the probability as being less than .02, and he would be undecided at about .02.

To calculate the threshold value of the benefit of not complying, we likewise set $(+Z_1)(.99) + (-\$10,000)(.01)$ equal to $(-Z_1)(.99) + (+\$10,000)(.01)$, and then solve for Z_1, where Z_1 equals the absolute value of either B_n or C_c. Doing so reveals a threshold Z_1 of $101. One could show algebraically that $101 can be arrived at more simply by just dividing .01 times $10,000 by .99, or $Pd/(1 - P)$. The $101 means that if the would-be robber perceived the store take as being less than $101, then he would be better off not robbing the store, given the .01 probability of being imprisoned at $10,000 worth of suffering.

To calculate the threshold value of the benefits of complying, we set $(+\$200)(.99) + (-Z_2)(.01)$ equal to $(-\$200)(.99) + (+Z_2)(.01)$ and then solve for Z_2, where Z_2 equals the absolute value of either B_c or C_n. Doing so reveals a threshold Z_2 of $19,800. One could show algebraically that $19,800 can be arrived at more simply by just dividing .99 times $200 by .01, or $(1 - P)(a)/P$. The $19,800 means that if the would-be robber perceived the suffering costs of being imprisoned as greater in value than $19,800, then he would be better off not robbing the store, given the .01 probability of being imprisoned and the $200 robbery take. In other words, with these hypothetical data, we could convert a prorobbery decision to an antirobbery decision by approximately doubling the .01 probability of being imprisoned, halving the $200 robbery take, or doubling the $10,000 imprisonment cost to the would-be store robber.

C. Increasing Compliance

The most useful purpose of this decision theory perspective probably is not the above quantitative uses, which do help understand the model, but rather the use of the perspective in generating insights on how to decrease wrongdoing behavior. Given our simple model, basically only three general approaches can be followed to increase compliance and decrease noncompliance. Those three general approaches stem from the fact that there are only three variables in the model to be manipulated namely, P, Z_1, and Z_2.

Stated in words rather than symbols, we can try to (1) increase the probability of being arrested, convicted, and imprisoned; (2) decrease the absolute value of cells a or c, which means decreasing the benefit of noncompliance or the cost of compliance; or (3) increase the absolute value of cells b or d, which means increasing the cost of noncompliance or the benefit of compliance. Any one of those three approaches will increase the likelihood that the expected value of compliance will become greater than the expected value of noncompliance, and then the complying behavior will be more likely to occur.

Merely pointing out those three approaches, however, does not in itself determine what policies to adopt since there are many ways of furthering each of those three subgoals and because there is nothing inherent in the deductive logic of the model as to which policies or combinations of policies are most effective. Under each of the three approaches one could talk in terms of a conservative or prosecution orientation, or in terms of a liberal or defendant orientation. A conservative orientation with regard to increasing the probability of being arrested, convicted, and imprisoned might emphasize reducing due-process restrictions on each of those three sets of procedures. Thus, one might argue in favor of making arrests, stops, or searches easier by requiring less than probable cause of wrongdoing, such as mere suspicion when someone is seen looking in a store window who looks too poor to be a customer of that store. Likewise, convictions could be made easier by allowing evidence that is based on an illegal seizure, a confession without warnings, or questionable hearsay. Imprisonment upon conviction could be guaranteed by abolishing probation, suspended sentences, and community-based corrections regardless of the circumstances. On the other hand, a more liberal orientation might emphasize increasing the probability of arrest, conviction, and imprisonment by developing more professionalism on the part of police, prosecutors, and other criminal justice personnel. That might include automatic suspensions of police officers who engage in illegal searches on the first occasion and automatic dismissals on the second occasion, especially if illegally seized evidence tends to decrease the chances of obtaining convictions.

A conservative orientation toward decreasing the benefits of noncompliance is reflected in the policies of the Law Enforcement Assistance Administration (LEAA) under Richard Velde. It emphasizes what is sometimes referred to as "hardening the targets." In the context of store robberies, this might mean developing systems of computerized credit via pushbutton telephones so as to minimize the cash carried in the cash register or by customers. It might also mean building bulletproof glass walls through which sales people transact business with customers in order to decrease the access of a would-be robber to the cash register. A more liberal orientation, although not necessarily mutually exclusive with target hardening, might emphasize decreasing the peer-recognition benefits received by many successful store robbers. More specifically, the typical robber of certain types of stores or the typical mugger may tend to be someone between the age of 15 and 25 who engages in such behavior at least partly because it brings a kind of prestige among fellow gang members. Thus what may be helpful in decreasing the benefit of successfully "knocking over" a gas station or a "mom and pop" grocery store is to somehow change how prestige is obtained among such people. The Office of Economic Opportunity Community Action Program attempted to do that among the Black Peacestone Rangers on Chicago's South Side in the 1960s by redirecting their aggressiveness into rent strikes, consumer boycotts, election campaigning, and picketing government agencies. That type of antipoverty gang work was, however, stopped largely as a result of the negative reaction of Senator McClellan's investigating committee, which some people interpreted as being more bothered by that kind of community action than by the robbing and mugging it may have decreased.

On the matter of increasing the cost of noncompliance and thus the opportunity benefits of complying, a conservative orientation might emphasize having longer prison sentences, more use of the death penalty, and more severe prison conditions. A liberal orientation, on the other hand, might equally recognize the need for increasing the cost of noncompliance, but instead emphasize a different set of costs, namely, the opportunity costs one suffers as a result of being arrested, convicted, and imprisoned, or even just arrested. Middle-class business executives do not rob stores or mug people in parks. They probably do not refrain from doing so because of fear of lengthy and severe imprisonment, since they may be likely to receive probation if a first offense is involved. A more important reason for their restraint is probably the fear of losing all the opportunities available to them in the middle-class business world. What may be needed is to give typical, would-be store robbers more alternative opportunities that they risk losing if they are arrested for robbery or other crimes. This may require changing our educational institutions, neighborhood housing patterns, hiring procedures, and other socioeconomic institutions in order to make those alternative opportunities more meaningful. If the gang member had more employment opportunities, not only would he suffer greater opportunity costs from getting arrested, buy also he would receive less incremental benefits from an extra dollar obtained from a store robbery, and he would have less need for antisocial peer recognition. Clearly, however, the opportunity costs approach to increasing the cost of noncompliance is a much larger social undertaking than the approach which emphasizes longer and more severe sentences.[5]

One can readily see from the above example and numerous others that a decision theory model can be heuristic, suggestive, or provocative of ideas that might otherwise be overlooked in the absence of such an organized model. The model, though, is no substitute for thinking and for understanding the subject matter. Some people who use this type of deductive approach would, however, have us think that their conclusions at the Roman numeral level of figure 8-1 logically follow from the basic premise of the model that individuals choose alternative decisions that maximize their perceived benefits minus costs. Thus, they might argue that to decrease criminal behavior, we should decrease its benefits and increase its costs (which makes sense), and then conclude prison sentences need to be lengthened (which does not necessarily follow from the model). The important value of this decision theory perspective is that it provides a kind of checklist of categories from which to generate ideas and on which to hang or organize the ideas that have been generated. The model can be made more elaborate than a simple four-cell payoff matrix by adding additional rows and columns, as previously mentioned, or by having cells that are not the same as other cells in absolute value. Nevertheless, a model as simple as this one can be useful in encouraging socially desired behavior even in the absence of quantitative data.[6]

II. Business Regulation Applications

In discussing criminal law applications of using decision deterrence theory to encourage socially desirable behavior, we started with a problem and used the decision deterrence theory perspective to suggest a variety of solutions or means for lessening the problem. An alternative use for decision deterrence theory is to start with a set of suggested solutions to a problem and then analyze their effectiveness in light of the theory. The field of environmental pollution lends itself nicely to that approach.

Pollution is determined largely by business practice, rather than by individual, nonbusiness behavior. For example, water pollution primarily comes from the wastes of such industries as paper, chemicals, petroleum, electrical, steel, and mining. It also comes from agricultural wastes in the form of runoff from feedlots, fertilizers, and pesticides. Municipal waste treatment could be substantially improved with regard to residential wastes, but most municipal wastes come from industrial and commercial establishments within municipal areas. Air pollution problems are partly associated with factories, but even more with the transportation industry, especially how automobiles are made. The solid waste problem also can be viewed as one of trying to change business practices with regard to returnable containers and the recycling of steel, but also encouraging better government landfills and solid waste collection. Radiation pollution is associated with the nuclear energy industry, and noise pollution with industrial and transportation noises. To the extent that individual wrongdoing is responsible, the criminal law applications of the model may be applicable, as discussed in the previous section. To the extent that governmental wrongdoing is responsible, the governmental applications may be applicable, as discussed in the forthcoming section.[7]

A number of incentives have been proposed for encouraging compliance with environmental standards. They include pollution taxes, injunctions, civil penalties, fines and jail sentences, tax rewards and subsidies, selective government buying, publicizing polluters, and conference persuasion.[8] Each such incentive, however, is likely to be effective only if it can have a favorable influence on one of the three key variables mentioned in figure 8-1. In other words, to be effective, these incentives or procedures must (1) increase the perceived cost of noncompliance or the benefit of compliance, (2) decrease the perceived benefit of noncompliance or the cost of compliance, and/or (3) increase the perceived probability of occurrence of the cost or benefit.

Often the idea of a pollution tax is mentioned as an especially effective incentive. Its effectiveness is largely due to the fact that it would directly increase the cost of noncompliance since the tax would be proportionate to the amount of pollution caused by the business taxpayer. A common formula with regard to water pollution involves determining the total cost needed to keep a river segment at a given level of water quality, and then assessing each business firm on that river segment a portion of the total cost equal to the ratio between the firm's pollution and the total pollution in the river segment. By reducing its pollution, each firm thereby lowers its tax assessment, and that lowered assessment represents an increased benefit of compliance. Thus, a pollution tax increases the cost of noncompliance and the benefit of compliance. The effectiveness of pollution taxes is also enhanced by virtue of automatic monitoring systems which are often a part of such proposals. Those systems increase the probability of the above costs and benefits occurring by making the assessment and collection of the tax or fee relatively automatic, as compared to proposals that require more active judicial action to enforce.

Proposed judicial action against polluters tends to be of three kinds: injunctions, civil penalties, or criminal sanctions. Like pollution taxes, the effectiveness of all three tends to depend on how they influence the costs of noncompliance (and the complementary benefits of compliance) and also the probability of those benefits and costs occurring, although all three have different influences. Injunctions to cease or suspend operating are the most costly to the polluting business firm, but they have the lowest probability of occurring. If an injunction is requested by a government agency, a private group, or an individual, normally a judge would be quite reluctant to order a steel mill or other manufacturing establishment to shut down in view of the economic damage such a decision might mean to the employees, consumers, stockholders, and community of the business firm. Civil damages are normally easier to obtain, especially if they are brought under a legal procedure that limits defenses available, such as in workmen's compensation actions. Civil damages are, however, normally less costly to the business firm than injunctions, unless a large class action is involved which decreases the probability of success. Criminal penalties in the pollution context are almost exclusively fines, rather than jail sentences. Such fines are easier to obtain than injunctions since they are not so economically disruptive to third parties, but they are more difficult to obtain than civil damages since they involve the more stringent due-process standards associated with criminal law. Such fines also tend to be in the middle between injunctions and individual damages with regard to the costs to the polluting firm if imposed, although fines can range from low, easily absorbed business expenses to assessments comparable to pollution taxes on up to the unlikely possibility of highly punitive fines.

Other proposals place emphasis on decreasing the money saved by noncompliance and decreasing the cost of compliance, rather than increasing the cost of noncompliance. Such proposals include tax rewards and subsidies. For example, installing equipment to decrease air, water, and other forms of pollution is normally an expensive cost of compliance. Government policy, though, can ease that cost by providing extra large business deductions or even credits for doing so, or the government can provide outright grants or no-interest, long-term loans to further reduce the cost of compliance. Those benefits are likely to occur if such government programs are instituted. In other words, business firms are likely to make the changes if the government, in effect, makes them cost-free or combines a cost-reducing program with one that provides enforced penalties for noncompliance. Large government subsidies to private industry, however, may not be so likely to get through the legislative process because of opposition from those who feel business should be doing more on its own, just as pollution taxes are not so likely to get through the legislative process because of opposition from those who feel they are too much of a burden on business.

Other proposals are likely to be less effective than the ones mentioned above because of their lack of influence on the key benefits, costs, and probabilities of the benefits and costs occurring. For example, selective government buying power, in theory, rewards nonpolluters for complying (a benefit of compliance) and makes polluters suffer an opportunity cost (a cost of noncompliance). In practice, however, too many polluting firms are not greatly affected by government purchases. Legislators and government purchasing agents also find it difficult to have pollution criteria override criteria relating to the cost and quality of the products purchased. Likewise, government publicizing of the names of polluters in order to get private consumers to engage in selective buying also has a low probability of the benefits and opportunity costs occurring, especially where the product is not a name brand or not a product bought by ultimate consumers. Conference persuasion is an especially ineffective approach, although it was a major part of water pollution enforcement prior to 1972. Merely trying to convince business polluters of the social harm they are doing is not likely to encourage any socially desired behavior since it causes no increase in the costs of noncompliance, decrease in the benefits of noncompliance, or change in the probability of either of those costs or benefits occurring.

The above discussion is rather general in the sense that it is primarily concerned with discussing a series of proposals in terms of what costs, benefits, or probabilities they effect. The discussion can be made more precise by talking in terms of more specific proposals and more specific types of business firms. One can develop for the pollution field a series of payoff tables showing specific dollar amounts, probabilities, and expected values. One could then determine how much the costs, benefits, or probabilities have to be changed to make the expected value of compliance with the environmental standards greater than the expected value of noncompliance. Even the above general discussion, though, can be helpful in organizing one's ideas and in making a preliminary assessment of the relative value of alternative proposals for encouraging socially desired business or other behavior. The basic ideas can also be applied to other forms of business regulation besides environmental protection such as consumer fraud, worker safety, produce safety, antitrust practices, unfair management or union practices, stock manipulation, and landlord abuses.[9]

III. Applications to Noncomplying Public Officials

This book has already discussed one application of decision deterrence theory to encouraging socially desired behavior on the part of government personnel. That application involved encouraging arraignment judges to be more willing to release defendants prior to trial in accordance with the presumption of innocence and with legal rules that say doubtful cases should be resolved in favor of releasing rather than holding.[10]

In that application, we mentioned raising and clarifying the probability of appearance through screening, notification, and statistical studies and prosecuting those who fail to appear. We also mentioned making more visible the costs of holding defendants who would appear (that is, the costs of not complying with the presumption of releasing). That possibly can be done by publicizing for each judge the percentage of defendants he holds and the appearance percentage he obtains, on the assumption that the high holders will be embarrassed by not being able to show any greater appearance rate than the low holders. The judicial system can also make more visible the costs and drawbacks of holding defendants in jail such as jail maintenance, lost income, bitterness from having one's case dismissed after a lengthy wait in jail, welfare costs due to loss of family income, the increased wrongful conviction probability, and jail riots due to overcrowding. We also mentioned decreasing the cost of releasing defendants who fail to appear (that is, the costs of complying with the presumption of releasing). That could be done by pretrial supervision which facilitates rearrest, decreasing the time from arrest to trial, and decreasing pretrial crime committing through proposals like those associated with the criminal law applications of decision deterrence theory.

All the previous decision theory models have involved simplified payoff tables in which we assume that the costs of noncompliance equal the benefits of compliance but are opposite in sign, and likewise that the unsigned benefits of noncompliance equal the costs of compliance. A more sophisticated and often more realistic payoff table recognizes that with four possible outcomes, one could have four different magnitudes, not just two. This is how the payoff tables are developed in the plea bargaining model of chapter 3 and in a detailed version of the jury decision-making model of chapter 6. At this point, we would like to apply that kind of analysis to the problem of how to increase the likelihood that prosecutors and other court personnel will make time-saving rather than time-lengthening decisions in order to decrease judicial delay and congestion.

Figure 8-2 applies that type of decision deterrence analysis to the problem of how to get prosecutors and assistant state's attorneys to make decisions to accelerate the slow and difficult cases so they do not exceed a maximum time threshold. Doing that could involve (1) increasing the benefits and decreasing the costs from making time-saving decisions, (2) decreasing the benefits and increasing the costs from making time-lengthening decisions, and (3) increasing or decreasing the probabilities of relevant contingent events. To encourage favorable time consumption decisions, assistant state's attorneys can be given monetary rewards (to increase the benefits) and work-saving resources (to decrease the costs). Likewise, to discourage unfavorable time consumption decisions, state's attorneys can, in effect, by punished by providing for an absolute discharge not subject to reprosecution of excessively delayed defendants, and they can be deprived of the plea bargaining benefits of lengthy pretrial incarceration by providing more release on recognizance. These devices are more specifically described in figure 8-2. They may incur substantial monetary and nonmonetary speed-up costs to the system which may outweigh the delay costs. Decision deterrence theory, however, does stimulate one's thinking with regard to how decision makers can be influenced to make time-saving decisions if one is, at least for the moment, primarily concerned with time saving.

Using Decision Deterrence Theory

	Alternative Occurrences		
	Being Penalized for Lengthening Time (P)	Not Being Penalized for Lengthening Time ($1 - P$)	Benefits Minus Costs
Time-saving Decision (S)	B_S Benefits from S	C_S Costs from S	$B_S - C_S$
Time-lengthening decision (L)	C_L Costs from L	B_L Benefits from L	$(B_L)(1 - P) - (C_L)(P)$

Alternative Decisions

To Increase the Likelihood that Time-saving Decisions Will Be Chosen:

I. Increase the benefits from making time-saving decisions (that is, increase B_S).
For example, reward assistant state's attorneys with salary increases and promotions for reducing the average time consumption per case.

II. Decrease the costs of making time-saving decisions (that is, decrease C_S).
For example, establish a computerized system that informs assistant state's attorneys concerning actual and predicted times at various stages for all cases to minimize the trouble involved to the attorney in keeping track of cases. Also, provide more investigative and preparation resources.

III. Increase the costs incurred from making time-lengthening decisions (that is, increase C_L).
For example, provide under the speedy-trial rules for absolute discharge of the defendant whose case extends beyond the time limit rather than just release on recognizance.

IV. Decrease the benefits from making time-lengthening decisions that is, decrease B_L).
For example, increase release on recognizance so that lengthening the pretrial time will not make the jailed defendant more vulnerable to pleading guilty.

V. Raise the probability of the decision maker being penalized for lengthening time (that is, increase P).
For example, allow fewer exceptions to the speedy-trial rules such as suspending their application "for good cause" or "exceptional circumstances."

Abbreviations: P = probability of being penalized, B = benefits, C = costs, S = time-saving decision, L = time-lengthening decision.

Figure 8-2. Increasing the Likelihood that Prosecutors will Reach Time-Saving Decisions.

A similar decision theory analysis could be applied to the decisions made in the public defender's office or the offices of private defense attorneys. The suggestions there for encouraging time-saving decisions may, however, conflict with the decisions applicable to the state's attorney. For example, one might recommend more pretrial release to decrease the benefit the prosecutor receives from the increased willingness to plead guilty by defendants held in jail. On the other hand, one might recommend less pretrial release in order to make the defendant (and indirectly his attorney) suffer more from delaying the case. In such conflicting situations, one has to decide which side is more responsible for the delay or decide on the basis of criteria other than saving time. There are also benefit-cost suggestions stimulated by this analysis applicable to the defense side that do not conflict with the previous suggestions applicable to the prosecution. For example, providing monetary rewards to assistant public defenders and more resources does not conflict with the prosecutor suggestions, unless one assumes there is a fixed quantity of resources available to the criminal justice system, and that whatever the prosecutor gets must be taken away from the public defender or other parts of the system.

A similar decision theory analysis could also be applied to judicial decisions that affect delay. For example, as of now, judges incur virtually no personal costs from granting repeated continuances or making other delaying decisions. If, however, records were publicized showing for each judge in a given court system how long on the average he or she takes to process cases of various types, that visibility might cause the especially slow judges to change their ways so as to come closer to the averages. Such a publicizing system (even just among the judges rather than among the general public) would increase the costs of making time-lengthening decisions. That kind of recordkeeping can also be done for making comparisons across assistant state's attorneys and assistant public defenders in a given court system, or across court systems if one calculates separate averages for cases of different types of severity and different expected time consumptions.

Numerous other applications could be developed of decision deterrence theory applied to noncomplying public officials. For example, one could talk about how to encourage police officers to issue more summons and make less formal arrests when they observe minor wrongdoing. Some of the same proposals that apply to the pretrial release decision would also apply there. Likewise, those proposals might apply to encouraging probation officers or parole boards to give the benefit of doubtful situations to the applicant for probation or parole as the law generally implies. Decision deterrence theory has been applied to discussing how to obtain greater compliance on the part of school board officials with regard to court desegregation school prayers, and disciplinary procedures. The model can be applied not only to governmental administrators, but also to legislators with regard to discouraging corrupt behavior. That type of application may involve a combination of proposals directed simultaneously at legislators, business firms, and bribe-offering individuals, thereby combining all three types of applications dealt with in this chapter.[11]

IV. Some Conclusions

In this chapter, we have discussed applying decision deterrence theory to encourage socially desired behavior largely through the use of examples rather than general principles. The general principles of decision deterrence theory consist basically of three overlapping ideas relating to assumptions, predictions, and prescriptions concerning behavior. On the assumptions level, the theory assumes all people, when faced with a set of alternative choices, will choose the alternative that maximizes their perceived benefits minus costs, discounted by the probability of the benefits or costs occurring, including nonmonetary benefits and cost like the security of not taking risks or the fun of taking them. On the predictive level, the theory says people will change their behavior if the perceived expected value of the new behavior becomes greater than the perceived expected value of the old behavior. On the prescriptive level, the theory says if society or public policy makers want to encourage socially desired behavior, they should arrange for such behavior to have a higher perceived expected value than the corresponding socially undesired behavior.

That kind of theory is virtually tautological in that it says, in effect, that people do what they think will give them the greatest satisfaction, and satisfaction is what people seek to maximize. That kind of theory is also quite in conformity with common sense, at least when the language is further simplified. In spite of its simplicity, however, decision deterrence theory can serve many useful purposes. First, in random order, it can help suggest specific prescriptive proposals for encouraging socially desired behavior. This is illustrated by the example of encouraging prosecutors to make time-shortening decisions, which is summarized in figure 8-2. Second, the theory can generate predictive hypotheses. This is illustrated by the example of encouraging arraignment judges to release defendants prior to trial by publicizing their holding rates and appearance rates in anticipation that doing so will cause the high holders to do more releasing. Third, the theory can help organize ideas into categories, as in the store robbery example summarized in figure 8-1.

Fourth, the theory can help test the meaningfulness of prescriptive proposals, as in the pollution reduction example. Fifth, the theory can provide explanations for data-based findings. A good illustration of that relates to the finding mentioned in chapter 2 that the optimum percentage of defendants to hold in jail prior to trial (about 4 percent) is substantially lower than the actual percentage which is held (about 27 percent). An important explanation seems to be that arraignment judges are making release-hold decisions more on the basis of their personal costs and benefits (including the embarrassment of a no-show defendant), rather than on the basis of social costs and benefits (including the high costs of holding defendants in jail). Sixth, the theory can be helpful in suggesting what data to gather in data-based legal process research. For example, the juror decision theory model of chapter 6 suggest the value of gathering data on how jurors might respond to different types of judicial instructions in order to encourage them to apply desired standards of guilt beyond a reasonable doubt.

Not only does decision deterrence theory have many potentially useful purposes, but it is also broadly applicable regardless of subject matter and regardless of the availability of relevant data. With regard to subject matter, we have seen some ways the theory can be applied to criminal behavior, business regulation, and noncomplying government officials. There are also many other applications as varied as discouraging unretrieved dog droppings, and unreturned cafeteria trays, negligent driving, and nonsupport.[12] With regard to available data, the theory is useful whether the payoff tables contain actual numbers (as in the data-based pretrial release example) or hypothetical numbers (as in the store robbery example). It is also useful whether the payoff tables contain absolute amounts (as in the store robbery example) or relative amounts (as in the basic pretrial release example). The theory is even useful regardless whether the payoff tables contain numbers (as in either the store robbery or pretrial release examples) or merely symbols in cells (as in the time-shortening example) or a purely narrative approach without drawing payoff tables (as in the pollution example).

On a broader level than decision theory applied to deterrence situations, it is hoped that this book will stimulate the development of the potential which a decision theory perspective has for increasing effectiveness, objectivity, and understanding of the legal process. All the uses mentioned above for decision deterrence theory are also applicable to general decision theory where there is no deterrence concern. For example, figure 5-3 illustrates the use of decision theory to predict the effect of judicial system changes on the likelihood of a plea bargaining settlement being reached and at what level. Likewise, that same chapter 5 uses decision theory to make policy proposals concerning how plea bargaining can be made to result in the same sentences that would be arrived at if all cases went to jury trials without the time, expense, and lessened predictability of actually having jury trials.

As mentioned, such a perspective merely involves viewing individuals as decision makers seeking to maximize their perceived benefits minus costs discounted by the probabilities of the benefits and cost occurring. Although the perspective is a simple one, it can help planners deduce the effects of policy changes before the policies are adopted so the policies can be more effective, and it can help policy makers develop policies that will achieve given goals under varying conditions including the goals of more objectivity and legal conformity across cases. What may be especially needed now are more researchers and practitioners to apply that basic perspective to a variety of legal process situations and policy problems.

Notes

1. Items that contain examples or reviews of regression analysis studies which attempt to relate criminal behavior to punishment severity and the probability of being caught include Lee McPheters and William Stronge, eds., *The Economics of Crime and Law Enforcement* (Thomas, 1976); Charles Tittle and Charles Logan, "Sanctions and Deviance: Evidence and Remaining Questions," 7 *Law & Society Rev.* 371-392 (1973); Morris Silver, *Punishment, Deterrence, and Police Effectiveness: A Survey and Critical Interpretation of the Recent Econometric Literature* (CCNY Crime Deterrence and Offender Career Project, 1976); Alfred Blumstein, ed., *Deterrence and Incapacitation: Estimating the Effects of Criminal Sanctions on Crime Rates* (National Academy of Sciences, 1978); Philip J. Cook, "Punishment and Crime: A Critique of Current Findings concerning the Preventive Effects of Punishment," 41 *Law & Contemp. Prob.* 164-204 (1977); and Soloman Kobrin et al., *The Deterrent Effectiveness of Criminal Justice Sanction Strategies* (USC Public Systems Research Institute, 1972).

2. For general discussions of decision theory, see Wayne Lee, *Decision Theory and Human Behavior* (Wiley, 1971); Ruth Mack, *Planning on Uncertainty: Decision Making in Business and Government Administration* (Wiley, 1971); Rex Brown et al., *Decision Analysis for the Manager* (Holt, Rinehart and Winston, 1974); and R.C. Jeffrey, *The Logic of Decision* (McGraw-Hill, 1965).

3. For general discussions of deterrence theory, see Franklin Zimring and Gordon Hawkins, *Deterrence: The Legal Threat in Crime Control* (University of Chicago Press, 1973); Franklin Zimring, *Perspectives on Deterrence* (NIMH Center for Studies of Crime and Delinquency, 1971); Jack Gibbs, *Crime Punishment and Deterrence* (Elsevier, 1975); and William Chambliss, "Types of Deviance and the Effectiveness of Legal Sanctions," 1967 *Wisc. L. Rev.* 703-719 (1967).

4. This example assumes our would-be store robber is just faced with a choice of committing or not committing a store robbery. The situation would be different if he were faced with a problem of how to spend his time over a given time period, such as whether to spend the coming year engaged in store robberies that might net $20,000, if he gets away with them, or engage in being a shipping clerk that would net a certain $5,000, or about $100 per week. In that situation, our would-be wrongdoer would be risk-neutral if he chooses the store robbery career only when he perceives the probability of getting away with it as being greater than .25. He would be a risk preferrer if he is willing to be a store robber when the probability of getting away with it is less than .25. He would be a risk avoider if he foregoes being a store robber when the perceived probability of getting away with it is greater than .25. This assumes the only cost of noncompliance is

the lost $5,000 a year in certain income. If the probability of getting away is .25, then the probability of being caught is .75. That figure is substantially higher than the .01 shown in figure 8-1. The .01, however, is the probability of being caught, convicted, and jailed, not just being caught. More important, the .01 is the probability of being caught, convicted, and jailed on a single store robbery, rather than on a whole year's worth. A year of store robberies is much more likely to result in being caught. The decision theory situation that involves one risky choicse and one nonrisky choice is featured in Robert Behn and James Vaupel, *Analytical Thinking for Busy Decision Makers* (Basic Books, 1979).

5. For examples of relatively conservative applications of decision deterrence theory to reducing criminal behavior, see Gordon Tullock, "Does Punishment Deter Crime?" 36 *The Public Interest* 103-111 (1974); and James Wilson, *Thinking about Crime* (Basic Books, 1975). For relatively liberal applications of decision deterrence theory, see Sheldon Danziger and David Wheeler, "The Economics of Crime: Punishment or Income Redistribution," 33 *Rev. Social Econ.* 113-131 (1975); and David Greenberg, "Crime Deterrence Research and Social Policy," in *Modeling the Criminal Justice System,* ed. Nagel (Sage, 1977).

6. Other examples of explicit or implicit decision deterrence theory applied to criminal behavior include Gary Becker and William Landes, eds., *Essays in the Economics of Crime and Punishment* (Columbia University Press, 1974); Gordon Tullock, *The Logic of Law* (Basic Books, 1971); Billy Wayson and Gail Monkman, eds., *Readings in Correctional Economics* (ABA Correctional Economics Center, 1975); Lawrence Kaplan and Dennis Kessler, eds., *An Economic Analysis of Crime* (Thomas, 1976); Simon Rottenberg, ed., *The Economics of Crime and Punishment* (American Enterprise Institute, 1973); A.J. Rogers, *The Economics of Crime* (Dryden, 1973); Robert Birmingham, "A Model of Criminal Process: Game Theory and Law," 56 *Cornell L. Rev.* 57-73 (1970); and Joseph Little, "A Theory and Empirical Study of What Deters Drinking Drivers, If, When and Why," 23 *Admin. L. Rev.* 23-57, 169-193 (1970-71).

Most of the above studies concentrate on the decision making of the individual wrongdoer or potential wrongdoer rather than use an aggregate data regression analysis approach like the studies referred to in note 1. The aggregate regression analysis approach generally involves crime rates as the dependent variable with arrest, conviction, or imprisonment rates as a measure of the contingent probability and sentencing severity as a measure of the costs of noncompliance. The units of analysis are generally cities or states. The benefits of compliance could be measured by obtaining data on job openings in the cities or states, but researchers generally use unemployment figures as an easier proxy measure. The benefits of noncompliance could be measured for property crimes by how much gets stolen in the average property crime in each of the cities or states, and the costs of compliance could be considered the opportunity of foregoing that stolen money. Neither of those variables, however, is normally measured in the statistical analyses.

7. On the extent to which business firms are the main source of pollution, see *Environmental Quality: The First Annual Report on the Council on Environmental Quality* (Government Printing Office, 1970).

8. For discussions of proposed incentives for encouraging compliance with environmental standards, see Frank Grad, George Rathjens, and Albert Rosenthal, *Environmental Control: Priorities, Policies, and the Law* (Columbia University Press, 1971); Stuart Nagel, "Incentives for Compliance with Environmental Law" in *The Politics of Environmental Policy,* eds. Lester Milbrath and Frederick Inscho (Sage, 1975); Paul Downing and William Watson, *Enforcement Economics in Air Pollution Control* (Government Printing Office, 1973); and Robert Witherspoon et al., *Government Approaches to Air Pollution Control: A Compendium and Annotated Bibliography* (National Technical Information Service, 1971).

9. Other examples of decision deterrence theory applied to pollution and business regulation include William Baumol and Wallace Oates, *The Theory of Environmental Policy* (Prentice-Hall, 1973); R.M. Dawes and J. Delay, "The Decision to Pollute," 6 *Envir. & Planning* 3-10 (1974); Richard Posner, *Economics Analysis of Law* (Little, Brown, 1977); James Anderson, "Public Economic Policy and the Problem of Compliance: Notes for Research," 4 *Houston L. Rev.* 62-72 (1966); Simeon Kriesberg, "Decisionmaking Models and the Control of Corporate Crime," 85 *Yale L. J.* 1092-1130 (1976); John Gleason and Darold Barnum, "Effectiveness of OSHA Penalties: Myth or Reality?" 7 *Interfaces* 1-13 (1976); Ronald Matheny, "Bayesian Techniques for Public Management and Decision Making" (American Society for Public Administration Annual Meeting, 1978); and Judah Gribetz and Frank Grad, "Housing Code Enforcement: Sanctions and Remedies," 66 *Columbia L. Rev.* 1254 (1966).

10. See chapter 1 and Nagel and Neef, "Decision Theory and the Pretrial Release Decision in Criminal Cases," 31 *U. Miami L. Rev.* 1433-1491 (1977); "Bail, not Jail for More Defendants," 60 *Judicature* 172-178 (1976); and "Improving Human Behavior on the Bench," 6 *Human Behavior* 72 (1977).

11. Other examples of decision deterrence theory applied to noncomplying public officials include Robert Stover and Don Brown, "Reducing Rule Violations by Police, Judges, and Corrections Officials," in *Modeling the Criminal Justice System,* ed. Nagel (Sage, 1977); Samuel Krislov and Melcolm Feeley, *Compliance and the Law* (Sage, 1970); Harrell Rodgers and Charles Bullock, "School Desegregation: A Cost/Benefit Longitudinal Analysis" in *Public Law and Public Policy,* ed. John Gardiner (Praeger,

1977); James Levine, "Implementing Legal Policies through Operant Conditioning: The Case of Police Practice," 6 *Law & Society Rev.* 195-222 (1971); Susan Rose-Ackerman, "The Economics of Corruption," 4 *J. Public Econ.* 187-203 (1975); and David Aaronson et al., "Improving Police Discretion Rationality in Handling Public Inebriates," 29 and 30, *Admin. L. Rev.* 447-485, 93-132 (1977-78).

12. Examples of decision deterrence theory applied to discouraging socially undesirable behavior that is not criminal, business regulation, or governmental include Leonard Jason et al., "Prompting Dog Owners to Pick Up Dog Droppings," (Unpublished paper available from the senior author at DePaul University, 1977); Lloyd S. Etheredge, *The Case of the Unreturned Cafeteria Trays* (American Political Science Association, 1976); Guido Calabresi, *The Costs of Accidents: A Legal and Economic Analysis* (Yale University Press, 1970); and David L. Chambers, "Men Who Know They Are Watched: Some Benefits and Costs of Jailing for Nonpayment of Support," 75 *Mich. L. Rev.* 900-940 (1977).

Bibliography

The purpose of this bibliography is to provide references which are relevant to applying decision theory to the legal process. By *decision theory* in this context is meant an analytic perspective which assumes that individuals are seeking to maximize their perceived benefits minus costs, where both the benefits and the costs are discounted by the probability of their occurring. That assumption or perspective enables one to deduce how the decisions of individuals would change as a result of system changes that affect their perceived benefits minus costs. That assumption also enables one to deduce what decisions ought to be reached in light of what the individuals or others consider to be benefits and costs. By *legal process* in this context is mainly meant the procedures whereby police, plaintiffs, defendants, attorneys, judges, jurors, and court administrators arrive at decisions.

I. General Items

Becker, Gary, and William Landes, eds., *Essays in the Economics of Crime and Punishment* (Columbia University Press, 1974).
Bohigian, Haig, *The Foundations and Mathematical Models of Operations Research with Extensions to the Criminal Justice System* (Gazette, 1971).
Bottomley, Keith, *Decisions in the Penal Process* (Rothman, 1973).
Brounstein, Sidney, and Murray Kamrass, eds., *Operations Research in Law Enforcement, Justice, and Societal Security* (D.C. Heath, Lexington Books, 1976).
Chaiken, Jan, et al., *Criminal Justice Models: An Overview* (Rand, 1975).
Cowan, T.A., "Decision Theory in Law, Science, and Technology," 17 *Rutgers L. Rev.* 499-530 (1963).
Gottfredson, Don, ed., *Decision Making in the Criminal Justice System: Reviews and Essays* (NIMH Center for Studies of Crime and Delinquincy, 1975).
Greenberg, David, *Mathematical Criminology* (Princeton University Press, 1978).
McPheters, Lee, and William Stronge, eds., *The Economics of Crime and Law Enforcement* (Charles Thomas, 1976).
Nagel, S., *Improving the Legal Process: Effects of Alternatives* (D.C. Heath, Lexington Books, 1975).
Nagel, S. ed., *Modeling the Criminal Justice System* (Sage, 1977).
Nagel, S. and M. Neef, *Decision Theory and the Legal Process* (D.C. Heath, Lexington Books, 1978).

—and—, *Legal Policy Analysis: Finding an Optimum Level or Mix* (D.C. Heath, Lexington Books, 1977).
—and—, *The Legal Process: Modeling the System* (Sage Library of Social Research, 1977).
—and—, *Operations Research Methods: As Applied to Political Science and the Legal Process* (Sage Quantitative Applications to the Social Sciences, 1976).
Posner, Richard, *Economic Analysis of Law* (Little, Brown, 1977).
Robert, P., *Operational Research in the System of Criminal Justice* (Council of Europe, 1971).
Tullock, Gordon, *The Logic of the Law* (Basic Books, 1971).
Wolfgang, Marvin, and Harvey Smith, "Mathematical Methods in Criminology," 18 *Int. Soc. Sci. J.* 200 (1966).

II. The Decision to Arrest and Pretrial Treatment

Forst, Brian, "A Model of Policy Operations from the Court Perspective," in Brounstein and Kamrass, *Operations Research in Law Enforcement, Justice, and Societal Security* (D.C. Heath, Lexington Books, 1976), 55-64.
LaFave, Wayne, *Arrest: The Decision to Take a Suspect into Custody* (Little, Brown, 1965).
Landes, William, "The Bail System: An Economic Approach," 2 *J. Legal Stud.* 79-105 (1973).
—, "Legality and Reality: Some Evidence on Criminal Procedures," 2 *J. Legal Stud.* 287-337 (1974).
Levine, James, Michael Musheno, and Dennis Palumbo, *Evaluating Alternatives in the Criminal Justice System* (Center for Political Research, 1974).
Locke, J., et al., *Compilation and Use of Criminal Court Data in Relation to Pretrial Release of Defendants* (National Bureau of Standards, 1970).
Marx, Gary, "Alternative Measure of Policy Performance," in Viano, *Criminal Justice Research* (D.C. Heath, Lexington Books, 1975), 179-193.
Nagel, S., M. Neef, and S. Schramm, "Decision Theory and the Pretrial Release Decision in Criminal Cases," 31 *U. Miami L. Rev.* 1433-1491 (1977).
Nagel, S., K. Reinbolt, and Eimermann, "A Linear Programming Approach to Conflicting Legal Values like Free Press versus Fair Trial," 4 *Rutgers Computers & Law* 420-461 (1975).

Nagel, S., P. Wice, and M. Neef, *Too Much or Too Little Policy: The Example of Pretrial Release* (Sage Administrative and Policy Studies Series, 1977).
Robertson, John, and Phyllis Teitelbaum, "Optimizing Legal Impact: A Case Study in Search of a Theory," *Wisc. L. Rev.* 665-726 (1973).
Rovner-Pieczenik, Roberta, *Pretrial Intervention Strategies: An Evaluation of Policy-Related Research and Policymaker Perceptions* (ABA Commission on Correctional Facilities and Services, 1974).
Tiffany, Lawrence, Donald McIntyre, and Daniel Rotenberg, *Detection of Crime: Stopping and Questioning, Search and Seizure, Encouragement and Entrapment* (Little, Brown, 1967).

III. The Decision to Prosecute and Out-of-Court Settlements

Birmingham, R.L., "A Model of Criminal Process: Game Theory and Law," 56 *Cornell L. Rev.* 57-73 (1970).
Brams, Steven, "Applying Game Theory to Antitrust Litigation" (New York University Department of Politics, 1978).
Forst, B., and K. Brosi, "A Theoretical and Empirical Analysis of the Prosecutor," 6 *J. Legal Stud.* 177 (1977).
Fried, Michael, "A Decision Theoretic Model of Plea Bargaining," (Paper presented to the meeting of the Midwest Political Science Association, 1974).
Friedman, A., "An Analysis of Settlement," 22 *Stan. L. Rev.* 67 (1969).
Horowitz, Ira, "Decision Theory and Antitrust: Quantitative Evaluation for Efficient Enforcement," 52 *Ind. L. J.* 713-733 (1977).
Lachman, Judith, "An Economic Model of Plea Bargaining in the Criminal Justice System," (Unpublished Ph.D. dissertation, Michigan State University).
Lachman, Judith, and William McLauchlan, "Models of Plea Bargaining," in Nagel, ed., *Modeling the Criminal Justice System* (Sage, 1977), 145-159.
Landes, William, "An Economic Analysis of the Courts," 14 *J. Law & Econ.* 61 (1971).
Miller, Frank, *Prosecution: The Decision to Charge a Suspect with a Crime* (Little, Brown, 1969).
Nagel, S., and M. Neef, "Plea Bargaining, Decision Theory, and Equilibrium Models," 51 and 52 *Ind. L. J.* 987-1024, 1-61 (1976).
—and—, "Allocating Resources among Court Cases by Legal Counsel" (Presently unpublished manuscript, available from the authors, 1978).
Newman, Donald, *Conviction: The Determination of Guilt or Innocence without Trial* (Little, Brown, 1966).

Posner, Richard, "The Behavior of Administrative Agencies," 1 *J. Legal Stud.* 305-247 (1972).
—, "An Economic Approach to Legal Procedure and Judicial Administration," 2 *J. Legal Stud.* 399-458 (1973).
Ross, H. Laurence, *Settled Out of Court* (Aldine, 1970).
Schwartz, and Mitchell, "An Economic Analysis of the Contingent Fee in Personal Injury Litigation," 22 *Stan. L. Rev.* 1125 (1970).

IV. Jury Decision Making and Determining Guilt

Bush, J.W., M.M. Chen, and A.S. Bush, "No-Fault Malpractice Insurance: Proximate Cause and the Quality of Medical Care," 122 *Western J. Medicine* 262-270 (1975).
Cullison, Alan, "The Model of Rules and the Logic of Decision," in S. Nagel, ed., *Modeling the Criminal Justice System* (Sage, 1977), 225-246.
Finkelstein, M.O., "The Application of Statistical Decision Theory to the Jury Discrimination Cases," 80 *Harv. L. Rev.* 338-376 (1966).
Finkelstein, and Fairley, "A Bayesian Approach to Identification Evidence," 84 *Harv. L. Rev.* 489 (1970).
Fried, Michael, Kaiman Kaplan, and Katherine Klein, "Jury Selection: An Analysis of Voir Dire," in Simon, ed., *The Jury System in America: A Critical Overview* (Sage, 1975), 47-66.
Friedman, H., "Trial by Jury: Criterial for Convictions, Jury Size, and Type I and Type II Error," 26 *Am. Statistician* 21-23 (1972).
Gelfand, Alan, and Herbert Solomon, "Argument in Favor of 12-member Juries," in S. Nagel, ed., *Modeling the Criminal Justice System* (Sage, 1977), 205-224.
Grofman, Bernard, "Jury Decision-Making Models," in S. Nagel, ed., *Modeling the Criminal Justice System* (Sage, 1977), 191-204.
Kaplan, John, "Decision Theory and the Factfinding Process," 20 *Stan. L. Rev.* 1065-1092 (1968).
Lempert, Richard, "Modeling Relevance," 75 *Mich. L. Rev.* 1021-1057 (1977).
Lindley, D.V., "Probability of the Law," 26 *The Statistician* 203-220 (1977).
Marshall, Catherine, and James Wise, "Juror Decisions and the Determination of Guilt in Capital Punishment Cases: A Bayesian Perspective," in Wendt and Vlek, eds., *Utility, Probability, and Human Decision Making* (Reidel, 1975).
Nagel, S., D. Lamm, and M. Neef, "Decision Theory and Juror Decision-Making," in Sales, ed., *The Jury, Judicial, and Trial Processes* (Plenum, 1978).

Nagel., S., and M. Neef, "Deductive Modeling to Determine an Optimum Jury Size and Fraction Required to Convict," 1975 *Wash. U. L. Q.* 933-978 (1976).

Roth, Arthur, Joseph B. Kadane, and Morris DeGrott, "Optimal Peremptory Challenges in Trials by Judges: A Bilateral Sequential Process," *Operations Research,* 25, no. 6 (November-December, 1977): 901-919.

Schum, David, "Contrast Effects in Inference: On the Conditioning of Current Evidence by Prior Evidence," 18 *Organ. Behavior & Human Performance,* 217-253 (1977).

Tribe, Lawrence, "Trial by Mathematics: Precision and Ritual in the Legal Process," 84 *Harv. L. Rev.* 1329 (1971).

Wendt, D., and C. Vlek, "Probability in Courtroom Decision Making," *Utility, Probability, and Human Decision Making* (Reidel, 1975), 219-273.

V. Judicial Decision Making and Determining Sentences

Aranson, Peter, "The Simple Analytics of Sentencing," in Tullock and Wagner, eds., *Deductive Reasoning in the Analysis of Public Policy* (D.C. Heath, Lexington Book, 1977).

Dawson, Robert, *Sentencing: The Decision as to Type, Length, and Conditions of Sentence* (Little, Brown, 1969).

Gottfredson, Don, et al., *Parole Decision-Making—The Utilization of Experience in Parole Decision-Making* (Law Enforcement Assistance Administration, 1973).

Grossman, Joel, and Joseph Tanenhaus, eds., *Frontiers of Judicial Research* (Wiley, 1969).

Hogarth, John, *Sentencing as a Human Process* (University of Toronto, 1971).

Jahnige, Thomas, and Sheldon Goldman, *The Federal Judicial System: Readings in Process and Behavior* (Holt, Rinehart, and Winston, 1968).

McEachern, Alexander, and J. Robert Newman, "A System for Computer-Aided Probation Decision-Making," 6 *J. Res. Crime & Delinquency* 184-198 (1969).

Nagel, S., *The Legal Process from a Behavioral Perspective* (Dorsey, 1969).

Nagel, S., M. Neef, and T. Weiman, "A Rational Method for Determining Prison Sentences," 61 *Judicature* 371-375 (1978).

Rainey, R. Lee, "The Decision to Remain a Judge: Deductive Models of Judicial Retirement" (Paper presented at the 1976 American Political Science Association meeting).

Schubert, Glendon, ed., *Judicial Behavior: A Reader in Theory and Research* (Rand McNally, 1964).

—, *Judicial Decision-Making* (Free Press, 1963).
—, *Quantitative Analysis of Judicial Behavior* (Free Press, 1962).
Ulmer, Sidney, "Modeling the Decisions of U.S. Supreme Court Justices: Some Deductive Approaches," in S. Nagel, ed., *Modeling the Criminal Justice System* (Sage, 1977), 247-264.
Wilkins, Leslie, et al., *Sentencing Guidelines: Structuring Judicial Discretion* (U.S. Department of Justice, 1976).

VI. Models Designed to Improve the Efficiency of the Legal Process

Blumstein, Alfred, and R. Larson, "Models of a Total Criminal Justice System," 17 *Oper. Res.* 199-232 (1969).
Flanders, Steven, *Case Management and Court Management in United States District Courts* (Federal Judicial Center, 1977).
Gillespie, Robert, "Economic Modeling of Court Services, Work Loads, and Productivity," in S. Nagel, ed., *Modeling the Criminal Justice System* (Sage, 1977), 175-189.
Hausner, Jack, Thomas Lane, and Gary Oleson, "Automated Scheduling in the Courts," in Brounstein and Kamrass, *Operations Research in Law Enforcement, Justice, and Societal Security* (D.C. Heath, Lexington Book, 1976), 217-228.
Nagel, S. and M. Neef, "Allocating Resources Geographically for Optimum Results," 3 *Pol. Method.* 383-404 (1976).
—and—, "Time-Oriented Models and the Legal Process: Reducing Delay and Forecasting the Future," *Wash. U. L. Q.* (1978).
Noam, Eli, "The Criminal Justice System: An Economic Model," in S. Nagel, *Modeling the Criminal Justice System* (Sage, 1977), 41-56.
Oberlander, Leonard, ed., *Quantitative Tools for Criminal Justice Planning* (Law Enforcement Assistance Administration, 1975).
Reed, John, and Ronald Slivka, "Operations Research and the Courts," in S. Nagel, ed., *Modeling the Criminal Justice System* (Sage, 1977), 159-174.
Shoup, Donald, and Stephen Mehay, *Program Budgeting for Urban Police Services* (Praeger, 1971).
Zeisel, Hans, Harry Kalven, and B. Bucholz, *Delay in the Court* (Little, Brown, 1959).

VII. The Decision to Violate a Social Norm or to Refrain from Doing So

ABA Correction Economics Center, *Readings in Correctional Economics* (1975).

Bibliography

Becker, Gary, "Crime and Punishment: An Economic Approach," 76 *J. Pol. Econ.* 169-217 (1968).

Brams, Steven, and Douglas Muzzio, "Game Theory and the White House Tapes Case," 13 *Trial* 48-53 (1977).

Breit, W., and K.G. Elzinga, "Antitrust Penalties and Attitudes toward Risk: An Economic Analysis," 86 *Harv. L. Rev.* 693-613 (1973).

Correa, Hector, "A Mathematical Model of Rational Choice between Criminal and Non-Criminal Activities" (University of Pittsburgh Annual Conference on Modeling and Simulation, 1975).

Downing, Paul, and James Kimball, "Enforcing Environmental Regulations" (Department of Economics, Virginia Tech, 1977).

Gibbs, Jack, *Crime, Punishment, and Deterrence* (Elsevier, 1974).

Greenberg, David, "Crime Deterrence Research and Social Policy," in S. Nagel, *Modeling the Criminal Justice System* (Sage, 1977), 281-296.

Kaplan, Lawrence, and Dennis Kessler, eds., *An Economic Analysis of Crime: Selected Readings* (Charles Thomas, 1976).

Kriesberg, Simeon, "Decision-making Models and the Control of Corporate Crime," 85 *Yale L. J.* 1091 (1976).

Nagel, S. and Stengel, "Using Decision-Deterrence Theory to Encourage Socially Desired Behavior" (Presently unpublished manuscript available from the senior author, 1978).

Rodgers, Harrell, and Charles Bullock, "School Desegregation: A Cost/Benefit Logitudinal Analysis," in Gardiner, ed., *Public Law and Public Policy* (Praeger, 1977), 158-176.

Rogers, A.J., *The Economics of Crime* (Dryden, 1973).

Rottenberg, Simon, *The Economics of Crime and Punishment* (American Enterprise Institute for Public Policy Research, 1973).

Stover, Robert, and Don Brown, "Reducing Rule Violations by Police, Judges, and Corrections Officials," in S. Nagel, *Modeling the Criminal Justice System* (Sage, 1977), 297-312.

Index of Names

Aaronson, David, 274
Abrams, 161, 247
Adams, L. J., 160
Alfini, James, 211
Alschuler, Albert, 68, 91, 100, 170
Anderson, James, 273
Andreas, R., 173
Aranson, Peter, 240, 248, 279
Ares, 4, 38

Baade, Hans, 242
Bailey, 170
Barnum, Darold, 273
Baumol, William, 4, 97, 108, 135, 243, 273
Becker, Gary, 173, 245, 272, 275, 281
Behn, Robert, 4, 203, 272
Bell, C., 160
Bent, D., 247
Berger, 163
Birmingham, Robert, 108, 172, 272, 277
Blackstone, William, 13, 34, 188, 189, 195, 201, 205, 207
Blalock, Hubert, 55, 68, 247
Blumberg, 162
Blumstein, Alfred, 271, 280
Bond, Jon, 67, 91
Borgatta, Edgar, 170
Bohigian, Haig, 275
Bottomley, Keith, 32, 275
Brams, Steven, 68, 277, 281
Bray, Robert, 203
Breit, W., 281
Brennan, Michael, 55, 68, 139, 243
Brosi, Katherine, 242, 244, 277
Brounstein, Sidney, 275
Brown, Don, 273, 281
Brown, Rex, 5, 204, 271
Buchholz, Bernard, 163, 280
Bullock, Charles, 273, 281
Bush, A. S., 278
Bush, J. W., 278
Byrd, Jack, 247

Calabresi, Guido, 274
Casper, Jonathan, 162
Chaiken, Jan, 275
Chambers, David L., 274
Chambliss, William, 271
Chanin, 67
Chen, M. M., 278
Church, Thomas, 170
Cochrane, J., 246
Conway, R., 247
Cook, Philip J., 271
Correa, Hector, 281
Costner, Herbert, 170
Covington, Cary, 91
Cowan, Thomas A., 275
Cressey, Donald, 67
Cross, James, 68, 135, 137
Cullison, Alan, 204, 278
Curran, W., 203

Danelski, David, 172, 185
Danziger, Sheldon, 272
Dash, Samuel, 170
Davis, James, 203
Davis, M., 68
Dawes, R. M., 273
Dawson, Robert, 279
DeGrott, Morris, 279
Delay, J., 273
Dickinson, J., 243
Dinwiddy, Caroline, 139, 160
Downing, Paul, 273, 281

Easton, Allan, 247
Ebersole, Joseph, 31
Eckart, 162
Eimermann, Thomas, 276
Ellsberg, David, 133
Elwork, Amiram, 203, 211
Elzinga, K. G., 281
Erlanger, Howard, 203
Etheredge, Lloyd S., 274

283

Fairly, 278
Feeley, Malcolm, 273
Finkelstein, M. O., 278
Finney, D., 38
Flanders, Steven, 280
Foote, Caleb, 32
Forst, Brian, 242, 244, 276, 277
Fortescue, John, 207
Frankel, M., 4
Franklin, 67
Freed, Daniel, 32
Fried, Michael, 5, 93, 108, 203, 204, 212, 277, 278
Friedland, 170
Friedman, A., 277
Friedman, 39, 159, 247
Friedman, H., 278
Fruchter, Benjamin, 245

Gallagher, 165
Gardiner, John, 273, 281
Gass, Saul, 68
Gelfand, Alan, 278
Gibbs, Jack, 271, 281
Gillespie, Robert, 280
Gleason, John, 273
Goldfarb, Ronald, 32, 68
Goldman, Allan, 31
Goldman, Sheldon, 279
Gottfredson, Don, 275, 279
Grad, Frank, 273
Greenberg, David, 272, 275, 281
Greenberger, Martin, 68
Gribetz, Judah, 273
Grofman, Bernard, 278
Grossman, Joel, 242, 279
Guilford, J., 96, 245

Hale, Matthew, 207
Hand, R., 242
Hausman, Warren, 38, 42
Hausner, Jack, 280
Hawkins, Gordon, 4, 271
Hermann, 161
Hoffman, 136
Himmelblau, D., 246
Hogarth, John, 242, 279

Hogue, Anthony, 204
Holt, Robert, 203
Horowitz, Ira, 277
Howard, R. A., 204
Huber, 33, 38, 95, 102, 206
Hull, C., 247
Hunting, R., 161
Hurwicz, Leonid, 103

Ilich, J., 137
Inscho, Frederick, 273

Jacoby, Joan, 95, 247
Jahnige, Thomas, 279
Jason, Leonard, 274
Jeffrey, Ray C., 271
Jenkins, J., 247
Johnson, 247
Johnston, 159, 162

Kadane, Joseph B., 279
Kahr, Andrew, 204
Kalven, Harry, 36, 163, 208, 280
Kamrass, Murray, 275
Kaplan, John, 204, 209, 278
Kaplan, Kalman, 204, 278
Kaplan, Lawrence, 173, 212, 272, 281
Kaplan, Martin, 203, 209
Karrass, C., 137
Kassouf, Sheen, 243
Kelly, 68
Kemmerick, Gwen, 209
Kenney, R., 246
Kessler, Dennis, 272, 281
Kimball, James, 281
Klein, 212
Klein, Katherine, 204, 278
Klevorick, Alvin, 248
Kotler, Philip, 33, 95, 102, 206
Kobrin, Soloman, 271
Kotler, Philip, 38
Kriesberg, Simeon, 273, 281
Krislov, Samuel, 273
Kuh, 165

Lachman, Judith, 108, 242, 247, 277
LaFave, Wayne, 276

Index of Names

Lamm, David, xviii, 278
Land, Kenneth, 170
Landes, William, 5, 106, 108, 163, 170, 242, 272, 275, 276, 277
Lane, Thomas, 280
Larson, R., 280
Lave, Charles, 68
Lee, Wayne, 4, 271
Lehman, 168
Lempert, Richard, 205, 209, 278
Lermack, 31
Levine, Felice, 203
Levine, James, 274, 276
Lichtenstein, Sarah, 206
Liebenson, H., 161
Lindley, D. V., 278
Lindsey, Peter, 209
Lippman, 161
Little, Joseph, 272
Lock, J., 5, 38, 276
Logan, Charles, 271
Louisell, 162
Luce, R., 68

Mack, Ruth, 4, 204, 271
MacKinnon, F. B., 161, 246
Mahan, Linda, 209, 211, 212
Mahoney, Barry, 32
Mansfield, E., 108
March, James, 68
Marcus, M., 67
Mark, 67
Marshall, Catherine, 204, 209, 278
Marshall, Prentice, 203
Martinson, Don, 4
Marx, Gary, 276
Matheny, Ronald, 273
Mather, Lynn, 107
Maxwell, W., 247
McCormick, Charles, 210
McDonald, William, 31, 170
McEachern, Alexander, 279
McGarry, L., 203
McIntyre, Donald, 161, 277
McKean, Roland, 165
McKensie, R., 137
McLauchlan, William, 277

McMillan, Claude, 243, 246
McPheters, Lee, 271, 275
Meehan, Eugene, 170
Mehay, Stephen, 280
Milbrath, Lester, 273
Miller, D., 97
Miller, 170
Miller, F., 161, 247, 277
Miller, Herbert, 31
Miller, L., 161, 247
Mishan, Ezra, 161, 165
Mitchell, 161, 242, 246, 278
Mitchell, Judge, 211
Monkman, Gail, 5, 204, 272
Moore, 139
Morris, William, 170
Mosteller, Frederic, 245
Mullen, J., 32
Murphy, Walter, 157, 172, 183, 185
Musheno, Michael, 276
Muzzio, Douglas, 281

Nagel, Joyce, xviii
Neuwirth, G., 161
Newman, Donald, 67, 136, 166, 277
Newman, J. Robert, 279
Newman, P., 68
Nie, Norman, 247
Niemi, R., 172, 185
Nimmer, Raymond, 91, 162
Noam, Eli, 243, 280
Norman, Donald, 209

Oaks, Dallin, 168
Oates, Wallace, 273
Oberlander, Leonard, 280
Oleson, Gary, 280
Ordeshook, Peter, 172, 185
Orton, Ivan, 133
Ostrom, Thomas, 208

Palumbo, Dennis, 276
Peterson, Cameron, 204, 208
Peterson, Karen, 204
Petty, C., 203
Posner, Richard, 159, 163, 164, 172, 273, 276, 278

Powell, M. J. D., 246
Prescott, Elizabeth, 203
Pritchett, Herman, 172, 185
Raiffa, Howard, 4, 68, 204, 246
Rainey, R. Lee, 279
Rankin, Anne, 4, 38
Rappaport, Anatol, 68, 133
Rathjens, George, 273
Reed, John, 280
Reeder, 162, 242
Richmond, Samuel, 4, 55, 68, 100, 102, 103, 105, 162, 243
Riker, William, 172, 186
Robert, P., 276
Robertson, John, 277
Rodgers, Harrell, 273, 281
Rogers, A. J., 173, 272, 281
Rohde, David, 157, 172, 183, 185
Rose-Ackerman, Susan, 275
Rosenberg, Maurice, 163
Rosenthal, Albert, 273
Ross, H. Laurence, 160, 278
Rossett, Arthur, 67
Rotenberg, Daniel, 277
Roth, Arthur, 279
Rottenberg, Simon, 173, 272, 281
Rovner-Pieczenik, Roberta, 277

Sales, Bruce Dennis, xviii, 203, 211
Samuelson, Paul, 172
Schaffer, S. Andrew, 56
Schramm, Sarah Slavin, xvii, xviii, 276
Schubert, Glendon, 96, 157, 172, 183, 185, 242, 279
Schum, David, 210, 279
Schwartz, 161, 242, 246, 278
Shoup, Donald, 280
Shubik, Martin, 68
Siegan, B., 248
Siegfried, 173
Silver, Morris, 271
Silverstein, Lee, 32
Simon, Rita, 5, 203, 204, 207, 208, 211, 212
Singer, R., 242
Singleton, R., 68

Sisson, Roger, 68
Slivka, Ronald, 280
Slovic, Paul, 206
Smith, Harvey, 276
Soloman, Herbert, 278
Starr, Martin, 97
Steinbrenner, K., 247
Stengel, James, xviii, 281
Stover, Robert, 5, 162, 273, 281
Strawn, David, 203
Stronge, William, 271, 275
Sturz, 4, 38

Tanenhaus, Joseph, 96, 242, 279
Tanter, Raymond, 33
Tapp, June, 203
Teitelbaum, Phyllis, 277
Tersine, 159, 162, 247
Thaler, Richard, 38, 42
Thomas, Ewart, 204
Thomas, T., 32
Thomas, Wayne, 32, 43
Tiffany, Lawrence, 277
Tittle, Charles, 271
Tribe, Lawrence, 204, 279
Tufte, Edward, 55, 245, 247
Tullock, Gordon, 5, 106, 172, 173, 204, 247, 272, 276
Tyndall, W., 68

Ulmer, Sidney, 157, 172, 186, 280

Vaupel, James, 4, 203, 272
Velde, Richard, 260
Vetri, D., 169
Vlek, Charles, 204, 279

Wald, Patricia, 4, 32
Walton, R., 137
Watson, William, 273
Wayson, Billy, 272
Weiman, Thomas, 206, 279
Weisberg, Herbert, 172, 185
Wendt, Dirk, 204, 279
Wheaton, R., 67
Wheeler, David, 272

Index of Names

Wice, Paul, 32, 36, 41, 43, 57, 173, 276
Wilkins, Leslie, 31, 280
Williams, J. D., 171
Wise, James, 204, 209, 278
Witherspoon, Robert, 273
Wolfgang, Marvin, 276

Wood, Arthur, 161, 247

Zeisel, Hans, 36, 172, 187, 208, 280
Zeleny, M., 246
Zimring, Frank, 4

Index of Subjects

Accepting clients, decision-making by attorneys, 232-235
Adjusted limits, in plea bargaining, 76-91
Agricultural wastes, 262
Air pollution, 262-265
Allocating resources among court cases by attorneys, 217-253
Alternatives to plea bargaining, 79-81
Appearance at trial: probability of, increasing, 26-27; publicizing rates of defendants held, 24-31
Arbitrary bond setting, 7-44
Arraignment judges: bond-setting decisions, 21-31; discretion in releasing defendants, 7-44; errors in holding defendants, 7-10, 10-21; nondiscretionary bond schedules, 45-49; optimum percentage of defendants to release, 50-51
Arrest, shortening time to trial, 30
Attitudinal characteristics of judges, pretrial release, 13
Attorneys: and plea bargaining, 71-186; decisions to accept clients, 232-235
Automatic bond schedules, 45-49
Automobile pollution, 262

Bail reform: bond-setting decisions, 21-31; discretion in releasing, judicial, 7-44; errors in holding defendants, 7-10, 10-21; in civil cases, 147-149; nondiscretionary bond schedules, 45-49; optimum percentage of defendants to release, 50-51
Bargaining for sentences, 65-180, civil analogies, 141-180; equilibrium models, 111-140; limits, 76-91; payoff matrices, 71-76
Bayesian probabilities, 102, 103, 199, 210, 245
Bench trials, 92, plea bargaining as alternative, 65-180

Beyond a reasonable doubt, guilt, 193, juror perceptions of, 187-215
Bitterness costs from jailing of innocent defendants, 7-21
Bluffing, in plea bargaining, 76-91, 120, 122-127
Bond-setting, 3-61, civil cases, 147-149; errors, 7-10, 10-21; judicial discretion, 7-44; nondiscretionary, 45-49; optimum percentage of defendants to hold, 50-51
Bonus factors: civil settlements, 151; plea bargaining, 71-186
Brady v. United States, 100
Business regulation, 262-265

Calculating limits in plea bargaining, 76-91
Capital punishment, 65, 208
Cases, allocating resources among, 217-253
Categories of bonds, 45-61
Charge reduction in plea bargaining, 65-180
Civil cases: analogies to plea bargaining, 141-180; bail reform, 147-149; bonus factors in settlements, 151; discovery in, 147-149; equilibrium in, 141-143
Clarifying probability of appearance of defendants, 26-27
Clients, decision to accept, 217-253
Coalition models, 157-159
Collective decision-making, jurors, 187-215
Committing crimes, pretrial defendants, costs of, 7-21
Compliance with law, increasing, 255-274
Conduct, disorderly, 47-48
Conference persuasion, business, 262-265
Conformity with law in jury decision-making, 200-203

289

Congestion of courts: in civil cases, 147–149; reduction through plea bargaining, 30–31, 65
Consumer fraud cases, 193, 197–198, 208
Contingency fee cases, allocating time to, 217–253
Convergence in plea bargaining, determining, 111–140
Convicting defendants, xvi: standards for guilt, 195
Conviction probabilities, determining in plea bargaining, 83–88
Conviction threshold, jurors, 187–215
Corporate law, 236
Costs of holding or releasing defendants, pretrial, 3–61
Counteroffers in plea bargaining, 127–132
Court cases, allocating resources among, 217–253
Court congestion: in civil cases, 147–149; reduction through plea bargaining, 30–31, 65
Crime committing by defendants released, 7–21
Crime severity, plea bargaining, 96
Criminal behavior, deterring, 3–61, 255–274
Criminal law violators, 184
Criminal cases: attorneys' allocation of time to, 217–253; bond-setting in, 7–61; incentives for reducing, 255–274; juror decision making in, 187–215; plea bargaining of, 71–186

Damages to be awarded, 217
Death penalty, 261
Decision deterrence theory, 255–274
Decision to accept clients, 232–235
Decision to sue, 144–146
Decision trees, 93
Defense counsel: in civil cases, 147–149; in plea bargaining, 71–186
Delay reduction, 30–31, in civil cases, 147–149; through plea bargaining, 65
Detention, preventive, 3–61
Deterring criminal behavior, 3–61, 255–274, pretrial release, 3–61; incentives, 255–274
Developing objective bond schedules, 4; nondiscretionary, 45–49
Diminishing marginal utility, 75
Discount factors, in plea bargaining, 76–91
Discovery, 65; in civil cases, 147–149
Discretion of judges, bond-setting, 7–44, errors in releasing, 7–10, 10–21; civil cases, 147–149
Discriminant equations, 83–84, 102
Discrimination in bond-setting, minimizing, 45–61, racial, minimizing, 45–46
Disorderly conduct, 47–48
Disutility, sentencing, 75
Due process, 195, 260
Dynamic equilibrium, in civil case settlements, 141–143

Edgeworth box, use of, 134–135
Effectiveness of sentencing, 3–61
Effects of legal policy changes, xv
Empirical probabilities, Bayesian, 102, 103, 199, 210, 245
Encouraging socially desired behavior, 255–274
Energy, nuclear, 262
Environmental law, 31
Equal protection, 248
Equalizing marginal rates of return, 219–221
Equilibrium models: civil cases, 141–143; definition of, 66–67; plea bargaining, 111–140; probability of appearance, pretrial use, 10–21
Errors, risks of: juror decision-making, 187–215; pretrial holding or releasing of defendants, 7–10, 10–21
Exaggeration factors in plea bargaining, 122–127
Executives, xvi
Expenses of attorneys, 224
Expected values, calculation of: holding or releasing defendants, pretrial, 7–21, 24–31; jury decision making, 187–215

Index of Subjects

Failure to appear at trial, costs of, 7-44
Fall-back position in plea bargaining, 76-91
Fees, attorneys setting of, 217-253
Felony cases, 136
Fines, business, 262-265
Fidelity Mutual Loan Association v. Mettler, 207
Flat-fee cases, allocating time to, 217-253
Flat sentencing, 3-61, 167-168, 243-244
Fraud, consumer, 193, 197-198, 208

Game theory applications, 155-157
Government incentives for business compliance, 262-265
Group decision-making, 183-215
Guilt: beyond a reasonable doubt, standards, 193-195; juror perceptions of, 187-215; plea bargaining, perceptions, 71-91; pretrial bond-setting, 7-44

High bonds, reasons for, 22
Holding or releasing defendants, costs of, 7-61, publicizing, 24-31; optimum percentage of defendants to hold, 50-51

Illegally seized evidence, 65
Impact of judicial process changes on plea bargaining, 152-153
Imprisonment, life, 208
In re Meckley, 207
In re Winship, 207
Incentives for compliance with law, 255-274
Increasing objectivity in jury decisions, 200-203
Increasing visibility of wrongful holding by judges, 24-31
indeterminate sentences, 45, 167
Indigents, provision of counsel for, 65
Individual bond-setting decisions, 21-31, judicial discretion in, 7-44
Initial offers in plea bargaining, 122-127
Injunction, 262-265
Injury personal, allocating time to cases, 217-253

Innocence, juror perceptions of, 187-215, characteristics of jurors and cases, 196-200; judicial instructions, 200-203; measuring propensity to convict, 191-196
Instructions, judicial, 193
Intervals, bonds, 47-48

Judges, xv, conviction probabilities, threshold, 4; delay, reducing, 30-31, 65; discretion in bond-setting, 21-31; errors, minimizing, 7-10, 10-21; in civil cases, 147-149; plea bargaining context, 71-186; publicizing of holding of defendants, 24-31; instructions to juries, 200-203
Judicial process changes, effects on system, 152-153
Jurors, xv, xvii, 183-186: characteristics of jurors and cases, 196-200; judicial instructions, impact of, 200-203; measuring propensity to convict, 191-196; selection, 212; trials, 92

Law Enforcement Assistance Administration, 260
Law violators, xv, minimizing incentives for, 255-274
Lawyers: and plea bargaining, 71-186; decisions to accept clients, 232-235
Legislatures, xvi, nondiscretionary bond schedules, 45-61
Level of bond, determining: judicial discretion, 7-44; nondiscretionary, 45-61
Life imprisonment, 208
Likely sentences, plea bargaining, 76-91
Limits matrix, in plea bargaining model, 115-120
Limits of plea bargainers, general, 76-91
Linear prediction, 96
Litigation costs, 65, allocating resources among court cases, 217-253
Lower limit of prosecutor in plea bargaining, 76-91

Maintenance costs for jailed defendants, 7-21

Marginal utility, diminishing, 75
Markov chains, 93
Maximax strategy in plea bargaining, 80-81, 87, 100
Maximizing attorneys' income, 223-226
Measurement of variables, 191-196
Minimax strategy in plea bargaining, 80-81, 87
Minimizing attorneys' hours, 223-226
Minimizing discriminatory bond-setting, 45-61
Misdemeanor cases, 45
Multiple-judge courts, 183-186
Multivariate regression, 245
Municipal waste, 262
Mutual discovery, 65

Narcotics, sale of, 170
Negative sanctions, to increase compliance with law, 255-274
Noise pollution, 262
Nonappearance of defendants at trial, costs of, 7-44
Noncompliance with law, decreasing, 255-274
Noncomplying public officials, 184, 265-270
Nonconvergence in plea bargaining, 111-140
Nonlinear programming, 228
Nonlinear regression, 96
Nonmonetary values in releasing or holding pretrial defendants, 7-10
Nonsentence goals in plea bargaining, 86-91
Notification to defendants, pretrial, 65
Nuclear energy industry, 262

Objective bond schedules, 45-49
Officials, public, noncomplying, 184, 265-270
Opportunity costs, 94, 261
Optimally allocating resources, xvii, among court cases, 217-253; defendants to hold, 50-51; plea bargaining, 71-186
Optimism in plea bargaining, 85-86, 118-120
Optimum bond levels, 45-61

Optimum percentage of defendants to hold, 50-51
Out-of-court settlements, 111, 141-180

Pareto optimums, 140
Parole decisions, 3
Payoff matrices, construction of: juror, 191-196; pretrial release, 7-21; plea bargaining, 71-76
Penalties, business, 262-265
Penitentiary spaces, allocation of, 240
Personal injury cases, settlement of, 143-144, allocating time to, 217-253
Pessimism in plea bargaining, 85-86, 118-120
Plea bargaining, xvi, 71-186, bargaining limits, 76-91; civil analogies, 141-180; equilibrium models, 111-140; perceived payoff matrices, 71-76
Police: arrest, 3; bond-setting by, 45
Pollution, 262-265, taxes, 31; violators, 184
Portfolio analysis, 108, 217-253
Prediction techniques: for appearance rates of defendants, 38-39; of verdicts, 217
Presumption of innocence, 25
Pretrial notification to defendants, 65
Pretrial release, xvi, 3-61, bond-setting decision, 21-31; judicial discretion in releasing, 7-44, errors, judges' concerns with avoiding, 7-10, 10-21; nondiscretionary bond schedules, 45-49; optimum percentage to release, 50-51
Preventive detention, 3-61
Prison conditions, 261
Probability of appearance at trial, calculating, 7-21
Probability of guilt: beyond a reasonable doubt, standards, 193-195; juror perceptions of, 187-215; plea bargaining, perceptions, 71-91; pretrial bond-setting, 7-44
Probabilities, Bayesian, 102, 103, 199, 210, 245
Programming, nonlinear, 228

Index of Subjects

Prosecutors, xv, plea bargaining, 71-186, bargaining limits, 76-91; perceived payoff matrices, 71-76
Provision of counsel for indigent, 65
Public officials, noncomplying, 184, 265-270
Publicizing holding rates of judges, 24-31
Punishment: capital, 65, 208; severity of, 31

Race as variable, 45-46
Radiation pollution, 262
Raising probability of appearance of defendants, 26-27
Ranges for crime in setting bonds, 47-48
Rape cases, 193, 200-201, 208
Rates of defendants held, publicizing of, 24-31
Rationality: bond-setting, optimizing, 45-61; juror decisionmaking, 183-212; plea bargaining, 71-186; sentencing, 205
Rearresting costs, defendants, 7-21
Recognizance, release on: judicial discretion, 7-44; errors, 7-10, 10-21; optimum percentage to release, 50-51
Reducing wrongful holding by judges, 24-31
Reducing violations of law, 255-274
Reduction of charges in plea bargaining, 71-186
Reduction of time from arrest to trial, 30
Regression, 74, 76, 83-84, 96, 98, 101, 102
Regulation of business, 262-265
Releasing of defendants, pretrial, 3-61
Residential wastes, 262
Resource allocation models, 94
Results matrix, in plea bargaining model, 118-120
Risk-taking, plea bargaining, 76-91, 118-120
Robbery cases, 193, 208, decisions to commit, 255-262
Rule of law, promoting, 25

Santobello v. New York, 100
Sale of narcotics, 170
Sanctions, to discourage wrong-doing, 262-265
Schedules, bond-setting, 45-61
Scheduling of cases, 30, allocating attorney resources among, 217-253; reduction of court delay, 30-31
Screening of defendants, 65, pretrial, 7-61
Sentences: bargaining for, 65-180; civil cases, 149-153; disutility, 75; effectiveness of, 3-61; minimization, plea bargaining, 88-91; uniformity in, 3-61
Sequencing of cases, 30, allocating attorney resources among, 217-253; reduction of court delay, 30-31
Setting of bonds, 7-61, civil cases, 147-149; errors, 7-10, 10-21; judicial discretion, 7-44; nondiscretionary, 45-49; optimum percentage of defendants to hold, 50-51
Settlements of cases: costs, 65; out-of-court, 111, 141-180
Severity of punishment, 31, incentives for compliance with law, 255-274
Sondquist-Morgan automatic interaction detector, 102
Speedy trial, 14
Splitting rates in plea bargaining, 111-140
Standards in bond-setting: judicial discretion, 7-44; nondiscretionary, 45-61
State supreme courts and bond-setting schedules, 45-61
State v. Harris, 207
Store robbers, decisions of, 255-262
Subsidies, business, 262-265
Suing, decision, 144-146, 217-253

Taxes, as incentive for compliance, 262-265
Threshold probabilities for convicting defendants: juror perceptions of, 191-196; pretrial appearance, 10-21; store robbers, 258-259

Time discounting in civil settlements, 143-144
Time path graph, in plea bargaining, 120-132
Transportation industry, 262
Trial avoidance through plea bargaining, 65-180
Type 1 and type 2 errors: jurors' perceptions, 191-196; pretrial release by judges, 10-21, 24-31
Typology of decision making, construction of, xvi

Uniformity in sentencing, 3-61
U. S. v. McGuire, 207
Upper limit of defendant in plea bargaining, 76-91
Utility, sentencing, 75

Variables, measurement of, 191-196
Varying conviction probabilities, plea bargaining, 76-91
Verdicts, prediction of, 217
Violations of law, deterring, 184, 255-274
Visibility of pretrial holding costs, 24-31
Voting to convict by jurors, xv, xvii, 183-186, characteristics of jurors and cases, 196-200; judicial instructions, impact of, 200-203; measuring propensity to convict, 191-196

Waiting time in court, reduction of, 30-31
Wastes, pollution, 262
Water pollution, 262-265
Weight assigned to conviction of innocent or guilty defendants, 7-21
Workmen's compensation cases, 4, 244
Wrongful holding of defendants, costs of, 24-31

About the Authors

Stuart S. Nagel is a professor of political science at the University of Illinois and a member of the Illinois bar. He is the author with Marian Neef of *Policy Analysis and Social Science Research* (1978), *Legal Policy Analysis: Finding an Optimum Level or Mix* (1977), and *The Legal Process: Modeling the System* (1977). He is the author or editor of *Policy Studies Review Annual* (1977), *Modeling the Criminal Justice System* (1977), *Policy Studies and the Social Sciences* (1975), *Policy Studies in America and Elsewhere* (1975), *Improving the Legal Process: Effects of Alternatives* (1975), *Environmental Politics* (1974), *The Rights of the Accused: In Law and Action* (1972), and *The Legal Process from a Behavioral Perspective* (1969). He has been an attorney to the Office of Economic Opportunity, Lawyer's Constitutional Defense Committee in Mississippi, National Labor Relations Board, and the U.S. Senate Judiciary Committee. Dr. Nagel has also been a fellow of the Ford Foundation, Russell Sage, NSP, ACLS, SSRC, East-West Center, Illinois Law Enforcement Commission, and the Center for Advanced Study in the Behavioral Sciences. He has also been a grant recipient through the Policy Studies Organization from the Departments of Justice, Labor, HUD, Energy, Agriculture, Transportation, and HEW, and from the Rockefeller and Guggenheim Foundations.

Marian G. Neef teaches and does research in political science at the University of Illinois. In addition to the above coauthored books, she is the author with Stuart Nagel of such monographs as *Too Much or Too Little Policy: The Example of Pretrial Release* (1977); *Operations Research Methods: As Applied to Political Science and the Legal Process* (1976); and *The Application of Mixed Strategies: Civil Rights and Other Multiple-Activity Problems* (1976). She has also coauthored numerous articles in such journals as *Policy Analysis, American Bar Association Journal, Judicature, Political Methodology, Public Administration Review, Journal of Criminal Justice, Human Behavior, Journal of Legal Education, PS,* and various law reviews.